FRENCH MILITARY

Completely Revised Second Edition

FRENCH MILITARY AVIATION

compiled by Paul A. Jackson　　Midland Counties Publications

Edited and Published by
Midland Counties Publications (Aerophile) Limited
24, The Hollow, Earl Shilton, Leicester,
LE9 7NA, England.

Copyright © 1975, 1979
Midland Counties Publications (Aerophile) Limited

First edition published 1975
Completely revised new edition 1979

All rights reserved. No part of the contents of this publication may be reproduced, stored in a retrieval system or transmitted in any form or by any means electronic, mechanical, photocopying, recording or otherwise, without the prior written permission of the publishers.

ISBN 0 904597 17 2 (Hardback)
      0 904597 18 0 (Paperback)

Printed by W.T. Carrick (Printers) Limited
Westminster Trading Estate, Measham,
Leicestershire, England

Contents

6   Introduction and Acknowledgements
7   French Introduction and Abbreviations

9   **Part 1: Historical Background**
26   French Overseas Territories
30   The Future

33   **Part 2: Armée de l'Air**
34   Current Organisation
38   Current Units
67   Base Flights and Armée de l'Air Callsigns
69   Base Aérienne Numbers and Insignia

75   **Part 3: Aéronautique Navale**
76   Current Organisation
78   Current Units
86   Aéronautique Navale Callsigns

87   **Part 4: Aviation Légère de l'Armée de Terre**
88   Unit Organisation
89   Operational Units 1977 and 1979
90   Army Organisation 1979 (Order of Battle)
94   ALAT Callsigns

95   **Part 5: Other Services**
96   Gendarmerie
98   Sécurité Civile
99   CEAM/CEV/CNET/DCAN
100 ENSA/EPNER

101 **Part 6: Aircraft Review**
102 Serial Numbers, Markings and Radio Callsigns
103 Aircraft Service Histories and Illustrations

191 **Appendices**
     French Military Airbases, Callsign Blocks, 'F-Z' Registration Series, Unit Names, Named Squadrons, Escadrille Numbers in Current Use, Export Aircraft and Keeping Up-to-Date.

Cover photograph depicts Mirage F1 No.34 '30-FL' at Solenzara, in the markings of ECTT 3/30 (Arms of Lorraine) - white alerions on red (photo R.Cram)

5

Introduction & Acknowledgements

It is now three and a half years since the first edition of this book appeared as the first in the Midland Counties Publications 'Military Aviation' series, and since that time there have been many changes both in the organisation and equipment of the French aerial forces.

For those readers who have bought this volume to update their existing first editions or their own records, we hope that you will not be disappointed. What began as a simple revision and updating of 'French Military Aviation' has in fact developed into a completely re-written book containing a large amount of new information, entirely new photographic coverage, and over 250 additional insignia illustrations. For those readers who have bought this edition, or are encountering the 'Military Aviation' series, for the first time, it may be pertinent to offer some general comments concerning the aims of the series, and of this book in particular. We begin with a narrative section covering the history of French military aviation in order to give background and perspective which will assist in the interpretation of the main body of the book. This sets out to present in an easy cross-reference format, a current view, with particular emphasis on aircraft-operating units, and individual aircraft. In other books in the series it has been possible to cover the period from for instance, the Second World War up to date, but the size of the French forces renders this impracticable. We hope however that the information which is included, i.e. detailed coverage of all aircraft and units which are current or have been withdrawn since 1970, will provide adequate information for both historians and numerologists. A new feature in this edition is the inclusion of the full post-1945 history for all units now extant. Further historical information is published frequently by the excellent 'Le Trait d'Union', whilst data of a technical nature, such as aircraft performance, dimensions, and armament, which is deliberately excluded from this book, may be easily found in such publications as 'Janes' and the 'Observers' books.

The material which has enabled this volume to be so drastically improved and enlarged from the first edition has flowed in from many correspondents, to whom I am deeply grateful. In the first edition, I expressed thanks to the following long-term correspondents - Jean-Pierre Dubois, Tony Foster, Alan W. Hall, Jean-Michel Lefebvre, Ben Marselis, Eric Moreau, Eddy Ragas and Johan van der Wei, as well as to the members, magazine contributors and editors of the Midland Counties Aviation Society, British Aviation Research Group, Flash, West London Aviation Group, and Le Trait d'Union. To these names I am now pleased to add those of Jean-Louis Gaynecoetche and R.Cram for providing a host of photographs and highly-valued information; Vital Ferry, Patrick-Xavier Henry and Jean Delams (and many other members) of the French branch of Air-Britain for locating elusive insignia and correcting the original text, and to Walter Klein, Iain MacKenzie, Chris Pocock, Elfan ap Rees, Hans de Ree, Colin Smith, Colin M. Smith, and numerous others for their comments, corrections, photographs and news, all of which were most welcome.

It should be particularly noted that the compilation of this series is from unofficial, and largely amateur, sources, and it follows that without access to official records, then no pretence can be made that the information is totally complete or accurate, though every effort has been made to reach as high a standard as possible. Readers who compile their own records from reports in amateur magazines may note that some data on individual aircraft in this book is at variance with their own. It has become apparent that following the publication of the first edition of this book, some reporters ceased the practice of checking codes to serials on the aircraft, and took the information which we had published as being gospel, whereas in fact significant changes had taken place in the interim. Whilst it is highly flattering that our publications should be regarded in this way, it has led to a considerable amount of mis-information appearing in print in otherwise highly-respected publications, and thus perpetuated! We are confident that these aberrations have now been eliminated, but would ask all those who do report movements for magazines to please beware of this trap!

Before closing, it is worth drawing the attention of those readers who do spend their spare time at or near air bases, and particularly those who engage in the pastime of Spotting, to the Foreign Office warning which is reproduced overleaf. In France in particular, these hobbies are not at all widespread, and are frequently misunderstood, to the embarrassment of all concerned. We therefore suggest that in order that the hobby may become more accepted and widely understood by the relevant authorities, that those planning visits to military airfields take the trouble to go about it in a sensible manner, perhaps by making prior written contact with the base. In time this will work for the benefit of everyone.

Having said all that, may I close by welcoming via the publishers, any comments, corrections, news and photographs, all of which may enhance a third edition of this title at some future date.

Paul A. Jackson   March 1979
Enfield,
Middlesex

Introduction pour les Lecteurs Francais

Publié pour la première fois en 1975, voici la seconde édition d'un ouvrage traitant de l'aviation militaire Française, et faisant partie d'une série sur les forces aériennes européennes. J'espère que vous trouverez dans ce livre tout ce qui vous intéresse, soit que vous en découvriez un de ce genre pour la première fois, soit que vous connaissiez déjà la précédente édition.

En Grande-Bretagne, les passionnés d'aviation collationnent les sérials (numéros de production), les codes et les insignes des avions depuis de nombreuses annees et ce 'hobby' a maintenant atteint plusieurs pays en Europe. Ce livre a été écrit pour aider ces passionnés de tout pays à comprendre l'organisation de l'aviation militaire en France et également a leur faire découvrir des informations sur les avions qu'ils ont vu ou qu'ils pourront voir.

Bien qu'un grand nombre de pays possède déjà ces informations (et même, pour la plupart, beaucoup plus) une mise en garde est nécessaire. Tous les 'spotters' doivent constamment avoir présent a leur mémoire que la loi de leur pays considère ces informations comme secrètes. Aussi, ceux-ci doivent toujours demander l'autorisation pour photographier les avions militaires et ne doivent en aucun cas pénétrer sur les bases aériennes. Deux exceptions cependant existent: être muni d'une autorisation des autorités compétentes et les journées 'Portes Ouvertes' (où d'ailleurs la majorité des informations a été recueillie). En Grande-Bretagne, la police militaire connait fort bien l'intérêt des 'spotters' et il est possible aux associations de passionnés d'organiser des visites spéciales sur les bases aériennes. Si vous êtes considérés comme un ami d'une armée de l'air, et non comme un agent ennemi, tout est possible.

Je voudrais aussi avertir tous les Français qui trouveront ce livre interessant, de lire le magazine bimestriel 'Le Trait d'Union' qui est un excellent complément a des magazines commerciaux tels 'Le Fanatique de l'Aviation', 'Air Fan' etc.

Enfin, je souhaite que tout lecteur, possédant de nouvelles informations ou pouvant apporter des corrections à ce livre, m'écrive afin que je puisse les publier pour aider tous les autres 'spotters'.

Abbreviations

The abbreviations used in this book consist of those already familiar to most readers, viz:

c/n constructors number   w/o written off
ntu not taken up   wfu withdrawn from use

Please see also the introductions to the individual sections, where applicable.

Warning!

The hobby of aircraft spotting can be misunderstood in countries where it is not as widely accepted as in the UK and this has lead to a number of unfortunate incidents over the past few years.

We therefore remind readers of the advice contained in the official booklet *Essential Information for British Passport Holders:* 'Hobbies like *aircraft*, train or ship spotting, and even bird watching, are liable to misinterpretation and may lead to your being arrested for spying in some countries abroad. If in doubt you should enquire from the local authorities or a British consular officer'.

Part One

Historical Background

In the beginning...

Since the earliest days of manned flight, the French nation and its aviation pioneers have continually been in the forefront of aeronautical progress, and today's airmen are able to look back with pride to the achievements of their forefathers. Two centuries ago, on 21 November 1783, in a hot air balloon designed and built by the Montgolfier brothers of Annonay, the Marquis d'Arlandes and Pilatre de Rosier made the first manned flight from the Bois de Boulogne in Paris and ushered in a new era for mankind.

The Montgolfier balloon was capable of short flights only, as it left behind its source of hot air on leaving the ground, but the inventor M. Charles demonstrated a more practicable answer to this problem only a month later, when he made an ascent to 9,000 feet in a hydrogen balloon, again over Paris. By careful management of ballast, flights of many miles could be accomplished, but the direction of flight was governed by the wind. The ability to look upon the earth from a great height soon attracted the army, and a captive balloon was used in the battle of Fleurus in 1794, thus establishing a landmark in military history.

Outside of military deployments, the balloon had only a curiosity value, but the chemist Gay Lussac developed another use for it when he ascended to a previously unattained altitude of 23,000 feet for the purpose of taking atmospheric measurements. Napoleon's planned invasion of England envisaged the use of a fleet of troop carrying balloons as the first wave in conjunction with a tunnel under the Channel. This imaginative use of the air is now commonplace procedure amongst the armed forces of the world, and the sudden appearance of troops from the skies has won many battles where a conventional arrival would have meant defeat.

The restrictions on destinations imposed by the wind direction were combatted by M. Giffard of Paris who in 1852 devised a dirigible, or steerable, airship fifty years before Count von Zeppelin, but in the siege of Paris, during the Franco-Prussian war use was made of the free balloon to transport mail and important persons over the enemy lines.

Notable in the forward-looking attitude towards aviation which has typified French policy was the placing of the world's first contract for a heavier-than-air military aeroplane awarded to the pioneer Clément Ader on 3 February 1892. Although Italy was the first nation to employ an aircraft for the dropping of bombs, in 1912, this capability was clearly foreseen by the French war ministry, as a 75kg payload of explosives was mentioned in the specification. After five years of work, the aeroplane made its first hop of 300 metres on 14 October 1897, but was wrecked in the crash landing which ensued, whereupon the contract was terminated.

Hearing of a more successful flying machine in the United States, the war ministry despatched a representative to negotiate with the Wright Brothers in 1906. Orville, an ultra-cautious man, stipulated conditions for purchase similar to those which were offered to his own and other governments, requiring a large portion of the brothers' royalty to be paid even before the ability of the airplane to leave the ground had been established. Interested representatives, equally cautious because of the many cranks and hoaxers then claiming to have flown, were reluctant to part with any cash until the secrets of flight had been revealed to them. This stale-mate remained for two years until the progress made by such Frenchmen as Blériot and the Farman brothers convinced Orville and Wilbur that if they were not to relax their conditions of strict secrecy, they would be eclipsed by the home products.

Accordingly, Wilbur journeyed to Le Mans in August 1908 to demonstrate his aircraft and at the same time, the brothers made a more acceptable contract with the authorities resulting in an order for a Wright airplane which was delivered on 10 June 1910. A second Wright, two Farman and one Blériot were also received, all five the result of military aircraft trials held at Bétheny in August 1909. Volunteers soon came forward to learn the art of flying aeroplanes and, seconded to the Engineer Corps of the army, they were detached to the respective manufacturing firms for instruction.

The Artillery too, appreciated the value of the aircraft for observation, and placed a separate order for three Farmans, two Antoinettes and two Wrights whose pilots, once trained, were based at Vincennes with the Artillery Flying School. Anxious to prevent duplication of effort, the war ministry ordered the two air arms to merge under the command of Gen. Roques of the Engineers, whose school was established at Châlons in April 1910.

Experiments in photographic reconnaissance and artillery direction proved successful, and the military exercises of September 1910 were the first to feature aircraft playing an integral part in the manoeuvres. The large-scale demonstration of the value of the aircraft in warfare was not lost to the high command, and an immediate order for forty aircraft, equally divided between Blériot and Farman, was the outcome of the 1910 exercise.

Over the Channel, so symbolically bridged by Blériot the year before, the British Army was making-do with balloons and not until December 1910 did the Royal Navy receive its first two aircraft — as a gift from a patriotic individual. On 1 April 1911, the British Army established its first aeroplane squadron — No. 2 at Larkhill, at which time two small airships and a dozen aircraft of reasonable reliability were possessed by both Army and Navy. The British were well behind France and were to remain so for many years.

With the air element expanding rapidly, the time had now come to give the aviators some measure of autonomy, and so by Senatorial decree the Aéronautique Militaire was created on 22 October 1910, Gen. Roques becoming its first Inspector. The General exhibited considerable foresight in aviation matters for his day and this was reflected in the organisation and policies of his command.

In order that future aircraft would meet more exactly the requirements of the AM, a competition was held at Reims-Bétheny in October 1911, attract-

10

ing 140 entries from 43 companies, all of French origin. These were soon reduced to a more managable proportion by the trials, and the final was dominated by names which were soon to become known throughout Europe: Breguet, Deperdussin, Farman and Nieuport.

Civilian Aviators Certificates were no longer accepted as qualification to fly a military aircraft, being at the time merely a testimony to the ability of the holder to keep an aeroplane out of contact with the ground for a specified period without doing too great an amount of damage to life or property. Instead, four military flying schools were set-up, each for a particular make of aircraft; Châlons for Henri Farmans, Douai for Breguets, Pau for Blériots and Versailles for Maurice Farmans. The military certificate also demanded theoretical knowledge, and only on passing a written examination was Lt. de Rose granted the first licence on 7 February 1911.

The principle of homogeneous flying schools was extended to the operational squadrons as soon as the supply of aircraft permitted, and by 1912 the first five Escadrilles (squadrons) had been formed on this basis, each with six aircraft on charge, plus a permanent strength of men and equipment — this a full four years before the efficiency of such a system was impressed upon the British forces.

The escadrilles were numbered consecutively from 1, the number being prefixed by a letter or letters referring to the aircraft type operated. The first five were: 'HF 1' equipped with Henri Farman aircraft and based at Châlons, 'MF 2' with Maurice Farmans at Buc, 'Bl 3' with Blériots at Pau, 'D 4' with Deperdussins at St. Cyr and 'MF 5', also with Maurice Farmans at St. Cyr. These five formed the basis of the planned Aéronautique Militaire structure of three 'Groupes', based at Lyon, Reims and Versailles; each comprising flying units and the necessary support facilities to keep them operational.

The Great War

Enlightened though the French attitude to aviation undoubtedly was, other and more pressing reasons than inspiration and faith in the future of the aeroplane were responsible for the build-up of the Aéronautique Militaire. Whilst the early years of the twentieth century had witnessed an improvement in relationships between France and her traditional adversary, Britain, the attitude of Germany was giving cause for concern. The newly-formed German state (having taken from France the provinces of Alsace and Lorraine and their rich mineral deposits in the earlier Franco-Prussian war) was, like all adolescents, antagonising its elders by assertions of manhood, power and influence. In a situation which has parallels in today's Middle East and Africa, Germany offered her protection to several smaller European nations, whilst the remainder, fearful of German motives, formed an opposing alliance. By 1914, the stage had been set for war, and the players assembled in the wings.

The event which raised the curtain occurred in the remote Balkan town of Sarajevo on 15 June 1914 with the assassination of Archduke Ferdinand. A long-standing enmity between the Serbians and Austro-Hungarians escalated into war, Germany being allied to the latter, whilst Russia supported Serbia, and was itself allied to France. The French mobilised shortly after the killing of Ferdinand in anticipation of the course of events, and as joint guarantors of Belgian neutrality together with Britain were both brought into the conflict when German armies entered Belgium.

When Britain and France declared war on Germany on 4 August, the Aéronautique Militaire comprised twenty-one escadrilles totalling 132 aircraft, while reserves and impounded machines awaiting delivery to foreign governments totalled a further 136. The twenty-one escadrilles were assigned as under:

HF 1	Henri Farman biplane	Assigned to II Army
MF 2	Maurice Farman biplane	III Army
Bl 3	Blériot monoplane	I Army
D 4	Deperdussin monoplane	IV Army
MF 5	Maurice Farman biplane	I Army
D 6	Deperdussin monoplane	V Army
HF 7	Henri Farman biplane	III Army
MF 8	Maurice Farman biplane	II Army
Bl 9	Blériot monoplane	I Army
Bl 10	Blériot monoplane	I Army
C 11	Caudron G2 biplane	IV Army
N 12	Nieuport monoplane	V Army
HF 13	Henri Farman biplane	III Army
V 14	Voisin biplane	IV Army
Rep 15	R E Pelterie monoplane	V Army
MF 16	Maurice Farman biplane	III Army
Br 17	Breguet biplane	I Army
Bl 18	Blériot monoplane	I Army
HF 19	Henri Farman biplane	II Army
MF 20	Maurice Farman	II Army
V 21	Voisin biplane	IV Army

Each escadrille had a strength of six aircraft. In addition, there were three flights of three Blériots designated Bl C 2, Bl C 4 and Bl C 5 for cavalry reconnaissance. By the end of August, twenty-nine escadrilles were extant, this rising to thirty-four a month later.

Both in Britain and France the belief prevailed that it would 'all be over by Christmas' — the Kaiser proclaimed, however, that he would eat his next Christmas dinner in Buckingham Palace. The Aéronautique Militaire therefore took the drastic step of closing all flying schools in the mistaken belief that by the time their pupils had graduated, the war would have finished.

The General Staff was soon forced to revise its estimates as the opposing armies dug into their trenches, and the schools were re-opened, but with a serious delay.

From the start, the Aéronautique Militaire was employed by the Army in reconnaissance of German movements and the advancing troops and their supply lines were subjected to bombing attacks. On 12 August the first French airman was killed when Sgt. Bridou crashed on landing, and on 5 October, Sgt. Frantz shot down the first enemy aircraft by the French.

The importance of specialisation was realised early in the campaign and after only three weeks, the first specialised bombing wing was formed by escadrilles 14, .17 and 21 equipped with Voisins. These embarked on strategic missions such as the attacking of munitions factories and steelworks. Heavier bombers were ordered whilst fighter squadrons were re-equipped with. types such as the Nieuport Bébé, more manoeuverable than the unwieldy reconnaissance aircraft used hitherto.

Experiments with propeller deflector plates fitted to a Morane Parasol enabled pilots to direct more accurate machine gun fire by shooting through the disc of rotation, and the capture of such an aircraft prompted Anthoni Fokker to incorporate a mechanical interrupter to his famous fighters, resurrecting a pre-war patent which for some reason had never been adopted by any of the other air forces.

On both sides, larger and larger numbers of fighter aircraft were detailed to escort reconnaissances and were naturally intercepted by bigger enemy formations: thus were born the fighter wings which were to gain fame with the general public. Germany, of course, had the Baron von Richthofen and his 'Flying Circus', and France fielded the 'Cigognes' group, normally comprising escadrilles 3, 26, 73 and 103 but also incorporating 37, 62 and 103, all equipped with the Nieuport. The 'trademark' of the wing, later to be designated Groupe de Combat 12, was a stork painted on the side of each aircraft, individual squadrons having their own variation. Stork insignia will be found on several of the Armée de l'Air's supersonic fighters as a direct link between its first airmen and those of the present day.

Aircraft of other squadrons sported different badges and even individual pilots had their own personal markings. Again, those of the more famous units have been perpetuated. In one instance, 88 Squadron RFC, and Escadrille 88 found themselves near neighbours, striking up a friendship which resulted in both adopting the common insignia of a snake.

The British forces were also in France in great numbers, but the front line was divided into national sections with the air units to the rear, and little intermixture or co-ordination took place, save at the highest levels. Nearby friendly forces would be called upon to support a 'push' by the infantry, but this normally involved diversionary attacks rather than direct co-operation or joint manoeuvres.

There was, however, some interchange of equipment, the British continuing the pre-war practice of purchasing French aeroplanes to supplement their own, and the Aéronautique Militaire operating types such as the Sopwith 1A/1B bomber, 4,200 of which were built under licence. French aircraft engines deservedly had a high reputation over the Channel and these were incorporated in certain British types whilst Lewis and Vickers machine guns were mounted in French aeroplanes both for offence and defence. Of the sixty-three Royal Flying Corps aircraft delivered to the British Expeditionary Force in France between 13 and 18 August 1914, nineteen were of French design (twelve Henri Farman and seven Blériot) and every one had a French engine: an 80hp Gnôme for the BE8, Avro 504 and Tabloid (plus Farman and Blériot) and 70hp Renault in the BE2. Even later in the war other engines such as the Clerget (e.g. Sopwith Triplane) and Le Rhone (e.g. Pup and Camel) found widespread employment in British airframes.

France had other allies from nations not at war with Germany, these volunteers normally fighting in the Army, but soon after the opening of hostilities a group of nine Americans was attached to escadrille N124 where they were later joined by others of their countrymen. Appropriately the squadron insignia adopted was the head of an Indian chief, and more aptly still, in December 1916 the name 'Lafayette' was bestowed, commemorating the Frenchman who assisted the United States in the war of independence. When the USA entered the war on the Allied side, SPA124 (as it had later become) was transferred to the US Army Air Corps, its pilots having included Lt. G. R. Lufbery, one of the highest-scoring US airmen of the first world war, and a corporal by the name of James R. Doolittle who, much later, was to give the citizens of Tokio an unwelcome surprise with the assistance of an aircraft carrier and a squadron of B-25s.

As the campaigns of the Great War came and went, so the Aéronautique Militaire increased in strength. At the opening of the third battle of Ypres, in the early hours of 31 July 1917, 3,500 aircraft were on charge and plans were made to fix strength at sixty fighter squadrons of 15 aircraft, twenty bombing squadrons of 15 each, 140 reconnaissance and observation squadrons with ten aircraft and eight general duties squadrons, plus reserves. Britain at this time had fifty squadrons stationed in France. Many of the fighter wings received the Spad 7C1 of which 3,500 were eventually built, and most of today's fighter squadrons perpetuate the famous Spad units with their 'SPA' prefixes to the squadron numbers.

During the Spring of 1918, the Germans launched three offensives which gained them much ground, but in each case energetic flying by the Aéronautique Militaire and Royal Flying Corps denied the Kaiser's troops their air support and contributed materially to the halting of the spearheads. On 18 July the counter-attack began and in the absence of heavy artillery, Breguet bombers were used in the ground attack role. The Germans were pushed further and further back and this, coupled with economic and social disintegration in Germany induced them to ask for an armistice, which became effective at 1100 hours on 11 November, a moment in time remembered to this day. At the close of hostilities, the Aéronautique Militaire had grown to a force of 3,222 operational aircraft in 246 squadrons (plus reserve and training machines) as under:—

Fighter Groups

GC 11	Spad C1	4 squadrons
GC 12	Spad C1	4 squadrons
GC 13	Spad C1	4 squadrons
GC 14	Spad C1	5 squadrons
GC 15	Spad C1	4 squadrons
GC 16	Spad C1	4 squadrons
GC 17	Spad C1	4 squadrons
GC 18	Spad C1	4 squadrons
GC 19	Spad C1	4 squadrons
GC 20	Spad C1	4 squadrons
GC 21	Spad C1	5 squadrons
GC 22	Spad C1	4 squadrons
GC 23	Spad C1	4 squadrons
—	Spad C1	12 independent squadrons

Bomber Groups

GB 1	Farman F50	3 squadrons (night)
GB 2	Caproni 3	2 squadrons (night)
GB 3	Breguet 14	3 squadrons (day)
GB 4	Breguet 14	3 squadrons (day)
GB 5	Breguet 14	3 squadrons (day)
GB 6	Breguet 14	3 squadrons (day)
GB 7	Voisin 10	3 squadrons (night)
GB 8	Voisin 10	3 squadrons (night)
GB 9	Breguet 14	3 squadrons (day)
GB 10	Voisin 10	4 squadrons (night)
—	Caudron R11	4 squadrons (day bomber protection)

Artillery/Fighter-recce units.

—	Breguet 14	40 squadrons
—	Salmson 2	48 squadrons
—	Spad 11/16	29 squadrons
—	Caudron R11	2 squadrons
—	Voisin Bn2	5 squadrons
—	Breguet 14	11 squadrons (long range artillery)
—	Salmson 2	2 squadrons (long range artillery)
—	Spad A2	1 squadron (long range artillery)
—	Breguet 14	8 squadrons (long range artillery)
—	Salmson 2	8 squadrons (motorised artillery)

By way of comparison, the Royal Air Force possessed 188 operational squadrons of which ninety-nine were in France and thirty-four in other overseas theatres. The Aéronautique Militaire had 127,630 officers and men; the RAF 291,170.

Between the Wars

The welcome arrival of peace brought the expected contractions of the Aéronautique Militaire which was accompanied by a re-organisation of squadrons. Consecutive numbering was abolished and the air force established a more military method of numbering, in which the escadrille (squadron) was the basic unit, but subordinated to its parent group. At the top was the Air Division of the army which governed Brigades, Regiments, Groupes and Escadrilles. A typical example would be:—

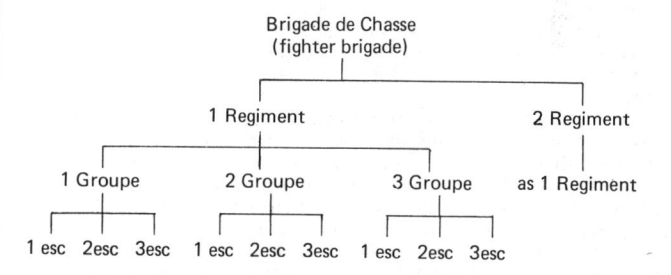

```
                    Brigade de Chasse
                    (fighter brigade)
              ┌───────────┴───────────┐
          1 Regiment              2 Regiment
       ┌──────┼──────┐                │
   1 Groupe 2 Groupe 3 Groupe     as 1 Regiment
   ┌─┼─┐   ┌─┼─┐   ┌─┼─┐
 1esc 2esc 3esc 1esc 2esc 3esc 1esc 2esc 3esc
```

Some fighter Groupes would have four escadrilles, whilst this number was normal for bomber squadrons. The reconnaissance regiments would sometimes have an extra groupe, but only two squadrons were attached to each. There were two Regiments de Chasse (fighter) Nos 1 and 2; two Regiments de Bombardement de Jour (day bomber) Nos 11 and 12; and two Regiments de Bombardement de Nuit (night bomber) Nos 21 and 22; plus a mixed brigade comprising 2nd Fighter, 13th Bomber and 31-37 Reconnaissance Regiments.

Throughout the 'twenties, the size of the Aéronautique Militaire remained static, operational action being confined to overseas territories. Some flying instruction was undertaken by civilian schools, but unlike the RAF system of reserve training this was restricted to young men who received a year's course before call-up into the full-time air force. Additionally a military school was established in 1924 for the refresher training of reservists and ground-duties officers, each of whom received a dozen hours in the air.

Changes in organisation also extended to the Naval Air Arm, the Aéronautique Navale, usually shortened to Aéronavale. This had been formed, initially with one Henri Farman, one Voisin, one Breguet and one Nieuport, on 12 March 1912, and by the outbreak of war had some fourteen seaplanes on strength. Its principal task was the protection of the French coastal waters against hostile penetration. It was to maintain a regular observation (surveillance) of the coastline, and a limited striking power against intruders and to provide air cover for the fleet. It depended on orders from the Ministère de la Marine (Ministry of the Navy), but was to work in co-operation with the army and the Aéronautique Militaire as far as possible.

During World War 1, aircraft — most of them being flying boats — were allocated to a number of naval air stations, such as Berre, Boulogne-sur-Mer, Brest, Cherbourg, Dunkerque, Le Havre, Lorient, Rochefort, Saint-Brieuc, Saint-Raphaël and Toulon in metropolitan France, and Bizerte and Oran in French Algeria. Single- or two-letter station codes were used — e.g. B Brest, BE Berre, C Cherbourg, D Dunkerque, H Le Havre, R Rochefort, SR Saint-Raphael — followed by an individual number. Each station had its own numbering sequence.

In the closing stages of World War 1, the Aéronautique Navale initiated a mutual assistance scheme with the US Naval forces, involving the availability of a number of air bases, and a limited amount of aircraft were transferred to the US Navy — fifty-eight Donnet-Denhaut, eleven FBA Type H, twelve Lévy-Lepen HB2, thirty-four Tellier T3 (all flying boats), and twenty-six Hanriot HD.2 C1 fighter seaplanes. The first base to be handed over to the US Navy was Le Croisic, on the mouth of the River Loire, which was commissioned on 27 November 1917, which was followed by a further seven, five of which being operational (Pauillac was reserved for repair and maintenance duties, and Paimboeuf had a complement of observation dirigibles).

The Aéronavale's structure was reorganised on 27 December 1921, with additional changes on 1 September 1924. The French territory was divided into Frontières Maritimes (Naval Fronts, or literally 'borders') — 1ère North Sea/English Channel, 2e Atlantic/Bay of Biscay, 3e Mediterranean, 4e North Africa; the number 7 was reserved for shipborne a/c, 8 for overseas units. The naval units were grouped into two Théâtres Maritimes (Naval Air Regions), each having a number of Arrondissements Maritimes (Naval Air Regions), as follows:—

Théâtre Maritime Mer du Nord/Manche/Atlantique *(N. Sea/Channel/Atlantic)*:

1er Arrondissement	Sectors: Boulogne, Cherbourg, Dunkerque, Le Havre	
	HQ: Cherbourg	
2e Arrondissement	Sectors: Brest, Saint-Brieuc	HQ: Brest
3e Arrondissement	Sectors: Loire, Lorient	HQ: Lorient
4e Arrondissement	Sectors: Charente, Gironde, French Morocco (Atlantic Coast)	HQ: Rochefort

Théâtre Maritime Mer Mediterranée *(Mediterranean)*:

5e Arrondissement	Sectors: Marseille, Nice, Port Vendres, Toulon, Corsica	HQ: Toulon
6e Arrondissement	Sectors: Alger (Algiers), Bizerte, Bône, Oran, Sfax. HQ: Bizerte (French Algeria)	

The Marine Nationale's first aircraft carrier, the *Béarn*, commissioned in May 1927 although it had been laid down in 1914 as a battleship upon which work had ceased the following year. Interestingly, landings and take-offs had been experimentally undertaken from her uncompleted main deck in 1921-22, before the construction of a proper flying deck had been begun in August 1923. She was followed by a number of battleships, cruisers and sloops which also had provision for light aircraft, and these included the battleships Dunkerque and Strasbourg, training cruiser Jeanne d'Arc and the Duguay-Trouin, Duquesne, Edgar Quinet, Jules Michelet, Lamitte-Picquet, Suffren and Tourville. Additionally, there was the seaplane carrier, the Commandant Teste.

When the Ministère de l'Air was formed on 15 September 1928, the Aéronavale came under its control for administrative purposes, although the service retained its identity, and its personnel remained under the orders of the Ministère de la Marine. The order of battle at this time is given below. Note that the escadrille designations comprise a Frontière Maritime number, a role designator and a unit number. Thus, Escadrille 4B1 was the first bomber escadrille of Frontière Maritime 4. Role designators were 'B' Bombardement (bomber), 'C' Chasse (fighter), 'E' Eclaireur (long-range reconnaissance), 'R' Reconnaissance, 'S' Surveillance (coastal patrol) and 'T' Torpillage (torpedo bomber).

Aéronavale Order of Battle for 15 September 1928

Escadrille 1B1	Cherbourg-Chantereyne	Farman 168 Goliath
2S1	Brest-Laninon	CAMS 55
3B1	Berre	Farman 168 Goliath

3B2	Berre	Farman 168 Goliath
3C1	Hyères-Palyvestre	Gourdou-Leseurre B
3S1	Berre	Latham 42
4B1	Bizerte-Karouba	Farman 168 Goliath
4B2	Bizerte-Karouba	Farman 168 Goliath
4B3	Bizerte-Sidi Ahmed	Farman 168 Goliath
4C1	Bizerte-Sidi Ahmed	Dewoitine D.1
4S1	Bizerte-Karouba	CAMS 55
7B1	aboard Béarn	Levasseur PL 7
7C1	aboard Béarn	Dewoitine D.1/Wibault 74
7S1	aboard Béarn	Levasseur PL 7

Centre Principal d'Hydravions (Main Seaplane Centre) — (one each) Berre, Brest, Bizerte-Karouba, Cherbourg-Chantereyne.

Centre d'Aviation Maritime (Naval Aviation Centre) — Lorient.

Centre Sécondaire d'Aviation Maritime (Secondary Naval Aviation Centre) — Hyères-Palyvestre.

Centre d'Instruction de l'Aéronautique Navale (Naval Air Training Centre) — (one each) Rochefort-Soubise, Hourtin.

Base d'Exercice de Saint Raphaël (Saint Raphaël Operational Training Base) — Saint Raphaël (including a research and development centre).

Centre Principal d'Aviation et de Dirigéables (Main Aircraft and Dirigible Centre) — Bizerte-Sidi Ahmed.

Centre Principal de Dirigéables (Main Dirigible Centre) — Cuers-Pierrefeu.

Centre de Ballons Captifs (Captive Balloon Centre) — (one each) Brest, Bizerte-Sidi Ahmed, Cherbourg, Toulon.

Entrepôt Général de l'Aéronautique Maritime (General Naval Aeronautical Depot) — Nanterre.

There was also a Centre Aéronautique at the Saint-Cyr military academy, which included a naval airship station.

The basic Aéronavale unit was at the time the Escadrille of twelve aircraft (fifteen for fighter escadrilles); two or more formed a Groupe, and two or more Groupes formed a Flottille.

Not until the early 'thirties did the air force cease to be the 5th Department of the army and was re-christened the 'Armée de l'Air' on 1 April 1933, gaining full autonomy on 2 July 1934. A further re-organisation was by that time complete and involved a return to the first world war system of subordinating the escadrilles to a groupe and escadre rather than a regiment.

The escadre being smaller than a regiment would all be based at one airfield, the chain of command being as under:—

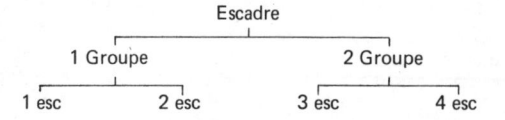

```
                    Escadre
           ┌───────────┴───────────┐
        1 Groupe                 2 Groupe
       ┌────┴────┐             ┌────┴────┐
     1 esc     2 esc         3 esc     4 esc
```

Some formations retained their regimental status with three groupes attached, but reconnaissance escadres lost their fighter-escort squadrons when they made the transition and would in future have to call upon a neighbouring fighter wing to mount a mission in defended territory.

At the time of its formation, the Armée de l'Air at home comprised three air divisions and two bomber formations: The Division Aérienne at Metz had been re-named 1 Division Aérienne and controlled 33 Escadre d'Observation at Nancy plus 1 and 4 Balloon Bataillons of 1 Régiment d'Aérostation. 2 Division Aérienne at Paris administered 2 Brigade Aérienne (7 Escadre de Chasse, 32 Escadre d'Observation, 52 Escadre de Reconnaissance) and 4 Brigade Aérienne (1 Escadre de Chasse, 34 Escadrille d'Observation, 54 Escadre de Reconnaissance and 2 and 3 Bataillons of 1 Régiment d'Aérostation). 3 Division Aérienne at Tours controlling 5 Brigade Aérienne (3 Escadre de Chasse, 5 Escadre de Chasse, 35 Escadre d'Observation, 55 Escadre de Reconnaissance) and 1 Brigade Aérienne (31 Régiment de Reconnaissance et Observation) and 6 Demi-Brigade Aérienne (36 Escadre d'Observation and 1 and 2 Bataillons of 2 Régiment d'Aérostation. The two bomber formations were autonomous: Groupement d'Aviation de Bombardement at Paris had 12 Brigade Mixte (11 and 21 Escadres de Bombardement plus 33 Escadre d'Observation seconded from 1 Division Aérienne) and 12 Brigade de Bombardement also at Paris (12 and 22 Escadres de Bombardement).

In addition to the overseas units which are detailed later, there were various schools and other establishments, principally the Ecole Militaire et d'Application l'Aéronautique at Versailles, the 'Central Flying School' of the Armée de l'Air; the Ecole de Formation des Sous Officiers Personnel Navigant — an NCO's flying school; l'Ecole Practique d'Aviation at Avord — elementary flying school; l'Ecole de Perfectionnement de Pilotage at Etampes — the advanced flying school; firing range at Cazaux; experimental and trials unit at Villacoublay, and 301 Entrepôt de l'Armée de l'Air at Chateaudun, the maintenance unit. In the ever important branches of ground support were the Ecole des Apprentis Mécanicien at Rochefort and the Centre d'Instruction des Spécialistes at Bordeaux, both technical training schools. Readers familiar with the current organisation of the Armée de l'Air will recognise many airfield names, some of which still host units performing the same tasks over forty years later.

15

Throughout Europe, the 'twenties and early 'thirties were a period of unhurried re-equipment, as aircraft types became obsolete. Whilst many of the models serving with the French air force were biplanes, there was no inbred mistrust of the monoplane as in Britain and even during the first decade of peace, front-line types included several of this variety. Fighters of the period were — in approximate chronological order — the Gourdou 32 C1 (the suffix indicating Chasse/fighter, single seat), a parasol monoplane; Wibault 7 C1 and 72 C1 of similar configuration; Nieuport Delage 62 C1/622 C1, an attractive streamlined sesquiplane and the Morane-Saulnier 225, another parasol design.

The bomber escadrilles flew such as the two-engined Lioré et Olivier 20 BN3 (and versions 203, 206 and 208) a three-seat night bomber of similar grotesqueness to the Beardmore Inflexible; Breguet 19 B2 (two-seat day bomber) single engine biplane; Potez 540, a shoulder wing monoplane with underslung engines in the manner of the modern Dornier Skyservant; Bloch 200/210 reminiscent of a monoplane version of the Boulton-Paul Sidestrand, and Amiot 143, another twin-engined monoplane.

Whereas the fighters represented all which was new and streamlined in aircraft design, the bombers were in contrast clumsy-looking attempts at producing heavy aircraft which would be capable of fighting their way to a target, attacked by enemy fighters. The wholesale slaughter of a generation in the trenches of 1914-18 had produced a profound effect upon the French people and their leaders, and they sought never again to permit such carnage. Accordingly, an immense fortified wall was constructed to close the frontier with Germany, and, fitted with underground barracks, storerooms and railways, blister turrets and strategically constructed approaches, it was considered the ultimate in defence. Over the 'Maginot Line', as this immense concrete barrier was named, would fly the long range bombers of the Armée de l'Air on their way to deal a crippling blow to any potential aggressor — or at least, that was the theory.

Supporting the bomber and fighter forces were the general duties types such as the Potez 25 A2 (co-operation, two-seat) single engined biplane, Potez 29 sesquiplane utility transport and the Mureaux 113/115/117 series of co-operation single engine parasols (best imagined as a Merlin engined Luton Minor). Training was capably handled by the Morane 230/315 Parasol.

When the Armée de l'Air became autonomous, it did so with equipment which was outdated and urgently in need of replacement. Since 1918, Germany had been in a state of confusion and unrest, both politically and economically, but as the effects of the depression lifted, shouts of a new slogan, 'Deutschland, Erwache!' were clearly to be heard west of the Rhine. 'Germany, Awake!' was an exhortation which generated great anxiety in every Frenchman, and as the message of National Socialism became increasingly clear, nations all over Europe began to re-arm.

Orders were placed for new types such as the Dewoitine D.500 series of monoplane fighter and the similar Morane-Saulnier MS 406, medium bombers of low wing design (Bloch 131) and twin-engined fighters e.g. Potez 630 series, remarkably like the Me 110. The speed with which aircraft manufacturers delivered new equipment was not to the Government's liking and thus occurred the paradoxical situation whereby the French Socialist Government (the Front Populaire) was threatening the industry with nationalisation unless they increased ouput, but the British Socialist party (the Labour Party) aided by the Liberals was voting against re-armament and instigating motions of censure at every opportunity.

On 11 August 1936, the French aircraft firms were nationalised and a drive for increased production was initiated. At first this bore little fruit and service deliveries for 1936 were 702 aircraft, exactly four more than in the previous year. By 31 December 1936, the Armée de l'Air had on charge 4,447 aircraft in the following categories (figures for 31.12.35 in parentheses): Fighters 639 (437), Bombers 707 (357), Reconnaissance 1,515 (1,368), Trainers 1,000 (1,632) and reserve 586 (559). Whilst the total numbers remained largely the same, the 'sharp end' had been strengthened and lengthened. This was by no means enough, and the aircraft industry became locked in a race against time to increase quantity and quality, a contest which was lost by the same 'narrow margin' by which Britain won her battle in the late Summer of 1940.

When the Front Populaire government came to power, it was planned to merge both air services, but this met with heavy opposition from the Aéronavale ranks. There were one or two instances when mergers did occur — for example, the fighter Escadrilles 3C2 and 4C1, equipped with the Dewoitine D.501, became the 1ere and 2e Escadrilles of the Armée de l'Air's GC I/8 in January 1936; the similarly-equipped Escadrille 3C1 (until then flying the Morane-Saulnier MS 225) becoming the 3e Escadrille of GC II/8 — but this was the exception rather than the rule. On the other hand, aircraft procured for the Armée de l'Air were diverted to Aéronavale service, or just handed over by the former air arm: the Loire-Nieuport L-N 411, which was to be the Armée de l'Air's version of the L-N 401 and as such had no provision for wing folding nor arrester gear, entered service with the Aéronavale Escadrille AB4 in April 1940, and the Potez 631 of GC II/8 were transferred to Escadrille AC1 early in 1940.

Parallel with the frenzied preparations for what was to become the Second World War, several of the major European powers were participating in a miniature dress-rehearsal in Spain, begun in July 1936, and volunteers came from many of the others not overtly aiding the opposing sides. France provided the Nationalists with Spad 510 and Dewoitine D.370 fighters and the Potez 540 bomber, at the same time taking an opportunity to study the tactics practised by the other nations. French pilots were able to fly a captured Me 109 and He 111, and gain impressions of their capabilities.

Whilst the aircraft industry was re-organising, an inevitable drop in production occurred, and in 1937 only 528 aeroplanes were accepted by the Armée de l'Air. Despite opposition from some quarters, France followed the lead set by Britain and placed her first orders with the United States (in secret) during the first months of 1938. One hundred Curtiss Hawk fighters were called for and began to arrive in January 1939, to be followed by almost two hundred of the ubiquitous T-6 Texan trainer. The Douglas DB-7 (Boston) was likewise ordered, but arrived too late to see service.

The Hawks and a small number of MS 406 and Potez 630 were the only aircraft of modern design serving with the Armée de l'Air in the early months of 1939. Much controversy surrounds the Anglo-French back-down over Hitler's invasion of Czechoslovakia in September 1938, claiming that Mr. Chamberlain's 'piece of paper' was either a necessary ruse to gain more time or a masterly confidence trick played by Hitler. Whatever time Britain bought, it was worth tenfold more to the Armée de l'Air.

Chamberlain's now famous 'Peace in our time' speech fortunately did not slow down the tempo of military expansion in Britain or France, and the air estimates for the latter country, made public in December 1938, totalled Fr10,822 milliards (£60 million at the values of those days). Wherever practicable, the French aircraft industry was working three shifts per day, and at last, modern types such as the D.520 and Bloch 151 fighters and the Bloch 131 bomber-reconnaissance aircraft were arriving in quantity.

Anglo-French Staff talks began in London on 29 March, and two days later, Britain and France jointly declared their support for Poland in the event of a German invasion of that country. Belatedly, the two allies commenced air exercises on 11 July with approximately one hundred RAF aircraft operating over France, and these were followed by a day and night exercise in which some 200 Armée de l'Air aircraft participated on 16/17 August.

In anticipation of the German attack on Poland, the French forces were dispersed to their war bases during the latter part of August, and air force squadrons dispersed to their operational airfields, where they came under the control of the various field armies. General mobilisation was ordered on 28 August and when news of the invasion of Poland was received early in the morning of 1 September, a joint ultimatum was issued, demanding the withdrawal of German troops. No reply was forthcoming, and at 11 am on 3 September, Britain was at war, France following suit at 5 pm.

The Second World War

At the commencement of hostilities with Germany, the Armée de l'Air possessed a total of 3,600 aircraft, of which 1,364 were front-line types, and of these only 494 were of modern design. The types in use are given below:—

Aircraft in service at commencement of hostilities

Fighters: Single engine 826 modern types (535 MS 405/406, 120 Bloch 151/152, 169 Hawk 75A-1/2, two Koolhoven FK58) plus a further 410 obsolescent aircraft (Dewoitine D.371/500/501/510, Nieuport 46, Spad 510) and a small number of obsolete Nieuport 622/629 and Morane 225. Twin engine — 288 modern types (78 Potez 630, 210 Potez 631).

Bombers: Twelve (ten LéO 451, two Breguet 691) and some obsolete LéO 206/257.

Bomber/recce: 890 obsolescent aircraft (Bloch 131/200/210, Amiot 143, Potez 540/542, Farman 221/222, Potez 633).

Reconnaissance: Sixty-five modern types (sixty Potez 637, five Potez 63.11).

Observation: 225 obsolescent aircraft (Mureaux 113/115/117) plus a small number of Potez 25/290/391 and Breguet 270/271 in the Army Co-operation role.

Transports: Six Farman 224, plus twenty-five obsolescent Potez 650.

On 2 September, with all units at their war stations, the Air Brigades were disbanded and fighter and bomber aircraft re-organised on a 'Groupement' basis. Thus, two escadrilles formed a 'Groupe', and two Groupes a 'Groupement'. There were in the front line twenty-two Fighter groups comprising 455 aircraft, plus 110 ageing aircraft in the nine Escadrilles Régionales (Air Force reserve); thirty-three Bomber groups totalling 322 medium, fifty heavy and twelve assault bombers; fourteen reconnaissance/co-operation groups with 172 aircraft; also forty-five Observation groups with 340 aircraft, of which 195 were autogyros. To these were added units of the British Expeditionary Force, the first ten Fairey Battles arriving on 2 September.

The Aéronavale, like the British Fleet Air Arm, had always been the Cinderella of air forces and comprised 159 shipborne and 194 shore-based aircraft — most obsolescent, and all poorly armed. Seagoing attack aircraft totalled forty-five: the carrier *Béarn* operated nine Vought 156F and four Loire-Nieuport 410/411 dive bombers and twenty-seven Dewoitine fighters, whilst the balance of four Levasseur PL101, thirteen Levasseur PL7 and fifteen Loire-Nieuport 210 seaplanes were allocated to various capital ships.

Thirty-two LéO 257 seaplane bombers flew from coastal bases and were complemented by a further thirty-nine long-range patrol/bomber flying boats — Breguet 521 (twenty), Loire 70 (six), LéO 470 (five), Latécoère 301 (one), Latécoère 302 (three), Latécoère 523 (three) and Potez 141 (one).

Seaplane torpedo bombers totalled forty-six, of which eighteen Latécoère

17

298B were intended for the seaplane carrier *Commandant Teste* and the balance were coastal-based Latécoère 298A/D. For reconnaissance, there was a motley collection of 164 aircraft, including sixty-nine which were shipborne, consisting of fifty-five Loire-Nieuport 130, twenty-four CAMS 55/2 and 55/10, thirty-three Gourdou-Leseurre 810/812/832, fourteen Potez 25, ten Potez 452, eight CAMS 37, five Levasseur PL15, four Farman NC.470, four Latécoère 290, four LéO-Cierva C30, two Breguet-Short S8/2 and a Mureaux MB411.

Facing the Armée de l'Air was the German Luftwaffe of approximately 4,250 aircraft, most of which were modern types. Propaganda had caused the British and French to over-estimate this force by 300%, and had they known the true figure *and* possessed imaginative and forceful political leaders, a bold strike at Germany whilst she was fully committed in Poland would in all probability have changed the course of history.

Instead, a limited-objective operation, partially occupying the Saar region was undertaken on 8 September. On the same day, a Mureaux 115 was shot down by flak and its two crew killed — the first Armée de l'Air victims of the war. A few hours later, the score was more than evened when two Me 109D out of a force of four were shot down by five Curtiss Hawks. Operations which could be described as no more than 'skirmishing' continued for the next eight months, and the only encounters were in the air. An American war correspondent coined the phrase 'Phoney War', which has now gone into the history books to describe this first period of the hostilities. By the beginning of May, the French had lost thirty-eight aircraft in air combat, eight to flak, and a further seventeen due to unknown causes over enemy territory. During the Battle of Britain, one air force could lose this number of aircraft in one day.

Valuable time was once more gained during the 'Phoney War', and aircraft deliveries continued to gather momentum. Comparison of numbers of certain of the newer types on charge on 3 September 1939 and 1 May 1940 show some considerable increases:—

Fighters: MS 406 373:1070, Bloch 151 srs 120:491, Hawk 172:206, Caudron 714 0:44, D.520 0:65.

Bombers: Breguet 691 srs 2:98, Martin 167F 0:109, Douglas DB-7 0:25, LéO 451 10:192, Amiot 351 srs 0:37.

Reconnaissance: Potez 63.11 5:603, Bloch 174 srs 0:42.

Some aircraft were to arrive from the factories faster than crews could be trained to fly them, for example a Dewoitine D.520 was being turned-out every hour during the last weeks of the Battle of France, and even in the last hours, pilots collecting replacements from maintenance units were able to choose from row upon row of factory-fresh machines. Bomber production was still behind schedule, but largely, the production race begun in 1936 was within a few steps of being won. Hitler, however, decided to take down the winning post and declare it a no-contest.

In the early hours of 10 May 1940, German armies began the invasion of Belgium, Holland and Luxembourg, wheeling then south to enter France. Ignoring completely the Maginot Line, an armoured spearhead pierced the French frontier in the Ardennes, a wooded and hilly area supposedly impenetrable to mechanised forces, and therefore thinly defended, and by the familiar Blitzkrieg system began to encircle the B.E.F. and French elements in the north of the country. At the time of the attack, the Armée de l'Air comprised four Air Zones, which in order of size were, North, East, Alpine (although containing many units re-equipping, and thus not operational) and South. Squadrons and aircraft were as tabulated:—

Zone d'Opérations Aériennes Nord

Fighters: Groupement de Chasse 21 (GC I/1 Bloch 152; GC II/1 Bloch 152; GC III/3 MS 406; GC II/10 and III/10 Bloch 151/152)
Groupement de Chasse 23 (GC I/2 MS 406; GC III/2 MS 406; GC I/4 Hawk; GC I/5 Hawk; ECMJ I/16 Potez 631)
Groupement de Chasse 25 (GC III/1 MS 406; GC II/8 Bloch 152)
Groupement de Chasse de Nuit (ECN I/13, II/13, III/13, IV/13 Potez 631)

Bombers: (under 1 Division Aérienne)
Groupement de Bombardement 6 (GB I/12, GB II/12 LéO 451)
Groupement de Bombardement 9 (GB I/34, GB II/34 Amiot 143)
Groupement de Bombardement d'Assault 18 (GBA I/54, GBA II/54 Breguet 693)

Reconnaissance: GR I/14 Potez 63.11; GR II/22 Potez 63.11; GR II/33 Potez 637/Bloch 174; GR I/35 Potez 63.11; GR II/52 Potez 63.11

Observation: GAO 501, 502, 503, 504, 505, 507, 510, 511, 515, 516, 518, 2/520, 544, 545, 547, 2/551, 4/551, 552 all with Potez 63.11 plus either Mureaux 115/117 or Breguet 27.

Zone d'Opérations Aériennes Est

Fighters: Groupement de Chasse 22 (GC I/2 MS 406; GC II/4 Hawk; GC I/5 Hawk; GC II/6 MS 406; GC III/7 MS 406; GC I/8 Bloch 152)

Reconnaissance: GR I/22 Potez 63.11; GR I/36 Potez 63.11; GR II/36 Potez 63.11 and Bloch 174; GR I/52 Potez 637 and Bloch 174)

Bombers: (under 3 Division Aérienne)
  Groupement de Bombardement 10 (GB I/38, GB II/38 Amiot 143)
  Groupement de Bombardement 15 (GB I/15, GB II/15 Farman 221/222)

Observation: GAO 1/506, 2/506, 2/508, 509, 512, 517, 520, 546, 548, 1/551, 3/551, 553 all Potez 63.11 plus either Mureaux 115/117, Potez 39 or Breguet 27.

Zone d'Opérations Aériennes Sud

Fighters: Groupement de Chasse 24 (GC III/6 MS 406; GC II/7 MS 406)

Bombers: nil

Reconnaissance: GR I/33 Potez 637/Bloch 174; GR I/55 Potez 63.11

Observation: GAO 513 Potez 63.11/Potez 39/Potez 25; GAO 543 Potez 63.11/Potez 540/Breguet 27).

Zone d'Opérations Aériennes des Alpes

Fighters: GC I/3 D.520; GC II/3 MS 406/D.520; GC I/6 MS 406; GC II/9 MS 406; GC III/9 Bloch 151; ECNV/13 Potez 631; GAM 550 MS 406/Potez 63.11

Bombers: Groupement de Bombardement 1 (GB I/62, GB I/63 Martin 167F)
  Groupement de Bombardement 6 (GB I/31, GB II/31 LéO 451)
  Groupement de Bombardement 7 (GB I/23, GB II/23 Bloch 210/LéO 451)
  Groupement de Bombardement 9 (GB I/21 GB II/21 Amiot 351/354/Bloch 210)
  Groupement de Bombardement 11 (GB I/11, GB II/11 LéO 451, Breguet 210)
  Groupement de Bombardement d'Assault 19 (GBA II/35 Potez 633/Breguet 691; GBA I/51 Potez 633/Breguet 691/693).
  (all in the process of re-equipping except GdB 1)

Reconnaissance: GR II/14, GR II/55 Potez 63.11

Observation: GAO 1/514, 2/514, 581, 1/589 Potez 63.11

With the Aéronavale, the urgent need for more aircraft had lead to the impressment of civilian aircraft, for example the three Farman 223 airliners operated by Air France (F-AGJM c/n 1 'Camille Flamarion', F-ARIN c/n 2 'Jules Verne' and F-AROA c/n 3 'Le Verrier'), were impressed in October 1939 for long-range reconnaissance duties (the Aéronavale's Escadrille 10E was allotted three basically similar Farman 222, transferred from the Armée de l'Air, in the next month), and 'Jules Verne' actually became the first Allied bomber to raid Berlin, on the night of 7-8 June 1940. The trio were then flown by Escadrille B5 from Paris-Orly since May 1940 (they were in fact the Escadrille); this became 5B on 1 August and shortly afterwards converted to Martin 167Fs, the Farmans then being returned to Air France.

During the early stages of World War II, the Aéronavale had a token fighter force, Escadrille de Chasse AC1, at Cherbourg-Chantereyne, flew the Dewoitine D.376 C1, re-equipping with ex-Armée de l'Air Potez 631 twin-engined fighters during the first four months of 1940 and receiving a few Dewoitine D.520 in June; it absorbed the Potez 631s of AC2 in August, and was transferred to French North Africa under the Occupation. Escadrille AC2 exchanged its Dewoitine D.373 and D.376 for Potez 631s early in 1940, and operated from Cherbourg and its satellite airfield Maupertus-sur-Mer; it received its first six Bloch 151 and a few Dewoitine D.520 in June 1940, and became 2AC in August, being transferred to Bizerte-Sidi Ahmed, and later to Oran-La Sénia, re-equipping with Dewoitine D.520 in September. It eventually went to Agadir (in 1942), where it was at the time of 'Operation Torch'.

Escadrilles AC1 and AC2 formed the 1ère Flottille de Chasse (F1C, later 1F), with HQ at Calais-Marck from March 1940. The units' Potez 631 operated over the North Sea, and between 10 and 21 May 1940 claimed twelve German aircraft for the loss of eight of their own machines.

Escadrille AC3 at Hyères-Palyvestre flew the Dewoitine D.510 until May 1940, when the first Bloch 151 arrived, but converted to Dewoitine D.520s in June, only to be disbanded in August. A similar fate befell Escadrille AC4, with Dewoitine D.520s. Escadrille AC5 was formed at Hourtin on 20 June 1940, with eleven ex-Armée de l'Air Morane-Saulinier MS 406, but saw no action.

The naval bomber units flew either the Martin 167F or the Douglas DB.7, with some Potez 63.11 and Lioré et Olivier LéO 451 also in use. The observation and torpedo Escadrilles were using the Latécoère 298 at the time of the Armistice.

The short and bitterly fought campaign which lead to the defeat of France saw the Armée de l'Air give a good account of itself, claiming 813 enemy aircraft shot down, of which 585 were positively confirmed. Almost 1,500 men were killed or wounded, and 1,200 aircraft written off by all causes including accidents.

A history of what became known as the Battle of France would fill an entire volume, but it will suffice to say that the task of maintaining air superiority over a large front was rendered increasingly difficult as time progressed by the inexorable advance of the Wehrmacht. Both the Army and Air Force were constantly plugging the gaps and transferring units to the scene of new threats as they emerged. From the start, the battle was a defensive one, and despite brave counter-attacks the Germans had advanced to a line Arras-Abbeville-Amiens in just eleven days (it had taken them three-and-a-half years to almost reach Amiens in the previous war).

Like the British and Belgians, the Armée de l'Air flew its share of 'suicide missions' in an attempt to destroy the infamous bridges over the Albert Canal and a later, more successful, attack on the bridges at Sedan to slow the principal German breakthrough. Otherwise the bombers were able to achieve little in the way of disabling the German Army and they were normally despatched in too small numbers to gain substantial results.

On 5 June, the Armée de l'Air claimed sixty-six aircraft shot down, but this was the high point of the fighters' brief war, and just a week later Paris was declared an open city; with the B.E.F. back in England via Dunkirk, northern France was in German hands. In the South, Italy now joined the conflict, eager to stab the reeling French in the back, and launching an offensive over the Alps. In the midst of the confusion, Prime Minister Reynaud resigned on 16 June and was replaced by Marshal Pétain who requested terms from Germany the following day. A separate peace was made with the Italians and at 0135 hours on 25 June all hostilities with the Axis ceased.

For the next two years there existed two French air forces, one fighting for the Allies, the other defending a neutral country. Still hoping to persuade Britain to agree to an armistice, Hitler granted what were (for him) generous terms to the French. The south-eastern portion of the country remained a nominally independent nation with a capital at Vichy and administrative control of the French Empire. Many aircraft had escaped to North Africa, but others flew to England where they joined the embryo Forces Aériennes Françaises Libres — Free French Air Force.

In July and August 1940, many Aéronavale units were redesignated — Escadrilles T1 to T4 became 1T to 4T, Escadrilles 1S1, 3S6, HB1 and HB2 became 1S, 12S, 1HT and 2HT respectively (T1 was ex 4T1, T2 ex 1T1, HB1 ex 7B2, etc), but the latter four were disbanded on 20 August, due to the reduction of military flying imposed by the German and Italian Armistice Commissions. The Aéronavale maintained a number of operational units, all of which (apart from isolated cases) shore-based, due to the destruction of the French fleet by the British during 'Operation Catapult', at Toulon, Oran, Algiers, Bizerte and Dakar.

Some time after 'Operation Torch' and the occupation of French North Africa by Allied forces, the Aéronavale units in the area came under Allied control and were relegated to the unexciting but important task of patrolling the Mediterranean coast. British equipment was gradually introduced into service, with deliveries of Walrus amphibians and later Sunderlands and Seafires.

The Vichy-administered Armée de l'Air de l'Armistice fought several campaigns against the Allies in North Africa and the Middle East before the remaining portion of France was taken over by the German troops on 11 November 1942. With France entirely subject to German domination, the agonising question of divided loyalty evaporated and all Frenchmen overseas gave their full support to the Allied cause.

Meanwhile, in Britain, escaped French airmen had been posted to St. Athan in Wales where a varied selection of aircraft was flown. Five suitably trained pilots were able to participate in the Battle of Britain and many others were trained on bomber and reconnaissance types. For some time they were to serve with various RAF squadrons, but eventually national squadrons were formed almost entirely of French personnel.

First of these was 340 Squadron, raised at Turnhouse, Scotland, with Spitfire IIs in November 1941. The French tradition of naming squadrons was perpetuated and the unit was alternatively known as the 'Ile de France' squadron. Ex-Vichy airmen in North Africa at the time of the German takeover in late 1942 increased numbers considerably and after training on RAF aircraft they formed several other units so that by the time the Allies had re-established themselves in Europe in June 1944, the position was:—

Squadron		Aircraft	Where Formed
326 Squadron 'Nice'	ex GC II/7	Spitfire	Ghisonaccia 1.12.43
327 Squadron 'Corse'	ex GC I/3	Spitfire	Campo del Oro 1.12.43
328 Squadron 'Provence'	ex GC I/7	Spitfire	Reghaia 1.12.43
329 Squadron 'Cigognes'		Spitfire	Ayr 5.1.44
340 Squadron 'Ile de France'		Spitfire	Turnhouse 7.11.41
341 Squadron 'Alsace'		Spitfire	Turnhouse 15.1.43
342 Squadron 'Lorraine'	ex GB I/20	Boston	West Raynham 7.4.43
343 Squadron	ex 7F	Sunderland	Dakar 29.11.43
344 Squadron	ex 7F	Wellington	Dakar 29.11.43
345 Squadron 'Berry'		Spitfire	Ayr 12.2.44
346 Squadron 'Guyenne'		Halifax	Elvington 16.5.44
347 Squadron 'Tunisie'		Halifax	Elvington 20.6.44

Other units remained in North Africa with US equipment and retained their original designations, and a group of airmen transferred to the USSR in August 1942, where as GC 3 'Normandie' they fought alongside the Soviet Air Force with their Yak fighters until the final victory. Also in Britain, but attached to the US Army Air Corps, were the Marauders of 31 Bomb Group (GB I/19, GB II/20 and GB I/22) and 34 Bomb Group (GB I/32, GB II/52 and GB II/63). These later moved to Lyon-Bron after D-Day and were assisted in their task of aiding the Allied armies liberating the home country by several spontaneously created squadrons formed in Southern France.

First of these was 'Groupement Patrie', equipped with Bostons and Marylands in North Africa and combined with a Forces Français de l'Intérieur squadron of ex-air force resistance members flying the Dewoitine D.520. From this unit evolved GB I/34 'Béarn' with Bostons, Marylands and an Me 110, and a second bomber squadron, Groupement Dor (later GB I/31 'Aunis') was formed with the Ju 88. Their aircraft wore a remarkable conglomeration of markings, namely Luftwaffe camouflage, French roundels and Invasion Stripes. The D.520 portion of this force was re-christened GC II/8 'Saintonge' and later received Spitfires, whilst reconnaissance duties were performed by GR Perigord with Fi 156 Storchs and a few Potez 631.

Although in what were very much 'scratch units', the men of the South acquitted themselves well and supported the Allied drive towards Paris. Hammered by Bomber Command and its two French squadrons of Halifaxes, molested by the 2TAF and its French Bostons, Marauders and Mitchells, and stung by the Spitfire and Thunderbolt fighters maintaining Allied air superiority, the Third Reich finally surrendered on 9 May 1945.

At the close of the war in Europe, the Armée de l'Air had thirty-six regular units serving with the British, US and Russian forces and the independent squadrons in Southern France. These were:—

Unit	Name	Aircraft type
GC I/2	Cigognes (329 Sq.)	Spitfire IX
GC II/2	Berry (345 Sq.)	Spitfire IX
GC III/2	Alsace (341 Sq.)	Spitfire IX
GC IV/2	Ile de France (340 Sq.)	Spitfire IX
GC I/3	Corse (327 Sq.)	Spitfire IX
GC II/3	Dauphiné	Thunderbolt
GC III/3	Ardennes	Thunderbolt
GC 3	Normandie-Niemen	Yak 3 (comprising 4 squadrons)
GC I/4	Navarre	Thunderbolt
GC I/5	Champagne	Thunderbolt
GC II/5	Lafayette	Thunderbolt
GC III/6	Rousillon	Thunderbolt
GC I/7	Provence (328 Sq.)	Spitfire IX
GC II/7	Nice (326 Sq.)	Spitfire IX
GT II/15	Anjou	C-45/B-25
GCB I/18	Vendée	Dewoitine D.520/Spitfire Vb
GCB II/18	Saintonge	Dewoitine D.520/Spitfire Vb
GB I/19	Gascogne	Marauder
GB I/20	Lorraine (342 Sq.)	Mitchell BIII
GB II/20	Bretagne	Marauder
GB II/22	Maroc	Marauder
GB II/23	Guyenne (346 Sq.)	Halifax BVI
GB I/25	Tunisie (347 Sq.)	Halifax BVI
GB I/31	Aunis	Ju 88A
GB I/32	Bourgogne	Marauder
GR I/33	Belfort	F-5G Lightning
GB II/33	Savoie	F-6C/D Mustang/Spitfire IX
GR III/33	Perigord	Storch/Potez 631
GB I/34	Béarn	DB-7/Martin 167F/Me 110
GB II/52	Franche-Comte	Marauder
GB II/63	Senegal	Marauder
GT Artois		C-47
GT Picardie		C-47

Some of these were prepared for service against Japan, but plans were overtaken by events at Hiroshima and Nagasaki.

Post War Progress

As soon as headquarters and a supply organisation could be re-established, the Armée de l'Air squadrons were detached from the temporary host air forces and took up permanent residence in their homeland. In most cases they brought their aircraft with them as a gift from the three powers, but it was principally to Britain that France looked to re-build her air force. Large numbers of Spitfires, Wellingtons, Mosquitos, Ansons, Tiger Moths, Halifaxes and even a few Martinet target tugs were provided during the immediate post-war years.

Western Union, a forerunner of NATO, bought Lancasters, Seafires and Sunderlands for the Aéronavale, and wartime American types such as the Thunderbolt, Kingcobra, Dakota and C-45 served in quantity. Production lines of the ex-German Ju 52, Si 208 and Me 108 were taken-over, and the aircraft produced as the Toucan, Martinet and Noralpha for Armée de l'Air use, but the eventual aim was to re-construct the aircraft industry and make France independent of foreign manufacture.

During the six years of war, the science of aircraft design had progressed by leaps and bounds and much had to be learned before the industry could catch-up. So that the air force would not be without modern interceptors, France was obliged to purchase and licence-produce her first jet type, the de Havilland Vampire 5. Initially, 180 ex-RAF examples were delivered commencing on 15 December 1948, and these were later augmented by 247 aircraft built by Sud Aviation. Vampires equipped EC 1 (re-numbered EC 7 on 1 November 1951), EC 2, EC 4, EC 5, EC 6 and EC 8 during the early 'fifties, and were not retired from EC 1/6 until the Autumn of 1960.

The majority of aircraft manufacturing firms remained in the groups which had been created by the 1936 nationalisation, and received governmental assistance, largely for aerodynamic and constructional research projects. In the decade following the war, few modern types entered large scale production, although the piston engined Noratlas achieved a creditable sales total, and it seemed to some that the French had an 'industry of prototypes'. Each of these one-off jobs advanced the science of design and construction and gradually reduced the lead gained by Britain and the USA, giving the country a firm foundation on which to build for the future.

Avions Marcel Bloch re-appeared after the war entitled Avions Marcel Dassault, and consistent with their current position as leading designers of jet interceptors, produced France's first indigenous jet fighter, the Ouragan. By the time the Ouragan entered service with 2 Wing at Mont-de-Marsan in 1951, a change in nomenclature had brought back the Escadre in place of the Groupement. The term 'Escadron' replaced 'Groupe' and henceforth the smallest indivisible unit was the Escadron, or squadron.

Each operational base normally housed an Escadre (or wing) made-up of two or three Escadrons each of which was named, usually after a unit which had distinguished itself in combat, such as 'Normandie-Niemen' or 'Cigognes'. The Escadron was, for administrative purposes only, further split into two escadrilles (or flights) each with the insignia of a First World War squadron — these badges being applied to opposite sides of the Escadron's aircraft.

The first major product of the post-war Dassault stable however was the piston engined Flamant, flown for the first time in 1947. Over three hundred were eventually built for use as both trainers and transports, but with the world market dominated by the United States, no overseas sales could be generated. The twin engined SO-30P Bretagne and four motor SE-161 Languedoc had a similar story, and although they gave good service to the Armée de l'Air and Aéronavale, only the latter was exported, in small numbers to the Polish airline, LOT. A few Flamant remain in use as twin-conversion aircraft, and until recently, a few others were employed as radar trainers by 30 Escadre. Bretagnes served both the air force and navy — principally the VIP transport wing, ET 60 at Villacoublay and 31S, the latter also having a few examples of the Languedoc, in common with multi-engine training unit 56S. It was however, the Toucan, Martinet, Noralpha and Dakota which served in quantity with the Escadres de Transport (ET 60-64) and the various Escadrilles de Liaison Aériennes numbered in the 40 and 50 range based at home, in North Africa and Indochina.

For pilot training, the Tiger Moths which had been supplied by the RAF at the end of the war were augmented by the Stampe SV4, and later MS 733 Alcyon, and in the mid 'fifties the Broussard began a production run that ran to 400 aircraft for the air force and army as a communications machine suited to short-field operations in the same category as the de Havilland Canada Beaver. These years were to see the Armée de l'Air achieve its greatest numerical strength, when the cold war was at its height, and a rapid build-up took place in most air forces of Western Europe.

With the entry of the USA into Western Union, the North Atlantic Treaty Organisation was born, and from the vast resources of the 'new world' ally came Thunderjets and T-33s by the hundred and in the Spring of 1951, Escadre de Chasse 3 at Reims became the first Thunderjet wing, followed by EC 11 and ER 33, the photo-reconnaissance wing.

The principal Thunderjet variant was the unswept F-84G, a development of the F-84E, and rapidly put into production as a result of difficulties with the swept wing F-84F Thunderstreak. When the 'Streak became available in 1955-56 it was promptly issued to the Thunderjet Escadres, EC 3 being the first recipient in November 1955. They were followed by EC 1, EC 4 and EC 9, whilst ER 33 received the photo-reconnaissance RF-84F Thunderflash.

The more potent F-100D Super Sabre displaced the F-84F in ECs 3 and 11 from 1958 onwards, but the trend now was towards two rather than three, squadrons per wing and when EC 1 and EC 9 disbanded in 1963 and 1965 respectively, they were not re-formed with another type. Each wing, or more correctly its resident base, operated a communications and instrument flying unit, first with such types as the Tiger Moth, Nord 1101, etc., and more recently the T-33, Broussard, Flamant and Magister. At regional level, Escadrilles de Liaison have similar types and additionally the Paris.

For night fighting, the Mosquito NF.30 was replaced by another British aircraft, the Meteor NF.11, the first deliveries of which arrived for EMICN 30 at Tours early in 1953, together with a small batch of mark T.7 trainers. The three Meteor squadrons were replaced by two of home-produced Vautour IIN in 1957, with a third based in North Africa. The Meteors re-grouped into a night fighter OCU (CIETT 346) which remained alongside EC 30 at Reims until 1963. Meteors are still in use, but now as chase and experimental aircraft with the CEV, and as late as 1974, a further six were bought from RAF stocks to act as a spares source.

All-weather fighter capability was further enhanced in 1956 by the arrival of the F-86K Sabre for the two squadrons of EC 13, a new wing formed at Colmar. In 1962, the availability of home-produced aircraft brought about their retirement and a small number were transferred to Italy where they continued in service for over a decade.

In 1952, a second Dassault jet fighter, the Mystère II appeared and was issued to ECs 5 and 10, remaining in use for the remarkably short period of two to three years before replacement by the swept-wing Super Mystère B2. The Mystere IVA went to EC 7 and EC 8 in North Africa, returning home in 1961, and those of EC 8 presently continue to serve in the fighter-training role.

Basic training switched to jet aircraft in 1956 with the arrival of the Fouga Magister at the Ecole de l'Air (later GI 312) and in North Africa the Division des Moniteurs de Pilotage (GE 313) and Ecole de Chasse additionally adopted the type. These schools also took up residence in France in 1961 when she evacuated her North African colonies, the EdC bringing back its T-33s to Tours where they now form GE 314.

During the 1950s, the Armée de l'Air and Aéronavale were almost continually engaged in operations overseas. These began with the war in what is now Vietnam in 1949-54, and continued with the Algerian rebellion of 1954-62 and the Suez attack of 1956.

The action in Suez was an Anglo-French affair with Israeli participation, born out of the nationalisation of the Suez Canal by Egypt's Colonel Nasser. The Canal, although in Egypt was (like the Panama Canal) the property of other nations, in this case France and Britain. Both were angered at the confiscation of their assets, France more so as a result of Nasser's help for the Algerian rebels, whilst Israel's relationship with Egypt at the time requires no further elaboration.

Prior to the operation, thirty-six Thunderstreaks of EC 1 deployed to Lydda on 25 October joining thirty-six Mystère IVAs of EC 2 which had arrived at Haifa two days before to provide fighter cover. Israel attacked on the 29 October, and on the 31st, British and French aircraft struck Egyptian positions near the canal, whilst a force of parachutists was dropped to capture strategic points along the length of the waterway. From Akrotiri in Cyprus, further support was obtained from Thunderstreaks of EC 3 and reconnaissance Thunderflashes of ER 33, plus several RAF units. From 1 November, Egyptian airfields were attacked, but the EAF wisely withdrew its force of twenty Il-28 light bombers to Luxor where it believed them safe. On the fifth of the month, a flight of eight Thunderstreaks flying at the limit of their range flew a dog-leg path to attack Luxor from an unexpected direction and destroyed all twenty of the bombers. The following day, world opinion forced a cease fire and the withdrawal of Anglo-French forces, and Colonel Nasser kept his canal.

By the time of the events at Suez, the Armée de l'Air had lost one of its principal duties, that of providing liaison and observation facilities for the Armée de Terre. The increasing importance of the aircraft and later the helicopter in army operations underlined the need for these to be under the direct control of the Army, and in November 1954, the Aviation Légère de l'Armée de Terre (ALAT) was formed.

In terms of numbers, the principal Army aircraft was the Piper Cub/Super Cub which had equipped several observation groups from 1943 onwards. Pilots and mechanics for these French-American units were provided by the Armée de l'Air, whilst aircraft and observers were the property of the Artillery. Duties involved the reporting of damage caused by fighter-bomber attacks and gun-ranging for the Army. With the end of the war, control passed entirely into French hands, with the Army supplying maintenance and support facilities, but pilots, now reduced to only four, were still from the air force.

During 1946, the first peacetime observation squadron formed at Mayence-Finthen in the French Zone of Germany with eighteen L-4 Cubs, two MS 500 and two autogyros. Next came the formation of eight L-4/MS 500 equipped Groupes d'Observation d'Artillerie: 1 GAOA at Nancy-Essey, 2 GAOA at Finthen, 3 GAOA at Setif Ain Arnat, 4 GAOA at Fez, 5 GAOA at Tunis, 21 GAOA at Touraine, 22 GAOA at Saigon and 23 GAOA at Hanoi. These latter three flights were soon to be involved in the Indochinese war of independence and during the first year (1949) 748 missions were flown including 288 of photographic reconnaissance and 202 co-operating with infantry.

A measure of autonomy for units serving in Indochina was gained on 3 March 1952 with the creation of the Aviation Légère d'Observation d'Artillerie which provided for the training of the first Army mechanics and pilots, the first of which arrived in Indochina as the war was drawing to a close.

American experience in Korea showed the importance of the helicopter in modern warfare, with the result that a small number were deployed in Indochina. In 1953, the ALOA began the training of its first three pilots at Issy les Moulineaux on the Bell 47D with two civilian instructors from Fenwick Aviation. Advanced instruction followed on the Hillers of Helicop-air and S-55 Whirlwinds of SNCASE at Buc before the newly-qualified pilots were posted to Indochina to fly ex-air force S-55s.

The first wholly ALOA helicopter squadron formed at Satory in 1954 designated 1 Groupement d'Helicoptères and equipped with the Hiller UH-12, Bell 47 and S-55, whilst 2 GH, which formed at Setif, Algeria in April 1955 operated the Bell 47, S-55 and the larger H-21, known universally as the 'Flying Banana'. Gradually the French aircraft industry made its presence felt, and Djinns and Alouettes replaced the S-55 and Hiller. Fixed-wing aircraft still retained their trans-atlantic bias, but the Cubs and Super Cubs were augmented by the NC 856 Norvigie in 1956, Nord 3400 in 1957 and Broussard in 1958.

During 1957, the Vautour also entered service as a bomber, in which role it offered a considerable improvement over the B-26 Invader then in use. France was still without her own strategic atomic bomb, but national pride dictated that she should possess one to increase her standing in the world, and work proceeded apace on both the weapon and delivery system, the bomb being first exploded in the Sahara on 13 February 1960. Meanwhile, French forces allocated to NATO's 4th Tactical Air Force (4TAF), were equipped with tactical nuclear weapons mounted on Super Sabres of the 3 and 11 Escadres.

The greatest single step towards self-sufficiency in aircraft manufacture occurred with the arrival of the Dassault Mirage. A Mirage I prototype flown in 1955 was followed by eleven experimental Mirage IIIA and a production series of ninety-five Mirage IIIC for tactical air command, the type also finding favour with the air forces of Australia, Israel and South Africa.

First recipients of the IIIC were the two strike squadrons of EC 2 at Dijon who relinquished their Mystère IVAs in the Spring of 1961; EC 13 following the next year. After replacement by later marks, the IIIC aircraft served

23

EC 5 in the air defence role and now remain only with EC 10 performing the same function.

A tandem-seat trainer, the IIIB was initially issued to Mirage III squadrons to assist in the work of crew conversion, but was later concentrated in a specialist OCU squadron, ECT 2/2. The strategic air command obtained ten of the variant to act as flight refuelling trainers, and a further version, the Mirage IIIBE incorporated the avionics of the major Armée de l'Air production model, the IIIE. On this occasion, EC 13 became the first wing to convert, during 1965 and was followed by EC 2. Tactical air command had also re-equipped EC 3 in 1967 (replacing the F-100 which was then concentrated in EC 11), EC 4 in 1966 (ex F-84F Thunderstreak), plus the reconnaissance Mirage IIIR for ER 33, beginning 1963.

A scaled-up version, the Mirage IVA, entered service with the Armée de l'Air in April 1964 to become the sole French Strategic nuclear bomber, when the first operational wing (EB 91) formed in October 1964. A total of sixty-two production aircraft were ordered and at peak strength equipped three wings each with three four-aircraft squadrons supported by twelve C-135F tankers. A proportion of the fleet was maintained at instant readiness, but this has now been reduced.

With the arrival of the Chance Vought Crusader in 1964, the Aéronavale achieved its long-held ambition of a front line composed entirely of modern types. As before the war, naval aviation was equipped with either inadequate numbers of up-to-date aircraft or semi-obsolete machines. Shipborne types had been mostly of ex-British or ex-US origin such as the Seafire, Helldiver or Hellcat with maritime patrol duties allocated to the Dornier Do 24, Sunderland or Nord Noroit flying boats. The old aircraft carrier, the *Béarn*, continued to serve as a ferry carrier, a role it had adopted in 1939 when the squadrons of Flottille F1A (AB1, AB2 and AB3) were put ashore and the vessel began a series of trans-Atlantic voyages bringing urgently required aircraft from the United States. When the French position became hopeless, the *Béarn* sailed for the West Indies where she was disarmed on 1 May 1942. With the German invasion of Vichy France, the carrier was overhauled in the USA but because of her slow speed was restricted to ferrying, a duty continued into 1946 supplying French forces in the Indochina war. In 1947-48, the ship was relegated to training, then becoming a submarine-fleet support ship until finally scrapped in March 1967.

First of the post-war aircraft carriers was the 8,200 ton *Dixmude*, launched as a cargo ship, the *Rio Parana* in December 1940, purchased by the US Navy in 1941 for conversion to an escort carrier, and handed to the Royal Navy as HMS *Biter* on 1 May 1942. On 9 April 1945 she transferred to the Marine National initially for fleet use, but by 1949 was relegated to an aircraft ferrying carrier in which role she delivered replacements to Indochina and brought MDAP aircraft over the North Atlantic. Finally, in 1959 the *Dixmude* was moored at St. Mandrier as a floating barracks.

The *Dixmude* was joined in October 1946 by the *Arromanches* (pennant number R95), launched on 30 September 1943 as HMS *Colossus* and transferred to France initially on a five year loan. This heavier vessel of 13,190 tons was bought outright in 1951 and during a refit in 1957-58 was fitted with a four degree angled flying deck and mirror-landing equipment in preparation for the Breguet Alizé. After a further short period of operations, armament was removed and the *Arromanches* became a training ship, finally disposed of in January 1964.

Carrier strength reached its peak in 1960 when for two months, six vessels were in service. The first of these additional carriers was the *La Fayette* (R96) launched on 22 May 1943 as the USS *Crown Point* (later USS *Langley* and USS *Fargo*) and handed over to France on 6 June 1951 under MDAP in time to participate in the Indochinese war. A similar craft, the *Bois Belleau* (R97) arrived on 5 September 1953 on five years' loan — later extended — and had been previously the USS *New Haven* and USS *Belleau Wood* when launched on 6 December 1942. The pair were replaced by French-built carriers and the *La Fayette* was handed back to the USN on 12 September 1960, the *Bois Belleau* following in March 1963.

As early as 1947, plans had been made for the construction of a new carrier to be named the *Clemenceau*, but not until 28 May 1954 was an order placed. The vessel commenced its trials on 24 November 1959, and was followed by sister ship *Foch* in July 1960, so that between the first voyage of the *Foch* and the return of the *La Fayette*, there were also the *Dixmude, Arromanches, Bois Belleau* and *Clemenceau* serving the navy. In 1958, the naval estimates included a new 30,000 ton carrier, but funds were not voted, and the ship was never built.

The *Clemenceau* and *Foch* enabled the Marine Nationale to begin operating high performance aircraft such as the Etendard and Crusader in place of its second post-war generation of Aquilons (Sea Venoms) and Corsairs. Ex-USN and RN Avengers were superseded by the Alize, whilst Alouettes and licence built HSS-1 Seabats replaced the HUP-2. Immediately prior to the introduction of the Crusader with 12F late in 1964, Aéronavale strength was as under:—

4F	Alizé	Hyères
6F	Alizé	Nimes-Garons
9F	Alizé	Hyères
11F	Etendard	Hyères
15F	Etendard	Hyères
16F	Aquilon	Hyères
17F	Etendard	Hyères
21F	P2V-6 Neptune	Nimes-Garons
22F	P2V-6 Neptune	Nimes-Garons
23F	P2V-7 Neptune	Lann-Bihoué
24F	P2V-7 Neptune	Lann-Bihoué

25F	P2V-7 Neptune	Lann-Bihoué
27F	P5M-2 Marlin	Dakar
31F	HSS-1	St. Mandrier
32F	HSS-1	St. Mandrier
33F	HSS-1	Lartigue
2S	Corse, Zéphyr, Expeditor	Lann-Bihoué
3S	Avenger, Alcyon, Flamant, Bretagne, Broussard	Cuers
9S	Lancaster, Expeditor	Noumea
10S	Alize, Alcyon, Flamant, Avenger, N2504, Aquilon	St. Raphaël
11S	Alcyon, Paris, Flamant	Dugny
20S	Alouette II, III, HSS-1	St. Raphaël
23S	Alouette II, III, HUP-2	St. Mandrier
31S	Bretagne, C-54	Dugny
50S	Corse, SV4C	Lanvéoc-Poulmic
55S	Expeditor	Ajaccio
56S	Dakota, Alizé	Lann-Bihoué
59S	Zéphyr, Aquilon	Hyères

Availability of a nuclear deterrent lead directly to the French withdrawal from NATO in 1966 when all squadrons assigned to the 4 TAF and based in Germany were transferred to home bases, and US and Canadian units requested to leave their stations in France. Thenceforward, the French adopted an independent policy of defence which brought much criticism from her former partners, based on the unrealistic assumption that she may be attacked from any direction. This nationalistic stance, typical of General de Gaulle, has in later years been modified, and now admits to the principal threat being in the East. A secondary stipulation that forces would only be used once foreign armies had set foot on French soil has equally been put aside, and it is now agreed that it will be in the national interest to fight with NATO on the German border, rather than alone on the French border when NATO's armies have been defeated.

It seems clear from recent events that the USA for one has not entirely forgiven France for leaving the organisation after receiving so much US aid. During the 'fifties, the Offshore Procurement Program paid for the development and production of many European aircraft, which although officially US property have never been claimed at the end of their service lives. Even American supplied aircraft such as T-33s and Thunderstreaks have remained in the country of use unless required by another NATO nation. Not so the Super Sabres, T-33s and Dassault Mystère IVAs of the Armée de l'Air, which have been recalled to USAFB at RAF Sculthorpe, England, even though only of scrap value. The US is clearly insisting that the conditions of supply are strictly observed where they apply to the French, although 1978 has seen some reciprocal visiting, with French and US aircraft displaying at each other's air shows for the first time in many years.

Redundancy of the above mentioned types has come about as the result of increased self-sufficiency in production for the Armée de l'Air, although the cost of developing present day aircraft has resulted in several joint ventures with other European partners. Dassault continues to dominate the fighter scene with the Mirage F1 and also has a new venture, the Mirage 2000; whilst the Anglo-French Jaguar provides hard-hitting tactical nuclear or conventional strike aircraft, which is ably supported in service by the older Mirage IIIE.

The French Army is at present in the process of receiving a welcome increase in anti-tank helicopter strength and re-organising its ground forces to meet the threat posed by the Warsaw Pact supremacy in armour. Fixed-wing aircraft have disappeared from use, and like many of its contemporaries, the French Army has become an all-helicopter force. The Bell 47 and Djinn were withdrawn gradually during the 'sixties as the Alouette II and III became more plentiful and in the middle years of the decade, large numbers of Super Cubs were sold for civilian use on completion of their military service. Additionally, the Nord 3202 and 3400 types have steadily declined in numbers, and in their place have come the Gazelle and Puma. Both of these are Anglo-French projects which achieved large-scale overseas orders and have been built on both sides of the Channel. The Puma has given the Army its first assault helicopter, capable of transporting sixteen-twenty armed troops rapidly to a battle zone, whilst the Gazelle serves as both a liaison and anti-tank helicopter.

At sea, the Marine National is spending much of its funding on a new class of destroyer, and with the recent withdrawal of HMS *Ark Royal,* will for a while, become the sole European navy with fixed-wing carrier-borne capability, with the exception of Spain's small Harrier force.

The principal addition to Aéronavale strength since the introduction of the Crusader has been the Breguet Atlantic maritime patrol aircraft, designed to NATO specification NBMR-2 and produced additionally for the German, Dutch and Italian navies. A prototype flown in 1961 was followed in December 1965 by the first delivery to 21F, at Nimes-Garons and its sister unit 22F, both of which disposed of their P2V-6 Neptunes. Next to follow were the slightly newer P2V-7 of 23 and 24F at Lann-Bihoué, leaving only 25F with the Neptune at home, and 12S in the Pacific.

In the inshore anti-submarine role, the H-34 was partly replaced by the French designed and built Super Frélon, which equipped 32F at Lanvéoc-Poulmic from January 1970. The Super Frélon is equivalent to the Sea King in possessing adequate accommodation for advanced detection equipment.

France is one of the few Western nations pursuing a one-for-one replacement policy in their armaments, and this appears to be having beneficial repercussions in overseas sales. French independence of NATO policy has not prevented her from continuing as an active member of all other European organisations to which she belongs, and additionally, apart from being

25

a matter of national pride, this 'go it alone' policy prevents politicians from exercising the excuse now heard in many NATO countries that someone else will plug the gap caused by their cuts in funding.

Whilst this individualistic stance provokes criticism from those used to relying upon corporate defence, it must be remembered that this attitude is not without precedent. One of the stranger manifestations of British public opinion occurred at the fall of France in June 1940, when despite sincere regret for the loss of a brave fighting companion, there was an uncanny feeling of relief throughout the country, expressing itself in the belief that without the need to constantly consult with her ally, Britain could best get on with the job of defeating Hitler if left to her own devices. History often repeats itself, but sometimes the participants' roles are reversed.

French Overseas Territories

France, like Britain, has granted independence to her former colonies since the end of the last war, sometimes peacefully, sometimes after a long military campaign. Friendly relations are maintained with several countries in the former category, to the extent of basing Armée de l'Air units to provide defence for the small nation of the Afars and Issas (Djibouti).

The following section briefly notes the history of military aviation in the main geographical regions of former French influence, and further information on bases still in use will be found under 'Overseas Units' in the main section on the Armée de l'Air's current organisation.

FRENCH EQUATORIAL AFRICA
Following the First World War, a small Aéronautique Militaire contingent was posted to French Equatorial Africa, consisting of one squadron of nine aircraft and a maintenance unit based at Bangui. By 1940, this unit was equipped with three Potez 25 and one Potez 29, and other squadrons had been formed at Fort Lamy, Chad (five Potez 25, two Potez 29, one Bloch 120); Pointe Noire, Gabon (six Potez 25 and one Potez 29); Douala, Cameroun (approximately six Potez 25 and one Potez 540), and one Bloch 120 at Brazzaville, Congo. British equipment was later added, notably the Westland Lysander, and some amalgamation took place: Escadrille 'Artois' formed on 31 August 1942 from the Gabon and Cameroun units, following the formation of Escadrille 'Bretagne' on 31 December 1941 with four Lysanders, two Potez 25 and three Potez 29 in Chad. The latter country was also defended by Escadrille 'Topic' and its Blenheims.

The war over, a minimal French presence was maintained until the constituent countries were given independence in 1960 as Chad, Cameroun, Central African Republic, Gabon and Congo. A detachment of Skyraiders was maintained in Chad by the Armée de l'Air from 1968 onwards at the request of the government because of guerilla activity, but direct dealing by the French with a rebel band holding French hostages offended the authorities and EAA 1/22 and the Army platoon of Pumas and Alouettes was asked to leave in October 1975. Relations gradually improved between the two countries, and late in April 1978 ten Jaguars temporarily based at Dakar because of guerilla activities in Senegal were detached to N'djamena to assist in the operations against Frolinat guerillas in Chad.

French air elements have also been active in the Congo in May 1978, ferrying paratroops (in conjunction with the Belgians) to rescue Europeans caught-up in fighting in the mineral-rich Shaba provence. No offensive sorties were flown or are believed to be contemplated.

FRENCH SOMALIA/DJIBOUTI
The port of Djibouti first attracted French interest in 1859, and since that time the area immediately surrounding the city has been known first as French Somalia (Côte Française des Somalis) and now as the Terretoire Français des Afars et Issas.

In 1933, a detachment of the 39 Escadre du Levant equipped with three Potez 25 was installed in a temporary aerodrome on the edge of the local salt marshes, becoming operational that April, but not moving to the new aerodrome south of the town until 1938. Declaration of war in Europe brought about an increase in strength in the form of the Potez 631, Amiot 350 and a single Latécoère 522 floatplane, and in the brief period of hostilities against Italy, a Martin 167 raided Italian Somalia, but was captured when it ran out of fuel.

Occupation by Free French forces in December 1942 permitted the establishment of a bombardment group of Martin 167 and a fighter group equipped with the Potez 631. Later in 1943, Escadrille 'Flandres' formed with the Potez 25 and 29 to undertake anti-submarine patrols for RAF Coastal Command. By the time of the German surrender, operational activity had moved elsewhere and only a Ju 52, Ju 88 and two MS 500 remained, and these were augmented by two more Toucans (Ju 52) when the resident escadron was re-named ELA 51 in 1947. Two replacement Flamants arrived in 1957, and having progressed through the various titles of ELA 51, EOM 88, and GAMOM 88, it became ETOM 88 on 1 April 1976; presently operated are the Noratlas, Broussard and Alouette II.

A long-standing border dispute with Somalia was responsible for the formation of the Skyraider squadron EAA 1/21 at Djibouti in October 1963, and these aircraft were replaced by the more potent Super Sabres of EC 4/11 in January 1973. The TFAI gained independence on 27 June 1977, but as a poor country relying on the trade passing through its harbour for revenue (and this reduced by the closure of the Suez Canal until recently) it requested the continued presence of Armée de l'Air and ALAT units. Original plans to replace the Super Sabres with Jaguars have now been abandoned and instead a new squadron, EC 3/10, has formed with the Mirage IIIC.

FRENCH WEST AFRICA

Shortly before the outbreak of the First World War, an escadrille of two Nieuports and two Henri Farmans was formed with local funding plus crews and mechanics from Metropolitan France. By 1933, three nine-aircraft escadrilles were in existence at Bamako, Gao and Thies and a maintenance unit was based at Dakar. After the French-German armistice, the Vichy government despatched bomber squadrons GB I/62 and GB I/63 to Bamako and GB II/62 and GB II/63 to Thies where they both joined GC I/4 and GC I/6 to participate in operations against the British in Freetown. For the rest of the war, West Africa remained outside the mainstream of operations, and thereafter a minimal military aviation presence was maintained until the component territories were granted independence, Guinea in 1958, Mali and Senegal in 1959, Mauritania, Niger, Upper Volta, Ivory Coast, Togo and Dahomey in 1960, most with French aid and military assistance. One squadron of Noratlas ET 1/63, stayed on in Senegal prior to disbandment, but in December 1977 the Armée de l'Air again returned to Senegal when a group of French nationals was captured by Polisario guerrilas. Jaguars of EC 11 refuelled by C-135 tankers, attacked the guerilla forces with the co-operation of the local government, forcing the release of the hostages.

During the early months of 1978, two squadrons of Jaguars were detached to Dakar at the request of the local government to continue harrassing the guerillas, at times operating inside northern Mauritania, one being claimed as shot down during a sortie by four aircraft on 3/4 May, on the fourth French strike.

INDOCHINA

Two Groupes, each with two nine-aircraft squadrons were based at Bien Hoa and Tong between the wars, and by 1940 they had been augmented by a small number of Farman 222 long-range transports and twenty MS 406 fighters. Axis pressure on Vichy France permitted a Japanese take-over of the area, but with the collapse of the empire in August 1945, GC I/7 and GC II/7 were shipped out to the Far East with their Spitfires to relieve the British and Chinese occupation forces, supported by GT I/15, GT II/15 and GT II/64.

The colonies of Tonkin, Annam and Cochinchina (what is now Vietnam) were soon to become involved in a war of several years' duration, for, reluctant to submit once more to French domination after the departure of the Japanese, Ho Chi Minh signed an agreement in March 1946, under which Tonkin, the northernmost state, would become the Democratic Republic of Vietnam under his leadership, but within a French federation. On December 14th of the same year, however, fighting broke out as the north attempted to take-over the southern states, and re-inforcements from France were hurriedly sent to the scene. Disapproving of colonialism, the United States gave no help to the French, but the 1949 Communist victory in China (which was supplying Ho Chi Minh with aid) and the dismissal of all but Communists from the Vietnamese government was soon to bring US assistance.

The Mosquitos of GC I/6 were replaced by Spitfires in 1950, and subsequently Bearcats and Hellcats, and B-26 Invaders arrived for GB I/19 in November of that year at Tan Son Nhut. GB I/25 at Cat Bi followed in 1952 and the type also equipped ERB 26, a reconnaissance unit. Bearcats formed the equipment of another reconnaissance unit, EROM 80, and fighter bomber GC I/21, whilst GC II/21 (ex GC II/9) had the Hellcat. By early 1953, US assistance had enabled the forces in Indochina to reach sixty-four fighter-bombers, thirty-two bombers, fifty-eight observation, fourteen reconnaissance and fifty-six transport aircraft, and eight helicopters (five Hiller UH-12 and three S-51).

An offensive at Dien Bien Phu, begun by the French in December 1953 was ensnared by stronger-than-anticipated Communist forces, and as the position grew steadily worse, the USA supplied C-119 Boxcars with American crews and Invaders to equip GB I/91. This was to no avail, and on 7 May 1954 Dien Bien Phu surrendered despite all attempts at relief. Peace negotiations in Geneva secured an agreement signed on 21 July, dividing Indochina along the 17th parallel into North and South Vietnam. French forces withdrew, to be replaced a decade later by those of the USA, with equally disastrous results.

The 1954 negotiations included neighbouring Cambodia and Laos which completed French Indochina, the whole territory having been taken-over by France between 1862 and 1907. The small military formations in these two countries were also disbanded, and the area was designated a neutral zone.

THE LEVANT (LEBANON AND SYRIA)

The defeat of Turkey in the First World War brought about the dismemberment of its empire in the Middle East, and its former colonies were handed over to France and Britain at the Versailles peace conference of 1919. Lebanon and Syria were allocated to the French and so, on 27 June 1920, the first Aeronautique Militaire units arrived, consisting of Breguet 14 bombers of 1 Groupe, 1 Day Bomber Regiment. These were incorporated into the 39 Régiment d'Aviation du Levant which built up into six escadrilles formed into three Groupes.

Not all the Syrian tribes agreed with French rule and the twelve months commencing mid-1925 saw the Regiment complete more than 6,000 operational missions including supply dropping to a besieged fort during a sixty-one day period. Main bases of the 39 Régiment were Aleppo, Damascus, Palmrye and Rayak.

In 1940, GC I/7 was stationed at Estabel, Syria with the MS 406, GB I/39 at Baalbek had the Martin 167F, GB III/39 at Baalbek the Bloch 200 bomber, whilst reconnaissance and observation were the duties of GR II/39 at Damascus and GAO I/583 at Aleppo both had the Potez 63.11. Further

27

reinforcements added shortly afterwards were five Groupes of Potez 25: GAO 592 at Rayak, GAO 593 at Aleppo, GAO 594 at Baalbek, GAO 595 at Palmrye and GAO 596 at Deir-ez-Zor, and in reply to British air raids on airfields which the Germans had been permitted to use, GC III/6 and its MS 406 arrived from Algeria.

Despite the departure of the German aircraft, both the British and General de Gaulle, leader of the Free French Forces, considered the invasion of the Levant worthwhile. This began on 8 June, and a hard-fought campaign ensued, an unfortunate result being that Frenchman fought Frenchman when Vichy Forces resisted the Allied advance. The LeO 451s of GB I/12 arrived at Aleppo on 13 June after a long flight from France, joining GB I/31 at Homs-Hamidiye the next day, and GR II/39 and GAO 592 were combined to form 'Groupement de Nuit Martini' at Rayak. In the next few days, GAOs 593 and 594 formed a second Groupement de Nuit, and LéO 451s of GB I/25 with D.520s of GC II/3 also arrived. The Aéronavale also took part in the fighting, Escadrille 6B moving in from Morocco with the Martin 167F, and 7B from Sidi Ahmed with similar equipment, these combining to form 4 Flotille.

By 15 July, Syria and Lebanon were in Allied hands, and those units which could, had evacuated to North Africa. A few airmen took the Allied side, and thus was formed 2 French Fighter Flight at Haifa with a Morane 406, Potez 63.11, Loire 130 and Miles Magister. The flight was instrumental in repulsing several Italian air raids during September 1940, and a second unit, the Escadrille 'Nancy' formed at Rayak on 26 July 1942 with Blenheims for convoy escort and anti-submarine work, operating from an advanced base at St. Jean. The flight disbanded on 6 September and its crews went to form a light bomber unit in Britain, but in February 1944, GC III/3 formed at St. Jean with Hurricanes, some detached to Beirut, and joined the action in North Africa in May 1944 when it moved to Bône.

During 1943, elections returned Nationalist Governments in Syria (July) and Lebanon (September), but French forces remained there even after the end of hositilities and only when a United Nations resolution was passed did the last garrisons leave Syria — on 17 April 1946, and Lebanon — in December of that year.

MADAGASCAR

Military Aviation in Madagascar centred around the base at Tananarive where one squadron of nine aircraft was formed during the 'twenties. At the fall of France this single unit was designated EC II/565, but early in 1942 its Potez 63.11 aircraft were augmented by some twenty Morane MS 406. In order to forestall Japanese ambitions in the Indian Ocean, Madagascar was invaded by Allied troops on 6 May 1942, at which time the resident squadron had been re-designated the Groupe Aérienne Mixte and was maintaining a detachment at Arrachart.

Faced with a numerically superior force of Sea Hurricanes, Martlets, Fulmars and Swordfish from British carriers and SAAF Beauforts, the GAM was unable to prevent the northern part of the island being over-run, and an armistice on the 8th conceded this region to the Allies. Talks with the Vichy Government over the occupation of the remainder showed little progress, and on 10 September a second advance began, opposed by three MS 406 and three Potez 63.11, survivors of the earlier battles, but ground engagements continued until 6 November, when all of Madagascar was in British hands.

A small contingent of French forces returned to the island at the end of the war and following independence in 1960 was invited to stay-on. The Skyraiders of EAA 2/21 and the Noratlas/Alouette equipped support squadron GAM 50 were requested to leave by the left-wing government in 1973, taking up temporary residence on the island of Réunion prior to disbandment.

NORTH AFRICA (ALGERIA, MOROCCO, TUNISIA)

Aviation first came to North Africa following a request from the commander of 19 Army Corps in Algeria for the founding of a desert air corps. Accordingly, a Fr 400,000 grant for six aircraft was made available, and the first military flight occurred at Biskra on 17 February 1912, in a Henri Farman. The re-organisation of the Aéronautique Militaire in 1920 resulted in the creation of 36 Régiment at Hussein Dey shared between Algeria and Tunisia, this having three groups, each of two squadrons specialising in army co-operation and reconnaissance. These were disposed four to Algeria (two in the desert, at Biskra and Laghouat, one operational training unit (OTU) at Constantine and one coastal patrol unit) and two in Tunisia (one squadron and an aircraft park (MU) based at Tunis and the other south of Gabès.) By 1933 the Algerian contingent had been increased to three Groupes under the Commandement de l'Aviation d'Algérie at Algiers: 1 Groupe de l'Aviation d'Afrique at Algiers, 2 GAA at Colomb Béchar and 3 GAA at Setif, whilst the 4 GAA was at Tunis, Tunisia.

Military aviation in Tunisia had followed the lead set in Algeria, and in 1912 a squadron was raised under the command of Capt. Reimbert. Tunisia remained largely unaffected by the First World War, and in 1920 received two squadrons of the 36 Régiment. In Morocco, shortly before the outbreak of the Great War, two squadrons were established, a unit of Blériots at Casablanca and one of Deperdussins at Oujda. The contingent was progressively strengthened and by 1920 the 37 Régiment had been formed with three Groupes, each of two squadrons of reconnaissance and army co-operation aircraft. By 1921, ten squadrons were present as a result of operations undertaken to quell what were euphemistically known during the 'twenties as 'dissident tribes'.

In 1920, the Riff and Chleuh tribes of Morocco were driven out of Ouezzan, occupation of which had given them control of the main Oudja-Meknès Road. In the following four years, support was again given to ground forces subduing tribes in the Atlas mountains who had rejected governmental authority. Early in 1925, a co-ordinated uprising by rebel forces put the French under serious pressure, and squadrons from Algeria, Tunisia and home swelled 37 Regiment to a peak of twenty-two squadrons which were kept busy evacuating wounded, supplying isolated garrisons, undertaking reconnaissances and attacking villages held by rebels.

At the start of the European war in 1939 there were 302 aircraft in North Africa, comprising ninety-five fighters, 130 bombers, twelve reconnaissance and sixty-five army co-operation. These were mostly semi-obsolete types, but by May 1940 the position had been slightly improved, and the North African command had the following units at its disposal:—

Fighters: GC I/9 and GC I/10 MS 406; GC III/4 and GC III/5 Dewoitine D.500/510, Nieuport 629, Spad 510, MS 406;

Bombers: Groupement 1 - GB II/62 and GB II/63 Martin 167F; Groupement 2 - GB I/19, GB II/19 and GB II/61 Bloch 210 and Douglas DB-7; Groupement 3 - GB I/32 and GB II/32 Douglas DB-7; Groupement 8 - GB I/25 LéO 451; GB II/25 LeO 257;

Reconnaissance: GR I/61 Bloch 131;

Observation: GAO 1/585, GAO 586, GAO 587, GAO 590 Potez 63.11, Potez 25.

Units retreating from France swelled the strength, and soon GC I/5 and GC II/5 and their Curtiss Hawks (later Dewoitine D.520) were at Rabat-Salé and Casablanca, GR II/33 with Bloch 174s at Tunis, GR II/52 with Bloch 175 at Oran, GR I/22 also with the Bloch 175 at Rabat and GR I/36 with the same type at Setif.

On 8 November 1942, Allied forces landed on the North African coast to take-over the Vichy French territories. In Algeria, they met with little resistance, but fighting in Morocco involved GC I/5 and II/5 operating against British and US aircraft before a cease-fire was agreed the following day. The invasion of the remaining un-occupied zone of France on 11 November prompted many airmen to transfer their services to the Allied cause, and soon LéO 451s were operating supply flights for the USAAF and GM 8 (ex GB I/11 and GB II/23) was bombing German units in the desert. GR II/33 was also flying from Algeria with its Bloch 174s to attack Axis troops in Tunisia.

GC II/5 'La Fayette', a US volunteer squadron during the Great War, was presented with Curtiss Warhawks, whilst GC II/3 re-equipped with Hurricanes at Taher, later moving to Reghaia, and then Bône, before converting to Thunderbolts in May 1944. In the same month, GC III/3 arrived from the Levant and took over II/3's Hurricanes. These were replaced by P-40 Warhawks, and the unit moved to Reghaia in July to receive the Thunderbolt, as did GC I/4. With the P-39 aircraft of GC I/5 and Lightnings of GR II/33, they moved to Italy with the USAAF to continue the fight against the Nazis.

French administration returned to North Africa after the war, the principal unit being GC 19 and its Mosquitos, which were transferred to Indochina in 1949. ECs 6 and 7 and their squadrons converted to the Mistral and were settling down with the new type when in November 1954 a general uprising threatened to develop into a war of independence. The Algerian rebels were equipped by Egypt, and full-scale military operations were required against them. As in Indochina, the B-26 Invader took-on much of the bombing and served with EB 1/91, ERP 1/32, GB 2/91 and EC 2/6 at Bône and Oran-La-Sénia.

For what is now known as 'COIN' and for forward air control work, Thunderbolts and the venerable T-6 were put into service with several Escadrilles d'Aviation Légère d'Appui based throughout North Africa to face the spreading rebellion. Another North American product, the Trojan, replaced the Harvard, and these were supplemented by the Skyraider.

At the start of 1958, the 746 Armée de l'Air aircraft and ninety-seven helicopters were directly involved in the area, including 295 Harvards, forty-four S-58 helicopters, thirty-seven Broussards and thirty-two Noratlas together with Army Alouettes, H-21s, Bell 47s, Broussards, L-19s and L-18/21s and Navy Neptunes and Aquilons. At the peak of North African operations, in 1960, the AA had the following units in North Africa:—

EC 6	Mistral/Vautour	Boufarik
EC 7	Mistral/Mystere IVA	Telergma
EC 8	Mistral/Mystere IVA	Rabat—Salé
EC 20	Skyraider	Telergma and dets.
EH 22	H-34	Telergma
ER 32	RB-26C	Bône
GLS 45	Flamant	Boufarik
ECN 71	B-26N	Tebessa
GSRA 76	Toucan	Colomb-Béchar and dets.
ET 62	Noratlas	Maison Blanche, Blida, Oran-La-Sénia
EC Martel	T-33/Mystère IVA	Meknès
BE 707	T-6	Marrakech
E Moniteurs	T-6/Magister	Marrakech

plus the T-6 equipped close-support units EALA 3/1 at Ain-Oussera, EALA 2/2 Oued Zenata, EALA 3/4 Telergma, EALA 3/5 Batna, EALA 3/9 Telergma, EALA 3/10 Thiersville, EALA 3/12 Blida, EALA 4/72 Tebessa, EALA 10/72 Orléansville, EALA 11/72 La Reghaia, EALA 13/72 Bir Rabalou, EALA 16/72 Biskra, EALA 19/72 Djelfa, EALA 2/73 Bangui, EALA 3/73 Paul Cezelles, EALA 5/73 Atar, ERALA 1/40 Algiers, ERALA 2/40 Oran-La-Sénia.

Most of the above were connected with the anti-terrorist operations, but training units Ecole de Chasse Martel, Ecole des Moniteurs and Base Ecole 707 were attracted by the good flying weather.

The question of Algerian independence was settled in a referendum during January 1961, but OAS terrorism continued until an uneasy cease-fire was organised on 19 March 1962. Independence was granted on 3 July that year and the French commenced a withdrawal, not completed until 1964. Many of the older types were left in North Africa, but EC 6, 7, and 8 and ET 62 returned home, whilst EC 20 and its Skyraiders was deployed elsewhere in Africa.

Algeria was the longest-lived of the French colonies in North Africa, having been conquered between 1830 and 1847. Tunisia became a French protectorate in 1883 and was granted internal autonomy on 2 June 1955, and full independence on 20 March 1956. Involvement with the Algerian war made France reluctant to withdraw her military units, and not until the late Summer of 1958 did the last of the French depart. Similar events took place in Morocco, a protectorate since 1912. The status was jointly renounced on 2 March 1956, preparatory to the establishment of a Moroccan government, but once more it was several years before the last air elements withdrew.

The Future

Having brought the history of the three flying services up to date, it is now necessary to look at plans for the future.

L'ARMEE DE L'AIR
Principal amongst the Armée de l'Air plans for the future are those concerning the increase in fighter and strike squadrons in order that each CAFDA and CATac wing should consist of three escadrons. In terms of numbers of front line aircraft the increase will not be as great as may first be imagined, as squadron strength has now been reduced from eighteen-twenty aircraft to fifteen-sixteen. Nevertheless, the withdrawal of the Super Mystère and Super Sabre in favour of more modern equipment will boost Armée de l'Air effectiveness and the formation of extra squadrons will place the air force in an almost unique position in Western Europe. The new units in prospect will be added to various wings currently operating two, or occasionally three, squadrons.

Plans to re-equip EC 10 with the Mirage F1 have now been shelved, and instead the unit is to wait until 1982/83 when it will be the first to receive the Mirage 2000. The remaining F1 aircraft which are scheduled for delivery up to 1983, will allow the formation of EC 3/5 (which will include fourteen Mirage F1B two-seaters), EC 3/12 and EC 3/30. Jaguar production is soon to be completed with the acceptance of the 200th aircraft, and final deliveries will replace the ancient Vautours of EB 92, which disbanded in September 1978. It was proposed that EC 1 should be re-activated to fly the Jaguar, but as the next wing to form is assigned to air defence, FATac will instead attach an extra squadron to two existing wings. These will be based away from the remainder of the unit, EC 4/7 at Istres and a new EC 4/11 at Bordeaux.

Joint production of the Alpha Jet is now in hand with German partners, but whereas the Luftwaffe will replace the Fiat G91 strike fighter, the Armée de l'Air examples will be delivered for advanced training, beginning in 1979, and will allow the T-33 to be phased-out between 1980 and 1983, although some of the latter have already been returned to the USAF for disposal. The Ecole de l'Air (GI 312) will receive its first flight of Alpha Jets in the Spring of 1979, and the type will soon be seen in the markings of the *Patrouille de France*. The final aircraft to be delivered, the 200th, is to be completed early in 1985.

The current Long Term Plan (4^e PLT) 1977-82 calls for the purchase of three new types of aircraft, notably the first 127 of an expected 200 Mirage 2000 air superiority fighters, of which the first ten are expected to have been delivered before the end of 1982, for evaluation by the CEAM. Secondly, a replacement for the CAP.10 light aircraft used for the initial evaluation of prospective aircrew and known as the 'Epsilon' will receive an order for sixty examples, all for post-1982 delivery. To meet this requirement, Aérospatiale have developed a 300hp version of the TB10 known as the TB30B, but flight-testing has been halted by the crash of the prototype early in 1978. Thirdly, a new helicopter of unspecified type (possible an Alouette II replacement) will receive a contract for an initial fifty, again for delivery after 1982. Funding has yet to be announced for a Magister replacement, for which the Fanjet 600 and Fouga 90 are contenders.

The final major purchase under the 4^e PLT will be of twenty-five Transalls for 64 Escadre de Transport to help replace the Noratlas which is expected to retire in 1985. The re-opening of the Transall production line was at one time conditional upon the receipt of additional civilian sales to ensure economic viability and it remains to be seen whether further military orders will be placed. Early production Noratlas aircraft have already been sold on the civilian market or scrapped, and another 'old faithful', the Flamant, is also rapidly approaching the end of its life as a twin-conversion aircraft. The Cessna Titan has been evaluated as a replacement, and the fact that it is available for licence production by Reims Aviation will undoubtedly be a point in its favour when a decision is made before the last Flamants are phased-out in 1981.

Overall, the period 1977-82 will see defence expenditure gradually increased from NF58,000m (£6,531m) in 1977 to NF114,575m (£12,902m) in 1982, an average of 14.8% per annum, which it is hoped will be sufficient to keep abreast of inflation. Of this sum, the Armée de l'Air will receive 22%, but increased personnel costs will mean that only 40% of the air force vote will be expended on aircraft and support facilities.

AERONAVALE

Two new types of aircraft are entering Aéronavale service at the present time, the Super Etendard and the Lynx. After consideration of the navalised Jaguar, the Marine Nationale decided upon an improved version of the Etendard to re-equip the carrier-based strike element; the first examples were delivered during the latter half of 1978. The current long term plan envisages a second batch of forty-four to be ordered and delivery of all seventy-one to be completed by the end of 1982. Linked with the building of a fleet of C70 Class destroyers is an order for twenty-six Westland Lynx shipborne anti-submarine helicopters, delivery of which began in 1978. The PA75 helicopter carrier will now not be completed until 1985, by which time further Lynx may have been supplied. A number of Alizé anti-submarine aircraft are currently being re-worked for service until 1990 when the carriers *Foch* and *Clemenceau* are expected to be retired.

The two carriers, transferred to the Mediterranean late in 1974 as a result of friction in the Middle East, have been employed off the Djibouti coast where the security of this former French colony is threatened by its aggressive neighbours. They will in all probability continue to make regular cruises to the East African coast for exercises.

AVIATION LEGERE DE L'ARMEE DE TERRE

The ALAT now regards anti-armour as its principal task, anticipating that any attack from the East will take the form of a mass tank 'steamroller' operation employing conventional arms. To this end, the original order for 166 Gazelle will be increased by a further 128 in the planning period 1977-82, over half of the grand total being the SA342 variant capable of firing six HOT missiles, although only four are normally carried. Other helicopters in service are 180 Alouette II now relegated to training and communication; the Alouette III which will augment the Gazelle/HOT force with its SS12 missiles and 125 Pumas in the troop transport role. Fixed-wing aircraft, thirty-five Broussards and ninety Cessna L-19s, will be relieved of their communications role by the availability of further Gazelles, and will remain for air experience and restricted training duties with the flying schools. The remaining Bell 47 helicopters have likewise been retired.

ALAT personnel totals 3,700 out of the army's 338,000 officers and men, of which 220,000 are one-year conscripts. In times of war, the sixteen existing divisions of the regular army can be increased by a further fourteen by drawing on reservists and training personnel. Although capable of taking the field, these fourteen would in practise take up the positions vacated by the sixteen regular units, all of which would transfer to the front, supported by the ALAT. Despite the ALAT re-equipement programme, the army as a whole has much equipment which is at the end of its useful life, and in the event of war the ALAT will be stretched to the full in order to meet its commitments.

Suggested further reading:
JACKSON, R. (1974) *Air War over France 1939-40*. Ian Allan.
VAN HAUTE, A. (1974) *Pictorial History of the French Air Force Volumes 1/2*. Ian Allan.

Part Two

Armée de l'Air

Current Organisation

Unit Designations

Before proceeding with any discussion of Armée de l'Air organisation, an explanation of the system of unit designations is appropriate.

In order to identify military aircraft units, a system of numbered escadrilles beginning at '1' was initiated, each having a prefix indicating the manufacturer of the unit's equipment. At the start of World War 1 in August 1914, Escadrilles 1 to 22 had been formed, and were quickly augmented by several more.

The first escadrilles created specifically for bombing duties formed in November 1914 as the components of Groupe de Bombardement 1. To avoid confusion, all three were re-numbered VB101-103 in early 1915. A system was then started with the numbers 1-100 reserved for fighter escadrilles, 101-200 for bombers and 201-300 for reconnaissance.

The principal Escadrille prefixes used during World War 1 were:—

AR	Dorand AR1/2
BM	Breguet BM2/4/5
BR	Breguet 14
C	Caudron
D	Deperdussin
DO	Dorand
F	Farman 30/40/50/60 series
HF	Farman 20 series
L	Letord
MF	Farman F7/11
MS	Morane-Saulnier
N	Nieuport
PS	P. Schmitt
R	Caudron R.11
RE	REP
SAL	Salmson Moineau
SOP	Sopwith
SPA	SPAD
V	Voisin
VB	Voisin 2

Each escadrille adopted its own insignia, many of which were both colourful and inventive, and when the military air arm was reorganised post-war these were perpetuated in the new system.

Between the wars, the basic air formation was the Groupe (Groupe de Chasse = fighter group; Groupe de Bombardement = bombing group etc.) For example:—

GC I/1
1 escadrille	SPA 31	Spartan archer
2 escadrille	N48	Head of cockerel

GC II/1
3 escadrille	C94	The grim reaper
4 escadrille	SAL 58	Fighting cock

GC III/1
5 escadrille	N84	Fox's head
6 escadrille	SPA 93	Flying goose

Post-war a similar system was used with each Groupe usually receiving the name of a French province, but in 1951 the 'Groupe' designation gave way to the 'Escadre'. This method of organisation is in use today, an escadre normally consisting of two, three or four escadrons, each of which has an authorised complement of aircraft, a name, and two attached escadrilles with their own badges. Therefore in current usage the following apply: Escadre = Wing; Escadron = Squadron; Escadrille = Flight. The escadrille is purely an internal division for pilots and crews, and thus all aircraft of a particular escadron carry both escadrille badges, usually 1 esc. on the left of the fin, with 2 esc. to the right.

Escadrons may be transferred to other wings, and do so by taking their escadrilles and name with them. Reconnaissance, night fighter, helicopter, transport and some smaller units are allocated only one escadrille, in addition to which some fighter escadrons carry the badge of their province on both sides of the fin. The 2 Escadre at Dijon is a good example as it has three different systems in use:—

EC 1/2 'Cigognes'
1 escadrille	SPA 3	Stork, head and wings down.
2 escadrille	SPA 103	Stork, wings raised.

EC 2/2 'Cote d'Or'
1 escadrille	SPA 57	Seamew
2 escadrille	SPA 65	Chimaera
3 escadrille	SPA 94	The grim reaper.

EC 3/2 'Alsace'
Shield of Alsace carried on both sides of the fin.

The name of EC 1/2 is unusual, this meaning 'Storks', and not a province name, whilst EC 3/2 uses no escadrille insignia. The wing also illustrates the present trend in building up wings with their pre-war escadrilles, as the aircraft of EC 1/2 and EC 2/2 carry the same badges as GC I/2 and GC II/2 between the wars. Of late, however, some opportunites to further this procedure have been lost.

Overall Organisation

Typically, the Armée de l'Air is divided into commands responsible for nuclear attack, interception, transport etcetera. In total some 470 first line aircraft are employed with about 1,400 more in second line duties. Manpower is about 104,000 and aircraft are operated from some seventy bases. Armée de l'Air Headquarters are 26 Boulevard Victor, Paris 15e, and the current chief of staff is Général Maurice Saint-Cricq. The principal commands are detailed overleaf.

FORCES AERIENNE STRATEGIQUES

Headquartered at Taverny near Paris where it formed on 1 January 1964, and commanded by General Delaval, a reorganisation of the FAS (colloquially referred to as the 'Force de Dissuasion') was brought into effect on 1 June 1976 whereby EB 93 was disbanded and the force reduced from three Escadres each of twelve Mirage IVA nuclear bombers plus four C-135F tankers to two Escadres de Bombardement (EB 91 and EB 94) with sixteen Mirage IVA each and the eleven remaining C-135Fs in one separate wing.

The magazines of 60KT bombs are maintained at each escadron base by a Dépôt Atelier Munitions Spéciales, and stocks are kept at the three former bases.

Also part of the FAS is CIFAS 328 at Bordeaux, the training unit of the Strategic Force, operating the Mirage IIIB, Mirage IVA, Noratlas and T-33A. Two or three of these Mirage III and T-33A aircraft are detached to each squadron for continuation training and communications, whilst the remainder join the Noratlas and Mirage IVA in the instruction of new FAS crews.

The Mirage bomber will be phased-out in 1985, when the nuclear deterrent will pass almost entirely to the Marine Nationale's submarines.

1er GROUPEMENT de MISSILES STRATEGIQUES

Headquartered near Avignon, the 1 GMS operates two escadrons of nine S-2 intermediate range missiles, but no aircraft. Instead, support facilities are provided by Alouette II and Puma helicopters of EH 4/67 based at BA200, Apt. 1 GMS became operational in 1971 complementing the Mirage IVA fleet, but the planned strength of three squadrons has not been attained because of budgetary difficulties. The squadrons are numbered and named as are those flying aircraft, the first of these being EMS 1/200 'Luberon'. The second unit is presumably EMS 2/200.

Between 1978 and 1982 the Group is converting to the S-3 missile. Work is underway on the nine silos of the 1er Post Centrale de Tir at Rustrel, and the 2^e PCT will commence conversion in 1980.

1er COMMANDEMENT AERIEN TACTIQUE

Previously based in Germany, CATac was relocated in France (Headquartered at Metz) after the withdrawal from NATO, and is now equipped with 15KT tactical nuclear weapons, and Martel and AS30 missiles. The present strength of CATac is:—
   EC 2   — Mirage III
   EC 3   — Mirage III, Jaguar
   EC 4   — Mirage III
   EC 7   — Jaguar
   EC 11   — Jaguar
   EC 13   — Mirage III, Mirage 5F
   ER 33   — Mirage III

This gives a total of fifteen tactical, three reconnaissance and two training escadrons. In addition, each escadre has a SLVSV (Section de Liaison et de Vol Sans Visibilité - Communications and Instrument Rating Flight) equipped with a mixture of types. The usual escadron complement is sixteen eighteen aircraft. Overall administration of the tactical air commands, the Force Aérien Tactique, (and of 1 Region Aérienne) is in the hands of Général Philippe Fleurot.

2ème COMMANDEMENT AERIEN TACTIQUE

2 CATac is the air component of a tri-service 'Force d'Intervention' and has its headquarters at Nancy. The Force d'Intervention is designed for rapid deployment in France or the Mediterranean area, and its sole permanent air unit was EB 92, consisting of one escadron (1/92) of Vautour IIB medium bombers, kept up to strength by transferred Vautour IIN fighters.

The Vautour unit disbanded in September 1978 and is to be replaced by two Jaguar squadrons (4/7 and 4/11), the second of which has already formed. Any other air unit can be attached to 2 CATac as a situation demands.

35

COMMANDEMENT AIR DES FORCES DE DEFENCE AERIENNE

Approximately 7,000 airmen are attached to CAFDA which is responsible for the air defence of France in an organisation including the other armed forces of the country. A liaison with NATO is maintained, through the NADGE system and a computerised warning and communications network (Système de Transmission et Représentation des Informations Radar-STRIDA) links all bases. Aircraft of CAFDA are equipped with the MATRA R.530, R.550 Magic, and Sidewinder air-to-air missiles with the Super R.530 following in 1978, whilst fifteen battalions of MATRA Crotale provide SAM defence for operational bases of all commands. The units of CAFDA are:—

EC 5	— Mirage F1
EC 10	— Mirage IIIC
EC 12	— Mirage F1
ECTT 30	— Mirage F1

Each escadre operates a SLVSV also. EC 10 will receive the Mirage 2000 in 1982-82, and during 1982-83 CAFDA will be equipped with Aladin and Centaure low-level radar installations.

COMMANDEMENT DU TRANSPORT AERIEN MILITAIRE

All communications, rescue and transport services are provided by CoTAM, operating both fixed-wing aircraft and helicopters. Communications duties are undertaken by Escadres ELA 41, ET 65, ELA 43 and ELA 44 on behalf of 1, 2, 3 and 4 Aerial Regions, ET 65 being also the Groupe Aérien d'Entraînement et de Liaison responsible for training and ambulance tasks. ET 60, the Groupe de Liaison Aériennes Ministerielles is engaged on VIP transport. Each of the above units uses a variety of aircraft types.

Freight and troop transport is provided by the Transalls of ET 61 and Noratlas of Escadre 64, with new ET 63 using small numbers of both types for crew training. The aged DC-6s of ET 64 (and overseas ETOM 82 were replaced by further DC-8 and Caravelle deliveries to ET 60 and ETOM 82 in 1976-77, and in addition, the C-135K tankers of the FAS may be used for transport in an emergency. On 1 May 1975, the two helicopter wings EH 67 and EH 68 combined to form a new enlarged EH 67 operating the Alouette II, Alouette III and Puma in five squadrons situated throughout the country. At the same time, training unit CIEH 341 was established to instruct both Air Force and Navy helicopter pilots.

Armée de l'Air helicopters are employed in the communications and SAR roles, whilst the army provides its own heavy assault Pumas. CoTAM personnel strength numbers 4,400 and is responsible for 250 aircraft and 100 plus helicopters, whilst the yearly total of hours flown in 1978 is expected to exceed the 1977 figure of 109,000 by some 5%. On 1 July 1978 the Noratlas equipped 62 Escadre disbanded and its two squadrons were attached to other units.

COMMANDEMENT DES ECOLES DE L'ARMEE DE L'AIR

Flying and technical training is administered by the newest command (formed 1 April 1962) the CEAA which is also responsible for the early stages in naval pilot instruction. After initial selection by the Escadron de Formation Initiale du Personnel Navigant (in GE 313), combat pilots will progress via GI 312 and GE 315 (Magister) and later to GE 314 (T-33). Operational training is provided by ET 8 at Cazaux flying the Mystère IVA (with Alpha Jets in Prospect) and by specialised sections within 2e and 7e Escadres, soon to be joined by ECT 3/5. Transport pilots undertake twin conversion at GE 319 (Flamant), and later ET 63.

Additionally, GE 316 (Noratlas) provides navigational instruction and GE 313 (Magister) trains instructors and foreign students. Technical training is centred at Rochefort and Saintes, (Air Base 721 and 722).

COMMANDEMENT DES TRANSMISSIONS DE L'ARMEE DE L'AIR

CTAA manages electronic countermeasures and currently operates eight specially equipped Noratlas of EC 54 and a DC-8 of EE 51 in the ECM role.

OTHER UNITS

Not mentioned above are GAM 56, operating transport (Noratlas, Broussard and Puma) and EdC 57, the radar calibration unit (Noratlas). At Istres the EPNER has a small flight of aircraft for test pilot training purposes.

The two principal test centres for aircraft are the Centre d'Expériences Aériennes Militaires and the Centre d'Essais en Vol. The former exists principally for the proving of military aircraft (under direct control of the Air Staff), whilst the latter is orientated more to research and development. In British terms, they would thus parallel the A&AEE and RAE respectively.

CURRENT OVERSEAS UNITS

EC 3/10	Mirage IIIC	Djibouti, Afars and Issas
ETOM 52	Puma	Tontouta, N. Caledonia
GAM 50	Noratlas	Réunion Is., Indian Ocean
ETOM 55	Noratlas, Alouette	Dakar, Senegal, Equatorial Africa
ETAG 58	Puma	Point-a-Pitre, West Indies
ETOM 82	Caravelle,	Papeete, Pacific
ETOM 88	Noratlas Alouette	Djibouti, Afars and Issas, Africa

Two squadrons of Jaguars detached to Dakar early in 1978, and of these, a flight moved to N'djamena, Chad, in April 1978 where Skyraiders of EAA 1/22 and Noratlas and Alouette of GMT 59 were based until 1975.

Coding and Callsigns

All aircraft in France and her colonies have a five-letter identification beginning 'F', whether they be civil or military, unlike in Britain where the series G-xxxx, G-(numbers), Mxxxx, and BGA.xxxx are all in use. The table on page 197 gives all French block allocations and usage, even though in some cases they are no longer in use, particularly where former French colonies now independent, have assumed their own prefix letters.

The civil registrations demand no explanation in this book, and the ALAT and Aéronavale call-signs are dealt with in detail under their respective sections.

Armée de l'Air aircraft codings normally use the final two letters of the call-sign, prefixed by the unit number, thus 'F-UGEA' (allocated to Mirage IIIE, No. 432) is arrived at as follows:

F — national identity
U — fighter aircraft
GE — Escadron 1/2
A — first aircraft

Mirage IIIE No. 402 F-UGLA is the first aircraft of Escadron 3/2, from which it may be seen that callsigns are not always in sequence. The two aircraft above would be marked 2-EA and 2-LA respectively on the fuselage sides.

In some cases only the 'last two' is carried, without a number, this normally being practised by the Force de Dissuasion (Mirage IVA etc), the CEV, and some small units. Examples are:—

Mirage IVA	No.2/F-THAA	'AA'	Esc. 91
CAP-20	No.1/F-TFVU	'VU'	GI 312
Cessna 310N	No.186/F-ZJBI	'BI'	CEV
Noratlas	No.207/F-RAXD	'XD'	GAM 56
Nord 262	No.55/F-ZVMH	'MH'	ENSA
Jodel D.140	No.509/F-ULQA	'QA'	4 Region

Other establishments use only one identity letter, eg:

Jaguar	No.E-02/F-ZWRC	'C'	CEV
Mystere 20	No.49/F-RAFJ	'J'	GLAM

The radio aids calibration unit EdC 57 is unusual in quoting the 'last three' on the aircraft, eg:
Noratlas   No.151/F-RCAR 'CAR'

A non-standard system appeared on some helicopters of the detachments of EH 67 and EH 68, consisting of the constructors or delivery number and part of the call-sign, eg:

Alouette II	No.1571/F-RBSD	'282-SD'	EH 67
S-58	No.SKY977/F-RBST	'977-ST'	EH 67

One further practice of the EHs, now discontinued, was that of number coding, thus:

Sud S-58	No.SA1/F-RAOX	'68-03'	EH 68
Sik'y S-58	No.SKY93/F-RAON	'68-04'	EH 68

In some cases where the unit in question has no number designation, one is devised, this normally being the air base number. The CEAM and CEV are noted in this connection, particularly the former. Examples are:—

Jaguar	No.A2/F-SDAE	'118-AE'	CEAM
S. Mystère	No.140/F-ZABB	'332-AB'	CEAM
Magister	No.136/F-RHHG	'125-HG'	BA 125
Broussard	No.182/F-RHEA	'722-EA'	BA 722
Noratlas	No.199/F-SDMD	'070-MD'	EC 070

The series F-RHEA/F-RHEZ is used for base-flight aircraft within 3 Region, in which BA 722 is situated, and may have several prefixes. Other similar series are allocated to 1, 2 and 4 Regions.

Wing Structuring

Wings of a particular function are numbered consecutively for ease of reference, and the following blocks of numbers are reserved.

1-13	Fighter wings
30	All-weather fighter wings
33	Reconnaissance wing
41-44	Regional communications flights
50-59	Miscellaneous transport flights
60-65	Transport wings
67-68	Helicopter wings
70	Ferry flight
80-89	Miscellaneous support squadrons
91-94	Bomber wings
301-319	Flying schools
328-346	Operational Conversion Units

The function of units in the OCU category may often be changed, as in the case of the latest formation, CIEH 341 which is a helicopter training school, but was before that a paratroop practice unit equipped with Noratlas. Numbers 301-311 were Auxiliary (volunteer reserve) training schools, disbanded in 1957.

37

Within an individual wing, squadrons, support units and even aircrew are numbered. as an example the departments of 1 Escadre would include:

00/001	Wing administration section
01/001	1 Escadron
02/001	2 Escadron
03/001	3 Escadron
08/001	Technical section
15/001	Aircraft maintenance section

Aircrew callsigns are permanently allocated and would be prefixed by a code name for the unit, eg. 'Mickey' for GE 314. The Commanding officer would be Mickey 15, his second in command, Mickey 16, etc. Where two or more aircraft are operating together, they would do so under a colour code, rather than the pilots' personal call signs, for example, 'Mickey Rouge' (red).

Occasionally a small flight of aircraft may be allocated to an air base, in which case the designation relates to the base number (see page 69). Thus, prior to the establishment of CPIR 339, the two long-nosed Mystère 20s were in the base flight of BA116, Luxeuil, which was designated CPIR 04/116. Similarly, it appears that the wing SLVSVs, whilst marking their aircraft with the code numbers of the unit to which they are attached, actually belong to the base in the manner of a Station Flight.

Insignia

Unit insignia as applied to fighter aircraft normally dates from World War 1, whereas other units have more recently devised their own, often descriptive of their function, eg. a bat for a radar training flight. Several types of badge are depicted on the following pages, and may be classified as hereunder—

Escadrille insignia: applied to aircraft of fighter units (different badge either side) or individual flights (same badge both sides).

Escadron insignia: normally combining the two escadrille badges in a divided shield. Rarely applied to aircraft, but EB 1/92 is an exception.

Escadre insignia: takes two forms, either a shield containing the escadre number and often bordered by the names of the component squadrons, or is a combination of all the escadrille insignia. The escadre badge may occasionally be found on the aircraft of the liaison and instrument flight (SLVSV). Transport wings will apply escadre insignia to all aircraft, irrespective of the squadron code letters which they carry, but Mirage IVA and C-135F of the FAS carry none.

Additionally, the various support units attached to each wing (technical, stores, etc.) will have their own badges, but they are not illustrated in this book. Air bases each have a badge, often depicting a local geographical feature, the insignia of the resident units or a representation of the based aircraft type, in which latter case it may be changed as new equipment is delivered (although St. Cyr displays a Giffard airship – hardly the last word in Armée de l'Air armament). Unlike RAF insignia which must be approved by the Chester Herald at the Royal College of Arms and the reigning monarch, Armée de l'Air badges are not subjected to such heraldic scrutiny. Nevertheless, they are submitted to Armée de l'Air headquarters and issued with a registration number which suffices to prevent the appearance of any of a frivolous nature, (although Donald Duck features in two badges of Aéronavale squadrons).

Unit badges are shown for most Escadrons, but it should be borne in mind that there is no set design for badges and these will often change slightly. An example is the 'Ardennes' Escadron (badge – a wild boar), which in the F-84F era decorated some of its aircraft with only the boar's head whilst others carried the complete animal. The current trend is towards simplification of the badges, but wherever possible the drawing shows the more detailed version.

For reasons of clarity, the correct tonal values have not been shown on drawings of a very small number of insignia. Reference should thus be made to the colour key for accurate information. Some badges, particularly those of the Mirage fighter wings, have unauthorised decoration surrounding the traditional part of the insignia, for example EC 1/5 has standardised the stork and the head of Joan of Arc by placing them both inside pennants. These variations are *not* shown except in the case of EC 2/5 which has dismembered the components of its badge and arranged them to cover the whole fin.

Current Units

Brief histories are given for wings and squadrons currently in existence. Where the components of a wing have remained unaltered for some time, the several histories will be largely the same, and so to avoid unnecessary repetition, detail in one or more of the entries has been cut to a minimum. For the purposes of research therefore, reference should be made to both the histories of the wing *and* its squadrons. Brief mention of now-disbanded components will be found in the revelant wing history, whilst the present designation for those currently serving in another formation will be provided as an aid to research. For ease of reference, recently disbanded units are also included but are marked '†'.

1 ESCADRE DE CHASSE (†)

1 Escadre was formed on 1 July 1947 by the renumbering of GC 7 and its two squadrons of Spitfires GC 1/1 'Provence' (ex GC 1/7) and GC 2/1

'Nice' (ex GC 2/7) in Germany. The wing received Vampires in 1950 at Sidi Ahmed in North Africa, and reverted to its original designation of 7 Escadre on 1 November 1951.

1 Escadre

Escadron 2/1

The 1 Escadre was the second to receive the F-84G Thunderjet in 1953, exchanging these for the F-84F Thunderstreak at its St. Dizier base in August 1955. Until its disbandment in December 1963 three escadrons were attached: EC 1/1 'Corse' (now EC 3/11), EC 2/1 'Morvan' and EC 3/1 'Argonne' (now EC 2/7). The 'Morvan' insignia comprises 'la Fauche le Mort' (SPA94) and a Fighting Cock (GCII/1-4e) and its F-84 aircraft carried the codes 1-NA/1-NZ. Its component escadrilles have now split, with the SPA94 insignia now forming a third escadrille within ECT 2/2.

2 ESCADRE DE CHASSE - 1 CATac

Groupe de Chasse 2 formed in Germany during November 1945 when escadrilles 'Cigognes' and 'Alsace' left the RAF still equipped with their Spitfires. On 3 August 1946, GC 2 became operational in Indochina, taking over from GC 7 and remaining operational until stood down in favour of GC 4 on 15 September 1947. The wing re-formed in Germany, this time with Thunderbolts, but with the same two component squadrons, later converting to the Vampire/Mistral, Ouragan, Mystère IVA and Mirage IIIC, with which latter type it was the first operational escadre when initial deliveries were made in the Spring of 1961, to the current base at Dijon.

EC 1/2 'Cigognes'
Codes: 2-EA/2EZ
Callsigns: F-UGEA/F-UGEZ
Aircraft: Mirage IIIE (2-EA to ET)
Fin insignia: Left SPA3 (GCI/2-1e) - a stork, neck and wings bowed, in black and white.
Right SPA103 (GCI/2-2e) - a stork in flight, wings raised, coloured black and white.

'Cigognes' bears two of the most famous escadrille badges in the Armée de l'Air, these being from units of the World War 1 fighter group all of whose squadrons adopted the insignia of a stork in a different attitude. The squadron's present period of existence began on 5 January 1944 when it formed as 329 Squadron, RAF, at Ayr, flying Spitfires. When returned to French control on 17 November 1945, it adopted the designation GC 1/2, later exchanging its Spitfires for the Thunderbolt, Vampire, Ouragan, Mirage IIIC and IIIE.

ECT 2/2 'Côte d'Or'
Codes: 2-FA/2-FZ and 2-ZA/2-ZZ
Callsigns: F-UGFA/F-UGFZ; F-UMZA/F-UMZZ
Aircraft: Mirage IIIB (2-FA/FT)
Mirage IIIBE (2-ZA/ZO)
Fin insignia: SPA57 (GCII/2-3e) - a seamew
SPA65 (GCII/2-4e) - a chimaera (dragon)
SPA94 (GCII/1-3e) la Fauche le Mort
All three coloured black and white.

The second escadron of EC 2 is unique in being the only Armée de l'Air escadron made up of three escadrilles, for which it qualifies by virtue of its over-size complement. The 'Escadre de Chasse et de Transformation 2/2', 'Côte d'Or' is the principal Mirage III training squadron and functions as an OCU, training French and overseas pilots. Until 1976, EC 2/2 retained five Mirage IIIC (between 2-FA and 2-FF) for advanced instruction, but has now standardised on the two seat IIIB and IIIBE, the latter from 1971 onwards. The two traditional 'Côte d'Or' escadrilles were joined by SPA94 from 'Morvan' escadron (see EC 2/1), two of the three appearing on each aircraft, eg. Mirage IIIBE No.216 - SPA57 & SPA65, No.262 - SPA94 & SPA57, No.263 - SPA94 & SPA65, etc. In 1976, the squadron saw the graduation of its 1,000th qualified Mirage pilot, over 100 of these being from other air forces. Côte d'Or formed as EC 3/2 on 1 October 1949 becoming EC 2/2 as the result of a squadron re-shuffle on 1 May 1951. Disbanded at the end of the Ouragan era, on 1 November 1957, it reformed in its current training role as ECT 2/2 on 1 July 1968.

EC 3/2 'Alsace'
Codes: 2-LA/2-LZ
Callsigns: F-UGLA/F-UGLZ
Aircraft: Mirage IIIE (2-LA/LT)
Fin insignia: Having no adopted escadrilles, EC 3/2 displays the arms of Alsace on both sides of the fin. The red shield has yellow crowns and diagonal.

Originally 341 Squadron of the RAF, 'Alsace' formed with Spitfires at Turnhouse on 1 January 1943, having previously been a flight attached to several RAF squadrons in the North African theatre from 1940 onwards. Returned to the post-war Armée de l'Air as GCIII/2 on 27 November 1945, the squadron has remained with 2 Wing to the present day, at first with codes 2-SA/2-SZ.

S.L.V.S.V.
Codes: 2-HA/2-HZ
Callsigns: F-UGHA/F-UGHZ
Aircraft: Magister (2-HA, HB, HE, HG, HI, HM)
T-33 (2-HC)
Flamant (2-HD, HN)
Broussard (2-HH).

---

3 ESCADRE DE CHASSE - 1 CATac

Formed at Reims in May 1950 with the Vampire/Mistral, EC 3 perpetuated the squadrons and designations of a Spitfire wing which had been based in Indochina from November 1948 until the preceding month. In 1951, EC 3 became the first French Thunderjet wing when the F-84E arrived under the auspices of the US Mutual Assistance Program. Commencing March 1952, these were replaced by the improved F-84G model, equipping the same three squadrons which currently form the wing.

The first Thunderstreak arrived on 4 November 1955, but exactly a year later the complement was reduced to two squadrons with the disbandment of 'Ardennes'. In November 1958, EC 3 received half of the F-100D Super Sabres allocated to France, moving to Lahr, Germany, in February 1961. The Mirage IIIE replaced the Super Sabre in September 1966, but after being declared operational in July 1967, EC 3 returned home to its current base at Nancy, just two months later, following French withdrawal from NATO. 'Ardennes' re-emerged in July 1974 flying the Mirage 5F, but these were passed on to EC 2/13 in April 1977 in exchange for Jaguars. The wing is allocated the task of 'pave-strike' and both aircraft types are fitted with the Martel anti-radar missile, the Jaguars having secondardy responsibilities for low-altitude air superiority and conventional attack.

EC 1/3 'Navarre'
Codes: 3-IA/3-IZ
Callsigns: F-UGIA/F-UGIZ
Aircraft: Mirage IIIE (3-IA to IS)
Fin insignia: Left SPA95 (GCI/4-1e) - a blue martlet on a black and yellow pennant.
Right SPA153 (GCI/4-2e) - a Lammergeyer, in red and white.

After finishing the war as GCI/4 with Thunderbolts, 'Navarre' and its sister unit 'Champagne' took up station in Indochina in November 1948 equipped with Spitfires for operations against the Communists. Disbanded in April 1950, it re-formed with Vampires the next month, going on to receive the types detailed in the EC 3 history above.

EC 2/3 'Champagne'
Codes: 3-JA/3-JZ
Callsigns: F-UGJA/F-UGJZ
Aircraft: Mirage IIIE (3-JA to JS)
Fin insignia: Left SPA67 (GCI/5-1e) - a black and white stork upon a pennant.
Right SPA75 (GCI/5-2e) - a falcon hovering, coloured yellow and black.

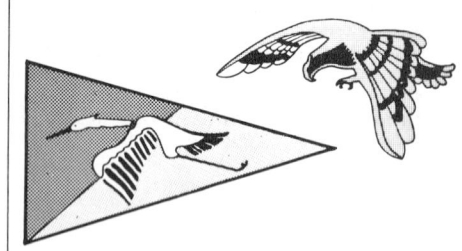

'Champagne' was equipped with Airacobras and later the Thunderbolt during the final two years of World War 2 designated GC 1/5. The history of its present period of existence is given under the EC 3 heading.

EC 3/3 'Ardennes'

Codes:	3-XA/3-XZ
Callsigns:	F-UGXA/F-UGXZ
Aircraft:	Jaguar A (3-XA to XP)
Fin insignia:	Left - a wild boars head in silver and blue bar.
	Right - a wild boars head in silver and red bar.

'Ardennes' was the last of the EC 3 escadrons to form, not doing so until 1 January 1953, when it adopted the F-84G. Its previous existence had been as the Thunderbolt equipped GCIII/3 until disbanded on 1 April 1946, but between January and October 1950 it transferred its allegiance to EC 4 at Mont-de-Marsan flying Vampires as EC 4/4. The squadron progressed to the F-84F in 1956, but disbanded on 15 November 1957 without having received the Super Sabre. The availability of confiscated Israeli Mirages permitted the re-formation of 'Ardennes' on 1 July 1974, with a new code range replacing the old 3-VA/3-VZ. In April/May 1977 however, these were replaced by the squadron's current type, the Jaguar, and forwarded to EC 2/13.

S.L.V.S.V.

Codes:	3-KA/3-KZ
Callsigns:	F-UGKA/F-UGKZ
Aircraft:	T-33A (3-KA, KB)
	Magister (3-KC, KD, KE)
	Broussard (3-KY).

4 ESCADRE DE CHASSE - 1 CATac

4 Escadre formed with Spitfires in July 1947 from ex-Thunderbolt squadrons 2/3 'Dauphiné' and 2/5 'La Fayette' and became operational in Indochina on 4 September that year, relieving 2 Escadre in its battle against the Communist forces of Ho Chi Minh. The two squadrons were stood down in November 1948 immediately re-forming at Friedrichshafen with Thunderbolts, but exactly a year later, GC 4 received its first jet aircraft, the de Havilland Vampire at Mont-de-Marsan in a four squadron wing comprising its two present escadrons plus EC 3/4 'Flandre' and GC 4/4 'Ardennes' (the latter currently EC 2/3), both formed on 1 January 1950. 'Ardennes' disbanded in October 1950, the remaining three squadrons transferring to Bremgarten, Germany in April 1954 where they shortly afterwards received the Ouragan. EC 4's Ouragans provided the 1955-56 'Patrouille de France' aerobatic team in the days before this was permanently the function of GI 312, but in November 1957, 'Flandres' (SPA160 and N155) was disbanded a few days before the wing converted to the F-84F Thunderstreak. In June 1961, it moved back to France, installing itself at the present base of Luxeuil, where during 1966 the 'Streaks were replaced by the new Mirage IIIE fighter bombers. From March 1968, these were camouflaged, and they are equipped with Martel missiles for anti-radar strike. In keeping with the current Armée de l'Air policy, a third escadron may soon be added to the wing.

EC 1/4 'Dauphiné'

Codes:	4-AA/4-AZ
Callsigns:	F-ULAA/F-ULAZ
Aircraft:	Mirage IIIE (4-AA to AS)
Fin insignia:	Left SPA37 (GCII/3-3e) - a condor in flight with a red head, yellow beak, white body and eye.
	Right SPA81 (GCII/3-4e) - a white greyhound.

Previous codes were 4-KA/4-KZ with the Ouragan, and 4-SA/4-SZ with the F-84F. The Thunderbolt-equipped GCII/3 'Dauphiné' was transferred to 4 Escadre in July 1947, and immediately converted to Spitfires. Its subsequent history followed exactly that of the parent wing, the current Mirage IIIE arriving in mid 1966.

EC 2/4 'La Fayette'

Codes:	4-BA/4-BZ
Callsigns:	F-ULBA/F-ULBZ
Aircraft:	Mirage IIIE (4-BA to BT)
Fin insignia:	Left N124 (GCII/5-3e) - the head of a Sioux,
	Right SPA167 (GCII/5-4e) - a black and white stork in flight.

Previous codes were 4-LA/4-LZ with the Vampire and Ouragan and 4-UA/4-UZ with the F-84F. One of the most famous squadrons of the Armée de l'Air, 'La Fayette' was originally a World War 1 escadrille manned by US volunteers — hence its Sioux insignia and name. After flying the Hawk and Warhawk in North America as GCII/5, 'La Fayette' converted to Thunderbolts for the last two years of the Second World War and in 1946 was re-designated GC 2/4. Like 'Dauphiné', GC 2/4 served in Indo China during 1947-48 and converted to Vampires with the rest of GC 4. Its later history is common to EC 4, with the Mirages being delivered in November 1966.

S.L.V.S.V.
Codes: 4-WA/4-WZ
Callsigns: F-UGWA/F-UGWZ
Aircraft: Magister (4-WB, WC)
T-33 (4-WG, WH)
Broussard (4-WZ)

Note that F-UGWL and F-UGWM are used by CPIR339, which see.

5 ESCADRE DE CHASSE - CAFDA

Current Insignia

Formed at its present base at Orange on 31 March 1951 from GC 5, the 5 Escadre flew both the Vampire and its French-built version, the Mistral, converting to the Mystère IIC in 1956, Mystère IVA in 1958, the Super Mystère B2, and late in 1968, the Mirage IIIC. A third squadron EC 3/5 'Comtat Venaissin' (SPA171 and ERC571, codes 5-WA/5-WZ) formed with Vampires on 31 March 1951, and disbanded when its Mystère IIs were withdrawn in April 1958. Late in 1974, 'Vendée' and 'Ile de France' passed their remaining Mirage IIIC aircraft on to EC 10 and took delivery of the Mirage F1C the second wing to do so. In mid-1977, the wing received an allocation of replacement F1s fitted with in-flight refuelling probes. 5 Escadre is shortly to form an OCU squadron for French and overseas converts to the F1, and this will revive 'Comtat Venaissin' under the designation ECT 3/5, either with one escadrille of the two-seat Mirage F1B and the remainder of the squadron with the single-seat version, or (now that a total of fourteen F1B have been funded) the unit *may* be totally F1B equipped.

The Escadre will probably revert to the old insignia, that of a shield divided into seven parts, as shown above.

EC 1/5 'Vendée'
Codes: 5-NA/5-NZ
Callsigns: F-UGNA/F-UGNZ
Aircraft: Mirage F1 (5-NA to NR)
Fin insignia: Left SPA124 (GCII/6-4e) - the head of Joan of Arc, in grey with a white face, Right SPA26 (GCII/6-3e) - a black and white stork in flight.

Originally a mixed bomber and fighter squadron GCBI/18, equipped with the Dauntless and D-520, 'Vendée' began its present existence on 10 February 1949 when GC 1/5 'Travail' with Vampires was re-named GC 1/5 'Vendée'. Since that time the squadron has flown the Mystère IIC and IVA, Super Mystère B2 and Mirage IIIC, prior to receiving the F1C in 1974.

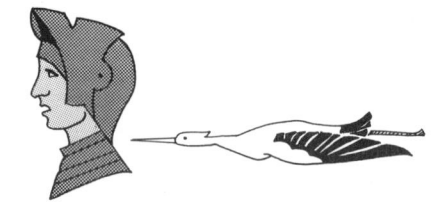

EC 2/5 'Ile de France'
Codes: 5-OA/5-OZ
Callsigns: F-UGOA/F-UGOZ
Aircraft: Mirage F1 (5-OA to OR)
Fin insignia: Both sides - Numerals '1941' in red on a black background. Yellow fleur de Lys on light blue diagonal.

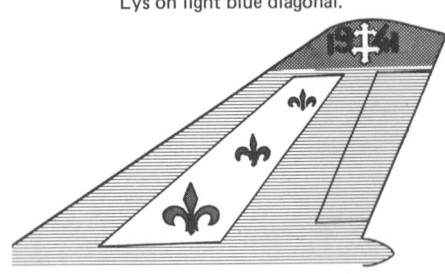

'Ile de France' was famous during World War 2 as the first Free French Spitfire squadron, formed on 7 November 1941 at Turnhouse as 340 Squadron, RAF, disbanding on 25 November 1945, following its transfer to French control as GCIV/2. On 10 April 1946, GCI/9 'Limousin' was re-named GCI/9 'Ile de France' and on 1 May was re-numbered GC 2/5 'Ile de France'. Spitfires were exchanged for Vampires and the subsequent types listed above under EC 5.

S.L.V.S.V.
Codes: 5-MA/5-MZ
Callsigns: F-UGMA/F-UGMZ
Aircraft: T-33A (5-MA, MF)
Magister (5-MC, MD, ME, MH)
Broussard (5-ML, MO, MP, MQ, MR)

6 ESCADRE DE CHASSE (†)

6 Escadron   *Escadron 1/6*

First of the overseas wings, EC 6 was based in North Africa throughout its existence. The Mistrals of EC 1/6 'Oranie' were withdrawn in the Autumn of 1960, the unit name later transferring to the Skyraider-equipped EC 3/20. EC 2/6 'Normandie-Niemen' re-equipped with the Vautour IIN in 1960, but left for France in 1962 whereupon EC 6 disbanded. The later history of 'Normandie' will be found under ECTT 2/30.

7 ESCADRE DE CHASSE - 1 CATac

In November 1945, escadrons 'Provence' and 'Nice' left the RAF to become 7 Wing, their pilots departing France for Indochina on 26 November 1945. Operations ceased on 1 August 1946 in anticipation of the activation of 2 Wing a couple of days later, and the two squadrons returned to Germany. They were designated 1 Wing on 1 July 1947, receiving the Vampire/Mistral in the course of 1950. On 1 November 1951, the unit reverted to its old title at Sidi Ahmed once again with its two squadrons 1/7 'Provence' and 2/7 'Nice', remaining in North Africa for a decade. The unit moved to Telergma in 1960 receiving the Mystère IVA here in March 1961, and following a brief period at Bizerte, returned to France that October. In December 1961, EC 7 settled at Nancy, transferring 'Nice' to EC 8 the same month, and receiving 'Languedoc' as EC 3/7 in return. In May 1973 'Provence' received its first Jaguars at St. Dizier, the Mystères of 'Languedoc' arriving at the same time for later replacement. A year later, the vacant EC 2/7 title was filled by a Jaguar OCU 'Argonne'. In late 1974/early 1975, the aircraft of 1 and 3 escadrons were modified to carry the AN53 nuclear weapon.

EC 1/7 'Provence'
Codes: 7-HA/7-HZ
Callsigns: F-UHHA/F-UHHZ
Aircraft: Jaguar A, Jaguar E (7-HA to 7-HP)
Fin insignia: Left SPA15 (GCI/7-2e) - a Bayard's helmet in light blue with white plumes.
Right SPA77 (GCI/7-2e) - the cross of Jerusalem, in yellow on a black pennant.

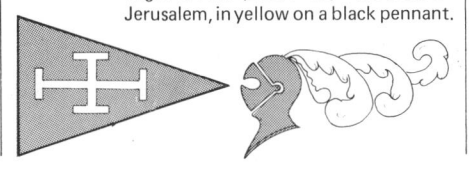

The present 'Provence' formed on 1 December 1943 as 328 Squadron of the RAF with the Spitfire, transferring back to French control as GCI/7 on 3 November 1945. The squadron immediately left for Saigon, French Indo China, arriving before its crated Spitfires and flying ex-Japanese 'Oscar' fighters as a temporary substitute. 'Provence' returned to Germany with EC 7 in August 1946, becoming GC 1/1 on 1 July 1947, and reverting to EC 1/7 on 1 November 1951, its subsequent history being as given above. The squadron left its Mystères (coded 7-AA/7-AZ) at Nancy in May 1973, moving to St. Dizier where the first six of its new Jaguars arrived on the 26th, making 'Provence' the premier Jaguar unit of the Armée de l'Air.

EC 2/7 'Argonne'
Codes: 7-PA/7-PZ
Callsigns: F-U PA/F-U PZ
Aircraft: Jaguar A, Jaguar E (7-PA/7-PW)
Fin insignia: Right SPA31 (GCI/1-1e) - a Spartan archer in yellow on a blue background.
Left SPA48 (GCI/1-2e) - the head of a cockerel in red and white.

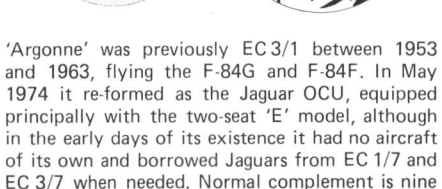

'Argonne' was previously EC 3/1 between 1953 and 1963, flying the F-84G and F-84F. In May 1974 it re-formed as the Jaguar OCU, equipped principally with the two-seat 'E' model, although in the early days of its existence it had no aircraft of its own and borrowed Jaguars from EC 1/7 and EC 3/7 when needed. Normal complement is nine aircraft of each version. 'Argonne' converts over fifty pilots per year to the Jaguar in four differing types of course:— 'Initial', for graduates from GE 314 or ECT 8 occupying 300 hours; 'Short' requiring fifteen hours for operational pilots; 'Intensive', six to ten missions for flight commanders and 'Special' for highly experienced pilots requiring only three days.

EC 3/7 'Languedoc'
Codes: 7-IA/7-IZ
Callsigns: F-UHIA/F-UHIZ
Aircraft: Jaguar A, Jaguar E (7-IA to 7-IP)
Fin insignia: Left SPA38 (GCII/8-4e) - a green thistle in a red and white pennant.
Right 3C-1 (GCII/8-3e) - a shark coloured blue and yellow.

'Languedoc', under the designation EC 2/8, moved from Indochina to Rabat in North Africa in 1955, receiving its present Mystère IVA aircraft there in 1958. In December 1961, it transferred to France with EC 8, and was immediately attached to 7 Wing as EC 3/7, codes 7-CA/7-CZ. Its Mystères were taken to St. Dizier on 1 June 1973 where they were replaced by Jaguars later in the year.

S.L.V.S.V.
Codes: 7-JA/7-JZ
Callsigns: F-UHJA/F-UHJZ
Aircraft: T-33A (7-JA, JB)
Magister (7-JE, JF, JG)
Broussard (7-JI)

8 ESCADRE DE TRANSFORMATION - CEAA

The squadrons of EC 8 left Indo China in 1955 for Rabat in North Africa where they were equipped with the Mistral: EC 1/8 'Maghreb' and EC 2/8 'Languedoc', codes 8-PA/8-PZ and 8-QA/8-QZ respectively. Withdrawn to Oran in 1960 and re-equipped with the Mystère IVA, EC 8 came home to Orange in December 1961 where 'Maghreb' (ERC 573 insignia) was replaced by 'Saintonge', and 'Languedoc' transferred to EC 7 in exchange for 'Nice'. Now stationed at Cazaux, ET 8 is a weapons training wing and is destined to receive Alpha Jets in 1979/80, finally retiring its Mystères in 1981.

ET 1/8 'Saintonge'
Codes: 8-MA/8-MZ
Callsigns: F-TEMA/F-TEMZ
Aircraft: Mystère IVA (8-MA to 8-MZ)
Fin insignia: Left 4C-1 (GCI/8-2e) - a lion in yellow and black.
Right 3C-2 (GCI/8-1e) - a black arrow flanked by red wings, the whole outlined in yellow.

Under the designation GCII/18, 'Saintonge' finished World War 2 flying the Dewoitine 520, converting to the Spitfire Vb in December 1945 for service in Indo China. Re-designated GC 1/22 and equipped with the Bearcat the squadron disbanded at Dien Bien Phu in 1955. 'Saintonge' was re-formed on 7 December 1961, taking over the aircraft of EC 1/8 'Maghreb', when all North African names were withdrawn from Armée de l'Air usage.

ET 2/8 'Nice'
Codes: 8-NA/8-NZ
Callsigns: F-TENA/F-TENZ
Aircraft: Mystère IVA (8-NA to 8-NZ)
Fin insignia: Left SPA78 (GCII/7-4e) - a black panther.
Right SPA73 (GCII/7-3e) - a black and white stork.

'Nice' formed as 326 Squadron, RAF, on 1 December 1943 flying the Spitfire Vc. Transferred to the Armée de l'Air on 3 November 1945 and taking-up its old designation GCII/7, 'Nice' left for Saigon in November 1945 where it served until re-established in Germany in August 1946 after its operational career in Indo China. On 1 July 1947, it was re-numbered EC 2/1 and as such received the Vampire/Mistral in 1950. It returned to its old designation EC 2/7 at Sidi Ahmed in North Africa on 1 November 1951, its aircraft receiving the codes 7-BA/7-BZ. 'Nice' moved to Telergma in 1960 where the Mystère IVA was received the following year, and with the gradual French withdrawal from Africa to Bizerte, prior to leaving for Nancy in October 1961. On 7 December 1961, the squadron was transferred to EC 8 in exchange for Escadron 'Languedoc'. Like ET 1/8, the unit flies approximately twenty aircraft.

S.L.V.S.V.
Codes: 8-OA/8-OZ
Callsigns: F-TEOA/F-TEOZ
Aircraft: Magister (8-OA, OB, OC, OD, OJ, ON)
T-33A (8-OE, OF, OG, OH)
Flamant
Broussard (8-OY, OZ).

From late 1976 onwards, strength has been augmented by the loan of Magisters (approximately five at any one time) from GE 315, these retaining their '315-' codes.

9 ESCADRE DE CHASSE (†)

EC 9 formed at Lahr in 1954 equipped with F-84G Thunderjets in two squadrons EC 1/9 'Limousin' and EC 2/9 'Auvergne', codes 9-AA/9-AZ and 9-BA/9-BZ respectively. The wing moved to Metz in 1956 where the F-84F Thunderstreak was received and flown until 30 June 1965 when the wing disbanded. 'Auvergne' now exists as EC 3/13, but 'Limousin' whose last period of existence was as GCI/9 at Meknès between September 1944 and April 1946, is currently dormant.

10 ESCADRE DE CHASSE - CAFDA

At the time of its formation, EC 10 was a reserve training wing flying the P-47 and MS 472 from Villacoublay and Dijon. This disbanded in 1954, whereupon EC 1/10 and 2/10 combined to form EC 2/17 at Creil, and EC 3/10 became EC 3/17.

The wing re-mustered as a Mystère IIC unit at Creil, its first squadron 'Parisis' forming on 1 December 1954, although it was without aircraft until July 1955. By late 1956, the wing was complete with 'Seine' and 'Valois' fully equipped, but with the disbandment of 'Parisis' in 1958 (see EH 3/67 for subsequent history), 'Valois' was re-numbered as the wing's first escadron. In 1958, EC 10 became the second Super Mystère B2 wing. The replacement Mirage IIIC fighters arrived with 'Seine' in 1969, although 'Valois' remained with the Super Mystère B2 until 1974. EC 10 was due to receive the Mirage F1 in 1978-9, in anticipation of which the Mirage IIIC were being grouped into the third escadron for service in Djibouti. Recent rumours however, suggest that EC 10 may well keep their Mirage IIICs until they are replaced by Mirage 2000s around 1982/3.

EC 1/10 'Valois'
Codes: 10-SA/10-SZ
Callsigns: F-UISA/F-UISZ
Aircraft: Mirage IIIC (10-SA to SV)
Fin insignia: Left SPA93 (GCIII/1-6e) - a goose in flight with yellow beak, neck, legs and feet; green head, tail and wing centre strips; black wing leading and trailing edges and brick red body.
Right N84 (GCIII/1-5e) - the red head of a fox.

Originally the third escadron of EC 10, 'Valois' received its first Mystère IIC in March 1956, phasing these out in March 1958 in favour of the Super Mystère B2 under the new designation of EC 1/10. The squadron disposed of its last Super Mystère to EC 12 in August 1974, receiving Mirage IIICs from EC 5 in return. In common with EC 2/10, the 'Valois' had an over-size complement of twenty-four aircraft.

EC 2/10 'Seine'
Codes: 10-RA/10-RZ
Callsigns: F-UIRA/F-URIZ
Aircraft: Mirage IIIC (10-RA to RX)
Fin insignia: Both sides (GCIII/10-3e) - a black and white cock with red comb and legs, a blue upper and red lower background, and white aircraft.

'Seine' formed in December 1955 as a component of EC 10, flying the Mystère IIC and later the Super Mystère B2. The first Mirage IIIC replacements arrived in 1969, but until the receipt of more of the type for EC 1/10, 'Seine' operated eighteen rather than the normal twenty aircraft. An unusual feature of the squadron insignia is that the old

45

Cercle de Chasse de Paris badge, the pre-war GCII/10-3e, appears on both sides of the fin, its companion escadrille, SPA76 (GCII/10-4e), an eagle within a pennant, not being worn.

EC 3/10 'Vexin'
Codes: 10-LA/10-LZ
Callsigns: F-UILA/F-UILZ
Aircraft: Mirage IIIC
Fin insignia:

In order to replace the Super Sabres of EC 4/11 at Djibouti, EC 10 formed a third squadron by reducing the strength of its existing components. The first aircraft to be noted in the new code range appeared in May 1978 camouflaged in a two-tone brown scheme, although more recently this has been described as 'sand and chestnut'. The choice of codes may not be unconnected with the series F-UHLA/F-UHLZ used by 'Parisis' during its time as EC 1/10. On 1 January 1979 'Vexin' officially formed at Djibouti with a small component of twelve aircraft, (its name being particularly appropriate as Vexin was one of France's smaller provinces).

S.L.V.S.V.
Codes: 10-KA/10-KZ
Callsigns: F-UIKA/F-UIKZ
Aircraft: Magister (10-KF, KG, KH, KI, KJ, KK)
Broussard (10-KW, KX, KY, KZ)

---

11 ESCADRE DE CHASSE - 1 CATac

11 Escadre formed at Reims on 1 August 1952 and worked-up three squadrons (Rousillon, Vosges and Jura) on the F-84G at Luxeuil, exchanging these for the F-84F in 1956. 'Jura' disbanded in 1958, prior to the arrival of the Super Sabre, and in June 1961 the two remaining squadrons transferred to Bremgarten, Germany, as part of NATO's 4ATAF. The French withdrawal from the North Atlantic Alliance brought EC 11 back to the ex-USAF base at Toul in 1966, where in the following year, the remaining Super Sabres of EC 3 joined the wing which was enlarged by the addition of 'Corse'. In January 1973, 'Jura' was re-formed as a detached flight in Djibouti. During 1976, the wing began to equip with the Jaguar, a transfer which was complete by the late Spring of 1977.

EC 1/11 'Roussillon'
Codes: 11-EA/11-EZ
Callsigns: F-UHEA/F-UHEZ
Aircraft: Jaguar A and E (11-EA to 11-EV)
Fin insignia: Left GCIII/6-6e - a mask of comedy, white with yellow and black face markings and wings. (Optionally in a blue disc.)
Right GCIII/6-5e - a black and white mask of anger.

'Roussillon' formed the first escadron of EC 11 on 1 August 1952 perpetuating the traditions of GCIII/6, a disbanded Thunderbolt squadron. It has remained with the wing as detailed above, becoming the second squadron to receive the Jaguar in the late Spring of 1976. The role of the squadron is conventional strike in support of the 1st Army and the authorised complement is fourteen 'A' and one 'E' version.

EC 2/11 'Vosges'
Codes: 11-MA/11-MZ
Callsigns: F-UHMA/F-UHMZ
Aircraft: Jaguar A and E
Fin insignia: Left SPA97 - a divided pennant, in red and white with black motifs.
Right SPA91 - a black vulture clutching a white skull.

Escadron 'Vosges' has been with EC 11 since its formation, and was the last of the three squadrons to convert to the Jaguar, doing so in late 1976/early 1977. By July 1977 the squadron was up to strength with fourteen 'A' and one 'E' Jaguars, and concentrating on its task of electronic countermeasures development for the Tactical Air Force. Deliveries began with No. 81/11-MA, the first to leave the production line with laser rangefinder and active ECM equipment.

EC 3/11 'Corse'
Codes: 11-RA/11-RZ
Callsigns: F-UGRA/F-UGRZ
Aircraft: Jaguar A and E (11-RA to 11-RX)

Fin insignia: Left SPA88 (GCI/3-1e) - a red snake with yellow striping on a white disc outlined in black.
Right SPA69 (GCI/3-2e) - a black mask outlined in yellow on a red disc.

'Corse' is the oldest component of EC 11, its present term of existence beginning on 1 December 1943 when it formed as 327 Squadron, RAF, at Ajaccio flying Spitfires under the alternative French title of GCI/3. The squadron was returned to the Armée de l'Air on 1 November 1945 and was re-formed as a Mosquito unit the same month for service in Indo China. In July 1947, 'Corse' was re-numbered GC 1/6 and began to receive Spitfires in April 1950, but kept these for only a few months, for on 18 November it received its first Hellcat. Together with the Bearcat this type continued the air war against the Communist guerillas until disbandment in April 1952.

In 1953, 'Corse' took the premier position as EC 1/1 at St. Dizier with the F-84G, exchanging these mounts for the F-84F in August 1955. Disbandment of EC 1 in December 1963 brought 'Corse' to a temporary end, but the concentration of all French Super Sabres within EC 11 in 1966 was responsible for its re-formation as EC 3/11. Shortly after formation, 'Corse' moved to Colmar in June 1966, joining the rest of EC 11 at Toul in October 1967. It became the first to receive the Jaguar early in 1976. The squadron has a non-standard complement of seven-single seat ('A') and eight two-seat ('E') Jaguars to permit intensive flight-refuelling practise by reason of its allocated task supporting French units deployed overseas.

EC 4/11 'Jura'
Codes: 11-YA/11-YZ
Callsigns:
Aircraft: F-100D and F-100F
Jaguar A and E
Fin insignia: Left SPA158 - a secretary bird (French: Serpentaire) in black and white, clutching a blue snake.
Right SPA161 - a sphinx.

Previously the third escadron of EC 11, 'Jura' flew the F-84G and later F-84F until disbanded in 1958. It re-formed at Djibouti on 1 January 1973 as a detached flight with seven F-100D and one F-100F (four of which are equipped for photo-reconnaissance) replacing the Skyraiders of the disbanded EAA 1/21. The small size of the unit qualified it for only one unit insignia, the serpentaire being carried on both sides. However, during 1978, the Super Sabres were noted with 'sharkmouth' markings, and with the standard presentation of one unit badge each side. Original plans called for the replacement of its Super Sabres by a version of the Jaguar equipped for flight refuelling in 1978, but it was instead decided to base the Mirage III of EC 3/10 at Djibouti, and accordingly 'Jura' disbanded on 12 December 1978. On 1 January 1979 a new EC 4/11 formed with Jaguars at Bordeaux to replace the Vautours of EB 92. It has now been confirmed that the codes 11-YA/11-YZ (F-UMYA/F-UMYZ) will be perpetuated.

S.L.V.S.V.
Codes: 11-OA/11-OZ
Callsigns: F-UHOA/F-UHOZ
Aircraft: Broussard (11-OB).
T-33A (11-OH, OJ).
Magister (11-OA, OC, OD, OE, OF, OI).
Insignia: A red and white bird on a light blue background. Yellow eyes with black centres and gold stars. Lettering black on yellow.

---

12 ESCADRE DE CHASSE - CAFDA

EC 12 received its first squadron when EC 1/12 formed at Mont-de-Marsan in April 1952 equipped with the Ouragan. The wing commenced a move to its current base of Cambrai in July 1953 with escadrons 1/12 'Cambrésis', 2/12 'Picardie' and 3/12 'Cornouaille' and in 1954 formed the first Armée de l'Air aerobatic team to operate a French built aircraft since 1940. By the Autumn of 1955, all three squadrons had completed the changeover to the Mystère IVA. Three years later, EC 12 became the first to convert to the Super Mystère B2, although by that time 'Picardie' (SPA172 and

47

SPA173 codes 12-XA/12-XZ had disbanded and 'Cornouaille' promoted to fill the vacant EC 2/12 position. In mid-1976, Mirage F1 training began at Reims with aircraft marked in 'Cornouaille' insignia, the changeover being complete by the Autumn of 1977. EC 12 is due to form a third escadron with aircraft included in the 179 F1s ordered up to and including the fiscal year 1978.

EC 1/12 'Cambrésis'
Codes: 12-YA/12-YZ
Callsigns: F-UHYA/F-UHYZ
Aircraft: Mirage F1 (12-YA to 12-YO)
Fin insignia: Left SPA89 - a hornet, black and yellow with white wings.
Right SPA162 - a tiger's head, in black and yellow with a red tongue.

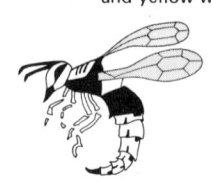

'Cambrésis' formed on 1 April 1952 within 12 Escadre, subsequently flying the Ouragan, Mystère IVA and Super Mystère B2. Having been the first unit to receive the latter type, 1/12 was also the last when its last three Super Mystères were retired on 9 September 1977.

EC 2/12 'Cornouaille'
Codes: 12-ZA/12-ZZ
Callsigns: F-UHZA/F-UHZZ
Aircraft: Mirage F1 (12-ZA to 12-ZO)
Fin insignia: Left - a bulldog's head in black and brown.
Right - a scorpion in black and white.

Previously EC 3/12, 'Cornouaille' was re-designated 2/12 with the arrival of the Super Mystère. Working-up on the Mirage F1 began at Reims in mid-1976 under the direction of ECTT 30, and the first eight aircraft arrived at Cambrai on 1 October that year.

Conversion was completed in April 1977 when EC 1/12 commenced the changeover.

S.L.V.S.V.
Codes: 12-XA/12-XZ
Callsigns: F-UHXA/F-UHXZ
Aircraft: T-33 (12-XA, XB, XC)
Broussard (12-XF, XI)
Magister (12-XJ, XK, XL, XM)
In 1978 T-33 '12-XC' was compromised by Broussard 'XC'.

13 ESCADRE DE CHASSE - 1 CATac

Newest of the Armée de l'Air wings, 13 Escadre formed at Lahr on 1 March 1955 and commenced pilot training with a small number of T-33A aircraft. Its first squadron formed in August 1956 and began to receive Sabres. The wing moved to its present base at the newly built Colmar air base on 1 April 1957 forming its second squadron the following month. During 1962, EC 13 became the second operator of the Mirage IIIC, but shortly afterwards commenced training on the IIIE in a special flight established at Istres. EC 13 was the first IIIE wing to become operational and was joined by a third squadron equipped with the Mirage 5F in 1972. During 1977, EC 2/13 also converted to the 5F although there are insufficient of this type to issue to 1/13.

EC 1/13 'Artois'
Codes: 13-QA/13-QZ
Callsigns: F-UHQA/F-UHQZ
Aircraft: Mirage IIIE (13-QA to QS)
Fin insignia: Left SPA100(GCIII/2-6e) - a swallow white body and black head.
Right SPA83 (GCIII/2-5e) - a black chimaera (dragon) on a red disc.

'Artois' formed in 1944 as an un-numbered Groupe de Transport equipped with the C-47, later flying the Bearcat in Indo China under the designation GC 1/21. On 1 August 1956, 'Artois' re-formed at Lahr as EC 1/13 and began to receive the F-86K single-seat all-weather fighter the following month. These were originally coded 13-GA/13-GZ, a series soon afterwards changed to the current 13-QA/13-QZ range, when the squadron transferred to Colmar on 1 April 1957. In September 1962 the first Mirage IIIC aircraft were delivered to EC 1/13, but they were retained only until 1965 when they were replaced by the IIIE.

EC 2/13 'Alpes'
Codes: 13-PA/13-PZ
Callsigns: F-UHPA/F-UHPZ
Aircraft: Mirage 5F (13-PA to PO)
Fin insignia: Left - a knight on a bay horse and a red background.
Right - a knight on a black horse and a white background.

Formed at Colmar on 1 May 1957, 'Alpes' is a new Armée de l'Air escadron with no inherited traditions. During the first few months of its existence the squadron's Sabres were coded 13-HA/13-HZ, but were soon changed to the present series. Withdrawal of the Sabre from EC 13 began with 1/13 in January 1962 and 2/13 disposed of its aircraft in April. Until the Mirage IIIC was available, a third escadron, codes 13-SA/13-SZ, existed from April to August 1962, designated EC 3/13 but with no name. In April 1965, 'Alpes' became the first squadron to receive the Mirage IIIE, and in April 1977 took over the Mirage 5F aircraft of EC 3/3.

EC 3/13 'Auvergne'
Codes: 13-SA/13-SZ
Callsigns: F-UHSA/F-UHSZ
Aircraft: Mirage 5F (13-SA to ST)
Fin insignia: Left SPA85 (GCII/9-3e) - a jester quartered in red and white with yellow bells, hands and face.
Right GCII/9-4e - a blue shield, yellow sword and white hand.

Following its disbandment in 1942, having been part if the Vichy forces, 'Auvergne' re-formed at Meknes in 1944 as a bomber unit, later moving to Vallon and Salon de Provence. In 1950 the squadron was established in Indo China as a Hellcat unit GM 2/9 becoming GC 2/21 in October 1953. Re-activated at Lahr in 1954 as EC 2/9, 'Auvergne' operated the F-84F until disbanded on 30 June 1965. The escadron re-formed on 1 May 1972 as the first of two Armée de l'Air squadrons to take up the embargoed Israeli Mirage 5 aircraft.

S.L.V.S.V.
Codes: 13-TA/13-TZ
Callsigns: F-UHTA/F-UHTZ
Aircraft: Broussard (13-TB)
T-33A (13-TC, TG)
Magister (13-TD, TE)

21 ESCADRON D'APPUI AERIEN (†)

Following withdrawal from Algeria, EAA 1/20 formed the basis for a Skyraider wing in Central Africa comprising two squadrons of six-seven aircraft at separate bases. The first of these existed on an operational footing in French Somalia (now Djibouti) until relieved by Super Sabres in 1973, defending the country against its unfriendly neighbours. The two components were:—

EAA 1/21 'Aures Namentcha' formed at Djibouti on 1 October 1963 out of the ex-Algerian EAA 1/20 'Aures Namentcha' disbanded the previous day. Squadron Skyraiders were coded 21-LA/21-LZ (F-TFLA/F-TFLZ) until the unit disbanded on 31 December 1972 when EC 4/11 became operational with Super Sabres.

EAA 2/21 formed at Chateaudun in April 1964 equipped with Skyraiders, transferring these to Ivato, Madagascar two months later. Aircraft codes were 21-ZA/21-ZZ (F-TGZA/F-TGZZ). As a result of the French departure for Madagascar, the squadron took up residence at St. Denis, Ile de Réunion on 1 August 1973, disbanding the following month.

22 ESCADRON D'APPUI AERIEN (†)

Following an outbreak of unrest in Chad during 1968, four Skyraiders were temporarily detached from EAA 1/21 at Fort Lamy. The flight was replaced by a full squadron from 1 March 1969 onwards, this adopting the name 'Ain' previously used by EC 3/10 in its days as a training wing. Aircraft codes were 22-DA/22-DZ (F-UIDA/F-UIDZ) and the 'Ramel' insignia was applied to both sides of the engine cowling. The squadron was the sole constituent of EAA 22 and disbanded in October 1975 following local rejection of continued assistance in the anti-guerilla campaign.

30 ESCADRE DE CHASSE TOUS TEMPS - CAFDA

The first French all-weather jet fighter wing was established at Tours in January 1953 and built up to a total of three Meteor NF.11 squadrons:

EMICN 1/30 'Loire' the FAW OCU, EC 2/30 'Camargue' and EC 3/30 'Lorraine'. Vautour IIN fighters arrived in 1957 resulting in the disbandment of 'Camargue'. Its vacant place was filled by a third Vautour squadron, 'Normandie-Niemen' in 1962. During 1965, 'Loire' (codes 30-OA/30-OZ) was detached to the Pacific, entitled GM 85. Phase-out of the Vautour began in 1974, and was complete by the Autumn, but 'Loire' is expected to re-join the wing, which will once more total three squadrons. From 1966, the whole of the wing has been based at Reims-Champagne.

ECTT 2/30 'Normandie-Niemen'
Codes: 30-MA/30-MZ
Callsigns: F-UIMA/F-UIMZ
Aircraft: Mirage F1 (30-MA to MU)

Fin insignia: Both sides - the arms of Normandie. A red shield, yellow lions and white flash.

'Normandie' formed in the USSR during 1942 from a party of French volunteers flying the Yak-1 and later Yak-9 and Yak-3. During the crossing of the river Niemen in 1944, the unit, by then of wing strength, was one of several which distinguished itself, and was awarded the name 'Niemen' by Stalin. Returned to France in June 1945, 'Normandie-Niemen' transferred to Rabat as GC 2/6 in March 1947 with Mosquitos and to Saigon with Kingcobras in September 1949. Following withdrawal from Indo China, the squadron re-formed as EC 2/6 at Oran in 1951, flying the P-47, Mistral and later B-26 Invader. Converted to Vautours (code 6-QA/6-QZ) at Oran during 1960, 'Normandie-Niemen' returned home to Orange in 1962 as ECTT 2/30, taking up station at Reims in July 1966. Training for the Mirage F1 began at Mont-de-Marsan under EC 24/118, and on 20 December 1973, the first seven aircraft arrived at Reims to commence re-equipment of the Armée de l'Air's first squadron.

ECTT 3/30 'Lorraine'
Codes: 30-FA/30-FZ
Callsigns: F-UHFA/F-UHFZ
Aircraft: Mirage F1 (30-FA to FO)
Fin insignia: Both sides - the arms of Lorraine. Three white alerions on a red diagonal.

Formed in the RAF as 342 Squadron at West Raynham on 7 April 1943, GB 1/20 was originally a bomber unit flying Bostons, and from April 1945, the Mitchell until disbandment on 2 December 1945. Re-formed at Rabat in November 1949, with Mosquitos as the Groupe de Reconnaissance et de Chasse de Nuit 1/20, the unit was re-titled GC de Nuit 1/31 in 1951. On 1 June 1952 it returned to France where it received Meteors at Tours during the following year under the title Escadron Mixte de Instruction et de Chasse de Nuit 3/30. In 1957, Vautour IINs were received under the slightly shorter title of ECTT 3/30, and the squadron moved to Reims in February 1961. During the Spring of 1974 the Vautours were retired in exchange for the current type, the Mirage F1.

S.L.V.S.V.
Aircraft: T-33A (30-QB)
            Magister (30-QC, QF)
            Broussard (30-QN)
            In early 1978 aircraft began to re-code in the series 30-WA to 30-WZ.
Fin insignia: A yellow head of a cat, yellow crescent, black sky and white stars.

For most of its existence, EC 30 has operated a radar interception training school, this originally being 1/30. The task was subsequently allocated to the Meteor-equipped CIPN 346 (later CIETT 346), but on its disbandment the wing SLVSV (codes 'LA/LZ' F-UILA/F-UILZ) was increased in size in January 1967 to form Escadrille de Entrainment 12/30 equipped with the T-33, Magister, Flamant and Broussard, codes 30-QA/30-QZ and adorned with the old CIETT 346 badge. EE 12/30 was adopted by the village of 'Hautvillers', this becoming the unit name. On 30 September 1972, 'Hautvillers' was disbanded and returned to SLVSV status (although still with the 'Q' codes).

33 ESCADRE DE RECONNAISANCE - 1 CATac

The three squadrons of ER 33 have been associated with each other since ER 33 was established at Freiburg in 1945, flying PR Mustangs and Lightnings. Moved to Cognac in May 1950, the wing received reconnaissance F-84G Thunderjets in the course of 1952, following these with RF-84F Thunderflashes in 1957, immediately prior to a move to Lahr in July of that year. The wing returned to France in 1960 and gradually converted to the Mirage IIIR which will be retained until replaced by the photo-reconnaissance Mirage F1-R from 1982 onwards.

ER 1/33 'Belfort'
Codes: 33-CA/33-CZ
Callsigns: F-UICA/F-UICZ
Aircraft: Mirage IIIR (33-CA to CV)
Fin insignia: Both sides - SAL33 - a 'Hache' (battle axe) in red.

ER 1/33 remained with the 2nd and 3rd squadrons of ER 33 until transferred to Luxeuil in 1959. It continued to operate the RF-84F until it re-joined the main unit at Strasbourg in January 1967 to take-up the Mirage IIIR.

ER 2/33 'Savoie'
Codes: 33-NA/33-NZ
Callsigns: F-UINA/F-UINZ
Aircraft: Mirage IIIR (33-NA to NT)
Fin insignia: Both sides SAL6 - a white seamew in a blue circle.

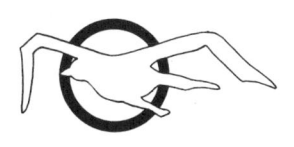

Last of the three squadrons to leave Lahr, 2/33 moved to Strasbourg in March 1960, and commenced conversion to the Mirage IIIR in March 1964.

ER 3/33 'Moselle'
Codes: 33-TA/33-TZ
Callsigns: F-UITA/F-UITZ
Aircraft: Mirage IIIRD (33-TA to TS)
Fin insignia: Both sides BR11 - an origami bird in red.

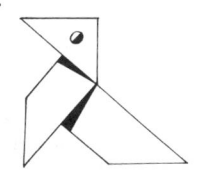

'Moselle' departed Lahr in 1959 for Strasbourg and became the first Mirage IIIR squadron when it took up temporary residence at Mont-de-Marsan between March to September 1963 for the duration of the changeover. In 1967-68, the IIIR aircraft were passed on to 1 and 2/33, and 'Moselle' equipped with the infra-red sensor equipped Mirage IIIRD, seventeen of which remain.

S.L.V.S.V.
Aircraft: Broussard (33-XB)
Magister (33-XC, XD)
T-33A (XH)   RT-33A (33-XG)

Codes: 33-XA/33-XZ
Callsigns: F-UIXA/F-UIXZ
Fin insignia: The three squadron badges within a Cross of Lorraine, (Escadre badge).

41 ESCADRILLE DE LIAISON AERIENNES - CoTAM

Responsible for communications within 1 Region, and principally for the 1ere CATac HQ, also at Metz, ELA 41 additionally provides facilities for continuation training. A detachment of the unit is based at Dijon. On 1 December 1974, Magisters 41-AU to 41-AX were transferred to the Metz base flight and continued to operate with code prefixes '128- '. In 1975, a single Rallye was employed for evaluation, but this was disposed of the following year.

ELA 41 'Verdun'
Codes: 41-AA/41-AZ
Callsigns: F-SCAA/F-SCAZ
Aircraft: Broussard (41-AA to AF, AI, AL)
Paris (41-AN to AU)

Official insignia:
A white castle
on a gold background

Unofficial insignia:
A pilot on a push scooter

51

43 ESCADRILLE DE LIAISON AERIENNES - CoTAM

HQ 3 Region at Bordeaux has at its disposal ELA 43 at the same base, for communications work.

ELA 43
Codes: 43-BA/43-BZ
Callsigns: F-SCBA/F-SCBZ
Aircraft: Paris (43-BA to BD)
Broussard (43-BM, BN, BP, BT, BU)
Fin insignia: A black stagecoach, on a blue background with a white cloud.

ELA 43 was allocated a Rallye for evaluation during 1975.

44 ESCADRILLE DE LIAISON AERIENNES - CoTAM

Communications for 4 Region, Aix, are provided by ELA 44 also at Aix with a detachment at Istres. A second detachment, ELA et le Sauvetage 1/44, at Solenzara, Corsica, has search and rescue as an additional responsibility.

ELA 44 'Mistral'
Fin insignia: Red 'ELA'; red 'Mistral' on white background; white '44' on gold. Golden bee.

Codes: 44-CA/44-CZ
Callsigns: F-SCCA/F-SCCZ
Aircraft: Broussard (44-CA to CF, CH to CJ)
Paris (44-CG, CM, CN, CO)
Nord 262 (CR to CU)
(Rallye 44-CZ was used for a trial period in 1975)

ELAS 1/44
Codes: 44-GA/44-GZ
Callsigns: F-RHGA/F-RHGZ
Aircraft: Puma (44-GA, GB, GF)
Noratlas (44-GD, GE)
Alouette (44-GC)
Fin insignia: On a map of Corsica, a boy on a dolphin.

During 1975, 1/44 received an infusion of new equipment, two Noratlas and two Pumas (later joined by a third) replacing a Broussard and an H-34. The H-34 was the last Armée de l'Air example still operational, and retired on 31 May 1976.

50 GROUPE AERIEN MIXTE - CoTAM

Based at St. Denis on the Isle of Réunion, since moving from Madagascar late in 1973, GAM 50 provides support for French and local units.

The codes 50-IA/50-IZ used by the Tananarive-based C-47s have been withdrawn, and the replacement Noratlas now employ a new sequence. The unit name is 'Mascareianes'.

GAM 50
Codes: 50-WA/50-WZ and LA/LZ (Alouette)
Callsigns: F-SDWA/F-SDWZ, F-SCLA/F-SCLZ
Aircraft: Noratlas, Alouette II
Fin insignia: An orange island and a white bird on a blue background. A black buffalo with white horns on a golden background. Black 'GLA 50' on a gold rectangle.

51 ESCADRILLE ELECTRONIQUE - CTAA

EE 51 formed at Evreux in 1977 equipped with one specially modified DC-8 which retains its original ET 3/60 code 'FE' (F-RAFE). The aircraft is designated 'DC-8 Sarig' and wears an eagle badge on the nose. The unit name is 'Aubrac'.

52 ESCADRON DE TRANSPORT D'OUTRE MER - CoTAM

On 1 April 1976, ETOM 52 formed at Tontouta Airport, Noumea, New Caledonia with a single Alouette II which had been detached from GAM 82 at Papeete the previous July. The first Puma arrived with the unit on 5 April 1976 and was joined by two more in March 1977. Codes used are 52-LA/52-LD (F-RALA/F-RALD) allocated in order of delivery.

Insignia consists of a silhouette of the island of New Caledonia and a Polynesian totem, and the unit name is also 'Tontouta'.

54 ESCADRILLE ELECTRONIQUE - CTAA

The eight Noratlas of EE 54 are based at Metz and equipped with special electronic countermeasures equipment for the confusion of an enemy force, under the designation 'N2501 Gabrielle'.

EE 54 'Dunkerque' applies no codes or badges to its aircraft, although the call-sign range F-RAYA/F-RAYZ was changed to F-RBTA/F-RBTZ in 1973. An ECM Puma is included in the 1978 defence procurements. The squadron originally formed on 1 January 1964.

55 ESCADRILLE DE TRANSPORT D'OUTRE MER - CoTAM

ETOM 55 'Ouessant' is based at Dakar to provide support for French army units in the area. The escadrille employs the Alouette II 55-BA/55-BZ (F-RBBA/F-RBBZ) and Noratlas 55-KA/55-KZ (F-RBKA/F-RBKZ).

The unit badge is a black cormorant over a black lighthouse standing on red ground in a blue sea and displaying a yellow beam.

56 GROUPE AERIEN MIXTE - CoTAM

GAM 56 'Vaucluse' operates a variety of types from Evreux, principally the Noratlas, Broussard and Puma. Only the former aircraft are marked with the 'last two' of the call-sign F-RAXA/F-RAXZ, a total of eight being a normal complement. Pumas are unmarked but employ call-signs in the range F-SCOA/F-SCOZ. The duty of the unit is unclear, but the total lack of any official data indicates an 'under-cover' function.

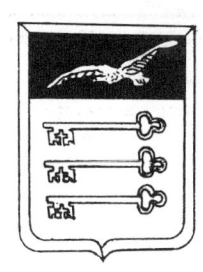

57 ESCADRILLE DE CALIBRATION - CTAA

EdC 57 'Commercy' is located at Villacoublay and operates four specially equipped Noratlas on radio-aids checking flights, replacing Dakotas withdrawn in 1968. The unit marks its aircraft with the 'last three' of the call-sign range F-RCAA/F-RCAZ. During 1977, Falcon No. 291 was operating with the unit.

Unit insignia shows three white maidens on a divided shield, upper portion blue, lower red and the unit originally formed on 1 August 1965.

58 ESCADRILLE DE TRANSPORT d'OUTRE MER - CoTAM

Communications in the West Indies are undertaken by ETOM 58 (previously known as Detachment Air 375) at Point-à-Pitre, equipped with the Alouette, Broussard and Puma. Four Noratlas (58-MI/58-MK) were returned to France in mid-1976 and replaced by Puma helicopters, the first of which arrived on 4 December 1976 and the remaining two on 1 July 1977. Unit callsigns are in the series F-RHMA/F-RHMZ and include Aztec 'MD'. The unit was designated Escadrille de Transport Antilles-Guyane until 1 April 1976. A small number of Transalls are operated on detachment from ET 61.

Insignia is a shield, upper part blue, left red, right green with black figures.

59 GROUPE DE MARCHE DU TCHAD (†)

Formed on 1 July 1969, GMT 59 'Orleans' provided support for Skyraider unit EAA 1/22 at N'Djamena (previously Fort Lamy) Chad and for local army detachments. The code range 59-CA/59-CZ (F-RBCA/F-RBCZ) was used by the Noratlas and HA/HZ (F-RAHA/F-RAHZ) by the Alouette II, H-34 and Broussard. The French presence in Chad was abruptly curtailed due to a political difference of opinion, and the unit was disbanded in October 1975.

60 ESCADRE DE TRANSPORT - CoTAM

GLAM 1/60

The Groupe des Liaison Aériennes Ministérielles (GLAM), is as its name suggests, responsible for the transportation of government ministers, including the president, and operates a variety of aircraft types for this purpose. ET 1/60 constitutes the major part of the 60th Escadre and is based at Villacoublay with the following types—

Caravelle (F-RAFG, H)
Mystère 20 K. L, M, N, P, T. (F-RAFK etc.)
Alouette II O, Q. (F-RAFO, F-RAFQ)
Puma R 'Carrousel', S 'Arc de Triomphe' (F-RAFR, F-RAFS) (Super Frelon F-RAFR has been sold and replaced by one of the above).

The insignia shows a black aircraft over a globe of blue oceans and white continents.

GAEL 2/60 see ET 65

ET 3/60 'Estérel'

Since the withdrawal of the DC-6 aircraft of ET 64 and GAM 82 the three DC-8 aircraft operated by ET 3/60 since 1966 have been increased to five, coded A-E (F-RAFA/F-RAFE). Originally based at Le Bourget, they transferred to Paris-Roissy (Charles de Gaulle) when this new airport opened, but in 1977 F-RAFE was seconded to EE 51. Insignia is coloured as ET 1/60.

61 ESCADRE DE TRANSPORT - CoTAM

Having been the first Noratlas wing, ET 61 commenced re-equipment with the Transall, its three component escadrons being as below.

The wing insignia comprises a silver eagle over three coats of arms; First a bat (escadrille V 113), a star (escadrille BR 101) and the arms of Touraine; second, the arms of Franche Comté, and third the arms of Poitou.

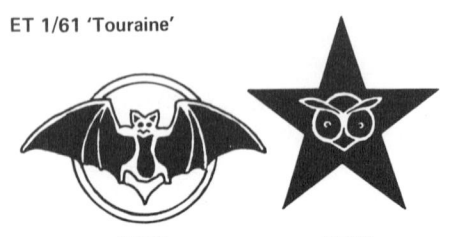

ET 1/61 'Touraine'

BR101

BR113

'Touraine' (ex 61-NA/61-NZ) previously GT 1/15 with Dakotas in Indo China, received Transalls between November 1967 and July 1969.

ET 2/61 'Franche Comté'

'Franche Comté' (ex 61-YA/61-YZ) previously GBII/52 with Marauders, 1945, and later GT 2/61 with Ju52/C-47 in Indo China. Received Transalls, August 1969 to May 1970.

ET 3/61 'Poitou'

'Poitou' (ex 61-QA/61-QZ). Received Transalls, October 1970 to May 1971. All are based at Orléans.

As a result of centralised servicing the aircraft of all three escadrons use only two callsign series 61-MA/61-MZ and 61-ZA/61-ZZ : F-RAMA/MZ and F-RAZA/ZZ.

62 ESCADRE DE TRANSPORT (†)

Based at Reims. ET 62 had two squadrons of Noratlas previously based in North Africa. A combined wing insignia carried on each aircraft beneath the cockpit consisted of a greyhound (SPA55) of ET 1/62 and the arms of Anjou for ET 2/62 superimposed upon the arms of Champagne. In September 1970, a third squadron, 'Escadrille Breguet' formed with four Br941 (62-NA/62-NZ) for intensive trials, and was later designated 'Ventoux' prior to disbandment in August 1974. The previous ET 3/62 'Sahara' flying the Noratlas disbanded in 1963. Components were—

ET 1/62 'Vercors'

'Vercors' codes 62-WA/62-WZ (eighteen aircraft) F-RAWA/F-RAWZ. Formed on 1 August 1945, as GT 1/62 and flying the Ju52 from Toussus the squadron was christened 'Algerie' in October 1945 and immediately moved to Maison Blanche where in 1954 it received the C-47 and in November 1955 began to augment these with Noratlas. With re-equipment complete the Dakotas were passed to ET 3/62 in March 1956 and 1/62 continued to serve in North Africa until withdrawn to Reims on 1 October 1963. The unit disbanded on 1 July 1978, together with 62 Escadre, and its nucleus combined with CIET 340 at Toulouse as the basis for the re-formation of ET 63.

ET 2/62 'Anjou'

'Anjou' became ET 2/64 on 1 July 1978.

The Escadre insignia, carried by the side of the cockpit is a dark blue shield within which are a black greyhound on a red cross of Lorraine, and three yellow Fleur de Lys.

63 ESCADRE DE TRANSPORT - CoTAM

Previously comprising Noratlas squadrons ET 1/63 'Bretagne' and ET 2/63 'Bigorre' (now ET 3/64), ET 63 disbanded on 1 July 1972.

The unit re-formed in mid-1978 from the OCU CIET 340 and Esc. 'Vercors', the latter having been Noratlas equipped as ET 1/62 until disbandment on 1 July 1978. CIET Noratlas in the series F-RAVA/VZ (approximately fifteen aircraft) have changed code prefixes to 63-VA etc, whilst the six Nord 262 Fregates commencing F-RBHL which flew with only their 'last two' due to the impending change will become 63-HL etc.

(See Disbanded Units under ET 62 and CIET 340.)

64 ESCADRE DE TRANSPORT - CoTAM

Since its formation at Le Bourget-Dugny in 1956, ET 64 has operated a variety of aircraft and of late

55

has additionally undergone some changes in complement. The second squadron, ET 2/64 'Maine', disbanded on 1 July 1977 this having been the squadron which operated the Breguet Sahara and DC-6, 64-PA/64-PZ (F-RAPA/F-RAPZ). Replacement was effected on 1 July 1978 when ET 2/62 'Anjou' arrived from the disbanded ET 62, and the code prefixes changed from '62-' to '64-'. At the same time, wing insignia was amended to include the three units, the arms of 'Béarn', 'Anjou' and the chamois of 'Bigorre'.

ET 1/64 'Béarn'

Codes 64-IA/64-IZ (F-RAIA/F-RAIZ). Equipped with the Noratlas, 'Béarn' was previously GBI/34 flying the Boston and Maryland in 1944 re-equipping with the Ju88 in 1945, re-forming with the N2501 Noratlas in 1956 at Le Bourget, and moving to Evreux in 1970.

ET 2/64 'Anjou'

'Anjou' formed in Bengal during 1944 as GTIt/15 equipped with the C-45 and B-25 (transport version) under the title Groupe de Marche en Extrême Orient receiveing the designation Groupe de Transport Aérien 2/15 'Anjou' at Tan Son Nhut in July 1946. On 1 July 1947 the squadron became GT 2/64 equipped with the Dakota, exchanging these for the Noratlas in 1954 and transferring to Blida on 17 July 1955 where it became GT 2/62. As a result of the French withdrawal from North Africa, 'Anjou' took up residence at Reims on 7 December 1961, there to be joined by its sister squadron, 'Vercors', two years later.

In 1971 the code range 62-KA/62-KZ (F-RAKA/F-RAKZ) was augmented by a second series 62-QA/62-QZ (F-RAQA/F-RAQZ) allowing an expansion of Noratlas strength to twenty-seven aircraft. Parent wing ET 62 disbanded on 1 July 1978 and 'Anjou' transferred to ET 64 where its aircraft began to receive new code prefixes and the new wing badge. It is expected that ET 2/64 will be the first recipient of the new Transall production batch, but will receive an initial allocation from ET 61 in December 1978.

ET 3/64 'Bigorre'

Codes 64-BA/64-BZ (F-RABA/F-RABZ). Formed on 1 April 1964 Escadron 'Bigorre' was originally a Dakota unit ET 2/63 based at Pau, which later transferred to the Noratlas. Following the disbandment of ET 1/63, which was on permanent detachment at Thies, Senegal, 'Bigorre' joined ET 64 at Evreux on 1 July 1972 changing its codes from 63-BA/63-BZ to their present form.

65 ESCADRE DE TRANSPORT - CoTAM

The newest of the transport wings formed at Villacoublay on 1 August 1972 when ET 2/60, the Groupe Aérien d'Entrainment et de Liaison, gained autonomy and was itself divided into two component escadrons. The GAEL performs two functions, those of communications for 2 (Paris) Aerial Region (paralleling ELA's 41, 43 and 44) and the training of communications aircraft crews.

ET 1/65 'Vendôme'

The middleweight aircraft squadron flies one Mystère and eighteen Fregates, of which several are permanently out on loan to the ELAs or the CEAM. During its currency as ET 2/60, the GAEL received Fregates F-RBOA/F-RBOF which were passed to

56

the Aéronavale in 1972, on arrival of the later models listed below.

Fregate   F-RBAA/F-RBAZ codes 'AA' to 'AR'
Mystère 20 F-RAEA/F-RAEZ code 'A'

Insignia: A shield divided, upper white, lower red, containing a black lion, gold star, wings and lettering.

ET 2/65 'Rambouillet'

The lightweight aircraft squadron operates the types which have served the GAEL since the early 'sixties, approximately eight Broussards, and twenty-two Paris. One Rallye, 65-CZ was used on an experimental basis in 1975.

Paris   F-RBLA/F-RBLZ codes 'LA' etc.
Broussard   F-RACA/F-RACZ codes 65-CA etc,
           (although some carry single letter codes)

Insignia: A shield divided vertically, on the left black with a white chevron. Right upper, a brown deer on a gold background; centre a grey sheep on red; lower, a green tree on white. Central shield gold, with white Fleur de Lys, gold star and GAEL.

---

67 ESCADRE D'HELICOPTERES - CoTAM

On 1 May 1975, helicopter wings EH 67 and EH 68 (both of which had formed on 1 September 1964) were combined in a new EH 67 of five squadrons, replacing the original disposition whereby EH 67 posessed two escadrons and one permanent detachment and EH 68 two escadrons and three detachments. At the same time, EH 2/68 was re-designated CIEH 341. As a replacement for the H-34, fifty Alouette III were received in 1973/74. Alouettes of both versions are used for communications, SAR and crash rescue, together with a proportion of the twenty-nine Pumas received by the Armée de l'Air in 1975/78, other heavy lift and assault duties being the responsibility of the Army. The old DPH 4/68 and 5/68 were detachments of EH 2/68 and so received new individual insignia in 1975. Note that great care must be taken with Alouette IIIs coded in the range 67-JA/67-JZ as this is used by both EH 1/67 and EH 1/67, and the insignia must be noted for positive identification.

EH 1/67 'Pyrénées'

On 31 August 1964, 22 Escadre d'Helicopteres disbanded, and on the following day was split into new units, EH 1/68 'Pyrénées' and EH 2/68 'Maurienne' (the latter now CIEH 341). EH 1/68 transferred to Cazaux on 1 July 1972 to replace Detachment d'Helicopteres 3/68 and became EH 1/67 on 1 May 1975, having received its first Puma on 5 December 1974. All three helicopter types are flown, with callsigns in the range F-RADA/F-RADZ and F-RBJA/F-RBJZ. Alouette IIs which were originally coded between 'DS' and 'DZ' prefixed by the aircraft serial number were repainted with a standard '67' prefix late in 1977. Two Pumas are coded '67-DE' and '67-DG', whilst the Alouette III occupies the block '67-JA' to '67-JF'. The squadron insignia is a leopard in red.

EH 2/67 'Valmy'

The ancestry of escadron 'Valmy' may be traced to the formation of Escadrille d'Helicopteres Legérs 5/57 in December 1956, this being raised to Escadron status on 1 March 1958 and renamed Escadron 1/23 on the last day of 1960, by which time it was already equipped with the Alouette II. The formation of 67 Escadre on 1 September 1964 brought about a further change of designation to EH 2/67, but not until 21 July 1967 was the name 'Valmy' bestowed. Unchanged by the 1975 re-organisation, the squadron remained at Metz, to which it had transferred from St Dizier on 1 September 1972, maintaining a detachment at the latter base, and continued to operate ten Alouette III (first delivered 21 November 1973) in the series '67-FA' to '67-FJ' (F-RBFA etc) whilst the Alouette IIs, scattered throughout the range F-RBMA/F-RBMZ, used until recently their serial as a prefix to the 'last two', but are now standardising on '67-'.

The squadron insignia is a gold crescent, shield and dagger handle, a black horse, white dagger blade, red cross, on a blue background.

EH 3/67 'Parisis'

'Parisis' is based at Villacoublay with a complement of fifteen Alouette II which during 1977 were re-

57

coded 67-SA/67-SP (F-RBSA/F-RBSP) having previously been prefixed by the aircraft serial number, eg. 04-SA, and eight Alouette III, 67-IA/67-IG (F-RBAI/F-RBIG) Unaffected by the 1975 changes, the unit insignia (SPA99) is the same as that previously used by EC 1/10 'Parisis' when formed at Creil in December 1954, flying the Mystère IIC. One Alouette III is detached to Abidjan on the Ivory Coast. Squadron aircraft are marked with a white Pegasus of EC 1/10-2e (EC 1/10-1e having had a black Pegasus). The first Alouette III was received on 21 November 1973.

EH 4/67 'Durance'

Cockpit badge   *Fin badge*

Formed on 1 May 1975 at Apt (previously the base of DPH 4/68, a detachment of EH 2/68) EH 4/67 took over responsibility for support facilities to the nearby strategic missile wing, the 1GMS. On 1 December 1976, the unit was allocated the insignia and name of the previous EH 1/65 which had existed in Indo China from July 1954 to February 1958. The first Puma was delivered on 12 January 1976 and the old EH 2/68 codes F-RAOA/F-RAOZ have been retained and are used by Alouette II 67-OH/67-OJ and Puma 67-OL/67-OO.

EH 5/67 'Alpilles'

On 1 May 1975, DPH 5/68, a detachment of EH 2/68, was re-designated EH 5/67 at its Istres base. Callsigns F-RAJA/F-RAJZ were retained for use by the Alouette III 67-JE/67-JH and Puma 67-JA/67-JC, the latter three are unusual in having the markings 'FRA-JA/JC' beneath the cockpit to differentiate them from the aircraft of EH 1/67 etc. The insignia is that of the 'Drakkar' previously of EH 1/67 at Bremgarten.

68 ESCADRE D'HELICOPTERES (†)

See 67 Escadre.

70 ESCADRILLE DE CONVOYAGE

EdC 70 is based at Chateaudun in support of the central overhaul and storage facility, EAA 601. The unit is responsible for the ferrying of aircraft and equipment throughout the Armée de l'Air and also acts as a test pilots' pool for aircraft flying from EAA 601 after overhaul or modification. A flight of aircraft is held for crew shuttling and the transport of ground equipment on behalf of the equipment depot CGMTAA 614, also at Chateaudun.

Types on charge are the Frégate (since 1976) 070-MA & 070-MB, Noratlas 070-MM (ex MA, MB and MD), Paris (since 1975) 070-MC (ex ME and MF) and Broussards 070-MG & 070-MH. The Noratlas, in use for several years, were coded 'M-D' etc, prior to 1972. Callsigns are F-SDMA/F-SDMZ.

In an unprecedented mixture of unit identification systems, EdC has recently been delivering Super Sabres to USAFB Sculthorpe marked with the original 11 Escadre prefix '11-' followed by code letters commencing 'MJ' (F-SDMJ). In addition, codes beginning at 'MJ' (without prefixes) were worn by Skyraiders returning from Africa in 1976.

Aircraft permanently allocated to the unit carry the insignia of a white globe in a blue sky, black aircraft and black wings around a yellow star.

82 ESCADRON DE TRANSPORT D'OUTRE MER - CoTAM

Formed at Papeete with the insignia of GCIII/7-5e, as Groupe Aérien Mixte 82, this unit provides support for the Nuclear Test Centre in the Pacific. Its earlier equipment included Saharas until April 1972, Cessna 411s 82-QC/QE until March 1974, and DC-6s 82-PU/PW & 82-PY/PZ withdrawn in 1977, plus Alouettes 82-RA etc, Noratlas 82-PA etc , an Aztec 82-QB, and a Mystère 20 F-RBQA on loan in 1974. In 1976 the mixed fleet was replaced by three Caravelle 11Rs, which all carry Polynesian names - F-RBPR/Torea, F-RBPS/Maire Nui and F-RBPT/Teva. Unit callsign range is F-RBPA/RZ and the badge is a black crocodile on green.

85 ESCADRON DE MARCHE (†)

'Loire' was formed at Tours in April 1953 as a night fighter OCU, EMICN 1/30 (codes 30-OA/30-OZ), later passing the instructional task to the specially formed CIPN 346 and re-equipping with Vautours. The squadron moved to Creil in February 1961 and disbanded here on 31 March 1965, re-forming with Vautours at Hao for air-sampling duties associated with the Atomic Test Centre in the Pacific. Six Vautour IIN and two IIB were used, until the unit disbanded on 1 May 1975, apparently leaving the aircraft on site. Since becoming EM 85, 'Loire' has used only the Trident insignia of escadrille C 46 (its 2nd escadrille when with ECTT 30) and the 'Chenonceaux' of ECTT 1/30 remains dormant.

88 ESCADRON DE TRANSPORT D'OUTRE MER - CoTAM

Support for government forces in Djibouti including the F-100 and later Mirages is provided by ETOM 88 with an assortment of transport types. Formed on the last day of 1958 as Escadrille d'Outre Mer 88 out of ELA 88, the unit was originally equipped with the MS500 and Ju52, subsequently using the Dakota 1959-67, H-34 1967-72. Current types are the two Broussard (from 1960), six Noratlas (from 1967), and four Alouette II (from 1965) coded in the range 88-JA/88-JZ (F-SCJA/F-SCJZ). The unit was known as Groupe Avions Mixte d'Outre Mer from April 1970 to April 1976.

Insignia details are a red sun on a yellow background with black ship and skyline.

91 & 94 ESCADRES DE BOMBARDEMENT - CFAS

The French strategic air arm is centred around a force of Mirage IVA bombers and their associated C-135F in-flight refuelling aircraft. As originally conceived, the FAS comprised three escadres (91, 93 and 94) each of four escadrons at dispersed bases, one with four C-135F, the other three with four Mirage IVA apiece. The force is supported by CIFAS 328 with which it interchanges its Mirage bombers, loaning in return the T-33A and Mirage IIIB for continuation training by the SLVSVs. The aircraft are coded by the last two of their callsign: Mirage IVA F-THAA/F-THCI and C-135F F-UKCA/F-UKCL. The second half of the latter range was previously used by communications aircraft, eg. Flamant, prefixed by escadre codes '91-' etc. No unit badges are worn by any of the bomber escadres of the FAS, except for CIFAS 328.

On 1 June 1976, economy forced the disbandment of EB 93, with some re-allocation of squadron numbers. The Escadrons de Ravitaillement en Vol (4/91, 4/93 and 4/94) were amalgamated into one wing, ERV 93, on the same day. The three bases now relinquished, Creil, Avord and Cambrai, have their FAS installations intact and available for use should the thirty-two-aircraft fleet need to be dispersed. The component units are—

EB 1/91 'Gascogne'

SAL28   *SPA79*

Base: Mont-de-Marsan. Insignia SAL28/SPA79. Previously GB 1/19, 'Gascogne', flew Marauders in 1944-45, re-forming at Touraine on 1 January 1951 with Invaders, still as EB 1/19. On 1 September 1956 it was established at Bône, Algeria, as EB 1/91 again with Invaders.

EB 2/91 'Bretagne'

Base: Cazaux. Insignia, the Arms of Bretagne. Another wartime Marauder squadron, GBII/20

'Bretagne' formed on 1 January 1942, and later flew Invaders as GBII/91, until disbandment at the end of the war. The name was subsequently used by Noratlas squadron ET 1/63 at Thies in Senegal, until EB 2/91 re-formed with the Mirage IVA on 1 December 1965.

EB 3/91 'Cévennes'

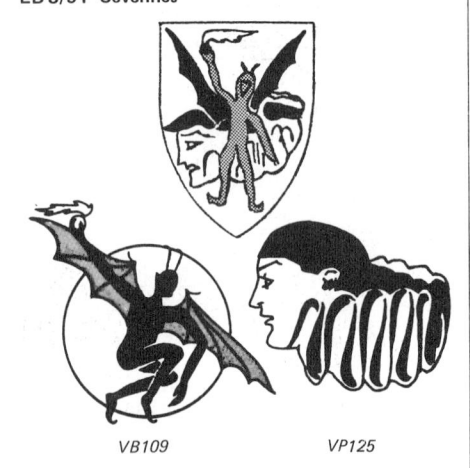

VB109   *VP125*

Base: Orange. Insignia VB109/VP125. 'Cévennes' inherits the traditions of GBI/22 'Maroc' which existed from 1 September 1943 to 30 April 1946, and formed as EB 2/93 with Mirages on 29 March 1965. The squadron adopted its present number on 1 July 1976 replacing the Creil-based EB 3/91 'Beauvaisis'.

EB 1/94 'Guyenne'

Base: Istres. Insignia BR66/BR129. Previously EBII/23 'Guyenne' formed at Elvington as 346 Squadron, RAF, with Halifaxes on 16 April 1944, disbanding on 27 November 1945. It re-formed in Algeria as EB 3/91 with Invaders in December 1956, and ultimately became EB 1/93 at Istres until re-

BR66   *BR129*

allocated to 94 Escadre on 1 July 1976. The original EB 1/94 'Bourbonnais' at Avord disbanded on the same day and was not re-allocated.

EB 2/94 'Marne'

BR107   *BR126*

Base: St. Dizier. Insignia BR107/BR126. Following the disbandment of GBI/12 in November 1942 (then a part of the Vichy AF), 'Marne' remained dormant until re-activated as EB 2/94 with the Mirage IVA on 1 October 1965 at its present base.

EB 3/94 'Arbois'

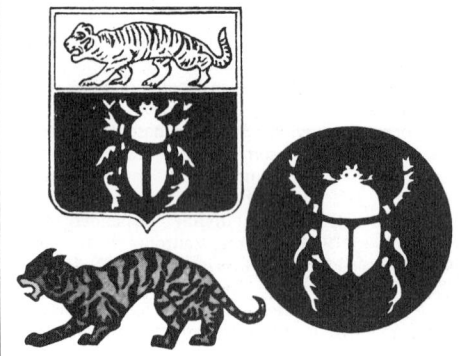

BR127   *BR128*

Base: Luxeuil Insignia BR127/BR128. The original 'Arbois', GBI/23, disbanded on 3 December 1942, and the unit did not re-form until EB 3/94 was established with Mirages at Luxeuil on 1 February 1966.

92 ESCADRE DE BOMBARDEMENT (†)

For many years the sole permanent component of the 2 CATac, EB 92 disbanded on 22 September 1978 to be replaced by two Jaguar squadrons

60

(EC 4/7 and EC 4/11). As formed, EB 92 comprised EB 1/92 'Bourgogne' and EB 2/92 'Aquitaine' (the latter inheriting the traditions of 'Tunisie' squadron, disbanded on 1 August 1955 and itself formed on 1 December 1958). Codes and callsigns were 92-AA/92-AZ and 92-BA/92-BZ (F-UKAA/BZ) respectively, but in 1970 all aircraft were pooled in the 92-A- series in order of c/n, irrespective of squadron, and with dual insignia applied to opposite sides of the nose. The Vautour IIB medium bombers at the wing's Bordeaux base were uprated to II.1B standard, some with photo-recce. noses, and in 1974 were augmented by a small number of Vautour IIN all-weather fighters from the re-equipped ECTT30. 'Aquitaine' disbanded on 1 September 1974 and the Vautours then carried the combined BR7/BR35 insignia of 'Bourgogne' depicting a Lorraine Cross and a clown with telescope, actually remaining in use for three months after the official disbandment of their squadron.

93 ESCADRE DE RAVITAILEMENT EN VOL - CFAS

93 Escadre was previously a bomber wing, equipped with the Mirage IVA (see 91 and 94 Escadre histories). On 1 June 1976 it was re-created out of the three air refuelling squadrons attached to each of the strategic bomber wings and operates the pool of eleven C-135F aircraft from detachments at Istres, Mont-de-Marsan and Avord. The original Mirage components, EB1/93 'Guyenne', EB 2/93 'Cévennes', EB 3/93 'Sambre' and ERV 4/93 'Aunis' have been altered, and the position now is:—

ERV 1/93 'Aunis'

Base: Istres. Insignia: GBI/31. Escadrilles: SAL277 and SAL10. 'Aunis' formed as a bomber squadron in 1939, existing until 1 October 1942. The squadron re-formed with the C-135F on 1 July 1965 at Istres as ERV 4/93, and received its present number on 1 July 1976.

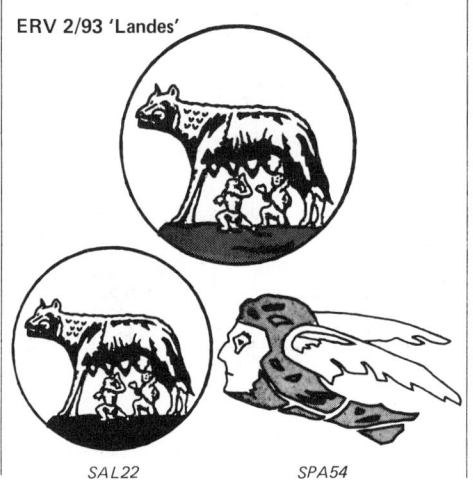

ERV 2/93 'Landes'

SAL22 *SPA54*

Base: Mont-de-Marsan. Insignia: SAL22. Escadrilles: SPA54 and SAL22. A new unit, 'Landes' formed as the refuelling squadron of 91 Wing, designated ERV 4/91 at Mont-de-Marsan, receiving the new title ERV 2/93 on 1 July 1976. The C-135F has been flown throughout its existence.

ERV 3/93 'Sologne'

BR44 *BR465*

Base: Avord. Insignia BR44/BR465. Over twenty-five years were to pass following the disbandment of EBII/11 'Sologne' on 15 August 1940, before the name was revived in the C-135F-equipped ERV 4/94 at Avord on 1 December 1965. The present title was bestowed on 1 July 1976.

Note The three squadrons which disappeared as a result of the 1976 reorganisation were *EB 3/91 'Beauvaisis'* (traditions of Escadron 'Senegal' 1939 to 30 April 1946) and re-formed with the Mirage IVA on 1 June 1965; *EB 3/93 'Sambre'* (traditions of GB 2/31 disbanded August 1940) and re-formed with Mirage IVA on 1 August 1965 and *EB 1/94 'Bourbonnais'* (traditions GBI/11 1939 to 1 August 1943) re-formed on 1 December 1965 with the Mirage IVA.

61

200 ESCADRON DE MISSILES STRATEGIQUES

1er Groupement de Missiles Stratégiques at Apt comprises two squadrons of S-2 missiles, of which the first is numbered 1/200 and named 'Luberon'. In March 1976 this was given the traditions of escadrille VB 137, which more recently operated in North Africa as ECN 1/71. The second unit is presumably 2/200.

312 GROUPEMENT INSTRUCTION - CEAA

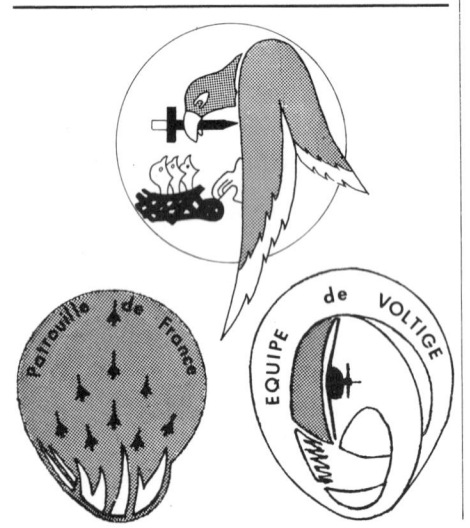

The Ecole de l'Air at Salon de Provence is the French equivalent of the RAF College, Cranwell and took up residence at its present base on 15 November 1937 when it moved from Versailles where the Ecole Militaire de l'Air had been established in 1925. Direct recruiting to the Armée de l'Air was made possible when the school changed to its present title on 3 June 1933, although more than two years were to pass before the necessary changes could be made to bring this to fruition. Post-war training re-commenced on a miscellaneous collection of Stampe SV.4 and Morane 230/315 trainers, with an Anson for good measure. Harvards were added in 1949, until the school completely re-equipped with the Sipa 111 and 12 in 1952, together with a small number of MS.733. In December 1954 a concrete runway was opened at Salon, and in May 1956 the first Magister was delivered. The Ecole de l'Air was the first school to equip with the type and in 1957 formed an aerobatic team, the *Patrouille de l'Ecole de l'Air'*, this becoming the famous *'Patrouille de France'* in 1964 when the task of providing a national aerobatic team was permanently allocated to the EdlA. The present title Groupement d'Instruction 312 was given on 1 September 1965.

Following succesful evaluation at the EFIPN 313, officer cadets of the Armée de l'Air and Aéronavale progress to GI 312 where basic flying training is undertaken on the Magister, a small flight of Mystère IVA aircraft (312-UR/312-UZ) being retired in 1976. Recreational flying and gliding is carried out by GAALEA 4/312 with a mixture of Jodel light aircraft and Wassmer gliders under the title 'Section de Vol a Voile'. To complement the *Patrouille de France*, the school has formed a second aerobatic team with CAP10 and CAP20 light aircraft entitled the *'Equipe de Voltige Aérienne'*, whilst a transport and liaison section flies the Broussard and Noratlas.

The regular training Magisters and the transport flight carry the badge of a dark blue bird on a light blue background, bringing a black dagger to its yellow chicks in a black nest. EVA CAP10/20 have the insignia of a white aircraft making a yellow slipstream in a light blue sky. The *Patrouille de France* badge shows nine black aircraft in a golden sky, above red flames, and this will doubtless be perpetuated when the PdF receives the Alpha Jet in 1979-80.

The codes and call signs are--

Magister	312-AA/312-AZ	F-TEAA/F-TEAZ
	312-BL/312-BZ	F-TEBL/F-TEBZ
	312-TA/312-TZ	F-TFTA/F-TFTZ
	312-UA/312-UZ	F-TFUA/F-TFUZ
Broussard	312-BA/312-BC	F-TEBA/F-TEBC
Noratlas	312-BD/312-BK	F-TEBD/F-TEBK
Patrouille de France	VA to VP	F-TFVA/F-TFVP
Equipe de Voltige	VQ to VZ	F-TFVQ/F-TFVZ
GAALEA 4/312	XA to YZ	F-SDXA/F-SDYZ

313 GROUPEMENT ECOLE - CEAA

Each year, the Armée de l'Air converts a small number of pilots to instructors, and it is the task of the 'Ecole des Moniteurs' to undertake the training of this group, and of overseas pilots. The badge of GE 313 is a black mountain in a blue sky, gold star and chevrons, and a white Magister, and is also that of the air base, BA745.

The history of GE 313 may be traced back to the formation of the Division des Moniteurs de Pilotage at Marrakech equipped with the T-6 Harvard in

62

1949. Training continued in the North African sunshine until the French withdrawal from the continent, when the school moved to Clermont Ferrand-Aulnat in the Spring of 1961. On 29 December of the same year, the first Magister arrived for the Division des Moniteurs de Pilotage 07/745, which eventually received twenty to be operated alongside the T-6, until the faithful Harvard retired in December 1964 and further Magisters were received. The creation of training command, the CEAA, brought about the numbering of flying schools, and on 1 April 1966 the DMP became GE 313. This will be the third unit to receive the Alpha Jet, following GE 314 and ET 8.

In 1971, the Escadron de Formation Initiale du Personnel Navigant (EFIPN) formed as a component of GE 313 equipped with the twin-seat CAP10, later gaining autonomy as EFIPN 307 'Gevaudan'. The unit administers a seventeen hour pre-selection course for the prospective pilots, enabling aptitude to be assessed before more costly training is begun. This has recently been extended to cover the first forty hours of instruction and the Aérospatiale TB30 is eagerly awaited as a CAP10 replacement and to ease the burden. Aircraft were coded 307-SA/307-SZ (F-SESA/F-SESZ), but in late May 1978, these were amended to 313-SA etc., indicating a re-absorption of the squadron into its parent unit. The unit insignia is a yellow and black shield, with a black eagle on a red inner shield. The Magister component of the school is divided into three squadrons, but these do not carry only the GE 313 insignia, that of the EFIPN being retained, however.

1 Esc.

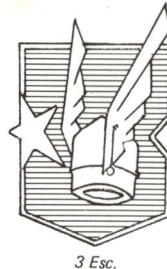

2 Esc.

3 Esc.

4 Esc.

Code range are—
313-SA/313-SZ	F-SESA/F-SESZ	CAP10
313-CA/313-CZ	F-TGCA/F-TGCZ	Magister
313-DA/313-DZ	F-TGDA/F-TGDZ	Magister
313-TA/313-TI	F-TGTA/F-TGTI	Magister
313-TX/313-TZ	F-TGTX/F-TGTZ	Broussard

(Liaison section. Flamant withdrawn)

314 GROUPEMENT ECOLE - CEAA

GE 314 is the direct successor the the fighter school established at Meknès, Morocco on 5 December 1943 with the Dewoitine D.520 aircraft of GCI/2 as the Centre d'Instruction à la Chasse. GCI/2 was the 'Cigognes' escadaron and thus donated its stork badge, against the background of a star, to the school. In December 1945, it was renamed the Ecole de Chasse and split into the Centre d'Instruction à la Chasse and the Centre de Perfectionnement à la Chasse, with three squadrons of aircraft, one each of Spitfires, Thunderbolts and Airacobras, and later a drogue towing flight of Miles Martinets, which together with other types gave a grand total of 210 aircraft on the base. As specialist training aircraft became available, the fighters were withdrawn and the school equipped with the T-6 Harvard, MS.475 and T-33A, receiving the Magister in February 1958 and achieving a full complement of the type by the end of the year. In February and March 1961, the French departure from Morocco brought the fifty-five T-33As and forty Mystère IVA of the Ecole de Chasse to Tours (see also GE 315).

Here it is responsible for advanced jet training under the new title GE 314 'Ecole de Chasse Christian Martel', and now operates only the T-33, having retired the Mystère IVA (314-TA/314-TZ and 314-ZA/314-ZZ) in 1973.

The school accepts pilots from GI 312 and GE 313 prior to them taking operational training with the OCUs attached to EC 2, EC 7, EC 11 and CIFAS 328. The course was previously of 250 hours, comprising one hundred with the T-33 and 150 on Mystères, but with the arrival of the Alpha Jet, the course will be reduced to 130 on this type alone. Between May and September 1979, the first fourteen aircraft will be delivered to re-equip one squadron, and the T-33 is to phase-out during the succeeding two years. The school is divided into six escadrons, each of which is named as well as numbered, although the aircraft carry only the stork insignia, in black and white on a green star.

1 Esc. 'Jean Lenglet'

2 Esc. 'Henri Jeandet'

3 Esc. 'Henri Arnaud'   4 Esc. 'Marin la Meslée'

5 Esc. 'Marcel Lefèbvre'   6 Esc. 'Jean Maridor'

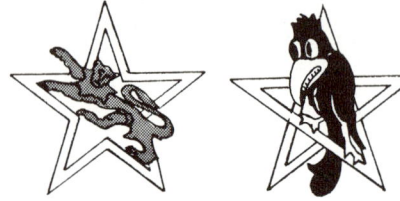

Liaison Section

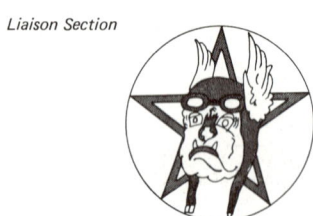

Callsigns are—
314-UA/314-UZ   F-TEUA/F-TEUZ
314-VA/314-VZ   F-TEVA/F-TEVZ
314-WA/314-WZ   F-TEWA/F-TEWZ
314-YA/314-YZ   F-TEYA/F-TEYZ

The liaison section uses codes in the range F-RHDA/F-RHDZ which are used for miscellaneous aircraft in 3 Region Aérienne. Aircraft are Broussard 314-DA and 314-DB, and Paris 'DD'.

315 GROUPEMENT ECOLE - CEAA

NCO and Naval Rating basic flying training takes place at Cognac on the Magister, totalling 150 hours dual and solo instruction. The unit badge carried on the aircraft is a combination of the four insignia of the components. The fourth eascadrille is commanded by a Naval officer, and a fifth formation the 'Escadrille de Transformation Broussard' handles conversion to that aircraft.

GE 315 is a combination of two flying schools, the first of which was the Magister element of the Ecole de Chasse (see GE 314). On returning from North Africa in February and March of 1961, the Ecole de Chasse Magisters established themselves at Orange under the title Escadron de Transition Réacteur 40/115 with thirty aircraft in the code range F-TGEA/EZ and F-TGRA/RZ. On 1 April 1962, the unit name was changed to Division d'Instruction et de Transition Réacteur 07/716, and remained thus until the school disbanded on 31 July 1965 and the majority of the aircraft transferred to Cognac. Here they joined the ex-Marrakech Harvards of the Ecole Elémentaire de Pilotage which had also returned to France in February/March 1961, but had begun to receive the Magister in August 1964 under the title Division Instruction du Cognac, changing its name to GE 315 on 31 May 1965, with the badge of a golden eagle and chicks on a red shield - (see Base Aerienne 709).

School aircraft wear a badge combining the four insignia of the component escadrilles in black on a red shield.

The individual badges are:—

1 Escadrille   2 Escadrille

3 Escadrille    4 Escadrille

Codes and callsigns:
Magister—
315-IA/315-IZ   F-TEIA/F-TEIZ
315-PA/315-PZ   F-TEPA/F-TEPZ
315-QA/315-QZ   F-TEQA/F-TEQZ
315-XA/315-XZ   F-TEXA/F-TEXZ
approximately seventy-five aircraft.
Broussard—
315-SA/315-SZ   F-TESA/F-TESZ
approximately three to four aircraft, eg 315-SL, ST.

316 GROUPEMENT ECOLE - CEAA

GE 316 is the Armée de l'Air Navigation School, based at Toulouse alongside the transport OCU, CIET 340. The Flamant was mostly withdrawn from use in 1974, (codes 316-KA/316-KZ F-TEKA/F-TEKZ), leaving only eight to ten Noratlas currently on charge, 316-FA/316-FZ (F-TEFA/F-TEFZ), plus possibly two to three Flamants.

Group insignia is on a blue background, with black continents, the remainder being yellow.

319 GROUPEMENT ECOLE - CEAA

Twin engined conversion for all the Armée del'Air takes place at Avord where GE 319, the sole large scale Flamant user, operates thirty-six aircraft in the ranges 319-CA/319-DZ (F-TECA/F-TEDZ). Most aircraft underwent a programme of overhaul and modification at Chateaudun during 1974 with the aim of extending their service lives upto 1981 at least. However, during 1977 a Cessna 404 Titan was evaluated by the school, and marked on the fin 'F-TEDL', as the first stage in selecting a replacement.

328 CENTRE D'INSTRUCTION DES FORCES AERIENNES STRATEGIQUES - CFAS

Conversion and continuation training for the Force Aériennes Stratégiques (Escadres de Bombardement 91 and 94) is undertaken by CIFAS 328 at Bordeaux, previously the Centre de Instruction de Bombardement 328 at Cognac. Four Mirage IVA are loaned from the FAS, but the unit maintains an allocation of fifteen Mirage IIIB, twelve T-33A and ten Noratlas. Two types of Mirage are used, five IIIB for regular conversion tasks and ten IIIB-RV (Ravitaillement en Vol) equipped with a refuelling probe for practise in fuel transfers. The 'RV' variant uses codes 'DA' to 'DF' and 'DN' to 'DQ', the others occupying vacant codes between these batches.

CIFAS 328 Noratlas are of the N2501SNB (Système Navigation-Bombardement) variety, fitted with a Mirage IVA radar in a bulged nose. The T-birds are allocated to FAS bases for communications work.

Codes and callsigns are:
Mirage IIIB	DA-DZ	F-UKDA/F-UKDZ
T-33A	WA-WZ	F-UKWA/F-UKWZ
Noratlas SNB	328-EA/328-EL	F-UKEA/F-UKEL
Mirage IVA	AA-CI	F-UKEP/F-UKES

(The Mirage IVAs retain their normal codes - see EB 91 and EB 94 sections - and use part of the Noratlas callsign range.) Insignia is a black eagle holding two red bombs.

338 CENTRE D'ENTRAINEMENT EN VOL SANS VISIBILITE - CEAA

CEVSV 338 operates the headquarters of blind flying instruction based at Nancy with twenty T-33A aircraft on charge marked 338-HA/338-HZ; callsigns F-UJHA/F-UJHZ. The unit badge consists of a black devil with red hands and face, a white cloud, a green playing card in the right hand and a white in the left.

339 CENTRE PREDICTION ET INSTRUCTION RADAR - CEAA

Equipped with two Mystère 20SNA long-nose radar trainers, CPIR 339 is based at Luxeuil alongside EC 4 and codes its aircraft in the sequence reserved for SLVSV EC 4 as 339-WL and 339-WM (F-UGWL/F-UGWM).

The Mystères provide interception training for Mirage fighter pilots and are marked with the unit insignia of a black and yellow bat on a green and blue globe first used on CPIR 4/116 when the flight was under the direct control of BA116, Luxeuil.

340 CENTRE D'INSTRUCTION DES EQUIPAGES DE TRANSPORT (†)

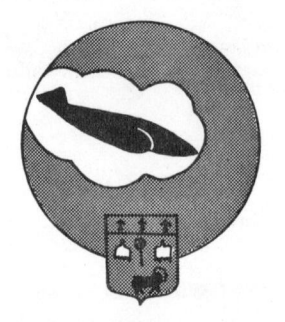

CIET 340, the heavy transport operational conversion unit, was based at Toulouse and had a fleet of Noratlas, numbering fifteen, augmented by four Transalls on loan from ET 61.

The unit badge depicts an aircraft flying in a cloud, whilst the coding system employed is 340-VA/340-VZ (F-RAVA/F-RAVZ). The previous sequence F-RBHA/F-RBHZ had been taken up once more by the six new Nord 262 Frégates delivered from 1977 onwards and commencing at 'HL' with no number prefix. Markings are a blue sky, white cloud, black aircraft above a red badge with yellow detail. On 1 July 1978, Noratlas wing ET 62 disbanded and its first squadron, 'Vercors' was transferred to CIET 340, apparently in name only. The two units then became 63 Escadre de Transport.

341 CENTRE D'INSTRUCTION DES EQUIPAGES D'HELICOPTERE - CoTAM

Formed on 1 May 1975 by the re-naming of EH 2/68 'Maurienne', CIEH 341 is the central helicopter school of the Armée de l'Air and Aéronavale, based at Chambéry. EH 2/68 had previously managed helicopter training under the title of GE 309, and the old 'Maurienne' insignia is perpetuated on the CIEH helicopters.

The unit evolved from 2 Escadre d'Helicoptères, formed in November 1956, and was later re-named 22 Escadre. On 1 September 1964, EH 2/22 became the 68 Escadre with 'Maurienne' as its second squadron. Original callsign ranges have been perpetuated, with the substitution of a '341-' prefix to the last two, replacing the '68-', or in the case of the Alouette II, the serial number. The Alouette IIs of the school were, in 1976, the first to adopt codes in the normal (unit identification) format. Code sequence for the Alouette II is 341-RM to 314-RZ (F-RARM etc.) whilst the Mk.III are 341-EA to 341-EN (F-RBEA etc.). In 1975, two Pumas were attached to GERMaS 15/067 followed by a further three (341-EU to 341-EZ, originally without number prefix) for training and civilian medevac duties, but most, if not all, have been passed on to other units. CIEH 341 provides ab-initio training for helicopter pilots (including overseas students) who arrive with 250 hours basic experience and their 'wings'. Following a thirty hour course with seventy hours on the Alouette II and fifteen on the Alouette III they qualify as second pilots and after a further 250-300 hours operational flying can return for crew chief training lasting nine weeks (thirty five hours). The insignia is a black panther, yellow wings and sword and a red cross.

601 ENTREPOT D'ARMEE DE L'AIR

Based at Chateaudun, EAA 601 acts as a maintenance unit for French military aircraft, combining storage, repair and disposal facilities. Test flying and ferrying is the responsibility of Escadron de Convoyage 70 situated at the same base. A third base resident is CGMTAA 614, (Centre de Gestion du Materiel Technique de l'Armée de l'Air), the central technical equipment store.

See also page 70 for other Entrepôt bases.

Base Flights

Most aircraft allocated to Armée de l'Air bases are for the use of a resident fighter wing and will be found under the heading 'SLVSV' in various places in the main part of this section. Occasionally, where base aircraft are not for the exclusive use of the resident wing or there is no other flying unit on the airfield the aircraft bear the Base Aérienne number (see page 69) as a prefix to the last two letters of the callsign. As detailed below, there are certain ranges of callsigns which are reserved for miscellaneous use on a regional basis. Usually no badge is carried, with the exception of BE721 and BE722 whose insignia will be found on page 73. Note that in the recent examples which follow, the numerals 126, 273 and 725 do not appear on the aircraft, and are therefore in parentheses.

Recent examples are noted below:—

118   Base Aérienne 118, Mont-de-Marsan, See CEAM entry on page 99.

125   Base Aérienne 125, Istres. Only one example is known, Magister 125-HG, callsign F-RHHG (in the 4 Region callsign range) allocated in February 1972.

(126) Base Aérienne 126, Solenzara. Two Magisters F-RHHA and 'HHB are used by Moyens Operationels 05/126 coded 'HA' and 'HB' without prefix. The isolated nature of Solenzara qualifies it for its own recreational gliding detachment, the Section Vol à Voile de la BA126 with Jodel 140R tugs and Wassmer gliders coded between 'QA' and 'QZ' (F-ULQA/F-ULQZ).

128   Base Aérienne 128, Metz. On 1 December 1974, the base flight took over ELA 41 Magisters 41-AU to 'AX' and re-coded these 128-AU/128-AX possibly with the same callsigns, F-SCAU/F-SCAX. These joined Jodel 140R glider tug 128-VZ, callsign unknown and in 1978 were re-coded from 128-VM onwards.

(273) Base Aérienne 273, Romorantin. On 1 March 1973 the Centre de Vol à Voile CVA 55/273 formed at Romorantin with two D.140R glider tugs F-UMFA and FB coded by their last two and a small complement of sailplanes. The task of the unit is to evaluate gliders for the Armée de l'Air and train a team of pilots to take part in gliding competitions.

332   See CEAM entry on page 99.

721   Base Ecole 721, Rochefort. The ground training school at Rochefort possesses, in addition to a large fleet of defunct airframes, a small communications flight of Flamant and Broussard. These are coded 721-Ex in the series F-RHEA/F-RHEZ used by all miscellaneous aircraft within 4 Region.

722   Base Ecole 722, Saintes. BE722 maintains an airworthy Broussard for communications, coded 722-EA in the 4 Region callsign series F-RHEA/F-RHEZ. BE722 is the home of the Ecole d'Enseignement Technique de l'Armée de l'Air.

(725) Base Aerienne 725, Chambéry. A Broussard allocated to the base carries only the code 'HR' (F-RHHR) without a prefix.

Armée de l'Air Callsigns

Within the overall allocation of 'F-' type callsigns to French civil and military agencies, (See Appendix 'D') the Armée de l'Air is allocated F-RAAA to F-UZZZ. This range was originally planned so that the final three letters would run consecutively throughout whilst the second letter changed to identify the function of the operating squadron, viz:—

F-RAAA to F-RBZZ transport squadrons
F-SCAA to F-SDZZ communications flights
F-TFZZ to F-TFZZ flying schools
F-UGAA to F-UHZZ fighter squadrons.

However, in practice, numberous exceptions have been made, and the main batches are as below:—

F-RAAA to F-RBZZ transport squadrons
F-RCAA to F-RCZZ calibration squadron
F-RDAA to F-RGZZ not used
F-RHAA to F-RHZZ miscellaneous (base flight, etc.)
F-RIAA to F-RZZZ not used
F-SAAA to F-SBZZ not used
F-SCAA to F-SDZZ communications flights
F-SEAA to F-SEZZ miscellaneous (electronics/ training)
F-SFAA to F-SZZZ not used
F-TAAA to F-TDZZ not used
F-TEAA to F-TGZZ flying schools
F-THAA to F-THZZ nuclear bombers
F-TIAA to F-TQZZ not used
F-TRAA to F-TRZZ ambassadorial aircraft
F-TSAA to F-TZZZ not used
F-UAAA to F-UFZZ not used
F-UGAA to F-UHZZ fighter squadrons
F-UIAA to F-UMZZ miscellaneous
F-UNAA to F-UZZZ not used.

The following table lists the callsign series in current or recent use. In each case the batch runs from A to Z, but obviously not all are taken up. Reference should be made to the Current Units section to establish present day usage.

Callsign	Unit	Callsign	Unit	Callsign	Unit	Callsign	Unit	Callsign	Unit	Callsign	Unit
F-RAAA	ET 1/63	F-RBTA	EE 54	F-SDMA	EdC 70	F-TRAA	Embassy Aircraft	F-UICA	ER 1/33	F-UIWA	CIFAS 328
F-RABA	ET 2/63	F-RBVA	EH 2/67	F-SDWA	GAM 50			F-UIDA	EAA 1/22	F-UIXA	CEVSVER 33
F-RACA	ET 2/65	F-RBXA	EH 2/67	F-SDXA	GAALEA 4/312	F-UGDA	SLVSV EC 2	F-UIEA	EOM 84	F-UJGA	ELA 41
F-RADA	EH 1/67	F-RCAA	EdC 57	F-SDYA	GAALEA 4/312	F-UGEA	EC 1/2	F-UIFA	ECTT 2/30	F-UJHA	CEVSV 338
F-RAEA	EH 1/67	F-RHDA	GE 314			F-UGFA	ECT 2/2	F-UIGA	EOM 87	F-UKAA	EB 1/92
F-RAFA	GLAM	F-RHAA	1 Region*	F-SDZA	EAA 615	F-UGGA	EC 3	F-UIKA	SLVSV EC 10	F-UKBA	EB 2/92
F-RAGA	GAEL	F-RHBA	1 Region*	F-SEBA	CNET	F-UGHA	SLVSV EC 2	F-UILA	EC 3/10	F-UKCA	ERV 93
F-RAHA	GMT 59	F-RHCA	2 Region*	F-SEDA	ELA 53	F-UGIA	EC 1/3	F-UIMA	ECTT 1/30	F-UKDA	CIFAS 328
F-RAIA	ET 1/64	F-RHEA	3 Region*	F-SEEA	ELA 54	F-UGJA	EC 2/3	F-UINA	ER 2/33	F-UKEA	CIFAS 328
F-RAJA	EH 5/67	F-RHFA	3 Region*	F-SESA	EFIPN 307	F-UGKA	EC 3/3	F-UIPA	EC 1/8	F-ULAA	EC 1/4
F-RAKA	ET 2/64	F-RHGA	ELAS 1/44	F-TEAA	GI 312	F-UGLA	EC 3/2	F-UIQA	EC 1/8	F-ULBA	EC 2/4
F-RALA	ETOM 52	F-RHHA	4 Region*	F-TEBA	GI 312	F-UGMA	SLVSV EC 5	F-UIRA	EC 2/10	F-ULQA	4 Region*
F-RAMA	ET 61	F-RHMA	ETAG 58	F-TECA	GE 319	F-UGNA	EC 1/5	F-UISA	EC 1/10	F-UMYA	EC 4/11
F-RANA	ET 3/62	F-SCAA	ELA 41	F-TEDA	GE 319	F-UGOA	EC 2/5	F-UITA	ER 3/33	F-UMZA	ECT 2/2
F-RAOA	EH 4/67	F-SCBA	ELA 43	F-TEEA	GE 319	F-UGPA	GC 1/6				
F-RAPA	ET 2/64	F-SCCA	ELA 44	F-TEFA	GE 316	F-UGQA	SLVSV ECTT 30				
F-RAQA	ET 2/64	F-SCDA	GLA 45	F-TEIA	GE 315	F-UGRA	EC 3/11				
F-RARA	CIEH 341	F-SCEA	ELA 46	F-TEKA	GE 316	F-UGSA	EC 3/2				
F-RAUA	CIET 340	F-SCFA	ELA 47	F-TELA	GE 315	F-UGVA	EC 3/3				
F-RAVA	ET 63	F-SCGA	ELA 88	F-TEMA	EC 1/8	F-UGWA	SLVSV EC 4/ CPIR 339				
F-RAWA	ET 1/62	F-SCHA	ELA 90	F-TENA	EC 2/8						
F-RAYA	EE 54	F-SCIA	ELA 91	F-TEOA	SLVSV EC 8	F-UGXA	EC 3/3				
F-RAZA	ET 61	F-SCJA	ETOM 88	F-TEPA	GE 315	F-UHAA	ER 33				
F-RBAA	GAEL	F-SCKA	ELA 352	F-TEQA	GE 315	F-UHDA	EC 9				
F-RBBA	ETOM 55	F-SCLA	GAM 50	F-TERA	GE 315	F-UHEA	EC 1/11				
F-RBCA	GMT 59	F-SCMA	ELA-382	F-TETA	GE 314	F-UHFA	ECTT 3/30				
F-RBFA	EH 2/67	F-SCNA	ELA 372	F-TEUA	GE 314	F-UHHA	EC 1/7				
F-RBHA	ET 63	F-SCOA	GAM 56	F-TEVA	GE 314	F-UHIA	EC 2/7				
F-RBIA	EH 2/67	F-SCQA	ELA 387	F-TEWA	GE 314	F-UHJA	SLVSV EC 7				
F-RBJA	EH 1/67	F-SCTA	ELA 54	F-TEXA	GE 315	F-UHKA	EC 1/4				
F-RBKA	ETOM 55	F-SCXA	GAM 50	F-TEYA	GE 314	F-UHMA	EC 2/11				
F-RBLA	GAEL	F-SDAA	CEAM	F-TEZA	GE 314	F-UHNA	EC 1/1				
F-RBMA	EH 2/67	F-SDBA	CEAM	F-TFLA	EAA 1/21	F-UHOA	SLVSV EC 11				
F-RBOA	GAEL	F-SDDA	CEAM	F-TFTA	GI 312	F-UHPA	EC 2/13				
F-RBPA	ETOM 82	F-SDIA	CEAM	F-TFUA	GI 312	F-UHQA	EC 1/13				
F-RBQA	ETOM 82	F-SDKA	CIEES 343	F-TFVA	GI 312	F-UHSA	EC 3/13				
F-RBRA	ETOM 82	F-SDLA	Ambassador to Laos	F-TGCA	GE 313	F-UHTA	SLVSV EC 13				
F-RBSA	EH 3/67			F-TGDA	GE 313	F-UHUA	GC 2/6				
				F-TGTA	GE 313	F-UHXA	SLVSV EC 12				
				F-TGZA	EAA 2/21	F-UHYA	EC 1/12				
				F-THAA	EB 91/94	F-UHZA	EC 2/12				
				F-THBA	EB 91/94	F-UIAA	EROM 80				
				F-THCA	EB 91/94	F-UIBA	EOM 82				

Note: An asterisk in the above list indicates Base Flights.

As the last two letters of the callsign often appear in paint on the aircraft, a given identity can remain with the same aeroplane for several years.

For transport and communications aircraft flying outside the country, certain ranges of number callsigns prefixed 'FM' are issued, independently of the 'F-Rxxx' allocation. These change rapidly, usually after each flight but are of use in identifying the unit. Known examples are:—

FM0001 - FM0050 ET 1/60 Mystère 20
FM0490 - FM0499 GAM 56   Noratlas & Puma
FM0500 - FM0550 ET 1/65 Mystère 20 & Nord 262
FM0560 - FM0590 ET 2/65 Paris
FM0710 - FM0719 ELA 41   Paris

Numbers in the series FM9900 - FM9999 have been used by several heavy transports of different wings and are possibly flight numbers.

A third system, of which little is known, concerns operational aircraft, each wing being allocated a code name, eg. EC 10 'Viseur', EC 12 'Condor' following which the pilot will append his personal identification number within that wing. The method of allocating number designations is discussed on page 37 under the heading 'Coding and Callsigns'.

Base Aérienne Numbers

All Armée de l'Air bases including schools, supply and radar sites are allocated a Base Aérienne number in a unified sequence. Below are listed all known airfields and some of the more significant ground stations.

001-099 Flying units

Wings and autonomous squadrons are numbered in this range, beginning at EC 1 and concluding at EARS 99 (SAR unit) both of which are currently dormant.

BA101-BA200 Operational airfields

Wherever possible, numbers are allocated on a geographical basis. eg. 190-196 were in French Indochina. Numbers may be re-allocated, such as BA136 which was previously Bremgarten, until resident unit EC 11 was transfered to the ex-USAF airfield at Toul, which then conveniently took up the designation BA136. Other re-allocations take place when the function of a base is changed, as with BE705 (Base Ecole - school base) Tours, home of GE 314 the T-33 flying school which was BA109 in its days as an operational base. Note also that BA numbers are occasionally used as a code prefix for base flight aircraft. Current numbers are indicated *

101*	Toulouse-Francazal
102*	Dijon-Longvic
103*	Cambrai-Epinoy
104*	Le Bourget-Dugny
105*	Evreux-Fauville
106*	Bordeaux-Mérignac
107*	Villacoublay-Velizy
108	Marignane
109*	Tours-St. Symphorien
110*	Creil-Senlis
111	Lyon-Bron
112*	Reims-Champagne
113*	St. Dizier-Robinson
114*	Aix-en-Provence/Les Milles
115*	Orange-Caritat
116*	Luxeuil-St. Saveur
117*	Paris/Boulevard Victor (HQ only)
118*	Mont-de-Marsan
119	Pau-Uzein
120*	Cazaux
121	Nancy-Essey
122*	Chartres-Champhol
123*	Orléans-Bricy
124*	Strasbourg-Entzheim
125*	Istres-le Tube
126*	Solenzara
128*	Metz-Frescaty
129	St. Jean d'Angely
130	Toulouse-Balma
131	Mourmelon
132*	Colmar-Mayenheim
133*	Nancy-Ochey
134	Versailles
135	Cognac-Chateaubernard
136*	Toul-Rosières
137	Coblence (Koblenz)
139	Lahr-Hugsweier
140	Blida
141	Oran-La Sénia
142	Boufarik
143	Batna
145	Colomb-Béchar
146	La Reghaia
148	Algiers-Hussein Dey
149	Algiers-Maison Blanche
150	Rabat
151	Rabat-Salé
152	Agadir
153	Oujda
154	Mediouna
155	Casablanca-Cazes
156	Bizerte-Sidi Ahmed
157	Tunis-El Aouina
158	Gabes
160*	Dakar-Yoff
161	Thies
162	Bamako
164	Atar
165*	Berlin-Tegel
167	Reggan
168	Bouake
170	Brazzaville-Maya Maya
171	Bangui
172	Fort Lamy
173	Pointe Noire
174	Douala
177	Auxerre-Moneteau
178*	Friburg-Achern
180	Bou Sfer
181*	St. Denis, Réunion ex Ivato, Madagascar
185*	Hao
188*	Djibouti
190*	Tahiti ex Hanoi-Bach Mai
191	Saigon-Tan Son Nhut
192	Saigon-Bien Hoa
193	Haiphong
194	Nha Trang
195	Cat Bi
196	Senu
197	Papeete
198	Hanoi-Gia Lam
199	Cap St. Jacques
200*	Apt-St. Christol

BA201-BA299 Non-operational airfields

These are normally reserve bases, but Brétigny and Chateaudun are obvious exceptions.

201	Sidi Slimane
202	Ben Guerir
203*	Cenon
204*	Mérignac-Beauséjour
205	Dijon-Kriern

206*	Bordeaux-Fauché	607*	Rocamadou	EMDA900*	Taverny (Etat Major de la Defense Aerienne - Air Defence HQ)
209	Toulouse-Balma	608*	Toulouse		
210	Algiers	609*	Cinq Mais la Pile	BA901*	Drachenbronn
211	Telergma			CDC05/901*	Drachenbronn
213	Bône			CDC05/902*	Contrexeville
217*	Bretigny-sur-Orge			BA903	Friedrichshafen

BE701-BE799 Schools

Training establishments with or without an attached airfield are included in this listing.

240	Nimes-Courbesac		
246*	La Rochelle	701*	Salon-de-Provence
250	Le Bourget	702*	Avord
257	Friedrichshafen	705*	Tours-St.Symphorien
261	Crepey	706	Cazaux
265*	Rocamadour	707	Marrakesh
271	Rennes	709*	Cognac-Chateaubernard
272*	St. Cyr l'Ecole	720	Caen
273*	Romorantin	721*	Rochefort-Soubise
274*	Limoges	722*	Saintes-Thenac
275	Le Blanc	723	Auxerre-Montenau
276	St. Astier	725*	Chambéry-Aix les Bains
277*	Varennes	726*	Nimes-Courbessac
278*	Ambérieu	727	Toulouse-Balma
279*	Chateaudun	740	Nantes
290	Ris-Orangis	742*	Echonbaulain (Initial training school - female)
292*	L'Hers-Toulouse		
		745*	Clermont Ferrand-Aulnat
		748*	Bordeaux-Beauséjour (Hospital)
		749*	Grenoble (Initial training school)

CICO910*	Dijon (Centre d'Instruction des Controleurs d'Operations ex Mont-de-Marsan, 1977)
BA914*	Romilly-sur-Seine
CDS15/914*	Prunay (Centre de Detection Satellite)
DMC80/920*	Orly
BA921*	Taverny
BA923	Meaux
BA925*	Doullens
CDC05/925	Doullens-Lucheux
CDC07/927*	Cinq Mais la Pile
CDC08/927*	Brest
CDC04/930*	Mont-de-Marsan
DMC80/940*	Aix-en-Provence
CMC85/940*	Istres
BA941	Giens
BA942*	Lyon
CDC05/942	Lyon-Mt. Verdun
CDC05/943*	Nice-Mt. Angel
CDS15/944*	Narbonne
EMSA01/950*	Istres (Escadron de Missiles Sol Air)
CI987*	St. Cyr
PAENAC988*	Toulouse (Permanence Air de l'Ecole National d'Aviation Civile).

Plus 762, 770, 773, 781, 790 and 799 all current headquarters units.

301-400 Flying Schools and OCUs

See section on current flying units, which begin at 312, the numbers 301-311 being reserve units with Harvards, all re-numbered on 1 January 1957.

401-600 Not used

601-700 Depots (Entrepôt d'Armee de l'Air - EAA)

The eight current bases supply the entire Armée de l'Air with their entire requirements from Atomic bombs to Zips (Flies, trousers, airmen for the use of).

601*	Chateaudun
602*	Romorantin-Pruniers
603*	Limoges (services the Jaguars of EC 7)
604	St. Cyr-l'Ecole
605*	Savigny-en-Septaine
606*	Varennes

800-899 Miscellaneous

Bases 800-822 are allocated to establishments of the Commandement des Transmissions (CTAA), and 834-840 to hospitals. A few later numbers cover administrative offices.

900-999 CAFDA

Air Defence Headquarters and radar sites. Main bases are prefixed by the usual 'BA', whilst CDC indicates Centre de Détection et de Controle, DMC Detachement Militaire de Controle, and CMC Centre Militaire de Controle.

AIRFIELD NAMES

French practise in naming airfields normally results in a double-barrelled designation, the second part of which is the nearest village to the airfield (as is the British way) and the first, the nearest principal town. It is normally the first part of the name which is used for everyday purposes, but care is sometimes required with neighbouring establishments such as BA121 Nancy-Essey (now closed) and BA133 Nancy-Ochey. Others readily lend themselves to confusion, as in the case of BA106 Bordeaux-Merignac, BA204 Merignac-Beauséjour and BA206 Bordeaux-Fauché.

BASE AERIENNE NUMBERS

Some current badges

OPERATIONAL AIRFIELDS

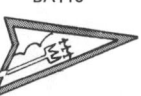

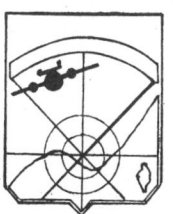

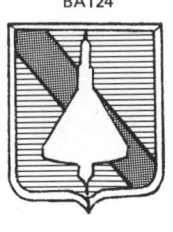

| BA101 | BA103 | BA105 | BA106 |

| BA107 | BA109 | BA110 | BA112 | BA113 | BA114 | BA115 |

| BA116 | BA118 | BA122 | BA123 | BA124 | BA125 | BA126 |

| BA128 | BA132 | BA133 | BA136 | BA165 | BA188 |

| | NON-OPERATIONAL AIRFIELDS | BA203 | BA204 | BA206 | BA272 | BA273 |

| BA278 | BA279 | BA292 | | DEPOTS | 601 |

| 602 | 605 | 606 | 609 |  | SCHOOLS | BE701 |

| BE709 | BE721 | BE722 | BE725 | BE726 | BE745 |

| CAFDA | BA901 | CDC05/901 | BA921 | BA942 | CDC05/943 | CDS15/944 |

73

Part Three

Aéronautique Navale

Current Organisation

Headquartered at 2 Rue Royale, Paris 8, the Aéronavale, with a personnel strength of 12, 000, and about 400 aircraft on charge, is an important component of the Marine National.

The Aéronavale flies from two aircraft carriers, one helicopter ship, and several vessels equipped with helicopter platforms, in order to provide protection for the fleet from air and submarine attacks, and ensure the continued freedom of the shipping lanes to the merchant navy. Coastal bases house maritime reconnaissance aircraft for naval patrol and submarine detection, these also being the location of second-line training and support units.

A far-reaching programme of improvement has been laid down for the Marine National, but the force receives less than one sixth of the defence budget and must necessarily be highly cost-effective.

Types of Unit

Operational tasks are performed by Flotilles (squadrons) equipped with approximately twelve aircraft each. The number of the unit will indicate its function:—
 1F to 10F anti-submarine, carrier-based,
 11F to 20F fighter and fighter/bomber,
 21F to 30F maritime patrol,
 31F to 39F helicopter.
Flotilles are homogeneous in aircraft complement.

Escadrilles de Servitude provide training and communications functions from shore bases. Again, numbers are allocated to indicate the unit task:—
 1S to 19S communications,
 20S to 29S helicopter,
 51S to 59S training.
Note that in only three cases do the actual numbers used duplicate those of Flotilles. Aircraft complements normally include several types per unit.

For establishments with a smaller fleet the title Section de Soutien (ex Section de Liaison) is given, followed by the unit base name. Sections de Soutien are unnumbered.

Experimental work is undertaken by CEPA which utilises the aircraft of the S.E.S. and 20S for its trials.

Overall Organisation

EMBARKED UNITS
The Breguet Alizé, to be replaced later by the SA-321 Super Frélon, flies with two Flotilles and carries the AS-12 missile in the offensive role. The F-8E(FN) Crusaders of 12F and 14F, have received wing modifications, and as such should continue in service to the end of the decade, but the three Etendard squadrons (two strike, one reconnaissance) will phase out their aircraft in favour of the Super Etendard as this becomes available instead of the Jaguar M as originally proposed.

Two Flotilles of HSS-1 helicopters remain in service, one for ASW and the other in the assault role, whilst a third unit uses the larger Super Frélon for ASW work. Section Jeanne d'Arc equipped with Alouette IIIs and HSS-1s for operation from a vessel of that name completes the normal seagoing component of the Aéronavale, whilst 32F has recently received its first Lynx which will soon be allocated to destroyers, replacing Alouettes.

SHORE-BASED ANTI-SUBMARINE UNITS
Four Atlantic and two Neptune units provide ASW and patrol facilities including the Hao-based 12S which is additionally involved with nuclear test duties in the Pacific. The remaining five units maintain surveillance of the Atlantic and Mediterranean.

COMMUNICATIONS UNITS
Five Flotilles employ a variety of types for communications work between shore stations and for plane guard duties from the two carriers. The Flamant has been withdrawn from this work and replaced by the Piper Navajo.

TRAINING UNITS
Initial training for aircrew is undertaken by the Armée de l'Air, but the Aéronavale maintains units responsible for deck landing, navigation, and twin conversion experience. The Army helicopter training school at Dax handles helicopter training with experience in heavier types being gained with the Armée de l'Air at CIEH 341, Chambéry.

UNITS BASED ABROAD
Three communications sections are currently in commission in the Pacific.

MISCELLANEOUS UNITS
St. Raphael, home of the CEPA, is the base for trials units for fixed and rotary wing aircraft. Naval cadets gain flying experience with the SVSEN Rallyes at Lanvéoc-Poulmic and those of the SEN at St. Raphael, and there is in addition a ferry unit, with no permanent complement of aircraft.

Aircraft and Helicopter-Carrying Vessels

The Marine National operates principally in the Atlantic and Mediterranean. The Atlantic fleet operates from Brest, with a secondary base at Cherbourg, and comprises the capital ship *Colbert*, most of the newer destroyers and frigates and one tanker. The Mediterranean fleet at Toulon has aircraft carriers *Clemenceau* and *Foch*, capital ships *Duguesne* and *Suffren*, plus the older destroyers and frigates and one tanker.

The vessels listed below are capable of operating aircraft or helicopters. The number quoted prior to the name is the pennant number, a permanent code allocated to each ship for ease of identification.

AIRCRAFT CARRIERS

R98 *Clemenceau*
(launched 21.12.57; completed 22.11.61)
R99 *Foch*
(launched 28.7.60; completed 15.7.63)

Both carriers are of the same class with a deck 543 feet long and ninety-seven feet wide, the flying portion of which is angled at eight degrees. Upto forty aircraft may be carried, normally a Flotilla each of Etendards, Crusaders and Alizés. The *Clemenceau* entered dry dock in the Spring of 1978 for a re-fit, and when she re-emerged in January 1979 was equipped to operate the Super Etendard.

A nuclear powered helicopter-carrier, the as-yet unnamed PA75, was to have been laid down by DCAN at Brest in 1975, for completion in 1980. This 18,400 ton vessel will now be begun in 1980-81, and when commissioned will be capable of operating twenty-five Lynx, or ten Super Frelon, or fifteen Pumas. Technically, it will replace the helicopter carrier *Arromanches* (ex HMS 'Colossus') which retired in January 1974.

HELICOPTER CRUISER

R97 *Jeanne d'Arc*

The *Jeanne d'Arc* is normally used for training by the Naval Academy. Launched on 30 December 1961 and completed on 1 July 1963, the vessel was known as *La Resolute* until 28 July 1964 when the 'old' *Jeanne d'Arc* retired. The flying deck is 203 feet long and sixty-nine feet wide and the ship operates its own flight of four helicopters, the Section Jeanne d'Arc, although in a war situation, eight helicopters and 700 commandos can be accomodated. Long term plans foresee the vessel equipped with the Lynx helicopter.

DESTROYERS

C70 class D640 *Georges Leygues*
           D641 *Dupleix*
           D642 *Montcalm*

The above trio are the first of thirty class C70 destroyers for the Marine National, to be equipped with two Lynx helicopters. Of the twenty-four planned for completion before 1985, eighteen will be the anti-submarine version and the remaining six, anti-aircraft (where the Lynxes will possibly be omitted). Three of the former type will be ordered in the 1977-82 plan plus three anti-aircraft variants later. *Georges Leygues* was laid down on 16 September 1974, launched on 18 December 1976 and commissioned in 1978.

F67 class D610 *Tourville*
           D611 *Duguay-Trouin*
           D612 *de Grasse*

To be equipped with two Lynx each, the three vessels were originally classified as corvettes, but are called Frigates and carry destroyer pennant numbers. The first was laid down on 16 March 1970, and the last commissioned in July 1976.

T56 class D638 *La Galissonnière*
Commissioned in July 1962, this may operate one helicopter if required.

T53 class D633 *Duperre*
           D635 *Forbin*
Now twenty years old, two of the T53 class have been fitted with a helicopter platform in place of one gun turret.

CRUISER C611 *Colbert*

Originally commissioned in May 1959, the *Colbert* was equipped with a helicopter platform on the quarter deck during a re-fit in 1970-72. There is no hangar, and thus no permanent allocation of a helicopter.

FRIGATES Commandant Riviere class

F725 *Victor Schoelcher*
F726 *Commandant Bory*
F727 *Admiral Charner*
F728 *Doudart de Lagrée*
F729 *Balny*
F733 *Commandant Rivière*
F740 *Commandant Bourdais*
F748 *Protèt*
F749 *Enseigne de Vaisseau Henry*

The above nine have been converted to carry one helicopter on a platform, but without the benefit of hangarage. Helicopters are allocated only for specific missions are not permanently on board.

AUXILIARIES

Tanker   A629 *La Durance*
         A... *Meuse*

Both the above will be capable of operating one light helicopter. *La Durance* commissioned in July 1976, and the *Meuse* is yet to enter service.

Depot   A615 *Loire*
Ship   A618 *Rance*
        A621 *Rhin*
        A622 *Rhone*

Four of the five Rhin Class vessels are equipped for helicopter operation. The laboratory and radiological services ship *Rance* has provision for three light helicopters and the remainder have accomodation for one each. The *Rhin* is an electronics maintenance ship, *Rhone* is for fishery patrol and the minesweeper support *Loire* is also temporarily performing this duty.

Command Ship
        A626 *La Charente*
Bought in 1964, the vessel is the flagship of the Indian Ocean fleet also functions in its former role as a tanker. A helicopter platform is fitted.

Maintenance and Repair Ship
        A620 *Jules Verne*
Commissioned in March 1976, the *Jules Verne* has accomodation for two light helicopters.

Trials and Research Ship
        A603 *Henri Poincare*
A tanker converted for missile tracking duties at the Landes Range in southern France, the vessel was commissioned in 1967 and may operate two heavy or five light helicopters with hangarage provided.

Submarine Support Ship

   A646 *Triton*

Commissioned in 1972, the *Triton* is a support ship for experimental submarine work. There is a platform fitted for one light helicopter.

LANDING SHIPS

LS (Dock) L9021 *Ouragan*
   L9022 *Orage*

Up to four heavy helicopters can be carried in each vessel. The *Orage* is presently detached to the Pacific Nuclear Test Centre.

LS (Light Transport)
   L9030 *Champlain*
   L9031 *Francis Garnier*

Classified as 'Batral' class barges, each has a small helicopter platform.

LS (Tank) L9003 *Agens*
   L9004 *Bidassoa*
   L9007 *Trieux*
   L9008 *Dives*
   L9009 *Blauet*

Each with accomodation for two Alouette III.

Note: The ability to carry a helicopter does not indicate that the vessel does so at all times, this particularly applying to support ships.

Current Units

4 FLOTILLE

Callsigns: F-XCDA/F-XCDZ
Insignia: A white bird, black tortoise, light blue sky and dark blue sea.
Base: Lann-Bihoué
Aircraft: Alizé.

4F re-formed in July 1944 with the SBD5 Dauntless serving in Indochina during 1947, progressing to the TBM-3E Avenger in October 1953 and Breguet Alizé at Hyères late in 1959. The Flotille moved to its present base at Lann-Bihoué in July 1964 and is responsible for SAR and ASW duties from its shore base or either of the two carriers. Normal complement is twelve aircraft.

6 FLOTILLE

Callsigns: F-XCFA/F-XCFZ
Insignia: A cross of Lorraine in red outlined in gold on a white background and surrounded by a blue square outlined in gold.
Base: Nimes-Garons
Aircraft: Alizé

Apart from performing operational duties in SAR and ASW, 6F also acts as the Alizé operational conversion unit and employs a dummy deck at Nimes for landing practice. Twelve aircraft are used, equipped, like those of 4F, with the AS-12 missile. The squadron received the Alizé at Hyères in 1960, taking up residence at its current base the following year.

11 FLOTILLE

Callsigns: F-XCKA/F-XCKZ and 'Kimono'
Insignia: A seahorse
Base: Landivisiau
Aircraft: Super Etendard

11F traces its ancestry in an unbroken line to August 1926 with the formation of escadrille 7C1, this later becoming AC 1 in 1940, 1F in 1945, and adopting its present title in 1954. Equipped with the Seafire in October 1946, the unit joined the Dauntless dive bombers of 4F on the *Arromanches* in October 1948, and commenced operations against the Communists from Bien Hoa in December. After returning home, Hellcats were received in 1950 and a further spell of service on the same carrier off Indochina began in August 1951, followed by a third in August 1953. Back at Hyères in August 1954, 11F was created and immediately began conversion to the Aquilon (Sea Venom) transferring to Karouba, Tunisia in November 1957 and Bizerte, Algeria the following year, from where it participated in the Algerian war, later moving to Maison Blanche. Taken out of the line in September 1959, 11F went to sea on the *Clemenceau* in March 1960, but disbanded on 1 April 1962 re-forming exactly a year later to receive its present type, the Etendard. On 3 May 1967, 11F transferred to Landivisiau, where it has on charge twelve aircraft for strike duties, these being regularly operated from the two carriers. The first Super Etendards were noted with the unit in October 1978 prior to embarkation on the *Clemenceau* in early 1979 with a strength of seventeen aircraft.

12 FLOTILLE

Callsigns:	F-XCLA/F-XCLZ
Insignia:	Donald Duck holding a blunderbuss
Base:	Landivisiau
Aircraft:	F-8E(FN) Crusader

12F formed in August 1948 when the Seafire-equipped 1F at Hyères was divided into two units.

F-6F Hellcats arrived for the squadron in the Spring of 1950 and between October 1952 and May 1953, these operated in Indochina. The first F-4U-7 Corsair entered service on 10 June 1953, and 12F returned to the Far East for a further period of operations. Following a period in North Africa, the unit disbanded early in 1963.

Re-formed at Lann-Bihoué on 1 October 1964, 12F received its first Crusader on 20 November and embarked on the *Clemenceau* in May 1965. Based at Landivisiau from July 1968, the unit regularly spends periods afloat and whilst ashore is integrated with the Armee de l'Air's fighter command, CAFDA. Unit strength is twelve aircraft but will be increased by transfers from 14F in 1979.

14 FLOTILLE

Callsigns:	F-XCNA/F-XCNZ and 'Negus'
Insignia:	A white skull and red scarf on a black background
Base:	Landivisiau
Aircraft:	F-8E(FN) Crusader

Formed at Karouba in 1953 with the Corsair, 14F was soon transferred to Indochina where it was engaged in the struggle against Communist forces until returned home in July 1955. In the following year the squadron was engaged in both the Algerian and Suez campaigns remaining in North Africa until transferred to Cuers in 1962 where it disbanded early in 1964. Following the re-equipment of 12F with Crusaders, 14F formed with the type at Lann-Bihoué in April 1965 moving to Landivisiau on 1 August 1968. Unit strength is twelve aircraft, and these are frequently detached to the two aircraft carriers. In 1979, 14F will re-equip with the Super Etendard and pass its Crusaders to 12F.

16 FLOTILLE

Callsigns:	F-XCPA/F-XCPZ and 'Pirate'
Insignia:	A black flamingo
Base:	Landivisiau
Aircraft:	Etendard IVP.

Previously an all-weather fighter squadron, 16F formed out of the Aquilon trials squadron at Hyères on 3 January 1955, and joined sister unit

79

11F at Karouba, Tunisia in August 1958. After returning home, the Flotille again moved to North Africa for a short time in September 1961, when it based a detachment at Karouba following unrest in Bizerte. 16F was regularly at sea on the *Clemenceau* and *Foch*, its Aquilons operating as missile carriers until the unit disbanded on 1 April 1964. On 1 May 1964 it re-formed at Istres with the photo reconnaissance Etendard IVP, and when fully equipped, returned to Hyères in September of that year. It transferred to Landivisiau on 1 April 1968 from where it provides detachments to the two Marine National aircraft carriers, and whilst ashore, co-operates with the Armée de l'Air's Mirage IIIR wing, ER 33.

17 FLOTILLE

Callsigns: F-XCQA/F-XCQZ and 'Laziar'
Insignia: A black bird on an arrow
Base: Hyères
Aircraft: Etendard IVM.

The Corsair-equipped 17F disbanded at Hyères in 1962, re-forming at the same base in January 1964, flying the Etendard. The Flotille operates alongside 11F in the strike role, sharing detachments afloat with a complement of twelve aircraft. The unit is expected to be equipped with the Super Etendard by the late summer of 1980.

21 FLOTILLE

Callsigns: F-XCUA/F-XCUZ
Insignia: A gazelle's head in red, black and white.
Base: Nimes-Garons
Aircraft: Atlantic

21 Flotille was formed out of 3F in 1953 and operated the P2V-6 Neptune in Algeria until withdrawn to France in 1961. The Flotille was the first to receive the Atlantic, in December 1965, and eight of the type are now used for maritime reconnaissance and SAR work.

22 FLOTILLE

Callsigns: F-XCVA/F-XCVZ
Insignia: Three black and white birds, a red sun and blue sea.
Base: Nimes-Garons
Aircraft: Atlantic

Like 21F, this unit was formed by the division of 3F in Algeria, and moved to Nimes in 1961. Eight Atlantics received in 1966 are used for maritime reconnaissance and SAR.

23 FLOTILLE

Callsigns: F-XCWA/F-XCWZ
Insignia: A white and blue seagull, black shark and blue sea.
Base: Lann-Bihoué
Aircraft: Atlantic

Originally designated 2F, this unit remained at Dakar throughout World War II, afterwards using the Wellington and Lancaster. Re-named 23F in 1953, it received the P2V-6 Neptune and in 1959 the P2V-7, and withdrew to its present base in 1961. 23F aircraft are often deployed to the Pacific test ranges where a detachment of Atlantics is based.

24 FLOTILLE

Callsigns: F-XCXA/F-XCXZ
Insignia: A black and white bird, over a red and black buoy in a dark blue sea.
Base: Lann-Bihoué
Aircraft: Atlantic

The first Lann-Bihoué Flotille to receive the Atlantic was 24F, previously operating the P2V-7 Neptune. In common with the similarly equipped units at Nimes, the eight aircraft of 24F are responsible for maritime reconnaissance and SAR duties.

25 FLOTILLE

Callsigns: F-XCSA/F-XCSZ
Insignia: A black bird over a rising sun.
Base: Lann-Bihoué
Aircraft: Neptune

25F formed out of the Lancaster-equipped 11F at Lartique, Algeria in 1953 and moved to Lann in the same year to equip with the Neptune. Now the last home-based P2 Flotille, the unit uses eight aircraft for maritime reconnaissance and SAR.

31 FLOTILLE

Callsigns: F-XCAA/F-XCAZ
 A to Z
Insignia: A pegasus over the Southern Cross.
Base: St. Mandrier
Aircraft: SH-34J   Lynx

The twelve aircraft of 31F are unusual in carrying letter codes on the fuselage side. 31F provides detachments to both carriers when at sea, specialising in anti-submarine warfare.

Formed in July 1956, 31F saw operational service in Algeria equipped with the H-34, before moving to its present base in September 1961. The unit's first Lynx was delivered on 28 September 1978.

32 FLOTILLE

Callsigns: F-XCBA/F-XCBZ
 A to Z
Insignia: An eagle on a rock.
Base: Lanvéoc-Poulmic
Aircraft: Super Frelon

Formed at Lartique, North Africa, with the H-34 in January 1958, 32F moved to St. Mandrier in August 1962 and to Lanvéoc in 1964. Super Frelons were delivered for anti-submarine duties from January 1970 onwards, and 32F provides ASW detachments for the Marine National, an additional task being the protection of the French nuclear submarine base at l'Ile Longue.

33 FLOTILLE

Callsigns: F-XCCA/F-XCCZ
Insignia: A dove on a flash of lightning.
Base: St. Mandrier
Aircraft: SH-34G

33F employs twelve H-34 helicopters, some armed with SS-11 air-to-ground missiles for assault duties. The unit transports Marines or army soldiers, and has previously been detached to Chad for anti-guerilla work.

34 FLOTILLE

Callsigns: 'Moloch'
Insignia: A sea monster
Base: Lanvéoc-Poulmic
Aircraft: Alouette III.

The newest unit in the Aéronavale, 34F was formed in 1974, providing ASW helicopters for detachment to vessels of the Marine National, with seven Alouette III.

2 ESCADRILLE DE SERVITUDE

Callsigns: F-YDAA/F-YDAZ and 'Vega'
Insignia: A phoenix clutching a bomb.
Base: Lann-Bihoué
Aircraft: Nord 262 (4)   Navajo (3)

2S established at Lann-Bihoué in 1955 and operated the Wellington, Spitfire, Aquilon, Catalina and Beech SNB-5. Seven Flamants were withdrawn in 1972 and replaced by the Navajo and Nord 262. The unit provides a liaison service for 1 and 2 Maritime Regions.

3 ESCADRILLE DE SERVITUDE

Callsigns: F-YDCA/F-YDCZ
Insignia: A swan on a lake.
Base: Hyères
Aircraft: Nord 262 (4)   Alizé (6)
           Navajo (3)   Falcon 10 (1)

Communications work for 3 Maritime Region is undertaken by 3S, which in addition provides training facilities when its aircraft are not in use on official business. The Nord 262 also performs as a radar trainer as does the Alizé, whilst the Navajo has assumed the instrument-flying duties of the earlier Flamants. The Falcon 10 was delivered to the unit on 2 May 1978.

9 ESCADRILLE DE SERVITUDE

Callsigns:
Insignia: A white bird with yellow edging, surmounting a yellow cows head with a black face, all on a green background.
Base: Tontouta
Aircraft: C-47 (2), C-54E (1), P-2H Neptune (1)

9S was first formed at Tontouta in 1957 with Avro Lancasters for liaison and SAR duties. MS.500s and SNJ-5s were also operated, and on 2 January 1964 Douglas C-54E 49148, formerly General de Gaulle's personal aircraft arrived, remaining in service with the unit until the present day. It was joined later in 1964 by a C-54B 10454, but this was withdrawn in 1969, when 9S was re-named as the 'Section de Liaison de Nouvelle-Calédonie'. A C-47 Dakota was delivered in 1970, but after tests in 1974 involving P-2H Neptune 147570 on detachment from 25F, 9S was re-activated on 1 May 1975 with P-2H 146432. Further Neptunes have served with the unit, which did however retain the C-47 and C-54, the latter converted in 1976 to carry weather radar similar to that fitted in the Aéronavale's Lynx helicopters.

The unit is responsible for maritime surveillance and liaison duties in the area, but is particularly involved in mapping and survey work using oblique camera in the C-54, and vertical installations in the P-2H. Secondary roles are VIP transport with the C-54, and SAR.

82

10 ESCADRILLE DE SERVITUDE

Re-named Section Expérimentale et de Servitude.

12 ESCADRILLE DE SERVITUDE

Callsigns: F-YDGA/F-YDGZ
Insignia: A black shark with red mouth on a radar scope (green sea, blue sky) on a black shield with red lightning flash.
Base: Faaa, Tahiti.
Aircraft: Neptune (8).

The unit formed at Lann-Bihoué on 15 April 1969 to operate Neptunes in support of the atomic test programme. Six aircraft were modified as 'AMOR' versions with missile-tracking equipment in the nose, and four of these were operated at any one time for the Landes range off the French Atlantic coast; all were re-converted to standard configuration later. Other aircraft were involved in the ECM experiments and training. In 1972, 12S moved to Hao in the Pacific, and later to Faaa, from where detachments are made to Hao and Mururoa. The principal duties of the unit are maritime patrol and surveillance, particularly in connection with the Pacific Nuclear Test Centre, but SAR and liaison flying are both important secondary tasks.

20 ESCADRILLE DE SERVITUDE

Callsigns:
Insignia: A helicopter rotor and a '?' mark.
Base: St. Raphael
Aircraft: Alouette II   Alouette III
Super Frelon   H-34   Lynx.

The rotary wing department of CEPA's test flight is designated 20S, and participates in experiments and operational trials.
The first Lynx, 05-04 was delivered in May 1978, and is due to be joined by 05-03.

22 ESCADRILLE DE SERVITUDE

Callsigns: F-YDKA/F-YDKZ
Insignia: The arms of Brittany.

Base: Lanvéoc-Poulmic
Aircraft: Alouette II   Alouette III

22S Alouettes provide communications and SAR for aircraft carriers in 2 (Atlantic) Region. The Alouette III VSV is also operated in the training role.

23 ESCADRILLE DE SERVITUDE

Callsigns: F-YDLA/F-YDLZ
Insignia: A seagull dropping a lifebuoy.
Base: St. Mandrier
Aircraft: Alouette II   Alouette III

The escadrille is responsible for support and SAR for carriers in 3 (Mediterranean) Region. 23S also operates Alouettes on behalf of the CERES engine research establishment for missile recovery.

27 ESCADRILLE DE SERVITUDE

Callsigns: F-YDNA/F-YDNZ
Insignia: The 'radiation' warning sign.
Base: Mururoa
Aircraft: Super Frélon (5)

Of the initial Super Frélon order, five cargo examples were delivered to 27S in 1968 and designated SA.321Ga. The unit provides heavy lift helicopters for the Nuclear Test Centre.

55 ESCADRILLE DE SERVITUDE

Callsigns: F-YDOA/F-YDOZ
Insignia: Donald Duck flying a twin-engined aircraft.
Base: Aspretto
Aircraft: Nord 262 (8)

After advanced flying training under the direction of the Armée de l'Air, prospective pilots of twin-engined aircraft transfer to Corsica for conversion to the Nord 262.

56 ESCADRILLE DE SERVITUDE

Callsigns: F-YDPA/F-YDPZ
Insignia: A flying fish on the sun.
Base: Nimes-Garons
Aircraft: C-47 Dakota (12)

56S is attached to the Ecole du Personnel Volant for the navigational training of Aéronavale aircrew. The escadrille is the last in France to use the Dakota.

59 ESCADRILLE DE SERVITUDE

Callsigns: F-YFKA/F-YFKZ
Insignia: A white bird with yellow beak and feet over a turtle with black shell and yellow head and eyes on a light blue sky and dark blue sea. (The previous insignia was a black mask with red eyes on a grey background).
Base: Hyères
Aircraft: Etendard (12) Alizé (6) Zéphyr (14)

New and old insignia

59S formed at Hyères from the Section d'Entrainement à la Chasse de Nuit on 1 February 1956 as an all-weather fighter pilot's school equipped with the F6F-5N Hellcat and SO30P Corse, replacing the former with Aquilons in February 1957. These were augmented by the Zéphyr from October 1959 and in 1962 the unit formed an aerobatic team, the Patrouille de Voltige d'Hyères, on the type. On 8 March 1965 the last Aquilon was retired and 59S was re-designated as the training unit for all carrier fighter pilots. To assist in this task, ten Etendards were introduced from 1 October 1965 onwards but in 1972 the Alizé was also added and the Escadrille assumed responsiblity for all classes of embarked pilots. At the same time, unit insignia of a black mask was replaced by the bird and turtle badge of 54S. The Alizé also undertake SAR duties for 3 Maritime Region and two are permanently detached to the Section Expérimentale at St. Raphael.

SECTION REACTEUR LEGER

Callsigns: F-YETA/F-YETZ, 'Tenor' (and 'Tokio', Falcon only).
Insignia: Nil.
Base: Landivisiau
Aircraft: Paris (10)   Falcon 10 (2)

The SRL operates a small fleet of jet aircraft for proficiency and continuation training, additionally functioning as a communications unit. The two Falcons were added to the strength in 1975, augmenting the entire remaining Naval Paris stock.

SECTION JEANNE D'ARC

Callsigns:
Insignia: not carried
Base: St. Mandrier
Aircraft: Alouette III   H-34

Formed in 1969, the SJA provides a helicopter detachment to the *Jeanne d'Arc* whilst it is performing its peacetime role as an officer-cadet training ship.

SECTION DE SOUTIEN DE DUGNY

Callsigns: F-YEFA/F-YEFZ
Insignia: Nil.
Base: Le Bourget/Dugny.
Aircraft: Nord 262 (3) Navajo (1)
DC-6 (1)

Formed by the renaming of 11S in 1968, the SSD provides VIP transport for the Naval headquarters in Paris.

SECTION ALOUETTE DU PACIFIQUE

Callsigns: F-YDAA/F-YDAZ
Insignia: Nil.
Base: Hao
Aircraft: Alouette III (4)

The Sectalpac provides four support helicopters for the Nuclear Test Centre, CEP. According to the callsign allocation, the unit is a detachment of 2S.

ESCADRILLE DE RECEPTION ET DE CONVOYAGE

Callsigns: F-YFLA/F-YFLZ
Insignia: An aircraft over a factory.
Base: Toussus-le Noble.
Aircraft: All types.

The ERC is the Aéronavale's ferrying unit and thus flies all types in service. It uses a detached Navajo of 2S as a ferry aircraft when required, this sometimes to be seen at Toussus.

SECTION DE VOL SPORTIF ECOLE NAVALE

Callsigns: F-YECA/F-YECZ and 'Canari'
Insignia: Nil.
Base: Lanvéoc-Poulmic.
Aircraft: Rallye 100S.

Previously equipped with MS 733 Alcyon, ten Rallyes were handed over to this Section in April 1974. The SVSEN provides initial flying training to cadets of the Naval Academy, on an informal basis.

SECTION EXPERIMENTALE ET DE SERVITUDE, BAN St. RAPHAEL

The SES has assumed some of the duties of the disbanded 10S and operates an unusual mixture of aircraft from St. Raphael. Six Rallyes replaced the MS 733 air experience aircraft of the Naval Ratings'

Insignia of the former 10S

School in 1976 and these are maintained alongside N.2504 Noratlas (tip-jet version) No. 01, previously used by 10S. In addition the section services detachments of Alizés from 59S at Hyères and a Dakota of 56S. The 10S callsigns F-YDEA/F-YDEZ are perpetuated, but the continued use of the 10S insignia is not confirmed.

OTHER ESTABLISHMENTS

DCAN, St. Tropez	See page 99.
GI 312, Salon	) Fixed wing training is
GE 313, Clermont	) given to Aéronavale
GE 314, Tours	) personnel at all these
GE 315, Cognac	) Air Force schools.
ESALAT, Dax	Basic helicopter training with the ALAT.
CIEH 341, Chambéry	Heavy helicopter training with the Armée de l'Air.
BA721, Rochefort	Ground training school, Non-airworthy aircraft.
BA722, Saintes	Electrical and Radio school.
CEV, Bretigny	The Aéronavale provides a proportion of aircraft and personnel for this experimental establishment.

85

Aéronautique Navale Callsigns

Two systems of callsigns are in use for Aéronavale aircraft, a letter sequence commencing 'F' and an operational series consisting of a code-word followed by a number or letter.

ALL-LETTER SERIES
This is further sub-divided into two series, commencing 'FX' for front line units and 'FY' for second line establishments.

First line Flotilles use F-XCAA to F-XCZZ where the penultimate letter is indicative of the Flotille number, and the last identifies the individual aircraft, eg F-XCNx is employed by 14F, as 'N' is the fourteenth letter of the alphabet.

Second line Escadrilles used F-YCxx upto 1972 when these were changed to F-YDxx and F-YExx. Higher unit numbers designations precluded a rigid adherence to a system similar to that above, but some regularity does remain.

The final letter of the callsign is frequently changed and cannot be used as a reliable guide to aircraft serial numbers.

Those used in recent years are listed below. In each case the series runs from A to Z, although not all are necessarily taken up.

F-XCAA	31F
F-XCBA	32F
F-XCCA	33F
F-XCDA	4F
F-XCFA	6F
F-XCIA	9F
F-XCKA	11F
F-XCLA	12F
F-XCNA	14F
F-XCOA	15F
F-XCPA	16F
F-XCQA	17F
F-XCUA	21F
F-XCVA	22F
F-XCWA	23F
F-XCXA	24F
F-XCYA	25F
F-YALA	ex *S.S. Madagascar*
F-YCAA	ex 2S
F-YCBA	ex 2S
F-YCCA	ex 3S
F-YCEA	ex 3S
F-YCHA	ex *S.S. Pacifique*
F-YCIA	ex 9S/S.S.N.C.
F-YCJA	ex 10S
F-YCKA	ex S.S.D.
F-YCLA	ex 12S
F-YCSA	ex 59S
F-YCTA	ex 20S
F-YCVA	ex 22S
F-YCWA	ex 23S
F-YCXA	ex 27S
F-YCZA	ex D.C.A.N.
F-YDAA	2S
F-YDCA	3S
F-YDEA	10S/C.E.P.A./SESSt. Raphael
F-YDGA	12S
F-YDKA	22S
F-YDLA	23S
F-YDNA	27S
F-YDOA	55S
F-YDPA	56S
F-YECA	S.V.S.E.N.
F-YEEA	D.C.A.N.
F-YEFA	S.S.D.
F-YEGA	9S
F-YETA	S.R.L.
F-YFFA	ex 55S
F-YFGA	ex 56S
F-YFKI	59S
F-YFLA	E.R.C

OPERATIONAL CALLSIGNS
Designed to be of a more cryptic nature, the system is partly self-defeating because of its regularity. The original allocation followed an alphabetical/numerical pattern in a manner similar to the 'FY' sequence above, in which the identification name for each Flotille began with the penultimate letter of its callsign. Thus 14 Flotille (F-YCNA/F-YCNZ) used 'Negus' followed by a number for each aircraft or mission. Occasionally the identification name is followed by a letter, as with 16F and the SVSEN. Some re-allocation of letters makes a complete listing impossible, but known examples are listed. Where two types of aircraft are operated, two different names may be used, both beginning with the same initial (see S.R.L.).

Canari	S.V.S.E.N.
Kimono	11F
Lasiar	17F
Moloch	34F
Negus	14F
Pirate	16F
Tenor	S.R.L. (Paris)
Tokio	S.R.L. (Falcon 10)
Vega	22S.

In view of the above, the unknown callsign range for 34F may be F-XCMA/F-XCMZ.

Part Four

Aviation Légère de l'Armée de Terre

The Army Aviation Section, usually referred to as ALAT, has its headquarters at 25 Boulevard Gallieni, Issy-Des-Moulineaux, near Paris, and since formation in November 1954 has provided observation and liaison services for the Armée de Terre. Personnel strength of the ALAT is 3,700.

Helicopters operate in the anti-tank role, the Alouette II/SS10 combination having been replaced by the Alouette III/SS11. The modification of 110 of the original 166 SA341F Gazelles to SA341M standard (capable of carrying HOT missiles) will permit the equipment of three RHCs with this missile before the specialised SA342 Gazelle/HOT becomes available in late 1979. The first to be re-equipped with the SA341M/HOT was 3RHC, with first deliveries beginning in September 1978.

Various army units are equipped with Honest John, Pluton and Hawk short-range nuclear missiles, but these are not under ALAT control.

Unit Organisation

The ALAT is currently undergoing a change in structure and grouping to match the revised army order of battle in which the brigade formation is eliminated. This process began in 1977 and is to be complete by the end of 1979, although only those units at the 'sharp-end' will be involved and training/support squadrons and some attached flights are to remain as before.

Parent units for ALAT aircraft may be deduced by reference to a three-letter code applied to all types in service. When prefixed by 'FM', this becomes the callsign, and a full list of those in use is given below. To clarify the position vis-a-vis the re-grouping of units, the orders of battle for 1977 and 1979 are listed separately.

ALAT Operational Units - 1977

GROUPE D'AVIATION LEGERE DE CORPS D'ARMEE (GALCA)

The GALCA is attached to an army corps, of which two are in existence, in France and in Germany. Each consists of four escadrilles: an EHL (Escadrille d'Helicoptères Légers) for liaison, an EHAC (Escadrille d'Helicoptères Anti-Chars) anti-tank flight and two EHM (Escadrille d'Helicoptères de Manoeuvre) for assault transport and heavy lift.

GALCA 1 (Phalsbourg)		Callsign range
1 EHL	10 SA341 Gazelle	FMAEA/FMAEZ
2 EHAC	12 Alouette III	FMAEA/FMAEZ
3 EHM	11 Puma	FMCYA/FMCYZ
4 EHM	11 Puma	FMCYA/FMCYZ
GALCA 2 (Friedrichshafen, West Germany)		
1 EHL	10 SA341 Gazelle	FMASA/FMASZ
2 EHAC	12 Alouette III	
3 EHM	11 Puma	FMASA/FMASZ
4 EHM	11 Puma	FMASA/FMASZ

Personnel strength is fixed at: EHL eighteen pilots including fifteen NCOs; EHAC fifteen pilots including twelve NCOs and EHM fifty-two pilots and second pilots including forty-four NCOs.

With regard to the numbers of aircraft on charge, it is doubtful if GALCA 2 ever achieved full strength. The occasional fixed wing type has been used, eg Cessna L-19 'ASG' and Broussard 'CYB'.

GROUPE D'AVIATION LEGERE DE DIVISION (GALDiv)

Six GALDivs, each with approximately forty helicopters, are attached to army divisions in the area of the divisional HQ. Unlike the GALCA, which is predominantly Puma-equipped, the GALDiv specialises in observation and anti-tank work with only a modest heavy helicopter contingent. The squadrons are designated 'Pelotons' (platoons) and are PHL, PHAC and PHM with duties as delegated to the GALCA units. Bases are in parentheses.

1 GALDiv (Trier, W. Germany)		Callsign range
1 PHL	10 SA341 Gazelle	FMCVA/FMCVZ
2 PHL	10 SA341 Gazelle	FMCVA/FMCVZ
3 PHAC	10 Alouette III	FMCVA/FMCVZ
4 PHM	7 Puma	FMCUA/FMCUZ
3 GALDiv (Freiburg, West Germany)		
1 PHL	10 Gazelle	FMCQA/FMCQZ
2 PHL	10 Alouette II	FMCMA/FMCMZ
3 PHAC	10 Alouette III	FMCRA/FMCRZ
4 PHM	7 Puma	FMAPA/FMAPZ
4 GALDiv (Verdun)		
1 PHL	10 Alouette II	FMCXA/FMCXZ
2 PHL	10 Alouette II	FMCXA/FMCXZ
3 PHAC	10 Alouette III	FMCXA/FMCXZ
4 PHM	7 Puma	FMCPA/FMCPZ
7 GALDiv (Mulhouse)		
1 PHL	10 Alouette II	FMBWA/FMBWZ
2 PHL	10 Alouette II	FMBWA/FMBWZ
3 PHAC	10 Alouette III	
4 PHM	7 Puma	FMBUA/FMBUZ
8 GALDiv (Compiègne)		
1 PHL	10 SA341 Gazelle	FMACA/FMACZ
2 PHL	10 SA341 Gazelle	FMACA/FMACZ
3 PHAC	10 Alouette III	FMACA/FMACZ
4 PHM	7 Puma	FMADA/FMADZ
11 GALDiv (Pau and Dinan)		
1 PHL	10 SA341 Gazelle	FMBPA/FMBPZ
2 PHL	10 SA341 Gazelle	FMBPA/FMBPZ
3 PHAC	10 Alouette III	FMBPA/FMBPZ
4 PHM	7 Puma	FMBQA/FMBQZ

GALDiv 11 is equipped for long-range intervention and maintains an extra Alouette Peloton at the amphibious operations HQ at Dinan, in addition to retaining the Broussard for liaison work (eg. 'BPA').

Note: Most units seem to have ten Pumas with the exception of 4 GALDiv which apparently has none, and only ten Alouette IIs.

GROUPE D'AVIATION LEGERE DE REGIONAL (GALReg)

Seven regional army headquarters have an attached Groupe for liaison and general duties. The Escadrilles Avions (EA) are the last users of fixed-wing aircraft in the ALAT, and are accompanied by an EHL. In addition, because of its increased workload as communications unit to 1 Region at Paris, 1 GALReg has a third squadron, designated Escadrille Helicoptères. Bases are:—

		Callsign range
1 GALReg (Mureaux)		
EA	2 Broussard,	FMABX
	5 Cessna L-19	FMAFA/FMAFR
EHL	4 SA431 Gazelle	FMABA·
		FMAFS/FMAFZ
EH	Alouette III	FMABB/FMABG
2 GALReg (Lille-Lesquin)		
EA	2 Broussard,	
	5 Cessna L-19	FMAMN/FMAMZ
EHL	4 Alouette II	FMAMA/FMAMM
3 GALReg (Rennes)		
EA	2 Broussard,	FMAGA/FMAGB
	5* Cessna L-19	FMAGN/FMAGZ
EHL	4 Alouette II	FMAGC/FMAGM
4 GALReg (Bordeaux)		
EA	2 Broussard,	
	5 Cessna L-19	FMAQA/FMAQM
EHL	4 Alouette II	FMAQN/FMAQZ
6 GALReg (Metz)		
EA	2 Broussard,	
	5 Cessna L-19	FMAOA/FMAOM
EHL	4 Alouette II	FMAON/FMAOZ
8 GALReg (Lyon-Corbas)		
EA	2 Broussard,	FMAHP/FMAHR
	5 Cessna L-19	FMAHA/FMAHE
EHL	4 Alouette II	FMAHJ/FMAHO
		FMAHS/FMAHZ
	2 Alouette III	FMAHH/FMAHJ
9 GALReg (Aix-en-Provence)		
EA	2 Broussard,	
	5* Cessna L-19	FMATA/FMATR and TZ
EHL	4 Alouette II	FMATS/FMATY

*Actual observation indicates approximately ten Cessnas.

In 1977, aircraft strength was given as 229 Alouette II, eighty-four Alouette III, 130 Puma, 140 Gazelle, eighty-five Bell 47 and 200 fixed-wing aircraft. The Bell 47 total appears suspect unless this number were in storage.

ALAT Operational Units - 1979

In 1976, it was decided to re-structure the Armée de Terre with the object of deleting the brigade as a battle formation, thus shortening the chain of command to units in the field. During the period of the fourth 5-year plan, Fr. 156,930m will be expended on the army in increasing amounts (eg. Fr. 18,400m in 1977 to Fr. 35,170m in 1980) enabling (amongst other things) the previously static territorial defence forces to become mobile.

By late 1979, the Corps, Divisional and Regional air units (GALCA, GALDiv and GALReg) will have been broken up and re-integrated as front-line Régiments d'Helicoptères de Combat (RHC) or regional Groupes d'Helicoptères Légers (GHL). The RHC will be much larger than the GALDiv which it replaces, but with emphasis now on the imbalance in tank strengths between NATO and the Warsaw Pact, the principal increase will be a 300% improvement in the anti-tank capability. The new formations are listed as follows:--

1979 Command Structure

'COMALAT'
Commandement ALAT
(HQ: Villacoublay)

FRONT-LINE GROUPS:

'COMALCA 1'
(HQ: Metz)
- 1 RHC
- 3 RHC
- 6 RHC
- 11 RHC

'COMALCA 2'
(HQ: Baden)
- 2 RHC
- 4 RHC
- .. GHL
- E CC FFA

SUPPORT GROUPS:

GROUPEMENT ALAT 103
(HQ: Versailles)
- 1 GHL
- 2 GHL
- 3 GHL
- EEAC

GROUPEMENT ALAT 104
(HQ: Aix-en Provence)
- 5 RHC
- 4 GHL
- 5 GHL
- 6 RAMA
- E EAA
- E EAI
- GM EA

COMALCA = Commandement d'Aviation Légère de Corps d'Armée

Army Organisation 1979

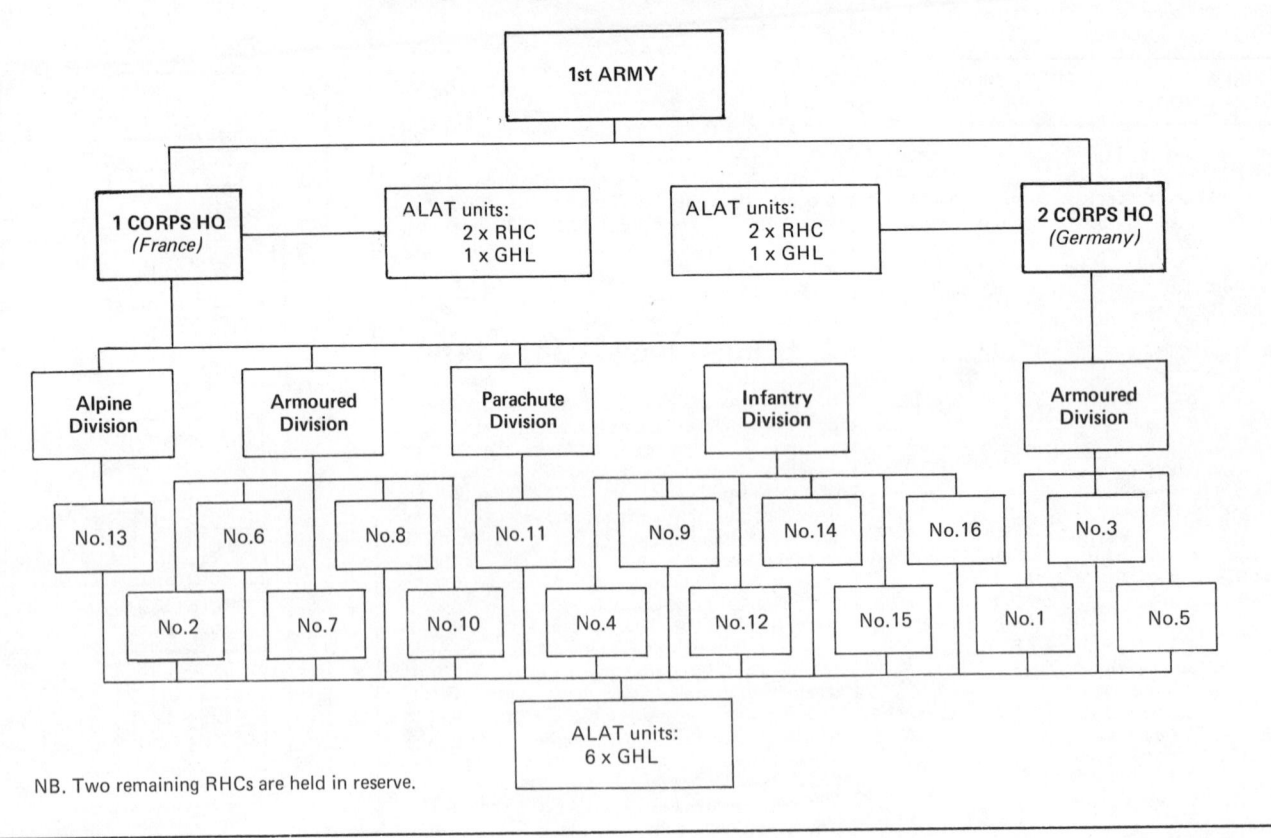

- **1st ARMY**
  - **1 CORPS HQ** *(France)*
    - ALAT units: 2 x RHC, 1 x GHL
    - Alpine Division
      - No.13
      - No.2
    - Armoured Division
      - No.6
      - No.7
      - No.8
      - No.10
    - Parachute Division
      - No.11
      - No.4
  - **2 CORPS HQ** *(Germany)*
    - ALAT units: 2 x RHC, 1 x GHL
    - Infantry Division
      - No.9
      - No.12
      - No.14
      - No.15
      - No.16
    - Armoured Division
      - No.3
      - No.1
      - No.5

ALAT units: 6 x GHL

NB. Two remaining RHCs are held in reserve.

REGIMENT D'HELICOPTERES DE COMBAT (RHC)

Six RHCs will assume the previous responsibilities of the disbanded GALDivs and will form, three in 1977, two in 1978 and one in 1979. Each will comprise a Commandement (HQ), an Escadrille de Soutien et Ravitaillement (supply and provision squadron) and seven Escadrilles of helicopters designated in the same manner as previously. Official statements indicate that all three EHAC will be equipped with the SA342 Gazelle/HOT anti-tank missile, but this is incompatible with the intention to retain the Alouette III/SS11 in some small measure, and it is possible that for the time being one EHAC will retain the Alouette until the SS11 becomes obsolete. Callsigns for the new formations contain a few alterations, but are basically the same as previously. Probable code ranges are given, but are as yet unconfirmed. For example, 2 RHC formed on 1 July 1978 with two escadrilles of Alouette III (AUK-AUS, AVA-AVI) and two of SA341 Gazelles (AUA-AUJ, CMA-CMJ), the Pumas of the former 3 GALDiv having been apparently withdrawn. It will obviously be some time before the RHCs achieve their authorised strength. Note, some units will have the SA341M substituting for the SA342.

1 RHC — COMALCA 1 (Phalsbourg)
  1 EHL   10 SA341 Gazelle
  2 EHL   10 SA341 Gazelle
  1 EHAC 12 SA342 Gazelle
  2 EHAC 12 SA342 Gazelle
  3 EHAC 12 SA342 Gazelle
            or Alouette III
  1 EHM   11 Puma
  2 EHM   11 Puma
Probable callsign ranges: FMCYA etc.

2 RHC — COMALCA 2 (Freiburg)
  1 EHL   10 SA341 Gazelle
  2 EHL   10 SA341 Gazelle
  1 EHAC 12 SA342 Gazelle
  2 EHAC 12 SA342 Gazelle
  3 EHAC 12 SA342 Gazelle
            or Alouette III
  1 EHM   11 Puma
  2 EHM   11 Puma
Probable callsign ranges: FMAUA, 'AVA, 'CMA

3 RHC — COMALCA 1 (Etain)
  1 EHL   10 SA341 Gazelle
  2 EHL   10 SA341 Gazelle
  1 EHAC 12 SA342 Gazelle
  2 EHAC 12 SA342 Gazelle
  3 EHAC 12 SA342 Gazelle
            or Alouette III
  1 EHM   11 Puma
  2 EHM   11 Puma
Probable callsign ranges: FMCPA, 'CXA etc.

4 RHC — COMALCA 2 (Trier)
  1 EHL   10 SA341 Gazelle
  2 EHL   10 SA341 Gazelle
  1 EHAC 12 SA342 Gazelle
  2 EHAC 12 SA342 Gazelle
  3 EHAC 12 SA342 Gazelle
            or Alouette III
  1 EHM   11 Puma
  2 EHM   11 Puma
Probable callsign ranges: FMCUA, 'CVA etc.

6 RHC — COMALCA 1 (Compiègne)
  1 EHL   10 SA341 Gazelle
  2 EHL   10 SA341 Gazelle
  1 EHAC 12 SA342 Gazelle
  2 EHAC 12 SA342 Gazelle
  3 EHAC 12 SA342 Gazelle
  1 RHM   11 Puma
  2 RHM   11 Puma
Probable callsign ranges: FMACA, 'ADA etc.

5 RHC — GA 104 (Pau)
  1 EHL   10 SA341 Gazelle
  2 EHL   10 SA341 Gazelle
  1 EHAC 12 SA342 Gazelle
  2 EHAC 12 SA342 Gazelle
  3 EHAC 12 SA342 Gazelle
  1 EHM   11 Puma
  2 EHM   11 Puma
Probable callsign ranges: FMBPA, 'BQA etc.

GROUPE D'HELICOPTERS LEGERS (GHL)

The GHL will replace both the GALCA and the GALReg by providing a detachment of liaison, observation and casualty evacuation helicopters to both the army corps and the military regions of France. Two strengths of GHL are envisaged:—

(a) Corps GHL
Two Groupes will replace the liaison element of GALCAs 1 and 2 but not their previously allocated assault helicopters or anti-tank helicopters.

GHL (Phalsbourg)
  EHL   10 SA341 Gazelle
  EHL   10 Alouette II
  EHL   10 Alouette III
Probable callsign ranges: FMAEA etc.

GHL (Freidrichshafen)
  EHL   10 SA341 Gazelle
  EHL   10 Alouette II
  EHL   10 Alouette III
Probable callsign ranges: FMASA etc.

(b) Regional GHL
A formation of twenty helicopters will be allocated to the military regions for liaison. These will replace the GALRegs with the exception of No. 6 at Metz which will be served by the GHL at Phalsbourg. 6 GALReg will move to Nancy to become 11 GHL and 9 GALReg has been replaced by the GdM EA ALAT situated at its former base of Aix-en-Provence. The flight at Mureaux (1 GHL) may possibly remain above normal strength because of its association with the COMALAT (HQ) at Villacoublay.

1 GHL — GA 103 (Mureaux)
  EH   10 SA341 Gazelle
  EH   10 Alouette II
Probable callsign ranges: FMABA, 'AFA etc.

2 GHL — GA 103 (Lesquin)
  EH   10 SA341 Gazelle
  EH   10 Alouette II
Probable callsign ranges: FMAMA etc.

3 GHL — GA 103 (Rennes)
EH   10 SA341 Gazelle
EH   10 Alouette II
Probable callsign ranges: FMAGA etc.
4 GHL — GA 104 (Bordeaux)
EH   10 SA341 Gazelle
EH   10 Alouette II
Probable callsign ranges: FMAQA etc.
5 GHL — GA 104 (Corbas)
EH   10 SA341 Gazelle
EH   10 Alouette II
Probable callsign ranges: FMAHA etc.
11 GHL — COMALCA 1 (Nancy)
EH   10 SA341 Gazelle
EH   10 Alouette II
Probable callsign ranges: FMAOA etc.

Note: 5 GHL combines the airborne elements of the Alpine brigades. A flight of four Alouette II was previously attached to 17 Alpine Brigade at Gap Tallard and a further six Alouette II/III to 27 Alpine Brigade at Le Versoux/Grenoble, the latter having callsigns F-MBGA/F-MBGZ. The Brigades have now been disbanded, but the Alpine Division now comprises the 5^e and 7^e Demi-Brigades to which the helicopters are attached.

Other Units

Several other ALAT units remain largely unaffected by the re-structuring:

DETACHEMENT D'HELICOPTERES ARMES, DJIBOUTI TFAI DU 6^e RAMA — GA 104

Although the Territory of the Afars and Issas (of which the city of Djibouti is capital) received its independence on 27 June 1977, the French presence has been strengthened rather than reduced as a result of the hostile intentions of its neighbour countries. The DHA, formed on 1 July 1972 to replace the H-34 helicopters of GOM 88 which were withdrawn the same month, now has on strength an undisclosed number of Alouette II and Pumas, coded in the range F-MKBA/F-MKBZ. (See also Armée de l'Air units EC 11 and ETOM 88 and Aéronavale aircraft carrier dispositions.)

ESCADRILLE ALAT ECOLE D'APPLICATION ARTILLERIE (EEAA) — GA 104

The Artillery school at Chalons-sur-Marne operates a flight of Alouette II in the range F-MCAA/F-MCAZ. The Bell 47 and Nord 3400 have been recently retired.

ESCADRILLE ALAT ECOLE D'APPLICATION, ACADEMIE DE CAVALERIE (EEAC) — GA 103

A flight of Alouette II attached to the Cavalry School at Saumur uses codes F-MCBA/F-MCBZ.

ESCADRILLE ALAT ECOLE D'APPLICATION INFANTRIE (EEAI) — GA 104

The infantry school at Montpellier used the Nord 3400 until recently, but the replacement type, if any, is not known. Codes allocated are F-MCCA/F-MCCZ.

ESCADRILLE ALAT DU COMMANDEMENT CENTRALE FORCES FRANCAIS ALLEMAGNE (ECCFFA) — COMALCA 2

The headquarters of French forces in Germany at Baden-Baden has a communications flight using several types. Examples are Alouette III F-MCWB, Cessna L-19 F-MCWC/WD/WE, Broussard F-MCWM/WP, SA341 F-MCWR/WV.

GROUPEMENT ALAT SECTION TECHNIQUE DE L'ARMEE DE TERRE

Established at Satory in 1954 as the Groupe d'Experimental ALAT, this experimental unit was transferred to its present base of Valence on 1 January 1966. GALSTA undertakes operational trials of all ALAT equipment with a pilot strength of fifteen officers and fourteen NCOs of which one is permanently detached to the CEV and another to the EPNER. Aircraft in use are two Puma (F-MBST/SV), three Alouette III (F-MBSJ/F-MBSM), four Gazelle (eg. F-MBSC/SE/SG), one Alouette II (F-MBSA), one Cessna L-19 (F-MBTQ) and one Broussard.

GROUPE DE MANOEUVRE DE L'ECOLE D'APPLICATION (GALAT 104)

Formed in 1977, the GMEA is a detached flight of the Ecole d'Application based at Aix-en-Provence and operating eight Pumas (possibly F-MBZA/F-MBZH) with Gazelles in prospect for later delivery. Aix is the headquarters of GALAT 104 and the unit replaces the disbanded 9 GAL Reg.

DIRECTION CENTRAL DU MATERIEL

The DCM is responsible for the storage and issue of all army equipment from depots at Paris and Bourges. The code range F-MMAA/F-MMJZ is occasionally used and recently noted types have been the Gazelle (F-MMAG, MDE, MDT), Nord 3400 (F-MMAB), Alouette III (F-MMDF), Puma (F-MMDG) and Broussard (F-MMAA, MGA and MJA, the latter apparently attached to 2 RHC).

OTHER OVERSEAS UNITS

A total of fifty-six helicopters is operated by army units in the overseas commands, which are: West Indies, West Africa, Central Africa, Afars and Issas (mentioned separately), Indian Ocean, New Caledonia and Polynesia. Callsigns for overseas units are in the range F-MKAA/F-MKCZ and have included the Dakar-based Tri-Pacers 'KAA-KAI' and Chad detachment of Pumas 'KCA-KCL' and Cessna L-19 'KCY-KCZ' both of which have now been withdrawn. Gendarmerie forces overseas operate Alouette II helicopters in the series F-MCSA/F-MCSZ.

Flying Training Schools

ECOLE DE SPECIALISATION

Flying training up to 'wings' standard is undertaken at the ESALAT at Dax on its fleet of one hundred aircraft and helicopters. The school instructs army officers and NCOs and also prospective pilots from the Aéronavale and some overseas countries. Training commences with familiarisation flying (as a passenger) on the Cessna L-19, followed by fifteen hours navigation training, 115 hours/twenty-two weeks on the Alouette II, after which officers only undertake forty hours/nine weeks observation training. All ranks then proceed to twenty hours/three weeks with the Gazelle at which stage 'wings' are awarded after the officers have completed 190 hours/thirty-eight weeks and the NCOs 150 hours/twenty-nine weeks.

The school has several ranges of codes attached, some of which have fallen into disuse:—

F-MAIA/F-MAJZ	Not used (ex Nord 3202)
F-MAKA/F-MALZ	Not used (ex Super Cub)
F-MBCA/F-MBCZ	Not used (ex Bell 47)
F-MBDA/F-MBDZ	Gazelle
F-MBIA/F-MBIZ	Alouette II
F-MBJA/F-MBJZ	Alouette II
F-MBVA/F-MBVZ	Alouette II
F-MCTA/F-MCTZ	L-19 and Broussard

Authorised strength is sixty Alouette II, ten Gazelle, nineteen Cessna L-19 and two Broussards, although an Alouette III (F-MBDB) has also been noted.

ECOLE D'APPLICATION

The EAALAT runs several advanced flying courses for army pilots at its base of Luc-Le Cannet des Maures. Here, officers will follow their qualification as pilots with a eighteen hour/three week course of 'pilotage tactique' or low level flying under operational conditions, and all ranks may return to qualify as a helicopter commander (Chef de Bord) requiring forty hours/ten weeks, a Puma co-pilot needing thirty-five hours/seven weeks, or after two years Puma experience to pass-out as a pilot, this requiring fifty-five hours/nine weeks including simulator and blind flying.

Aircraft types and codes are:—

F-MAXA/F-MAXZ	Gazelle
F-MAYA/F-MAYX	Broussard
F-MBAA/F-MBAZ	Puma
F-MBBA/F-MBBZ	Alouette II

A flight of eight Pumas is operated from Aix-en-Provence on behalf of the GALAT 104 HQ (see Groupement de Manoeuvre de l'EAALAT).

Note:

The following **Air Defence Squadrons** are known to be equipped with *Matra R.440 Crotale SAMs:*

Escadron		
	01/950	Istres
	02/950	Avord
	03/950	Apt

ALAT Callsigns

The series of callsigns listed have been employed by the ALAT during the last few years. Information on the type of aircraft using each series will be found in the 'Unit Organisation' section.

Callsign range	Unit/Operator	
F-MABA/F-MABZ	GALReg 1	
F-MACA/F-MACZ	GALDiv 8	
F-MADA/F-MADZ	GALDiv 8	
F-MAEA/F-MAEZ	GALCA 1	
F-MAFA/F-MAFZ	GALReg 1	
F-MAGA/F-MAGZ	GALReg 3	
F-MAHA/F-MAHZ	GALReg 5	
F-MAIA/F-MAIZ	ESALAT	
F-MAJA/F-MAJZ	ESALAT	
F-MAKA/F-MAKZ	ESALAT	disused
F-MALA/F-MALZ	ESALAT	disused
F-MAMA/F-MAMZ	GALReg 2	
F-MAOA/F-MAOZ	GALReg 6	
F-MAPA/F-MAPZ	GALDiv 3	
F-MAQA/F-MAQZ	GALReg 4	
F-MARA/F-MARZ	GALReg 3	disused
F-MASA/F-MASZ	GALCA 2	
F-MATA/F-MATZ	GALReg 9	
F-MAUA/F-MAUZ	2 RHC	
F-MAVA/F-MAVZ	2 RHC (ex EALAT 9 Brigade)	
F-MAXA/F-MAXZ	EAALAT	
F-MAYA/F-MAYZ	EAALAT	
F-MBAA/F-MBAZ	EAALAT	
F-MBBA/F-MBBZ	EAALAT	
F-MBCA/F-MBCZ	ESALAT	disused
F-MBDA/F-MBDZ	ESALAT	
F-MBGA/F-MBGZ	EALAT 27 Brigade	
F-MBHA/F-MBHZ	CISALAT	disbanded 1974
F-MBIA/F-MBIZ	ESALAT	
F-MBJA/F-MBJZ	ESALAT	
F-MBPA/F-MBPZ	GALDiv 11	
F-MBQA/F-MBQZ	GALDiv 11	
F-MBRA/F-MBRZ	PMAH (Phillipeville)	disbanded
F-MBSA/F-MBSZ	GALSTA	
F-MBTA/F-MNTZ	GALSTA	
F-MBUA/F-MBUZ	GALDiv 7	
F-MBVA/F-MBVZ	ESALAT	
F-MBWA/F-MBWZ	GALDiv 7	
F-MBZA/F-MBZZ	not known (Puma)	
F-MCAA/F-MCAZ	EALAT EAA	
F-MCBA/F-MCBZ	EALAT EA ABC	
F-MCCA/F-MCCZ	EALAT AEI	
F-MCDA/F-MCDZ	EALAT EAT	disbanded 1974
F-MCMA/F-MCMZ	GALDiv 3	
F-MCPA/F-MCPZ	GALDiv 4	disused
F-MCQA/F-MCQZ	GALDiv 3 (replaced in 2 PHL by F-MCMA/Z)	
F-MCRA/F-MCRZ	GALDiv 3	
F-MCSA/F-MCSZ	GFGOM	
F-MCTA/F-MCTZ	ESALAT	
F-MCUA/F-MCUZ	GALDiv 1	
F-MCVA/F-MCVZ	GALDiv 1	
F-MCWA/F-MCWZ	EALAT CC FFA	
F-MCXA/F-MCXZ	GALDiv 4	
F-MCYA/F-MCYZ	GALCA 1	
F-MCZA/F-MCZZ	not known (Gazelle)	
F-MJAA/F-MJBZ	see appendix on Gendarmerie	
F-MKAA/F-MKAZ	DMTMZOM (Dakar)	disbanded
F-MKBA/F-MKBZ	DHA.TFAI	
F-MKCA/F-MKCZ	DMTMZOM (Chad)	disbanded
F-MMAA/F-MMHZ	DCM	

Note:
GFGOM - Commandement des Forces de Gendarmerie Outre Mer.
DMTMZOM - Départment du Matériel des Troupes de Marine Zone d'Outre Mer.
PMAH - Peloton Mixte Avions-Helicoptères.
DHA.TFAI - Detachment d'Helicoptères Armés, Terretoire Français des Affars et Issas (Djibouti).

Part Five

Other Services

Gendarmerie

What in Britain would be regarded as 'police duties' are in France divided amongst three agencies, the Police Nationale, the CRS and the Gendarmerie. This apparent proliferation of law-enforcement agencies serves to segregate the armed forces from civilian areas of responsibility and equally ensures that the police do not need to involve themselves with affairs of a political nature such as demonstrations. The areas of operations are as below:--

(a) La Police Nationale. Civilian police under the Ministère de l'Intérieur. See the 'F-ZBDx' aircraft listed under 'Sécurité Civile'.

(b) Les Compagnies Republicaines de Sécurité (CRS). Also civilian, the CRS is organised into platoons and companies and is responsible for security at large airports, the anti-riot squad, anti-terrorist forces, assistance of motorway police at busy periods and life-saving detachments on the coast. No aircraft are used.

(c) Gendarmerie. Essentially military, the Gendarmerie acts as a civilian police force in peacetime and becomes the military police when the nation is mobilised. Manning some 10,000 posts throughout rural France and organised into fourteen areas: Alsace, Aquitaine, Basse-Normandie, Bourgogne, Bretagne, Centre, Champagne, Corse, Franche Comté, Limousin, Languedoc-Roussillon, Midi-Pyrénées, Picardie and Rhôn-Alpes (as illustrated below). The Gendarmerie also has various specialist sections, namely the 1, 2 and 3 Groupements Blinde de Gendarmerie Mobile (Mobile Armoured Gendarmerie), Commandement des Ecoles de Gendarmerie (Training Command), Centre Administratif et Technique de la Gendarmerie Nationale (Administration and Technical Centre), Gendarmerie Republicane de Paris, Gendarmerie de l'Air (Military Air Police), Gendarmerie des Transports Aériens (Civil Air Police), Musique de la Garde Republicane de Paris, and the Formation d'Helicoptères de la Gendarmerie.

FORMATION D'HELICOPTERES DE LA GENDARMERIE

Air operations are supervised by the FHG, both at home and overseas. The badge of an Alouette over mountain peaks appears on aircraft and helicopters, but may on occasion be replaced by one of the fourteen area command insignia. As with ALAT aircraft, the last three letters of the callsign are applied to Gendarmerie machines, these in the series F-MJAA to F-MJBZ for units at home and F-MCSA to F-MCSZ for overseas posts, the latter being Antilles/Guyana, Berlin, Polynesia and Indian Ocean (Djibouti having recently disbanded). Codes are frequently re-allocated, and it is notable that Alouette II helicopters purchases in military contracts are augmented by direct procurement.

The current Gendarmerie 'register', on which aircraft are sometimes re-allocated, is given on the next page, together with previous allocations and two known examples of overseas usage.

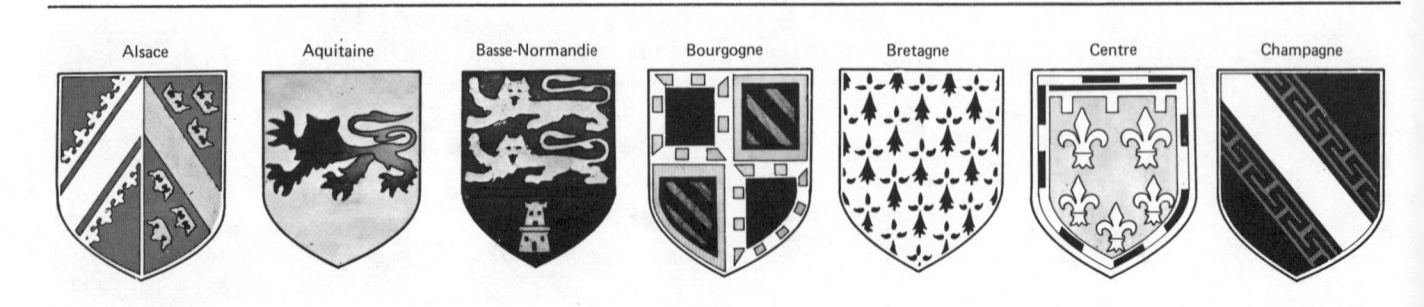

Serial	Type	C/n	
F-MJAA	U.206	2126	ex N71171, F-BRGI
F-MJAB	U.206	2147	ex N71140, F-BRGJ
F-MJAC	U.206	2193	ex N7405Q, F-BRGL
F-MJAD	Alouette II	1285	
F-MJAE	U.206	2173	ex N7325Q, F-BRGK
F-MJAF	U.206	2125	ex N71163, F-BRGH
F-MJAG	Alouette II	1654	
F-MJAH	Alouette II	1087	
F-MJAI	Alouette II	2154	
F-MJAJ	U.206	2194	ex N7411Q, F-BRGM
F-MJAK	Alouette III	1678	
F-MJAL	Alouette II	1729	
F-MJAM	Alouette II	1212	
F-MJAN	Alouette II	1716	
F-MJAO	Alouette II	1628	ex F-MJBD
F-MJAP	Alouette II	1717	ex F-MJBA
F-MJAQ	Alouette II	2022	
F-MJAR	Alouette II	1234	
F-MJAS	Alouette II		
F-MJAT	Alouette II	2153	
F-MJAU	Alouette II	1815?	
F-MJAV	Alouette II	1671	
F-MJAW			
F-MJAX	Alouette II	1807	
F-MJAY	Alouette II	1517	
F-MJAZ	Alouette II	1443	
F-MJBA	Alouette II	1715	
F-MJBB	Alouette II	1518	ex F-MJAV
F-MJBC	Alouette II	1806	
F-MJBD	Alouette II	1247	
F-MJBE	Alouette III	1160	
F-MJBF	Alouette III	1098	
F-MJBG			
F-MJBH			
F-MJBI	Alouette II		
F-MJBJ	Alouette II		
F-MJBK	Alouette II	2280	
F-MJBL	Alouette III	2009	
F-MJBM	Alouette III	2010	
F-MJBN	Alouette III	2033	
F-MJBO	Alouette III	2045	
F-MJBP	Alouette III	2057	
F-MJBQ			
F-MJBR			
F-MJBS			
F-MJBT			
F-MJBU			
F-MJBV	Nord 3400	96	
F-MJBW	Nord 3400	99	
F-MJBX	Nord 3400	105	
F-MJBY	Nord 3400	108	
F-MJBZ			

Previous allocations:

F-MJAB	A. Bell 47G	190	to F-GALT
F-MJAC	A. Bell 47G	191	to F-BTGQ
F-MJAE	A. Bell 47G	197	Written off 5.5.72
F-MJAF	A. Bell 47G	198	to F-BTGR
F-MJAO	A. Bell 47G	203	to F-BXXY
F-MJAP	Alouette II	1335	to F-MACN
F-MJAQ	Alouette II	1097	
F-MJAR	Alouette II	1758	
F-MJAT	Alouette II	1772	
F-MJAU	Alouette II	1093	
F-MJAV	Alouette II	1518	to F-MJBB
F-MJAW	Alouette II	1117	Written off 13.6.73
F-MJBA	Alouette II	1717	to F-MJAP
F-MJBD	Alouette II	1628	to F-MJAO
F-MJBG	Alouette III	1122	to F-MJBO
F-MJBH	Alouette II	1875	to F-MSCH
F-MJBO	Alouette II	1813	
F-MJBO	Alouette III	1122	ex F-MJBG

Gendarmerie Outre Mer

F-MCSH	Lama	315-09	ex F-MJBH
F-MCSI	Alouette II	2275	

Corse — Franche Comté  — Limousin  — Languedoc-Roussillon  — Midi Pyrénées  — Picardie  — Rhôn-Alpes

Sécurité Civile

Established under the title Protection Civile, the unit became the Sécurité Civile in 1976. Part of the Ministère de l'Intérieur and thus unconnected with the military, it nevertheless performs some functions which in other countries would be allocated to military forces.

Helicopters are used for coastguard, lighthouse and SAR duties, leaving the Gendarmerie to specialise in mountain rescue. The Canadair CL-215 (and previously the Catalina) is used for forest firefighting usually with a helicopter as co-ordinator, and flights are also undertaken on behalf of the Paris fire brigade by two ex-Gendarmerie Alouettes. Medevac is a third function, either from accident locations or the transfer of critical patients to special installations, eg. Central Lyons major burns hospital.

The F-ZBxx series is used for identification, the marks being painted on the aircraft, though the series F-ZBCA/CZ is not used by the Sécurité Civile. Also included in the series are a few aircraft used by the Customs (Douane), and Préfecture de Police. Current allocations are:—

Serial	Type	C/n	
F-ZBAA	PA-31 Navajo		
F-ZBAB	Alouette III	1353	ex F-BJHN
F-ZBAC	Alouette II	1407	ex F-BJOI
F-ZBAD	Alouette II	1451	ex F-BIFY
F-ZBAE	Alouette II	1550	ex F-BIFK
F-ZBAF	Alouette II	1647	ex F-BIET
F-ZBAG	Alouette III	1517	ex EI-ATO
F-ZBAH	Alouette III		
F-ZBAI	Alouette III		
F-ZBAJ			
F-ZBAK			
F-ZBAL			
F-ZBAM			
F-ZBAN	Alouette II	1820	
F-ZBAO	Alouette II	1867	
F-ZBAP	Aero Commander 680F	972-29	ex F-BJOM
F-ZBAQ			
F-ZBAR	CL-215	1021	
F-ZBAS			
F-ZBAT	Alouette II	1907	
F-ZBAU	Alouette II	1927	
F-ZBAV	Alouette III	1192	ex F-ZBAS
F-ZBAW	Alouette III	2306	
F-ZBAX			
F-ZBAY	CL-215	1023	
F-ZBAZ			
F-ZBBA	Alouette II	1773	Customs
F-ZBBB	Alouette II	1828	Customs
F-ZBBC	Alouette III	1791	
F-ZBBD	CL-215	1029	
F-ZBBE	CL-215	1005	ex CF-PQJ-X, CF-YWN
F-ZBBF	Dornier Do.28A-1	3032	Customs ex D-IBEH
F-ZBBG			
F-ZBBH	CL-215	1026	
F-ZBBI	CL-215	1027	
F-ZBBJ	CL-215	1028	
F-ZBBK	Dornier Do.28B	3111	Customs ex D-IBAC
F-ZBBL	Dornier Do.28B	3112	Customs ex F-IFAB
F-ZBBM			
F-ZBBN	Do.28B	3120	Customs
F-ZBBO	Alouette III	1793	
F-ZBBP	Alouette III	1795	
F-ZBBQ	Alouette III	1798	
F-ZBBR	CL-215	1001	ex CF-FEU-X
F-ZBBS	Alouette III	1978	
F-ZBBT	CL-215	1040	
F-ZBBU	Aero Commander	1082?	
F-ZBBV	CL-215	1046	ex C-GAOS
F-ZBBW	CL-215	1047	
F-ZBBX	Rallye	12532	
F-ZBBY	Rallye		
F-ZBBZ			
F-ZBDA			
F-ZBDB			
F-ZBDC	Alouette III	1435	Prefecture de Police on loan to Paris Fire Brigade.
F-ZBDD	CL-215	1024	
F-ZBDE	Alouette III	1630	ex Portuguese AF
F-ZBDF	Alouette III	1646	ex Port AF 9346
F-ZBDG	Alouette III	1749	ex Port AF 9357
F-ZBDH	Alouette III	1784	ex Port AF 9366
F-ZBDI			
F-ZBDJ			
F-ZBDK	Alouette III	2164	

Previous allocations are:

F-ZBAA	Alouette II	1165	ex F-BIFM
F-ZBAG	A. Bell 47G	*	
F-ZBAG	Alouette II	1517	ex/to F-MJAY
F-ZBAH	A. Bell 47G	1464	ex F-BHMG; to F-BTOH
F-ZBAI	A. Bell 47G	*	
F-ZBAJ	A. Bell 47G	217	ex F-BICA; to F-BIEH
F-ZBAK	Alouette II	1744	to F-BGDT
F-ZBAL	Alouette III	1036	written off
F-ZBAM	Alouette II	1819	to Lama C/n 1819/11 F-GAMF
F-ZBAQ	Catalina		
F-ZBAV	Catalina		
F-ZBAW	Catalina		
F-ZBAX	CL-215	1022	written off 4.7.70
F-ZBAZ	Catalina		ex CF-IZZ
F-ZBBG	CL-215	1025	written off
F-ZBBM	CL-215	1019	ex CF-TXM, written off 25.7.73
F-ZBBO	MH 1521	020M	ex F-ZWUA, F-MBCA; to F-MAYU
F-ZBBP	MH 1521	022M	to F-MAYS
F-ZBDB	Alouette II	1988	Paris Fire Brigade; to F-GBDV

* These two aircraft are c/n 1275 ex F-BGSS and 1465 ex F-BHKZ.

CEAM
CENTRE D'EXPERIMENTATIONS
AERIENNES MILITAIRES - EMAA

Under direct control of the Etat Major of the Armée de l'Air, the CEAM undertakes evaluation and research on all air force aircraft and ground equipment.

CEAM also trains operational pilots in the operation of new fighter aircraft, and it is usual that the first squadron to convert to a new type does so at Mont-de-Marsan under CAFDA controlled Escadre de Chasse 24/118. Routine research is carried out by CEAM 332 and support duties are undertaken by Escadron de Transport et de Liaison 26/118.

Aircraft codes, callsigns and unit types are:—

118-AA/118-AZ	F-SDAA/F-SDAZ	EC 24/118 (Mirage AA, AB; Jaguar AC, AF, AG, AI, AJ, AV; Mirage F1 AK-AN).
118-BA/118-BZ	F-SDBA/F-SDBZ	CEAM 332 (Magister BE; Transall BS, BT).
118-DA/118-DZ	F-SDDA/F-SDDZ	ETL 26/118 light jet transports (Paris DA, DB; Magister DD, DG).
118-IA/118-IZ	F-SDIA/F-SDIZ	ETL 26/118 propellor transports (Noratlas ID IF; N262 IT; Broussard IU-IW).

Aircraft in the latter three series have previously used '332-' prefixes, known examples being Super Mystère 332-BB/F-SDBB, Paris 332-DA/F-SDDA and Flamant 332-IL/F-SDIL. The number of aircraft coded in these three ranges have been reduced in recent years.

CEV
CENTRE D'ESSAIS EN VOL

The CEV functions as a research establishment akin to the British RAE, and using both civil and military aircraft, whilst the CEAM is more a parallel of the A & AEE. At the Brétigny base, many varied types are tested before they enter service, and these are allocated callsigns in the F-Z range Usually the 'last two' only are carried. Blocks allocated to the CEV are:—

F-ZABA/F-ZAEZ
F-ZJAA/F-ZJNZ
F-ZJPA/F-ZJTZ

A full list of allocations will be found in Appendix 'A' 'The 'F-Z' Registration series'.

CNET
CENTRE NATIONAL D'ETUDES
DES TELECOMMUNCATIONS

Although purely civilian in function, (paralleling the British GPO Telecommunications) the CNET aircraft are maintained by the Armée de l'Air and accordingly are allocated military-type callsigns.

The C-47, Alouette II and Bell 47 are identified by their c/ns or serials, but the single Friendship is marked F-SEBF on the fin, in the manner of a civil registration. CNET aircraft are based at Lannion-Servel.

DCAN
DIRECTION DES CONSTRUCTIONS
ET ARMES NAVALES

The Naval Dockyards and Armaments administration operates a small flight of aircraft from Cuers and other bases for communications purposes, whilst in addition, the Bell 47 helicopter is used by the Establishment des Constructions et Armes Navales for torpedo trials at St. Tropez.

Aircraft of the DCAN have their own separate numbering system commencing CAN1 and upto 1972 these were allocated the callsigns F-YCZA/F-YCZP in alphabetical/numerical order. The batch was then changed to F-YEEA etc, and aircraft current at that time received a new identity. Aircraft used since the inception of the series are:

Serial	Callsign	Type	C/n	Remarks
CAN1	F-YCZA	MS 502		
CAN2	F-YCZB	Nord 1002 (?)		
CAN3	F-YCZC	Nord 1203	154	scrap 1968

99

CAN4	F-YCZD	Nord 1203	155
CAN5	F-YCZE	Bell 47	
CAN6	F-YCZF	Bell 47G2	040 to F-YEEA
CAN7	F-YCZG	Bell 47G2	056 to F-YEEB
CAN8	F-YCZH	NC856	
CAN9	F-YCZI	Nord 1101	132 to F-YEEC
CAN10	F-YCZJ	Nord 1101	125 to F-YEED
CAN11	F-YCZK	Nord 1101	139 to F-YEEE
CAN12	F-YCZL	Nord 1101	181 to F-YEEF
CAN13	F-YCZM	Nord 1101	184 w'drwn 1975
CAN14	F-YCZN	Nord 1101	192 to F-YEEG
CAN15	F-YCZO	Nord 1101	197 to F-YEEH
CAN16	F-YCZP	Broussard	to F-YEEI
CAN17	—	HR.100/250(?)	
CAN18	F-YEEK	HR.100/250 533	

ENSA
ECOLE NATIONALE SUPERIEURE D'AERONAUTIQUE

A section of the CEV devoted to engine proving at Istres, the unit has now retired its Constellation F-ZVMV to the Musée de l'Air and this has been replaced by Caravelle F-ZACF. Three Nord 262s F-ZVMH, F-ZVMI and F-ZVMJ are currently in service, with Robin DR300 F-ZVMG and Rallye F-ZVMF.

EPNER
ECOLE DU PERSONNEL NAVIGANT D'ESSAIS ET DE RECEPTION

The EPNER was formed in 1946 as the French military test pilots' school, taking as its insignia a parody of the 'School' traffic sign situated outside its original headquarters at Istres. Several types of aircraft and helicopter are employed. No code prefix is used. (Further details in Appendix 'E').

Code	Callsign	Aircraft types/examples
AA-AZ	F-ZLAA/F-ZLAZ	Alouette II & III, Mirage IIIA, ex Canberra.
GA-GZ	F-ZAGA/F-ZAGZ	Nord 262, Alouette II & III, Mirage IIIB, Puma, Magister, ex C-45.
OA-OZ	F-ZJOA/F-ZJOZ	Alouette II, Meteor, Paris, Nord 1101 and Flamant (SAR).

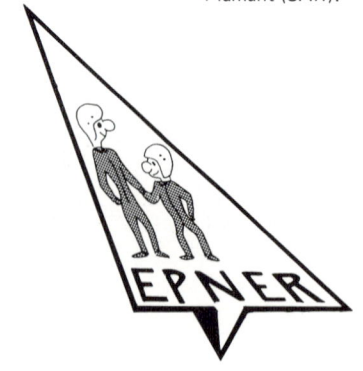

Insignia: On a yellow dart, two pilots in red overalls; helmets and faces white. Lettering and underside of dark blue.

Part Six

Aircraft Review

In this section will be found details of aircraft currently in French military service. The markings to be found on aircraft of the three services are summarised below.

Serial Numbers

Two methods of permanent identification are employed, the constructors number (c/n), and previous serial number.

The c/n and its function is familiar to aviation enthusiasts. In the case of a military aircraft type supplied exclusively to the Armée de l'Air these numbers are consecutive, e.g. the Mirage IV (Nos. 1 to 62). Production may be shared with another country, e.g. the Mirage IIIE, where certain aircraft were diverted to South Africa, Spain and Pakistan, and this has resulted in the gaps in the Armée de l'Air numbering sequence.

Occasionally the c/n is no indication of the time of entry into Air Force service, particularly with civil aircraft later taken up for military use. The widely differing c/ns of the Caravelles are sufficient evidence of this.

Aircraft prototypes or pre-production batches are allocated c/ns beginning with '00' or '0' but some care is required as this scheme is not standardised throughout the aircraft manufacturing industry. Officially, prototype c/ns begin at '001', pre-production at '01' and production aircraft at '1', this practice having been carried out properly on a civil aircraft, the Concorde. Some manufacturers will, however, label their prototypes from '01', and follow through to a 'production-type' series, whilst others begin pre-production correctly at '01', and omit the '0' once the full production series is commenced (viz 01 to 05, 6 onwards). Needless to say the upper limits of all three series will vary from type to type.

Prefixes to c/ns are unusual but not unknown. They include A and F prefixes to Transalls indicating pre-production and French deliveries respectively and manufacturer codes SKY and SA showing Sikorsky and licence-built Sud H-34s.

Markings and Radio Callsigns

Some general information on markings listed under l'Armée de l'Air is applicable to all three services.

ARMEE DE L'AIR

The representation of national insignia and data varies between types and manufacturers. Principal differences concern the tail insignia, which normally appeared on the rudder in the form of red, white and blue flashes, upon which were stencilled the aircraft manufacturer, mark number and c/n. In recent years the rudder flashes have been omitted from many aircraft and the c/n has often strayed to the fin or even rear fuselage on the Mirage IIIR. Reference to the illustrations will show ample variations, even among aircraft of the same manufacturer.

In the case of single-engined jets, the engine type and mark number is usually stencilled in the mid-fuselage position. Fighter types have now been camouflaged.

Five-letter callsigns are not generally applied in paint to aircraft except for the occasional Puma and experimental types in the F-Zxxx range. Their inclusion in the following listing is for the purpose of providing further information only.

AERONAVALE

Since 1 January 1976, naval aircraft have begun to be marked with the legend 'MARINE' on the fuselage side, the size of the characters varying as that of the aircraft. In addition, an anchor is superimposed on the national roundel.

No coding system is used and unlike several navies of the world the Aéronavale does not employ base or carrier code letters. Until 1961 the aircraft were marked with their unit designation and an identification number running onwards from 1 e.g. Alouette II c/n 1027 coded 58S-12. The aircraft constructors number is now used as the sole identity, and the unit with which it serves may only be determined by reference to the badge applied in the area of the cockpit. In rare cases the identity used is the last part of the previous serial or c/n where this is inconvenient because of its length.

Aéronavale Dakotas are a law unto themselves. Earlier deliveries used the last one or two numbers of the c/n or ex-USAF serial or Bu. number, but those later transferred from the Armée de l'Air have a three-figure identity comprising the first digit after the fiscal year, plus the last two, e.g. 44-76229 becomes '729'.

Callsigns are allocated in the F-XAAA to F-YZZZ range, with the first-line aircraft using 'F-X' and support units 'F-Y'; these are detailed in the section relating to individual units. In very rare cases codes have been applied to aircraft, but the only regular users of the callsign as a permanent identity are the Super Frelons of 32F and H-34s of 31F.

AVIATION LEGERE DE L'ARMEE DE TERRE

Army aircraft appear in olive drab with national roundels, but are devoid of insignia. Identification of units is by the last three letters of the callsign which are applied in white to the fuselage sides. In the following lists the 'F-M' prefix to the last three letters is given for reasons of clarity, but it should be borne in mind that this prefix is not worn on the aircraft or helicopter in question.

Aircraft Service Histories

Bearing in mind the changes in names of manufacturers due to take-overs and mergers, the various types are listed in alphabetical order, using what is believed to be the most common designation by which the aircraft is known.

In order to represent the information on individual aircraft in as concise a form as possible, the following conventions have been applied:-

1. Aircraft types with consecutive c/ns or serials:
    (a) Over 10-12 years service. Only the aircraft still in use or withdrawn after 1970 are listed, together with previous codes in which they may have been seen in the past few years.
    (b) For less than 10-12 year types, all c/ns are given.

2. Aircraft types with irregular c/ns or serials. All known aircraft are listed with recent codings.

Some aircraft will carry only part of their identity, and are shown as either:

(314-)WA i.e. only 'WA' appears, although the aircraft of the unit - GE 314 normally carry the number part of the coding, or

LA(65 E) - only 'LA' carried. The unit ET 65 does not mark any of its aircraft with numbers.

The following may be regarded as a comprehensive review of the individual aircraft currently in service, although brief service histories of another ten types withdrawn since 1970 are included for completeness of information and because in some instances a few examples remain in use for specialised duties. These withdrawn types are suffixed '(†)' in their respective heading, and it should be noted that their service code details follow the c/n (constructors number) in strict chronological order, whereas the *current* code/status on *serving* types has been extracted from an otherwise chronological sequence, to be presented first, i.e. immediately following its respective constructors number, and/or model no.

AEROSPATIALE (SOCATA) MS893 RALLYE

Employed by virtually every civilian flying club, the Rallye has additionally been used in small numbers by both the Aéronavale and Armée de l'Air, ENSA and Sécurité Civile. Naval aircraft are used for giving flying instruction to cadets, the first ten at the Ecole Navale at Lanvéoc-Poulmic to which they were delivered en masse on 18 April 1974, with the second batch of six on charge to the Section Experimental de Servitude de BAN St. Raphael for the use of the Course Préparatoire of the local Naval College. AdIA Rallyes were allocated to several communications squadrons in May 1975 for six months' evaluation as a Broussard replacement. They were sold in March 1976, and apparently no decision has yet been made as a result of these trials.

C/n	Model	Remarks
548	892A-150	CEV, ex F-BNBO
2462	893E-100S	62/Ecole Navale
2463	893E-100S	63/Ecole Navale
2464	893E-100S	64/Ecole Navale
2465	893E-100S	65/Ecole Navale
2466	893E-100S	66/Ecole Navale
2467	893E-100S	67/Ecole Navale
2468	893E-100S	68/Ecole Navale
2469	893E-100S	69/Ecole Navale
2470	893E-100S	70/Ecole Navale
2471	893E-100S	71/Ecole Navale
2582	893E-100ST	82/SES
2583	893E-100ST	83/SES
2584	893E-100ST	84/SES
2585	893E-100ST	85/SES
2586	893E-100ST	86/SES
2587	893E-100ST	87/SES
2601	893E-150ST	F-BXYO (sold), ex 312-B..
11438	893A	F-ZVMF/ENSA
12532	893E	F-ZBBK/Séc. Civile
12570	893E-180GT	F-BXYJ (sold), ex 65-CZ
12571	893E-180GT	F-BXYK (sold), ex 41-AZ
12572	893E-180GT	F-BXYL (sold), ex 43-BZ
12573	893E-180GT	F-BXYM (sold), ex312-B..
12574	893E-180GT	F-BXYN (sold), ex 44-CZ

AEROSPATIALE SA330 PUMA

The initial French order for the Puma was for 130 SA330B helicopters for the ALAT, followed by a further ten SA330H, an updated military production model. Additionally, the AdIA has received twenty-nine for the detachments of EH 67, GAM 56 at Evreux, and various overseas units, and including two VIP models for the GLAM. One extra aircraft will be ordered in fiscal 1979 for the Landes Missile Range as a support helicopter, and a further small order has been placed by the ALAT.

The prototype Puma flew on 15 April 1965, and the first production aircraft in September 1968, since which time the type has been supplied to many overseas airforces and to civilian contractors. In October 1977, the 500th Puma was delivered, and developments at that time included the twin-Makila-powered SA332 flown as a conversion of F-ZWWO in June 1977 under the temporary designation SA330Z. The prototype SA332-001 (which flew for the first time on 13 September 1978) uses the fuselage of c/n 1541. Late in 1977, a SA330R prototype, otherwise known as the SA331-001, was flown with a stretched cabin as the forerunner of the Super Puma, which the makers hope will be chosen by France, Britain, Germany and Italy as the new European Tactical Helicopter.

C/n	Callsign/Unit	Remarks
01	F-ZWWN	
02	F-ZWWO	
03	F-ZWWP	
04	F-BYAK	ex F-ZWWQ
05	F-ZWWR	To F-BRBU
06	F-ZWWS	
07	F-ZWWT	To c/n 1196
08	F-ZJUX	To XW241
1003		
1005	F-MBSV	ex F-ZKBL, F-BLOV
1006		ex F-ZKLO
1008		
1010		
1012	F-MBZB	
1013	F-MBAE	
1015	F-MBST	ex F-ZKBJ, F-MBAF
1017	F-MCYG	ex F-MBAG
1018	F-MBAH	
1020	F-MAPR	ex F-MBAI
1021	F-MCYG	ex F-MBAJ
1023	F-MBUN	
1024	(F-ZLAX)/EPNER	ex F-MBUO
1027	F-MBUQ	
1028	F-MBUR	
1029	F-MBUF	ex F-MBUS
1031		
1032		ex F-MADD
1034		
1036		
1037		
1038	F-MBUO	
1041	F-MCYR	
1043	F-MCYI	
1047	F-MCYU	
1049		
1051		
1052	F-MBSV	
1055		
1056	F-MCUD	
1057		
1060		
1062		
1063	F-ZKBK	
1066	F-MADD	
1067		
1069		
1071		
1073		
1075	F-MMDG	
1078		ex F-MCYZ
1079		

103

C/n	Callsign	Remarks
1081		
1085		
1087		
1088	F-MBAJ	
1092		
1093	F-ZKBT	
1094	F-MAPQ	
1100		
1102		
1103	F-MAPS	
1107	F-MBUM	
1108	F-MBQB	ex F-MCUJ
1109	F-MAPU	
1114	F-ZKBA	
1115	F-MAPZ	ex F-ZKBJ
1117	F-MAPW	
1121	F-MAPX	ex F-ZKBF
1122	F-MADA	ex F-ZKBL
1123	F-MAPY	ex F-ZKBK
1128	F-MBZA	ex F-MADC
1130	F-MADB	
1131		
1135		ex F-WKQC
1136		
1137		
1142		
1143	F-MCYW	
1145		
1149	F-MASR	ex F-MADE, F-MBAK
1150	F-MADF	
1151		
1155		
1156		
1158		
1159	F-MCUH	ex F-MCUI
1163	F-MASI	
1164	F-MCYK	ex F-MCUD
1165		ex F-MCUH
1171		
1172		
1173	F-MASW	ex F-MCUB
1176	F-MCUC	
1177	F-MADG	
1179	F-MCUF	ex F-MADE
1182	F-MCUG	
1184	EPNER	
1186	F-MBUU	
1189	F-MADH	
1190		
1192	F-MAPV	
1196	F-MBSU	ex SA330-07
1197		
1198		

C/n	Callsign	Remarks
1200		
1204	AX/EPNER	
1205	F-MADE	
1206	F-MADC	
1210		
1211	F-MBZD	ex F-MAPX
1213		
1214	F-SCOB/GAM 56	
1217		
1219		
1220	F-MCYZ	
1221	F-MADB	ex F-MBAE
1222		
1228	F-MCYH	
1231		
1232	F-MADJ	ex F-SCOB/GAM 56
1235	F-MASX	ex F-MAPL
1236	F-MADI	
1244	F-MASD	
1251	AW/EPNER	
1252	F-MCYT	
1257	R/GLAM (F-RAFR)	ex F-ZKBA
1263	F-MCUG	
1277	F-MCYF	
1288	67-ON	ex 341-EW
1297	67-DE	
1302	44-GF	ex 68-DF, 67-DF
1306	44-GA	
1311	44-GB	
1316	67-JA	
1321	67-JB	
1326	67-JC	ex F-SCOA/GAM 56
1346	S/GLAM (F-RAFS)	
1351	52-LC	ex F-SCOC/GAM 56, 341-EY
1354		
1362	52-LB	ex 67-OA
1367	67-OM	
1370	52-LD	ex EX/CIEH 341, 341-EX
1383	67-OO	ex EZ/CIEH 341
1387	67-DG	ex 341-EU
1394	–/GAM 56	
1399	67-OL	
1432	W/o 1.8.78	
1501		

Note: Integrated production at Hayes for the RAF and by Aérospatiale has resulted in some aircraft sharing the same c/n in error. XW233-237 are given as c/n 1205, 1206, 1213, 1217 and 1220, three of which have also been positively identified in ALAT service.

AEROSPATIALE SA341/342 GAZELLE

The first military model of the Gazelle for France, the SA341F, was developed from the SA340 prototype, flown on 7 April 1967. Production began at c/n 1001 which first flew on 6 August 1971, and examples have found buyers throughout the world. In Britain, Westland Helicopters who developed the Gazelle in conjunction with Aérospatiale, also have a production line principally for the supply of aircraft to all three services, but French models incorporate components built by Saunders-Roe, and Westland. Current orders for the ALAT are 166 helicopters, and a further 128 SA342M equipped with the HOT anti-armour missile will be delivered between 1979 and 1982. Additionally, 110 of the earlier batch are in the process of conversion to interim HOT-carrying standard, deliveries commencing September 1978. Over 900 Gazelles are now on order or have been delivered, and the last ALAT examples are due for delivery in 1984.

Prototypes
SA340-01   F-WOFH
SA340-02   F-ZWRA

Pre-production
SA341-01   F-ZWRH
SA341-02   F-ZWRI   Believed to SA342-01
SA341-03   F-ZWRK   To XW276
SA341-04   F-ZWRL

SA341F

C/n	Callsign	Remarks
1026		
1027	F-MBDI	ex F-MMDT
1028		
1037		ex F-ZARM, F-MBSH
1038		
1046		
1047		
1054		
1055		
1069		ex F-ZKBG
1070		ex F-ZKBH
1071		ex F-ZKBK
1077		
1080	F-MCWV	
1082		
1088		
1090		
1092		
1101		

1103		1335			1575	
1105	F-MAEH	1338			1576	
1115		1353	F-MCMB	ex F-MCWR	1580	
1117		1354			1583	
1119		1355			1593	
1129		1369			1594	
1131		1372			1597	
1133		1373			1598	
1147		1374			1607	
1149		1383			1608	
1151		1384			1611	
1153		1387	F-MABA		1612	
1171		1388	F-MAEK		1618	
1172		1399			1619	
1175		1400			1628	
1176	F-MBDA	1403			1629	
1179		1404			1642	
1180		1415	F-MMDE		1643	
1183		1416	F-MACP		1646	
1185	ex F-WTNA	1420	F-MABA		1649	
1186		1430			1657	
1189		1431	F-MCVH		1658	
1190	F-MAXD	1432			1659	
1193		1433			1660	
1194	F-MCQA	ex F-MBDA, F-MBSG	1447			1671	
1197		1448			1672	
1198		1451			1675	
1210	F-MAFX	1452			1678	
1211	F-MCQM	1462			1690	
1214		1463			1693	
1215		1467	F-MCMC		1694	
1229		1482			1702	
1232		1483			1703	
1234		1486			1706	
1251		1500			1707	
1252	F-MBSC	1501	F-MAUS		1717	F-MCMD
1255		1504			1718	
1266		1505				
1267		1508				
1270		1518	F-MBSC			
1281		1519	F-MCME			
1282	F-MBSC	1522				
1285	F-MAEH	1523				
1296	F-MBPR	1526				
1297		1537				
1300		1540				
1311		1541				
1312		1544				
1315		1557				
1316	F-MCMA	1558				
1326		1561	F-MCZV			
1327		1562	F-MBPN			
1334	F-MCWV	1565	F-MMAG			

Additionally, whilst undergoing trials by Aerospatiale, British example XW844 c/n 1005 was flown as F-ZKCW.

AIRBUS INDUSTRIE A300 'AWACS'

France has recently expressed concern over the vulnerability of her southern flank, and in typical patriotic style, announced late in 1978 that it intends to develop its own 'AWACS' system based on the A300 aircraft, rather than subscribe to the existing British (Nimrod E.3) or US/European (Boeing E.3) programmes.

AEROSPATIALE SA3210 SUPER FRELON

Developed from the SA3200 flown on 10 June 1959, the SA3210 prototype first flew on 7 December 1962 and the production examples began with No.101 on 30 November 1965. The Aéronavale order was for 17 aircraft for 32F and 27S, and further examples have been produced for South Africa (16), Israel (12), Iraq (10), China (16) and Libya (5). A further seven have subsequently been to France including one for the Armée de l'Air's GLAM, now withdrawn. Orders total 98 for all customers.

SA3200

001	'S'
002	'T'

SA3210

01	F-ZWWE	Preserved
02	F-ZWWF/CEV	
03	Written off 30.5.65 as F-WMCU, ex F-ZWWH.	
04	F-ZWWI/20S	
05	F-ZWWJ/CEV	ex CEPA
06	F-ZWWK/CEPA/20S	

SA321G

C/n	Callsign/Unit	Remarks
101	F-YCXA/27S	ex F-WJUX
102	F-XCBE/32F	ex F-ZKBE, F-YCXB/27S
103	W/o 22.8.66 as F-ZKBF	
105	F-ZKBG	
106	F-YCXD/27S	
112	F-XCBA/32F	
114	F-BTRP	ex F-WMHC, F-BMHC, F-OCMF, F-RAFR, F-OCZV, F-WKQC
118	F-XCBB/32F	ex F-ZQBG, F-YCTQ
120	F-XCBC/32F	
122	F-XCBD/32F	ex F-YCTR/32F
123	W/o 19.11.70 as F-XCBE/32F	
134	F-XCBF/32F	ex F-ZKBD
137	F-XCBG/32F	ex F-ZKBG
141	F-YCBH/32F	ex F-ZKBN, F-YCTU/20S
144	F-XCBI/32F	
147	W/o 17.3.76 as F-XCBJ/32F	
148	F-XCBK/32F	
149	F-XCBL/32F	
159	F-XCBM/32F	ex F-ZKBB
160	F-XCBN/32F	
161	W/o 18.5.77 as F-YCBO/32F	
162	F-XCBP/32F	
163	F-XCBQ/32F	
164	F-XCBR/32F	
165	F-XCBS/32F	

Note: C/n 150, Libya LC-150, seen in Aéronavale markings 1976. The essentially civilian aircraft, c/n 114, was used by ET 60 as F-RAFR pending the arrival of a Puma with the same identity.

AEROSPATIALE TB.30B

The Armée de l'Air is shortly to introduce new training aircraft at both ends of the instructional syllabus, the Alpha Jet and the TB.30B, which will supplement and then replace the CAP.10 as an initial selection aircraft and primary trainer, relieving the Magister of the first twenty hours of its instructional phase.
The TB.30 was developed for the AdIA under the project name 'Epsilon', and funding for sixty is included in the 1977-82 planning period. The civil version, which is to replace the Rallye on the production lines starting in 1979, began life in February 1975 as the SOCATA TB.10, the prototype, F-WZJP, flying on 23 February 1977 with an 160 hp Lycoming engine. A second aircraft, with the production 180 hp motor flew three months later, and the 300 hp TB.30 will do so in mid-1979.
Until the TB.30 enters service, the CAP.10 will be responsible for the initial 20 flying hours as before, but will provide a further 20 hours hitherto performed on the Magister. It will eventually be withdrawn when the TB.30 is in full service, the latter taking over the duties of initial selection, basic training, elementary instrument flying, VFR night flying and navigation, primary aerobatics, formation flying and post-basic stage grading.

BELL 47D/G and AGUSTA-BELL 47G (†)

The first helicopters to enter French military service were two Bell 47D delivered in 1950, followed by a further one in 1951 and five more the next year. US built Bell 47G were then received between August 1953 and September 1956, and augmented by Italian licence production. Principal user was the ALAT, and smaller quantities went to the Gendarmerie and the DCAN who continue to use at least two. Civilianised helicopters have appeared on the civil register, and those marked 'sold' below are recent sales awaiting overhaul and registration.

Agusta-Bell 47G

C/n	History
019	
022	F-MBDB
023	
024	ex F-BDVC, F-MBCQ. Sold
025	ex F-BDVH. To Senegal AF
026	
027	To Israel. To I-COLO
028	Sold
032	
034	To F-BMSP
036	Gendarmerie. To F-BNPJ, OO-BAW
038	F-MBDO. To F-BJDA
039	
040	CAN 6/F-YCZF. F-YEEA/DCAN (Current)
041	Gendarmerie. To F-BNPK
046	
047	F-MBJO
048	ex F-BGXB
050	ex F-BHGK. Gendarmerie. To F-BRHV
051	
052	F-BJDC. F-MBDL, F-MBCS
054	ex F-BJDD. F-MBDV
055	To F-BXXH
056	CAN 7/F-YCZG. F-YEEB/DCAN (Current)
067	ex F-BHPC. F-MBDD. To F-BJDE
068	ex F-BHPD
069	ex F-BHPG. To F-BXXK
070	ex F-BHPI
072	
075	F-MBDG
076	Preserved
078	F-SFFH, F-SFLN. To F-BXXS
079	To F-BXXI
082	
084	To F-BTST
085	
087	
088	
089	Written off 25.8.57
090	
091	Written off 19.3.58
092	Written off 22.8.58
093	
094	To F-BNFB
095	
096	
099	
102	F-MBMI, F-MASC. To F-BOFU
103	
106	F-MCAA. To F-BXXJ

108	F-MJAB. To I-MICO, F-GALQ
109	
111	To F-BXXD
112	F-MAHT. F-MBIW. To F-GALR
113	
114	F-MCMR, F-MBNU. To F-BXXL
115	
117	Sold
119	To F-BIFO, G-AYOG
120	To F-BILF
121	To Israel. To I-CIDI
122	To F-OCGB, G-AYOF, OE-AXT
124	
126	
128	Written off 14.11.56
129	Sold
131	F-MAHT. Sold
132	To F-BMSQ
135	
136	
139	To F-BXXM
140	
141	To Israel. To I-TIEZ
143	Sold
144	Sold
145	To F-BXXN
147	F-MCAB. To F-BTSX
148	To F-BXXE
149	F-MAVF. To F-BTSU
151	
152	To Israel
153	Written off 18.6.57
154	To F-BXXU
155	
156	To F-BXXF
157	CEV. Written off 24.1.60
158	To F-BXZU
160	
161	To F-BXXV
162	To Morocco
165	
166	Written off 7.9.56
168	To F-BTSQ
169	
174	To Israel
175	F-MBNY. F-MAZU. To F-GALS
179	F-MAFU
181	
183	To Senegal
184	F-SFWI. To F-BTSY
186	F-SFWJ. To F-BXXX
187	
188	

189	F-MAZF.To F-BXXO
190	F-MJAB. To F-GALT
191	F-MJAC. To F-BTGQ
197	F-MJAE. Written off 5.5.72
198	F-MJAF. To F-BTGR
199	To F-BTSV
200	To F-BTSZ
201	To F-BTSP
202	Gendarmerie. To F-BRAV
203	F-MJAO. To F-BXXY
204	Gendarmerie. To F-BUIG
205	To Israel. To D-HIPO
206	Written off 20.4.59
209	To F-BIFN
210	To F-BTSR
217	ex F-BICA. F-ZBAJ. To F-BIEH

Bell 47D

C/n	History
154	
157	
213	
483	
488	
608	
623	
634	

Bell 47G

C/n	History
543	ex 51-13902
673	To F-BMHY
682	
683	
684	To F-OAQO
685	F-MBCK. To F-BJDF
690	ex F-BGXY
708	
709	
710	
722	Sold
723	F-MBDW
724	
819	ex 51-14054
882	ex 54-14117
1275	ex F-BGSS. F-ZB.. To F-BIEI
1285	To F-BIEJ
1287	
1302	
1303	
1304	
1310	ex F-BHDS. CEV. To F-BVPX

1312	
1313	
1314	
1315	F-MBVB
1316	
1317	
1318	
1458	CNET. To F-BVXD
1464	ex F-BHMG. F-ZBAH. To F-BTOH
1465	ex F-BHKZ. F-ZB.. To F-BIEQ
1496	ex F-BHAD. To F-BMLZ
1622	ex N2841B
1623	ex N2842B. Sold
1624	ex N2843B. To N6761, EP-HAS
1625	ex N2844B. To F-BOFZ
1626	ex N2845B. To F-OBOK, F-BBOK
1627	ex N2846B. To F-BXXP
1628	ex N2847B. To N6762, EP-HAT
1629	ex N2848B. To F-MATO, F-BSIA
1630	ex N2849B.
1631	ex N2850B. To N6763, EP-HAU
1632	ex N2851B.
1633	ex N2852B. To N6764, EP-HAV
1634	ex N2853B
1635	ex N2854B. To N6765, EP-HAW
1636	ex N2855B. To F-BILG, D-HAFU, F-BXXZ
1637	ex N2856B. To Gabon, G-AYOH
1638	ex N2857B. To F-BXXG
1639	ex N2858B. To F-BXXQ
1640	ex N2859B. To N6766, EP-HAX
1641	ex N2860B

BOEING KC-135F

Twelve KC-135F flight refuelling aircraft were purchased from the USA and delivered in 1964. Distributed originally to ERV 4/91, ERV 4/93 and ERV 4/94, they form an important part of the FAS and are now based in one squadron at Istres and detached to Mirage IVA bases as required, under the title 93Esc R.V. The aircraft are identified by their US serial, and since 1970 by the last two letters of the call-sign applied to the rear fuselage. Both the Mirages and the KC-135s operate in a pool and have common call-sign ranges.

C/n	US serial	Code	Remarks
18679	63-8470	CA (F-UKCA)	
18680	63-8471	CB (F-UKCB)	
18681	63-8472	CC (F-UKCC)	
18682	63-8473	CD (F-UKCD)	Written off
18683	63-8474	CE (F-UKCE)	
18684	63-8475	CF (F-UKCF)	
18695	63-12735	CG (F-UKCG)	
18696	63-12736	CH (F-UKCH)	
18697	63-12737	CI (F-UKCI)	
18698	63-12738	CJ (F-UKCJ)	
18699	63-12739	CK (F-UKCK)	
18700	63-12740	CL (F-UKCL)	

63-8473 crashed in the Pacific on 1 July 1972 whilst on Nuclear Test Centre duties.

Aircraft are currently undergoing a programme of re-skinning of wing undersurfaces and will be re-engined with the CFM56 in the early eighties.

BREGUET 941S (†)

The Br941S was designed as a STOL transport for military use, employing a profusion of lift-assisting devices on the wing trailing edges. The prototype Br940 Integral first flew on 21 May 1958, and from this was developed the Br941, flown on 2 June 1961, and Br941S on 19 April 1967. Four of the latter model were evaluated by the CEAM, and then re-designated 'production' models with the deletion of the '0' prefix from the c/n. They were then passed on to the specifically formed ET 3/62 at Reims which accumulated 3,000 hours of flying before disbandment in 1973. The four were then stored at EAA 601, Chateaudun, from which one has been transferred to the Musée de l'Air and another has gone to Amberieu (in 1974), possibly as a fire-aircraft.

C/n	History
941-01	Z Scrapped, Toulouse
941S-01	K (F-ZJRK), 118-IX, re-serialled 941S-1, 62-NA Stored
941S-02	L (F-ZJRL), 118- re-serialled 941S-2, 62-NB, Stored
941S-03	M (F-ZJRM), 118-IH, re-serialled 941S-3, 62-NC, Dumped
941S-04	N (F-ZJRN), 118-IY, re-serialled 941S-4, 62-ND, Museum

BREGUET 1050 ALIZE

The Breguet Alizé was developed from the Br. 960 Vultur flown in prototype form on 3 August 1951. The second aircraft was later converted to Alizé standard, commencing flight trials on 26 March 1955, and it was followed by five pre-production examples (01 to 05). 01 first flew on 6 October 1956 and the initial production aircraft followed on 26 March 1959. Twelve were supplied to India as IN201 to IN212, and three secondhand aircraft followed in 1968. Several aircraft are currently being refurbished to allow them to remain in service until the two aircraft carriers retire in 1990. The work involves the fitting of Iguane radar, Doppler navigators and improved armament, and between May 1979 and February 1984 Nos 43, 50, 55, 64, 22, 17, 53, 30, 48, 25, 87, 28, 24, 44, 56, 76, 47, 68, 42, 41, 65, 31, 73, 37, 59, 49 and 72 will be thus modified, No 52 having acted as a prototype. A further twelve are expected to go to India in the near future.

C/n	Operated by	Remarks
01	Scrapped	ex 'SR-11'/CEPA, F-ZWUC/CEV
02	Instructional	ex 'SR-12'
03	Written off	ex 'SR-13'
04	Instructional	ex 'SR-14'
05	Scrapped	ex 'SR-15'
1	6F	ex 9F
2	Written off	
3	Instructional	ex 6F, 4F, 6F
4	4F	ex 6F
5	6F	ex 2S, 3S, 59S
6	Written off	
7	Scrapped	ex 9F, 59S, 6F
8	Instructional	ex 4F, 3S
9	4F	ex 4F, 9F
10	Preserved	ex 9F, 6F, 4F
11	6F	ex 4F
12	4F	ex 10S, 9F, 59S
13	6F	ex 6F, 3S, 59S
14	Written off	
15	Instructional	ex 6F
16	59S	ex 3S, 6F
17	4F	ex 9F, 10S
18	Written off	
19	4F	ex 3S, 6F, 9F
20	Written off	
21	Instructional	ex 9F, 6F, 4F
22	Store	ex 4F, 6F
23	Written off	
24	Store	ex 4F
25	4F	
26	59S	ex 6F
27	6F	ex 9F
28	6F	ex 10S, 4F
29	Written off	
30	4F	ex 10S, 4F, 6F
31	59S	ex 4F
32	Written off	
33	4F	ex 9F, 6F
34	3S	ex 6F, 59S
35	Written off	ex 6F
36	59S	ex 6F, 4F
37	6F	ex 10S, 4F
38	Written off	ex 6F
39	Written off 13.7.65	
40	6F	ex 4F, 3S, 59S
41	59S	
42	6F	
43	Store	ex 3S
44	Store	ex 4F
45	S.E.St.R	ex 4F, 3S, 10S
46	Written off	
47	59S	ex 3S, 4F, 10S
48	59S	ex 4F, 6F
49	4F	
50		ex 6F
51	4F	
52	CEV	ex 3S, 6F
53	4F	ex 3S, 4F, 6F
54	Written off 1965 (with 9F)	
55	S.E.St.R	ex 4F
56	6F	
57	Written off (with 4F)	
58	Written off	ex 9F
59	4F	ex 9F, 3S
60	4F	ex 10S, 6F, 59S
61	Written off	
64	Store	
65	4F	ex 9F
68	6F	ex 4F
69	6F	ex 4F, 2S
70	Written off	ex 9F
72	6F	ex 9F, 4F
73	6F	ex 9F
74	Withdrawn	ex 4F
75	4F	ex 10S
76	6F	ex 2S
77	Written off 1962	
80	3S	ex 4F, 59S
86	4F	ex 10S, 6F
87	4F	ex 10S, 9F

Alpha Jet No. 02 - the shape of things to come. Trainer versions of the Alpha Jet will enter service with GE 314 at Tours from May 1979 onwards and are also in prospect for the Patrouille de France, 8 Escadre and GE 313. The second prototype, illustrated here, was built by Dornier and transferred to France for Mauser cannon trials at Cazaux, having made its first flight in January 1974 in French markings and German flight-test registration D-9594. *(S.G. Richards)*

Aérospatiale Super Frélon No. 37 'G'. Long range anti-submarine duties are the speciality of the Super Frélon, illustrated here by No. 37 of 32F seen at Greenham Common Air Tattoo in 1977. 32F is one of the only two Aéronavale units to apply code letters to its aircraft, the other being 31F which employs the HSS-1 Seabat on similar duties. *(S.G. Richards)*

109

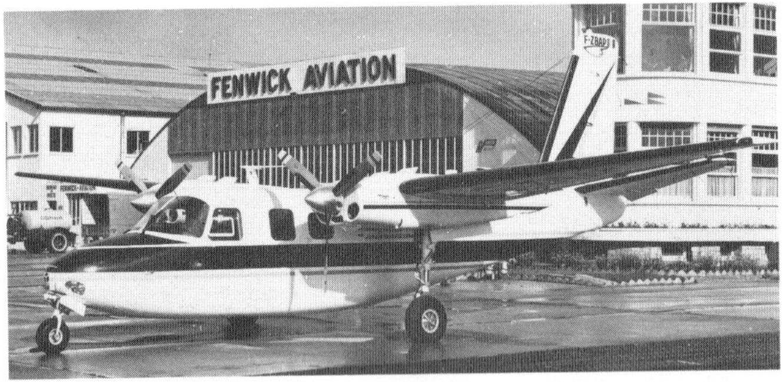
FENWICK AVIATION

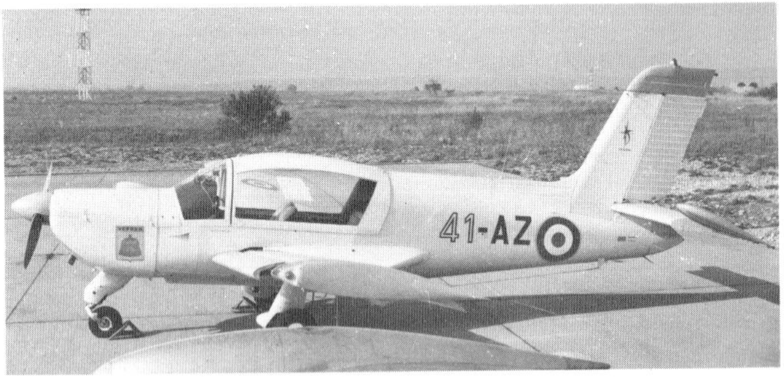
41-AZ

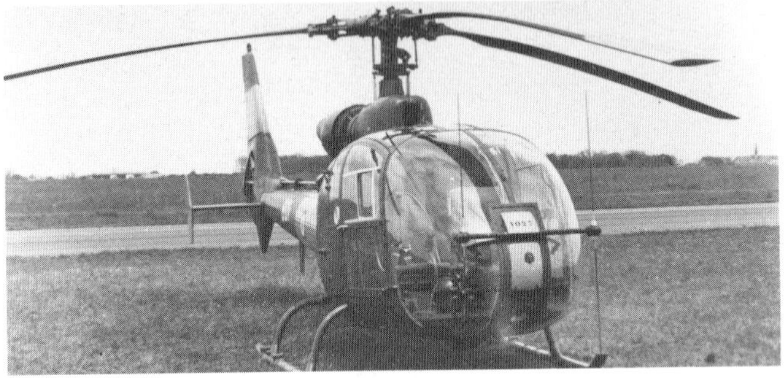

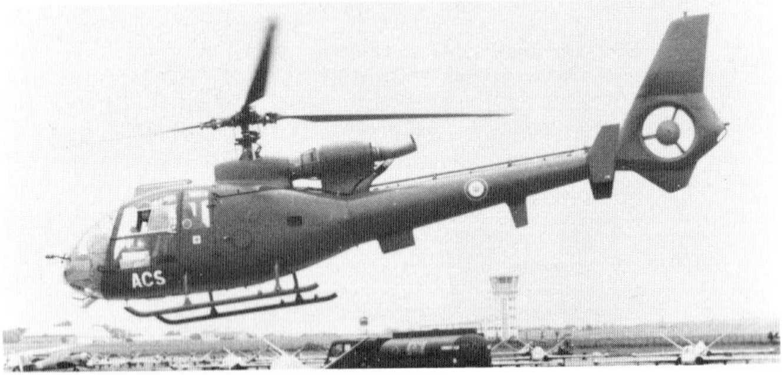
ACS

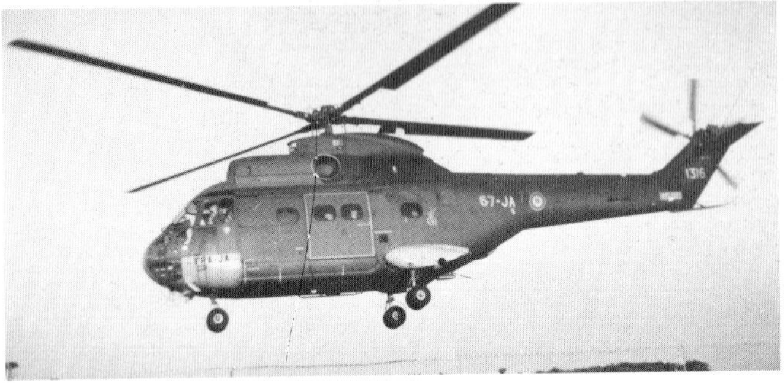
67-JA
1316

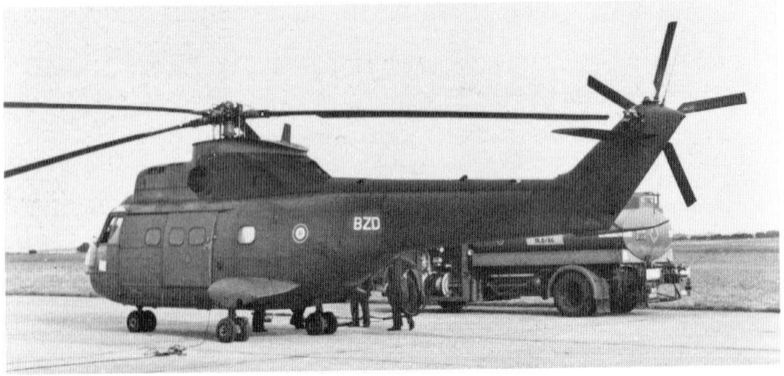
BZD

Aero Commander 680F F-ZBAP. Communications aircraft F-ZBAP has now been augmented by a second example, F-ZBBU. *(MAP)*

Aérospatiale SA341 Gazelle No.1027 'BDI'. Demonstrating the application of the c/n to the nose of the aircraft, 'BDI'' belongs to the ALAT's Ecole de Specialisation and was photographed in July 1977. *(J-L. Gaynecoetche)*

Aérospatiale SA330B Puma No.1316 '67-JA'. To avoid confusion with Alouette III '67-JA' (F-RBJA) of EH 1/67, the two Pumas of EH 5/67 have the full call-sign applied to the nose, complete with a novel positioning of the hyphen. *(R. Cram)*

Aérospatiale/SOCATA Rallye 180GT No.12571 '41-AZ' was one of six evaluated by the Armée de l'Air as a Broussard replacement, during 1975. *(via J-L Gaynecoetche)*

Aérospatiale SA341 Gazelle 'ACS'. Lifting off from Cognac in July 1976 is a visiting 8 GALDiv aircraft from Compiègne. *(J-L. Gaynecoetche)*

Aérospatiale SA330B Puma No.1211 'BZD'. From an as-yet unidentified Army unit, 'BZD' was first noted in September 1977, and the appearance of this new code-group is obviously connected with the re-structuring of the Army and ALAT which will be completed during 1979. *(J-L. Gaynecoetche)*

Aérospatiale SA330B Puma No.1311 '44-GB'. Flying over the impressive Corsican peaks, this Puma is one of three such helicopters allocated to ELAS 1/44 for SAR duties. *(R. Cram)*

Boeing C-135F No. 63-12738 'CJ'. Known as the 'sous-marin' (submarine) because of the absence of fuselage windows, the C-135F of the Armée de l'Air now serve exclusively with 93 Escadre de Ravitaillement en Vol to which they were attached in June 1976 when the FAS was reorganised. *(MAP)*

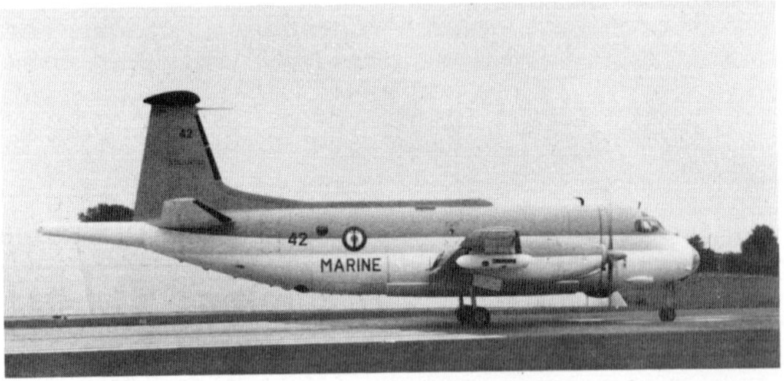
42
MARINE

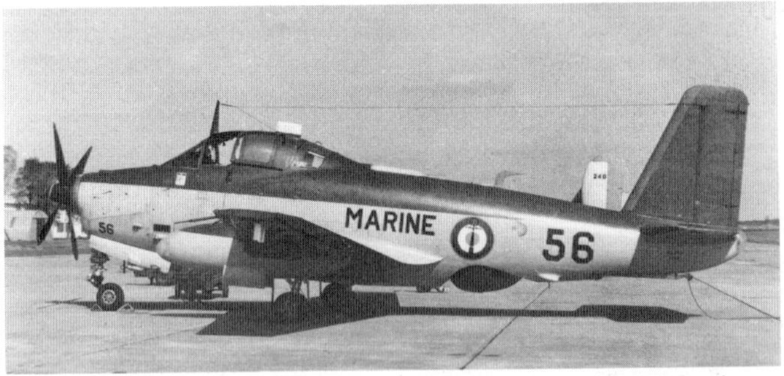
MARINE
56

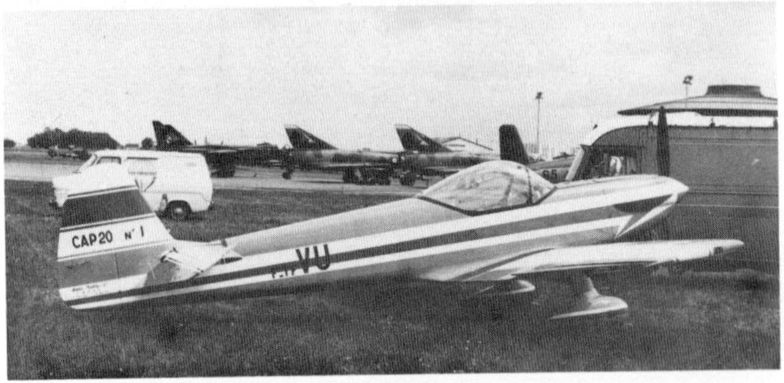
CAP20 N°1
VU

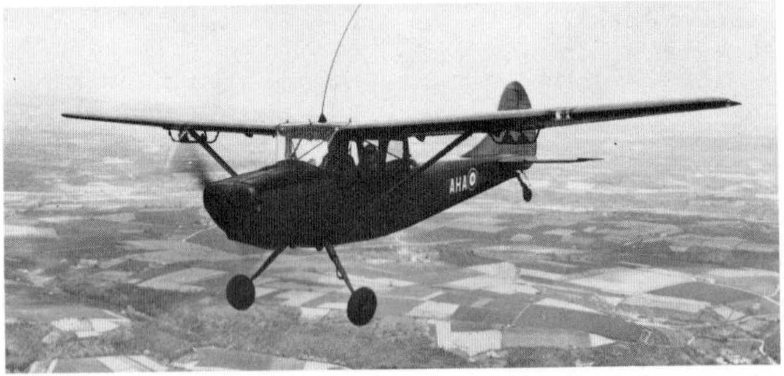
AHA

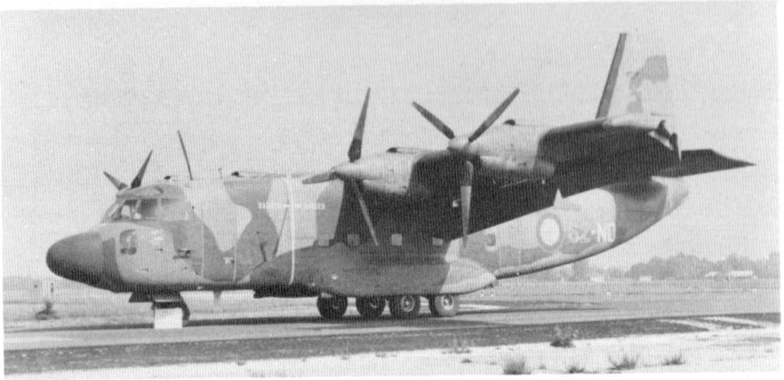

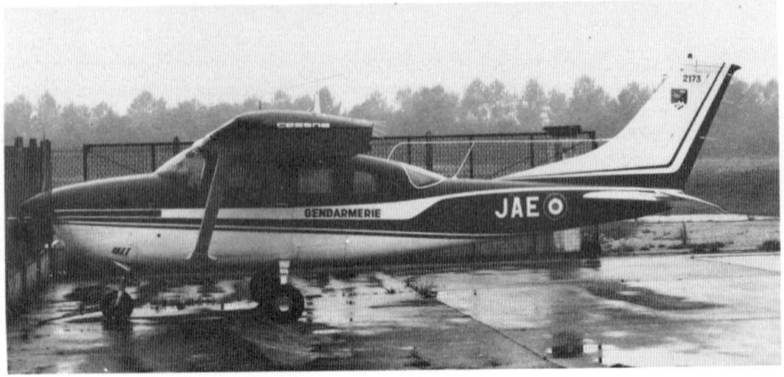
GENDARMERIE
JAE

Breguet Atlantic No.42 photographed landing at St. Athan in September 1977. *(S.G. Richards)*

CAP20 No.1 'VU' The Equipe de Voltige Aérienne principally operates the CAP20 from Salon de Provence, the home of its parent unit GI 312, in the distinctive team colours in September 1976. *(J-L. Gaynecoetche)*

Breguet Br941S No.4 '62-ND' Now withdrawn from service, Br941S No.4 resides in the Musée de l'Air collection at Le Bourget. *(S.G. Richards)*

Breguet Alizé No.56 was photographed in September 1977, wearing the Lorraine Cross badge of 6 Flotille. *(J-L. Gaynecoetche)*

Cessna O-1 Bird Dog 'AHA' The delivery of additional Gazelles to the ALAT will relegate the fixed-wing aircraft of the Army to the scrapheap or the most menial of tasks. Bird Dog F-MAHA of 5 GALReg serves as a reminder of better days. *(R. Cram)*

Cessna 206 No.2173 (F-MJAE). A rare bird in any military guise, this Cessna is one of six used by the Gendarmerie and registered in their own series of markings, of which it carries the 'last three'. *(MAP)*

CAP 10 No.5 Principally an aptitude evaluation aircraft, thirty CAP 10 serve the Armée de l'Air, mostly in the EFIPN. No.5 is pictured at Chateaudun in June 1977 and was originally '307-SC', but with the re-integration of the EFIPN into GE 313 in May 1978, this will become '313-SC'. *(S.G. Richards)*

Dassault Flamant No.253 '319-CQ'. One of three dozen aircraft operated by the twin-conversion unit GE 319. *(J-L. Gaynecoetche)*

114

Cessna 411 No.F001 'AC'. After six years with the Armée de L'Air, four Reims-Cessna 411 were transferred to the CEV. F001 carries the last two letters of its callsign, F-ZJAC. *(J-L. Gaynecoetche)*

Dassault Mystère IVA No.153 '8-NW'. The Mystère will remain in service beyond the end of the decade until Alpha Jets re-equip ECT 8 at Cazaux. No. 153 is a reserve aircraft, and has been in storage at Chateaudun since 1974. *(S.G. Richards)*

Dassault Super Etendard No.02. Photographed at the 1977 Paris Salon, No.02 is the second of three conversions from standard Etendards which acted as prototypes of this new strike fighter. *(MAP)*

Cessna 310N No.0192 'BM'. Celebrating its tenth year of service as a communications aircraft, No. 0192 is one of twelve Cessna 310 allocated to the various departments of the CEV. *(A. J. Brown)*

Dassault Flamant No.205 '113-DA'. Illustrating one of the more unusual code prefixes, this aircraft was until recently on the strength of the St. Dizier base flight. *(J-L. Gaynecoetche)*

Dassault Super Mystère B2 No.156 '12-YK'. Making a high-speed pass along the crowd line at the 1977 Greenham Common Tattoo. *(S.G. Richards)*

Dassault Etendard IVP No.115. Only twelve of the twenty-two reconnaissance derivatives of the Etendard remain in service with 16 Flotille, and will eventually be replaced by the 'Super'. *(S.G. Richards)*

Dassault Super Mystère B2 No.109 '12-YL'. Stored at Chateaudun in the Summer of 1977, No.109 was an early withdrawal from EC 1/12, and the last Mystères to leave the squadron did not do so until September of that year. Many are being redistributed as gate guardians. *(S. G. Richards)*

BREGUET 1150 ATLANTIC

The second aircraft designed to NATO specification was the Atlantic, first flown on 21 October 1961. Four prototype aircraft were built, followed by 87 production aircraft for Germany, Holland (c/ns 55-58, 61-65) and Italy (70-87). In 1978 after a protracted development period, the improved Atlantic M4 was put into production against an order for 42 for the Aéronavale, under the designation Atlantic Nouvelle Génération. Two older aircraft will serve as prototypes.

Prototypes

C/n	Code/Callsign	Remarks
01	A(F-ZWWA)	CEV. To the German Navy as UC+301, now 6100 (Instructional)
02	B(F-ZWWB)	Written off 19.4.62
03	G(F-ZWWG)	
04	M(F-ZWWM)	To 21/22F

Production

C/n	Unit	Remarks
1	22F	
3	23F	
5	24F	ex 22F
7	23F	ex 21/22F
9	23F	ex 24F, 21/22F
11	24F	ex 22F
13	24F	ex 24F, 23F, 21/22F
15	24F	ex 21F
17	24F	ex 21F
19	21/22F	
21	21F	
23	21/22F	ex 23F
25	22F	ex 23F
27	21/22F	ex 23F
29	21/22F	
31	23F	ex 24F, 21F
33	22F	
35	24F	
37	21F	
38	21/22F	ex 21F, 23F, 24F
39	W/o 31.8.67	
40	23F	ex 22F
41	21F	
42	23F	ex 22F
43	W/o 20.9.68	ex 22F
44	21/22F	ex 24F
45	24F	ex 21/22F
47	22F	
48	24F	
49	23F	ex 21/22F, 24F
50	23F	ex 22F
51	21/22F	ex 24F
52	21F	ex 21F, 24F
53	21/22F	
54	21/22F	ex 24F
66	24F	ex 24F, 21F
67	21F	
68	22F	
69	23F	ex 23F, 24F

Three aircraft, Nos. 32, 40 and 46 were allocated to Pakistan in 1975, and by June No. 32 was fully painted in Pakistani colours. It has since returned to the Aéronavale (eg.7/76) as has No. 40 (eg. 2/76).

CAP.10 and CAP.20

These two aerobatic light aircraft are essentially civilian in function, but are used by the Armée de l'Air for pilot selection and evaluation, and aerobatic practise and display. Following on from prototype CAP.10 c/n 01 F-BOPX, thirty were delivered from the first production run. The six CAP.20 fall between prototypes 01/F-BPXU, 02/F-BOPV and production 7/F-BTDO. The aircraft of GI 312, the Equipe de Voltige Aérienne, use the last two of the callsign as an aircraft identity, these following on directly from the Magisters of the Patrouille de France F-TFVA to VL. CAP.20 No.02 was a later delivery to replace No.2. The CAP.10 aircraft have been absorbed into GE 313 where they now provided the first 40 hours of pilot instruction as opposed to only the first 20 as hitherto. A replacement type, the Aérospatiale TB.30 is in the development stage.

CAP.10

C/n	Callsign/Code	Remarks
02	F-TFVQ/VQ	
03	F-TFVR/VR	
1	F-TFVS/VS	ex F-BTAA
2	F-TFVT/VT	ex F-BTAB
3	-SA	ex 307-SA
4	-SB	ex 307-SB
5	-SC	ex 307-SC
6	-SD	ex 307-SD
7	313 -SE	ex 307-SE
8	313 -SF	ex 307-SF
9	313 -SG	ex 307-SG
10	-SH	ex 307-SH
11	-SI	ex 307-SI
12	313 -SJ	ex 307-SJ
13	-SK	ex 307-SK
14		
15	-SM	ex 307-SM
16	313 -SN	ex 307-SN
17		
18	-SP	ex 307-SP
19	-SQ	ex 307-SQ
20	-SR	ex 307-SR
21		
22	-ST	ex 307-ST
23	-SU	ex 307-SU
24	-SV	ex 307-SV
25	-SW	ex 307-SW
26	-SX	ex 307-SX
27	-SY	ex 307-SY
28	-SZ	ex 307-SZ

CAP.20

C/n	Callsign/Code	Remarks
02	F-TFVV/VV	ex F-BOPV
1	F-TFVU/VU	ex F-BTAC
2	F-TFVV/VV	ex F-BTAD Written off 6.74
3	F-TFVW/VW	ex F-BTAE
4	F-TFVX/VX	ex F-BTAF
5	F-TFVY/VY	ex F-BTAG
6	F-TFVZ/VZ	ex F-BTAH

Note: code prefixes were amended to '313' in the Spring of 1978. Only those confirmed have been noted above.

CESSNA 0-1 BIRD DOG

A total of 147 O-1 aircraft was supplied to ALAT, comprising two batches of 90 and 36 new examples, and 21 ex-US Army aircraft. Approximately sixty remain in use, all identified by their constructors number. The type is due for imminent withdrawal but will probably remain in limited use for air experience flying.

Serial	Callsign	Remarks
23309	F-MAGZ	ex 51-12852, F-MAFA
23310	F-MAQL	ex 51-12853
23311		ex 51-12854
23312	F-MAGU	ex 51-12855, F-MCTI
23313		ex 51-12856
23314	F-MAFB	ex 51-12857
23316	F-MAHD	ex 51-12859
23317	F-MATG	ex 51-12860

116

C/n	Callsign	Remarks
23409	F-MBPC	ex 53-7988
23504		ex 55-4664
23509		ex 55-4669
23511	F-MCTZ	ex 55-4671
23512	F-MCTY	ex 55-4672
23516		ex 55-4676
23517		ex 55-4677
23533	F-MCTR	ex 55-4693
23538		ex 55-4698
23550		ex 55-4710
23557		ex 55-4717
23566		ex 55-4726
23567		ex 55-4727
23568		ex 55-4728
24501	F-MAGV	
24502	F-MAGX	ex F-MAFA
24503		
24504	F-MCTV	ex F-MALH
24505		
24506	F-MALQ	
24507		
24508	F-MCWC	
24509	F-MCTL	
24510		
24511		
24512	F-MAGS	ex F-MAKX
24513	F-MCTW	
24514		
24515		
24516		
24517	F-MAGP	
24518	F-MAGR	
24519		
24520		
24521	F-MCWD	
24522		ex F-MAOI
24523		
24524	F-MAOI	ex F-MATJ, F-MATD
24525	F-MCTX	
24526	F-MAGQ	ex F-MATJ, F-MBPN
24527	F-MCTO	ex F-MAMN
24528	F-MAGS	
24529	F-MCMM	ex F-MCWC, F-MAFD
24530		
24531	F-MATZ	
24532		
24533	F-MCWA	
24534		
24535		
24536		
24537		
24538		ex F-MAHD
24539		
24540		
24541		
24542	F-MCWC	
24543		
24544	F-MAPK	
24545		ex F-MAGO, F-MAGV
24546		
24547	F-MAGY	
24548		
24549		
24550		ex F-MAGS
24551		
24552		
24553		
24554		
24555	F-MAFB	
24556		
24557		
24558		
24559	F-MATF	ex F-MCWA
24560		
24561		
24562	F-MATC	ex F-MAGQ, F-MAGR
24563		
24564		
24565	F-MAGY	
24566		
24567		
24568	F-MAMN	
24569		
24570		
24571		
24572	F-MAHT	ex F-MATG
24573		
24574		
24575	F-MCWD	ex F-MAVO
24576	F-MBPC	
24577	F-MCTA	
24578	F-MBTQ	
24579		
24580		
24581		
24582	F-MKCZ	ex F-MBAM
24583		
24584	F-MAHE	
24585	F-MASG	
24586		
24587		
24588	F-MAHA	ex F-MATL
24589	F-MAQK	
24590	F-MASF	
24700	F-MAGT	
24701	F-MCTC	
24702	F-MAFF	
24703	F-MCWE	
24704	F-MATI	
24705		ex F-MKCY
24706		
24707		
24708		
24709	F-MATH	
24710		
24711		
24712	F-MAER	
24713		
24714	F-MAFG	
24715	F-MAGP	
24716		
24717		
24718	F-MATF	
24719		
24720	F-MATH	
24721	F-MATE	
24722	F-MBPI	
24723		
24724		
24725		
24726	F-MAFE	
24727		
24728		
24729	F-MAGN	
24730		
24731	F-MAGT	
24732		
24733	F-MAOX	
24734		

CESSNA 310

The imported Cessna 310 is employed as a communications aircraft by the CEV and its detachments. Callsigns are prefixed 'F-ZJ', with the exception of No.185 which clashes with a Cessna 411.
All aircraft are model 310N, except 0045/46 which are 310L, and 0242/44 which are 310K.

C/n	Callsign/Unit	Remarks
0045	AU/CEV	ex F-BOJR
0046	AV/CEV	ex F-BOJS
0185	AC/CEV	ex N5085Q, F-BPUM
0186	BI/CEV	ex N5086Q, F-BPUP
0187	BJ/CEV	ex N5087Q, F-BPUQ
0188	BK/CEV	ex N5088Q, F-BPUR

0190	BL/CEV	ex N5090Q, F-BPUS
0192	BM/CEV	ex N5092Q, F-BPUT
0193	BG/CEV	ex N5093Q, F-BPUN
0194	BH/CEV	ex N5094Q, F-BPUO
0242	AB/CEV	ex F-BOEJ
0244	AX/CEV	ex F-BOEK

CESSNA 404

One aircraft c/n 055 ex N5437G/F-BYAJ delivered for evaluation at Tours in June 1977 as a prospective Flamant replacement wearing the markings 'F-TEDL', reverted to civil registration immediately afterwards.

CESSNA 411

Six Cessna 411 were received by the Armée de l'Air between July 1966 and March 1969, divided between GAM 82 in the Pacific and ET 2/60 (now ET 65). The four survivors were transferred to the CEV, 001 and 002 early in 1973 and F6 and F8 in March 1974.

C/n	Code/Unit	Remarks
185/F001	AC/CEV	ex F-RAFY/ET 2/60
248/F002	AB/CEV	ex F-RAFX/ET 2/60, F-RAFX/ET 65
249/F004	Written off 4.6.71	ex F-RAFW/ET 2/60
250/F6	AD/CEV	ex 82-QC
250/F7	Written off 8.10.71	ex 82-QD
F8	AE/CEV	ex F-ZARC, ET 2/60, 82-QE

DASSAULT-BREGUET DORNIER ALPHA JET

Joint production of the Alpha Jet is shared between production facilities at Istres (Dassault/Bréguet) and Oberpfaffenhofen (Dornier). Four prototypes were ordered in 1972, and the first of these flew on 26 October 1973. Production examples are divided between the Alpha Jet E (Entrainement) the French variant, and the Alpha Jet A (Appui Tactique) for the Luftwaffe, and the first 'E' flew from Istres on 4 November 1977. The initial 'A' flew on 12 April 1978 and the type will replace the German Fiat G-91. France and Germany will receive 200 each, the initial firm orders being for 56 and 84 respectively, with additional quantities of 33 for Belgium, 24 for Morocco, 12 for Ivory Coast and 5 for Togo. The outstanding 144 AdlA aircraft will be ordered under the 1977-1982 long term plan, and 142 examples are expected to be in service by the end of 1982, with the remaining 59 to follow in 1983-84. Six were delivered to CEAM in 1978, and 1979 deliveries should be 14 to GE 314 in May, and 9 to the Patrouille de France in August/October. During 1980 GE 314 is due to receive a further 51 to replace ageing T-33s, and in 1981 CEVSV 338 should receive 14. ET8 will take 30 to replace Mystères in 1982, with GE 313 re-equipping on the type in 1982/3.

Prototypes

01	F-ZJTS (Larzac engine testbed)	
02	D-9594/CEV Cazaux (Mauser cannon and stores trials)	
03	40-01/Luftwaffe	ex F-ZWRV (Weapon delivery trials)
04	Written off 23.6.76	ex F-ZWRX

(01 and 03 built in France)

Production

French aircraft are numbered from E1, but the sequence may have gaps, marking the position of exports.

C/n	Status	Remarks
E1		
E2	W/o 15.9.78	ex 118-BQ

DASSAULT ETENDARD IV

Development of the Etendard was originally to a land-based specification which the Fiat G.91 was successful in fulfilling. The Etendard IV-01 first flew on 24 July 1956 and was followed on 21 May 1958 by the IVM-01 strike prototype. The seventh aircraft, IVP-07 flown on 19 November 1960 was the first photo-reconnaissance version. An example of the IVB, No.03, first flown 2 December 1959, survives as a static instruction aircraft. When the Super Etendard is established in service, some redundant IVM aircraft will be converted to IVP configuration to boost carrier-borne reconnaissance capability.

Etendard IVM

C/n	Unit/Status	Remarks
01	Instructional	
03	Instructional	
05	Instructional	
06	Instructional	ex 59S

1	11F	
2	59S	
3	17F	ex 16F, 59S
4	59S	
5	17F	ex 15F, 11F
6	59S	ex 11F, 59S, 17F
7	11F	ex 17F, 11F, 17F
8	W/o	
9	17F	ex 17F, 11F
10	W/o	(with 17F)
11	59S	ex 59S, 11F, 17F
12	W/o	ex 59S
13	Super Etendard ex 17F	
14	W/o 19.9.78	(with 17F) ex 11F
15	17F	ex 15F, 11F, 17F, 11F
16	17F	ex 59S
17	W/o 12.8.75	ex 17F, 11F
18	Super Etendard ex 17F	
19	W/o	
20	W/o	
21	17F	ex 16F
22	16F	ex 17F
23	W/o	ex 17F
24	W/o 1964	
25	W/o 1965	
26	W/o 1964	
27	W/o 28.6.73	ex 17F, 11F
28	W/o 1965	
29	11F	ex 17F
30	11F	ex 17F
31	W/o	ex 11F, 17F, 15F
32	59S	ex 11F, 17F, 11F
33	11F	ex 59S
34	11F	ex 17F
35	W/o 1965	
36	17F	ex 15F, 11F
37	59S	ex 17F
38	W/o 29.5.78	(with 17F) ex 59S, 17F
39	W/o	ex 16F, 17F
40	59S	ex 15F
41	59S	ex 17F
42	59S	
43	W/o	ex 17F
44	W/o	
45	W/o 13.8.74	ex 11F
46	W/o	
47	W/o	
48	W/o	
49	W/o 3.3.66	
50	W/o 13.8.74	ex 17F, 11F
51	59S	ex 59S, 17F, 11F
52	11F	
53	17F	ex 17F, 11F

C/n	Unit/Status	Remarks
54	W/o 15.11.72	ex 15F, 11F
55	W/o	
56	11F	ex 16F, 17F
57	11F	ex 17F
58	W/o 1964	
59	11F	ex 16F, 17F
60	11F	ex 59S, 17F
61	W/o 14.9.78 (with 17F) ex 11F	
62	17F	ex 11F
63	11F	
64	W/o	
65	W/o	
66	17F	ex 11F
67	W/o	ex 11F
68	Super Etendard	ex 59S
69	W/o	ex 17F

Etendard IVP

C/n	Unit/Status	Remarks
07	59S	ex 16F
101	16F	
102	W/o 26.8.71 (with 16F)	
103	W/o	
104	W/o 17.3.70 (with 16F)	
105	W/o	(with 16F)
106	W/o 11.6.77 (with 16F)	
107	16F	
108	16F	
109	16F	
110	W/o	(with 16F)
111	W/o 21.9.76 (with 16F)	
112	W/o	ex 16F, 59S
113	W/o 8.11.68 (with 16F)	
114	16F	
115	16F	
116	16F	
117	16F	
118	16F	
119	W/o 1.4.70 (with 16F)	
120	16F	
121	W/o	(with 16F)

DASSAULT SUPER ETENDARD

As implied by the name, the Super Etendard is a development of the Etendard, powered by the Atar 8K50 turbojet, and the three prototype aircraft were converted form standard airframes, the first flying on 29 October 1974. The first of 71 production examples was flown on 24 November 1977, and of this total, 44 will be financed in the 1977-82 PLT. The aircraft will be employed in tactical nuclear and anti-ship missile roles and additionally have a secondary interception capability. 11F will be the first to re-equip, and is due to embark on the *Clemenceau* late in 1979, the last aircraft leaving the production line two years later. Deliveries to the Aéronavale began on 28 June 1978 when No. 3 was handed over; fifteen are planned for delivery by the end of 1978, and 14F will be the next unit.

C/n	Unit/Status	Remarks
01		ex No. 68
02		ex No. 18
03		ex No. 13
1		
2		
3	11F	
4	11F	
5	11F	
6		
7		
8		
9		
10		
11		
12		
13		
14		
15		
16		
17		
18		
19		
20		
21		
22		
23		
24		
25		
26		
27		
28		
29		
30		
31		
32		
33		
34		
35		
36		
37		
38		
39		
40		
41		
42		
43		
44		
45		
46		
47		
48		
49		
50		
51		
52		
53		
54		
55		
56		
57		
58		
59		
60		
61		
62		
63		
64		
65		
66		
67		
68		
69		
70		
71		

DASSAULT FALCON 10

Four examples of this small executive jet have been ordered for the Aéronavale with one more on option. The first two are designated Falcon 10MER and are for use as radar trainers for Super Etendard pilots and for IFR and night-flying training. No. 32 was handed over on 15 April 1975 and serves with the Section Réacteur Léger. Two further aircraft were received in 1978, and although the first was delivered to communications unit 3S on 2 May, it is stated that both will participate in the Super Etendard training role.

C/n	Callsign	Unit
32	F-YETA	SRL
39	F-YETE	SRL
101		3S

119

DASSAULT (MYSTERE) FALCON 20

Essentially a civilian executive jet, the Mystère 20 is used by both the GLAM (ETI 1/60) and the GAEL (ET 1/65) as a VIP transport. Two are employed by the CEV and a similar number of Mystère 20SNA are equipped with the elongated Mirage IIIE nose as radar trainers for CPIR 339. Aircraft are allocated a dual c/n, and normally the first (sequential) number is used as an identity - the exception being No. 463. For some time, the calibration squadron, EdC 57, has been awaiting delivery of a Mystère 20 and in mid 1977, No. 291 was noted with an EdC 57 badge, but otherwise still in GLAM markings. In the same period, F-BMKK on c/n 22 was on loan to the GLAM.
The second part of the aircraft c/n is listed in the final column.

C/n	Code/Unit	Callsign	Remarks
49	J/GLAM	F-RAFJ	
79	–/CEV		ex F-WMKH, F-BNRH
93	N/GLAM	F-RAFN	ex F-WMKF, F-RAFN, F-RBQA/GAM 82
115	339-WL	F-UGWL	
124	CC/CEV	F-ZACC	
131	CD/CEV	F-ZACD	
138	CR/CEV	F-ZACR	ex F-WLCS, D-CALL, G-BAOA, F-BUIC
154	W/o 22.1.76		ex F-RAFK/GLAM, F-RAEB/GAEL
167	L/GLAM	F-RAFL	
238	M/GLAM	F-RAFM	
260	A/GAEL	F-RAEA	
268	K/GLAM	F-RAFK	ex F-RAEB/GAEL
291	P/EdC 57		ex F-RAEC/GAEL, F-RAFP/GLAM
463	339-WM	F-UGWM	

C/n
408
415
435
432
433
437
440
447
453
477
488
492
505
186

DASSAULT BREGUET FALCON 50

A three-engined development of the successful Mystère 20, the prototype Falcon 50 made its first flight on 7 November 1976 registered F-WAMD, followed by a second aircraft, F-WINR, on 16 February 1978. Production is scheduled to begin in the Spring of 1979, and c/n 5 is earmarked for the use of the French President. It is likely that it will be based at Villacoublay with the aircraft of the GLAM (ET 1/60).

DASSAULT FLAMANT

The first Dassault Flamant flew on 10 February 1947 and entered production in three versions. C/ns 1-135 were MD315 transports; 136-254 were MD312 six-seat transports; and 255-293 were MD311 bombing and navigation trainers. The final twenty-five, c/ns 294-318, were further MD312s, for use by the Aéronavale. The Flamant now serves in the training role, and some conversions to radar-interception trainer as MD315R have been made, particularly for ECTT 30.
Known remaining Flamants are listed below, many of the aircraft of the SLVSVs having been withdrawn and the Naval aircraft replaced by the Navajo. Flamants will remain in service with GE 319 at least until 1981, and the Cessna Titan has been evaluated as a prospective replacement. Those aircraft for which no current identity is known will almost certainly have been scrapped.

C/n	Current Status	Remarks
6	Scrapped	ex BR/CEV
17	Instructional	
30	Scrapped	ex BB
41	Preserved	ex 30-QR
43	Preserved	
50		ex 30-QQ
51	Preserved	ex 30-QS
52	Instructional	ex Q
58	Preserved	ex 118-IS
60	Scrapped	ex 30-QT, preservation
63		ex 44-CX
65	Instructional	
66	Preserved	
77	Scrapped	
79	Preserved	ex 30-QX
83	Scrapped	ex D
90	Instructional	ex H
91	Instructional	ex P
92	Preserved	
96	Instructional	
98	Scrapped	ex 2-HK
107	Instructional	ex N
113	Preserved	ex 30-QX
123	Instructional	ex M
124	Scrapped	
126	Preserved	ex 30-QU
127		ex F-ZABK
130	OF/CEV	
135	Instructional	ex 721-DO
138	AH/CEV	
140	Preserved	ex 7-JE
142	319-DI	ex DA/CEAM, 41-GH, 070-ME
143	319-CL	ex 30-QN, 332-IM
144	Instructional	ex 721-EO
145		ex A/GE 319, 8-OJ, 92-CU
146	319-CM	ex 41-GA
147		ex 8-OK
148	118-DE	ex 30-LA, M/GE 319, 319-DE
149	Preserved	ex 315-SW
150	Scrapped	
152	Scrapped	ex 319-DO
153	319-DV	ex 319-DK, EC 4
155	319-CH	ex H/GE 319
156	Bordeaux Base Flt.	ex 5-MJ
157		ex 94-CU, 5-ME
158	319-CF	ex 319-DL
160	319-DA	
161	Preserved	
163	319-CN	ex 30-LD
164	319-DB	ex 319-DJ
165	Preserved	ex 44-GI
166	319-DF	
167		ex F/GE 319, M-E/EC 70
168	Preserved	ex Z/GE 319
169	Preserved	ex 4-WA
170	Preserved	ex 319-CR
172	319-DD	ex C/GE 319
173	319-CR	ex CEV, 319-DG
174	319-DL	ex 118-IO
175	Preserved	ex 41-GB
176	Preserved	
177		ex 319-CE
178		ex D/GE 319
179		ex M/ET 2/60, 41-GG, B/GE 319
180	319-CT	ex 30-QL
181	319-DG	ex Q/GE 319, 10-KA
185	Preserved	ex 319-CO
187	319-CK	ex 12-XA
188	Preserved	ex 3-KZ, 41-GD
189	319-CU	ex 2-HL
191	Preserved	ex XA
194	Preserved	ex 30-QL
195		ex 118-DB, 319-DS
196	319-DZ	ex 319-DH, 5-MK
197	Scrapped	ex 332-IL
199	Scrapped	
200	Preserved	ex 13-TA
201	319-DJ	ex 5-MK, 3-KZ
202	319-CS	
203	319-CY	ex 319-DB
204		ex 113-DC
205		ex 113-DA
206	Scrapped	ex 118-IP
207	Instructional	ex 43-BL, 319-CV

120

208	319-CC			269	Preserved	ex 316-KD		03	W/o 28.10.68 ex CEAM, EPNER
209		ex 319-CL		270	Stored	ex 316-KC		04	Withdrawn ex CEV
210	319-CE	ex 319-CP		271	Preserved			05	W/o 13.10.60 ex CEV
211		ex 10-KB		272	Preserved	ex 316-KJ		06	Preserved ex F-ZLAY/EPNER
212	Instructional	ex 319-CB, 319-DD		273	Scrapped	ex P/CEAM		07	EPNER ex CEAM
213		ex 41-GF		274	—/GE 316			08	Withdrawn ex CEV
214	Scrapped	ex 319-DQ		275	Preserved	ex 316-KC		09	W/o 20.6.61 61
215	319-DP	ex 41-GI		276	Preserved	ex 316-KQ		010	CEV ex CEAM
216	319-DK	ex 313-CA, 313-TX		277	Scrapped				
217	319-CJ			278	—/GE 316	ex 316-KC			
218	319-CA			279	Scrapped	ex 316-KF			
219		ex 319-CP		280	Scrapped	ex 316-KM			
220	Preserved	ex 319-CK		281	Preserved	ex 316-KK			
221	319-CM			282	—/GE 316	ex 316-KY			
222	Preserved	ex 319-DY		284	Preserved				
223	Scrapped			285	Scrapped				
224	Scrapped	ex M/GE 319, 319-DV		286		ex 316-KO			
225	Scrapped			287	Stored	ex 316-KF			
226	319-CG	ex CEV		288	316-KP				
228	319-CP	ex F/GE 319, 319-CW		290	316-KL	ex 10-KB			
229	319-DW	ex 2-HD		291	—/GE 316	ex 316-KS			
230	Scrapped	ex 118-IN		293	Scrapped				
231		ex LA/EC 30, Z/GE 319, 5-MK		294	Instructional				
232	319-CB	ex 93-CT		295	Scrapped				
233		ex 8-OL		301	Preserved				
234	319-CW	ex 41-GE, 41-GC, 13-TA		302	Instructional	ex SLD			
235	319-DC	ex R/GE 319, 41-GJ		307	Scrapped	ex 2S			
236	Instructional	ex 721-EN		308	Scrapped	ex 3S			
237	319-DC			309	Scrapped				
238	Scrapped	ex 91-CW		311	Scrapped	ex SLD			
239	319-DN	ex 92-CV		314	Scrapped				
240	319-DY	ex E/GE 319, 30-QM		316	Scrapped	ex SLD			
241	Preserved	ex 319-CN, 319-CV		317	Instructional				
243	319-CD			318		ex 3S			
244	319-CO	ex 30-QN, 315-SX							
245		ex 44-GE							
246	319-DT	ex 3-KZ, 070-MF							
247		ex 2-HN							
248	319-DH	ex 12-XA							
249		ex CEV, 332-IQ, 2-HN							
250	319-CI								
251	319-CZ								
252	319-DQ	ex 319-DN							
253	319-CQ								
255	Preserved	ex 316-KN							
257	EAA 601	ex 316-KG							
258	EAA 601	ex 316-KA							
261	Preserved								
262	Bordeaux Base Flt.	ex 316-KZ							
263	EAA 601	ex 316-KN							
264	Scrapped	ex 316-KD							
265	Scrapped	ex 118-IK, 2-HD							
266	2-HD	ex 316-KJ							

Twin-seat trainer Mirage IIIB-01 was next to fly on 21 October 1959, and was followed by the production IIIB on 19 July 1962. Twenty-six were initially produced for the Mirage fighter and reconnaissance wings' training echelons, and were later joined by five for trials (Nos. 231-235), and ten for Mirage IVA training with 91, 93 and 94 Escadres. The IIIBE, equipped with the same instrumentation as the Mirage IIIE, began at No. 251.

Mirage IIIB

C/n	Unit/Status	Remarks
B01	CEV	
201	DG/C 328	ex 118-AV, 328-DC, 93-DC
202	CEV	ex CEV, 118-A, 33-N, 328-DG, EA/CEV
203	2-FG	ex 118-AW, —/C328
204	2-FO	ex 2-LY, 2-LV, 2-FL, 2-FD, 2-FU
205	DL/C 328	ex 13-QQ, 13-PX, 2-FE, 13-QQ, 94-DL
206	DD/C 328	ex 13-PN, 2-FF, 2-FH, 94-DL, 2-FM
207	118-AA	ex 328-DD, 2-FL, 2-FM, 2-FG, 93-DH, DH/C 328
208	W/o	ex 33-TZ, 33-NI, 3-KZ, 2-FH, 2-FS
209	2-FI	ex 2-LX, 2-FU
210	W/o 27.8.65	ex 33-TY, 33-NJ
211		ex 33-TX, 2-ED, 2-FO, 2-FK, 118-AA
212	2-FL	ex 33-TW, 33-NQ, 3-KR, 2-FR
213	2-FR	ex 2-ED, 2-FK
214	DK/C 328	ex 13-QW, 13-QP, 13-PR
215	DJ/C 328	ex 33-TV, 93-DH, 2-FT
216	Instructional	ex CEV, written off 11.9.63
217	2-FA	ex 33-TU, 33-NX, DJ/C 328, 33-TW, 2-FP
218	re-serialled 228/SAAF 816	
218	DM/C 328	ex 2-FO, 328-DE, ex C/n 227 (No. 1)
219	118-AB	ex 118-AF, 328-DM
220	2-FH	ex 13-QV, 13-PV, 13-QR, 2-FM
221	2-FN	ex 118-AN, 2-EM, 3-KB, 3-KR
222	2-FM	ex 118-AC, DI/C 328
223	W/o 18.9.68	ex 118-AE, 13-PY, 2-FM, 93-DI, CEV
224	2-FJ	ex 118-AG, 118-AB, 2-FM
225	CEV	Mirage IIIB-SV (variable stability)
226	2-FT	ex 13-PW, 13-QS, 2-FJ

DASSAULT MIRAGE III

Development of the Dassault Mirage began on 25 June 1955 with the first flight of the Mirage I trials aircraft, the ancestor of the world-famous Mirage III series. The Mirage III-001 first flew on 17 November 1956 and was converted to VTOL configuration in 1962. Ten Mirage IIIA evaluation aircraft followed, the first on 12 May 1958, and two of these still serve in an experimental role.

Mirage IIIA

C/n	Unit/Status	Remarks
01	Preserved	ex CEV (as IIIR)
02	Preserved	ex F-ZADY/CEV

121

227 re-serialled 218 (No. 2)
227 W/o 26.11.70 ex CEV, 2-FP, ex C/n 228 (No.1)
228 re-serialled 227 (No. 2)

Mirage IIIB-1

C/n	Unit/Status	Remarks
231	EPNER	ex CEV
232	–/CEV	ex CI/CEV
233	ZA/CEV	ex CJ/CEV
234	DT/EPNER	ex CK/CEV
235	CL/CEV	

Mirage IIIB-RV

C/n	Code/Unit	Remarks
241	DA/C 328	
242	DN/C 328	
243	DO/C 328	
244	DE/C 328	
245	DF/C 328	
246	DP/C 328	
247	DQ/C 328	
248	DB/C 328	
249	DC/C 328	
250	DD/C 328	

Mirage IIIBE

C/n	Code/Status	Remarks
257	W/o	ex 2-FV, 2-FD, 2-ZB
258	2-ZC	ex 2-FQ
259	W/o 2.1.72	ex 2-ZD
260	2-ZE	
261	2-ZF	
262	2-ZG	
263	W/o 25.9.73	ex 2-ZH
264	2-ZD	
265	2-ZI	
266	2-ZJ	
267	2-ZK	
268	2-ZL	
269	2-ZM	
270	2-ZA	
271	2-ZN	
272	2-ZO	
273	CEV	
274	2-ZB	
275	2-ZC	
276	2-ZH	

DASSAULT MIRAGE IIIC

The first fighter version of the Mirage III to enter service was the IIIC, the production model of which flew on 9 October 1960. The IIIC equipped 2 and 13 Escadres, and when EC 2 received the IIIE it transferred some of its aircraft to EC 2/10, whilst those of EC 13 were grouped in EC 5. As the aircraft of EC 5 were replaced by the Mirage F1 they went to EC 1/10 and to reinforce 2/10. A light blue camouflage has spread to the type, No.21 being the first in 1975. However the recently-formed 3/10 in Djibouti uses 12 aircraft (10-LA etc) in two-tone brown colours; these are also fitted with additional wing hardpoints to carry 'Magic' missiles.

C/n	Unit/Status	Remarks
1	Instructional	ex CEV, 2-FC, 10-SA
2	DX/CEV	ex 118-A.
3	Stored	ex K/CEV, 2-LN, 2-LA, 2-FA
4	W/o 3.2.67	ex 118-AE, 2-LM
5	Instructional	ex CEV, 2-FE, 10-RC
6	W/o 29.6.71	ex K/CEV
7		ex 118-AK, 2-FD, 10-RO
8	Stored	ex 118-AF, 2-FB
9	W/o 9.3.71	ex CEV, 2-FF, 2-EI
10	10-RJ	ex 118-AL, 5-NA, 5-ND
11	10-RA	ex 118-AM, 13-QC, 13-PC, 2-EC, 5-OC, 5-OL, 5-NM, 5-NA, 5-SL
12	10-SN	ex 118-AN, 2-EI, 2-LI, 2-LE, 5-OA, 5-NK, 5-NP
13	10-SS	ex CEV, 118-AM, 13-PN, 5-OB, 5-ON
14	W/o 23.6.67	ex CEV, 118-AU, 5-NB
15	W/o 30.1.63	ex 2-L.
16	10-SD	ex 2-EF, 2-LA, 5-OD, 5-OJ, 10-RA
17	W/o 18.3.65	ex CEV, 2-LE, 5-OE
18		ex CEV, 2-EJ, 2-EK, 5-OF, 5-NC, 5-NL, 10-SB
19	Scrapped	ex 13-PO, 2-LA, 5-OI, 10-SB, 10-RC
20	W/o 30.5.63	ex 13-QA
21	10-SC	ex 118-AP, 2-EK, 2-EO, 10-RA
22	10-..	ex 118-AO, 2-EE, 5-NG, 10-SQ
23	W/o 11.10.65	ex 2-EA
24		ex 2-EC, 2-LC, 2-LJ, 5-OG, 10-SA
25	10-SB	ex 2-ED, 2-LD, 2-LP, 10-RB
26	W/o 8.10.71	ex 2-EE, 2-EQ, 10-RC, 10-RO
27	10-LE	ex 2-LD, 2-EI, 10-RD, 10-SA
28	10-RU	ex 2-EQ, 2-EG, 5-OF, 2-FF, 5-OH
29	W/o 23.8.61	ex 2-E.
30	10-RE	ex 2-EM
31	10-RF	ex 2-LH, 2-EI, 10-RB
32	10-SK	ex 118-AR, 13-QT, 2-ET, 5-NF, 10-RJ
33	W/o 3.11.71	ex 2-EC, 13-QR, 2-LR, 5-OO, 5-NN
34	W/o 18.12.61	ex 2-ET
35	10-SE	ex 2-LK, 10-RL
36	10-SM	ex 2-EL, 5-NI
37	10-SL	ex 2-EM, 2-LK, 5-OE, 10-RV
38	W/o 6.10.78	ex 2-ET, 2-LT, 2-FA, 5-NI, 5-OC, 10-RW, 10-SJ
39	W/o 5.5.74	ex 5-OF, 5-NI
40		ex 2-ED, 10-RJ, 10-SU
41	10-SG	ex 118-AS, 2-EI, 2-FN, 5-OK, 5-NO, 10-RA
42	10-SF	ex 13-QB, 13-QF, 10-RN, 10-RI
43	10-RX	ex CEV, 5-OM
44	10-ST	ex 118-AT, 2-FG, 2-LF, 5-NQ, 5-NG
45	W/o 8.3.63	ex 13-QA, 2-LC
46	Instructional	ex 2-LC, 13-QH, 13-QA
47	W/o 2.11.62	ex 2-LL
48	Stored	ex 2-EF, 10-RK, 5-SG
49	10-SU	ex 2-LF, 2-LI, 5-OB
50		ex 2-LK, 13-PI, 13-PP, 10-RH, 5-NC, 10-SF
51		ex 2-LO, 5-OI, 10-RM
52	W/o 30.10.62	ex 2-LG
53	10-RM	ex 2-FC, 2-LH, 2-LN, 5-NR, 5-OA, 5-NP
54	W/o 13.11.63	ex 2-EH
55	10-RO	ex 2-LA, 5-NE, 5-OR
56	10-RP	ex 2-FD, 10-RF
57	W/o 14.8.64	ex 13-QC
58	10-RI	ex 13-QD, 2-LK, 10-RN
59	W/o 3.8.66	ex 13-QE, 13-PQ, 2-L.
60	10-RL	ex 13-QP, 2-FI, 5-OL, 5-NK
61	W/o 7.4.68	ex 13-QG, 2-EI, 2-FI, 5-OO, 118-AR
62	W/o 19.1.72	ex 13-PK, 10-RJ
63	W/o 4.3.69	ex 13-PT, 2-EN, 10-R.
64		ex 13-QJ, 2-LJ, 5-NK, 10-RR
65		ex 13-PJ, 2-EL, 10-RC, 10-RQ, 10-SI, 10-RO
66	W/o 3.3.71	ex 13-QL, 13-QR, 13-PR, 5-OF
67	10-RC	ex 13-QM, 2-EL, 10-RO, 10-SJ
68	W/o 1.2.65	ex 13-QN
69	Scrapped	ex 13-PS, 2-EP, 2-EA, 5-OO, 10-RY
70	10-RG	ex 13-PB, 13-PH, 5-NH
71	W/o 9.5.68	ex 13-PU, 2-EO
72	W/o 13.11.63	ex 2-EF
73	W/o 11.2.71	ex 13-PA, 2-EH, 2-LM, 5-NM
74	10-SV	ex 13-PE, 13-QY, 2-FA, 5-NJ, 5-NS
75		ex 13-PE, 2-LL, 5-OG, 5-OP
76	W/o 3.11.66	ex 13-PF, 2-LF
77	W/o 13.7.64	ex 13-PG, 2-L.
78	W/o 2.11.75	ex 13-PH, 2-EH, 2-LL, 5-NA, 5-OM, 5-NM, 10-SP
79	W/o 8.5.66	ex 13-QL, 2-E.

C/n	Unit/Status	Remarks
80	W/o 19.6.64	ex 2-EQ
81	W/o 12.2.65	ex 2-ED, 2-ER
82	10-RB	ex 2-ES, 13-PV, 5-OL, 5-NI, 10-SY
83	10-SO	ex 13-PL, 13-PI, 13-PQ, 5-NH
84	W/o 12.1.65	ex 2-EN
85	10-SH	ex 13-PM, 5-NB
86	10-RH	ex 118-AR, 2-EG, 2-FE, 5-NN
87	10-LB	ex 2-LO, 2-EO, 5-NF, 5-OR, 10-RK
88	W/o 23.7.69	ex 2-EH, 2-LG, 5-NR, 10-R.
89	10-RS	ex 2-FD, 2-LE
90	10-SR	ex 2-FB, 2-LA, 5-OO, 5-OD
91	10-RQ	ex 2-ED, 2-EV, 5-OQ
92	10-RT	ex 2-EX, 5-OJ, 5-OS
93	W/o 17.6.63	ex 2-EW, 2-L.
94	W/o 18.8.63	ex 2-LL
95	W/o 1.10.69	ex 2-EY, 10-RO

DASSAULT MIRAGE IIIE

The major Armée de l'Air Mirage variant, the Mirage IIIE flew on 5 April 1961 and was followed by two pre-production aircraft and the first production example on 14 January 1964. Deliveries have been made to 2, 13, 3 and 4 Escadres. the original order for twenty-four aircraft was progressively increased to 130, 150 and 180. Curiously, some overseas aircraft served with the Armée de l'Air prior to delivery, and in the case of Pakistan only the first six of the twenty-five Mirage IIIEP aircraft ordered received c/ns in this section. For this reason, exports in the 400-600 range are included in this listing instead of the appendix. The final AA aircraft were delivered in December 1972, and a total of 185 have served exclusively with the AA, CEV etc. The type will be phased out beginning in 1978, and is due to be completely replaced by 1985.

C/n	Unit/Status	Remarks
01	CEV	
401		ex 118-AA, 4-BA, 2-EO, 2-LD
402	2-LA	ex 118-A., 13-QR
403	2-LB	ex CEV, 4-AA, 2-EN
404	2-LQ	ex 118-AC, 13-PR, 2-LF, 2-LE
405	2-LC	ex 118-A., 2-EA
406	W/o 3.10.68	as IIICZ-01 ex 13-PQ
407		ex 118-AF, 13-PS, 13-PF
408	W/o 22.3.74	ex 13-PD, 2-LQ
410	2-EB	ex 118-A., 13-PU, 13-PN
412	2-EQ	ex 118-AE, 13-PT, 13-PN
414	W/o 22.9.68	ex 118-AF, 13-QS
415	W/o 19.1.68	ex 118-A., 13-PK
416	to SAAF 832	ex 2-ET
417	W/o 28.1.70	ex 13-PA
418	2-ET	ex 13-PB, 2-LB
419	W/o 28.7.75	ex 13-PC, 2-EF, 13-
421	W/o 31.8.66	ex 13-PD, 118-A.
422	W/o 18.6.71	ex 13-PE, 2-LO
423	2-EP	ex 13-PF, 13-QM, 2-LG, 2-EL
424	W/o 8.10.70	ex 13-PG
425	2-EE	ex 13-PH, 2-LG, 2-EL
426	2-LR	ex 13-PI, 2-LC, 2-EH
427	2-LG	ex 13-PJ, 13-QP
428	W/o 21.9.66	ex 13-PK
429	2-LO	ex 13-PL, 2-LG, 2-LD
430	2-LM	ex 13-PM
431	2-EG	ex 13-QA, 13-QD, 2-LE, 2-EH, 2-ED
432	2-EA	ex 13-PN, 2-EB, 2-EU
433	2-ED	ex 13-QP, 2-LD
434	2-ER	ex 13-QE, 13-PG, 2-LE, 2-LC
435	to SAAF 819	ex 13-PH, 2-LJ
436	2-ES	ex 13-PI, 13-QG, 2-ED, 2-LL
437	to SAAF 820	ex 13-PJ
438	2-LN	ex 13-QG, 2-EC, 13-PR
439	2-LS	ex 13-QI, 13-QH
440	2-EN	ex 13-QF
443	2-LF	ex 13-QE, 13-PF, 2-EH
444	to SAAF 823	ex 13-QI
445	2-LK	ex 13-QI, 2-EE
447	2-LH	ex 13-QJ, 2-LH
449	2-EJ	ex 13-PJ, 13-QM, 2-EF
450	to SAAF 826	ex 13-..
451	2-LT	ex 13-PO, 2-EG
452	W/o 16.1.75	ex 13-QC, 13-QN
453	2-EC	ex 13-QO, 2-EM
454	2-EK	ex 13-QK, 4-AB, 2-LN
455	W/o 16.12.68	ex 13-QL, 13-QM, 3-KA, 13-PQ
456	2-EM	ex 13-QL, 13-PM, 3-KA, 2-LH
457	W/o 8.11.67	ex 118-A., 4-AA, 13-QP
458	W/o 5.12.68	ex 13-PP, 2-LQ
460	2-LI	ex 13-QT, 4-AC, 13-PK, 13-PG
461	W/o	ex 13-PS, 13-QK, 2-LI
462	2-EH	ex 13-QQ, 2-LK, 2-LR
463	W/o 1.4.70	ex 4-BB, 2-LL
466	13-QE	ex 3-JA
467	13-QJ	ex 4-AL, 13-PL, 13-QC
468	W/o 6.3.67	ex 13-PL, 13-QC, 3-IA
469		ex 13-PJ, 3-IB, 13-PM
470	13-QR	ex 13-QB, 13-PD
471	13-QM	ex 3-IC
472	13-QN	ex 13-PF, 3-JB, 13-PC
473	W/o 18.8.66	ex 3-JD
474	W/o 24.6.74	ex 13-QE, 13-P.
475	W/o 24.6.75	ex 3-ID
476	13-QK	ex 3-JF, 13-PE
477	2-LL	ex 3-IE, 13-PA, 13-PK
478	W/o 17.6.75	ex 3-JL, 3-JC, 3-JG, 13-Q.
479	3-IH	ex 4-AC, 3-IF, 3-JH, 2-EI, 13-QO
480	13-QQ	ex 3-IF, 13-PF
481	13-QF	ex 3-JJ, 13-PN
482	13-QA	ex 3-IG
483	13-QH	ex 13-QI, 3-IH, 13-PL
484		ex 3-JJ, 3-IO, 13-PQ, 13-QR
485	13-QI	ex 3-II
486	W/o 5.3.71	ex 3-J.
487	W/o 24.6.74	ex 3-IJ, 13-PR
488	W/o 3.7.74	ex 3-JL, 2-EK
489		ex 3-IL, 13-QF
490	W/o 6.3.74	ex 4-BC, 3-J.
491	13-	ex CEV, 118-AL
492	13-QO	ex 3-IM, 3-JN, 13-PO
493	W/o 12.8.68	ex 3-IN
494	2-LD	ex 3-IO, 13-PA, 2-LQ
495		ex 118-AK, 118-AR
496	3-IF	ex 13-PG
497	3-JK	ex 118-AM, 118-AT
498	3-IA	ex 13-QK, 13-PB, 13-QL
499		ex 13-QN, 13-QB, 13-QN
500	13-QB	ex 4-AC, 13-QD, 13-PE
501	3-JE	ex 2-EK, 3-JH
502	3-IS	ex 4-AD, 13-QS, 4-BE
503	W/o 13.6.67	ex 4-AE
504		ex 4-BH, 2-LL, 3-IK, 13-QQ
505	Stored	ex 118-AH, 13-PP
506	3-JC	ex 118-AI, 13-QN
507		ex 118-AJ, 13-..
508		ex 118-AK, 13-PO, 3-JF, 3-JO
509	3-JE	ex 4-BE, 4-AF, 3-IH, 13-QB
510	W/o 9.8.67	ex 118-A., 4-BD
511		ex 118-AN, 13-QP
512	3-IC	ex 118-AO, 3-IL
513	3-IE	ex 2-EI, 3-JL
514		ex 4-BL, 2-EJ, 3-IO, 13-QH
515	3-JD	ex 4-AG
516	13-QP	ex 4-BF
517	13-QD	ex 4-BG, 4-AH, 2-LQ, 118-AU
518	3-JA	ex 13-, 4-AL
519	3-JG	ex 4-AL, 13-PC, 3-ID
520		ex 4-BG, 2-EG, 3-JG
521	3-JM	ex 4-AJ, 3-IC
522	W/o 28.4.72	ex 4-BI, 2-EA
523	W/o 25.4.68	ex 4-BK
524	3-IQ	ex 4-AK, 13-PB, 3-IG
525	W/o 27.6.71	ex 4-AM, 2-EP
526	3-IB	ex 4-BM
527	3-JF	ex 4-BN, 13-QP, 13-QA, 13-QL
528	3-JQ	ex 4-AN, 3-IQ
529	3-JS	ex 3-JF

530	3-IJ	ex 4-BJ, 3-JH, 3-JM
531	3-IR	
533	W/o 26.6.68	ex 13-PI, 4-AE
534	3-IL	ex 4-BO, 3-IF
535	3-IM	ex 3-IS
536	to Pakistan	ex 3-JT, 4-BJ
537	4-AK	ex 3-IE, 3-IF
538	3-ID	ex 3-JT, 3-IN
539	3-IN	ex 4-AP, 13-QI, 2-LP, 3-JA
540	to Pakistan	ex 4-AM
541	3-JR	ex 13-QO, 3-JM, 3-IM
542	to Pakistan	ex 4-AR
543	to Pakistan	ex 3-IF
544	to Pakistan	
545	3-JH	ex 13-PJ
546		ex 3-IA
547	3-JB	ex 13-QH
548	W/o 3.10.68	ex 13-
549	3-JJ	ex 13-PM
550	13-QS	ex 13-PH, 3-IG
551	W/o 11.12.68	ex 13-
552	W/o 26.2.69	ex 2-LJ
553		ex CEV, 13-PN, 13-PE, 13-PI
554	13-QG	ex 2-L.
555		ex 13-P., 13-QJ, 3-JG
556	3-IJ	ex 13-P.
557	to Saudi 1001	ex 2-LJ
558	to Saudi 1002	ex 4-BB, 4-BH, 3-JL, 3-JC
559	to Saudi 1003	ex 3-JR
560	CEV	(IIIRD nose)
561	W/o 22.12.75	ex 4-AK, 4-BK, 4-AK
562	4-AR	ex 4-AE, 4-AR, 4-BR
563	Instructional	ex 4-BK, w/o 4.6.71
564		ex 4-BL, 4-AD
565	4-AA	ex 4-B.
566	4-AS	
567	4-BD	
568	4-BH	
569	W/o 22.12.75	ex 4-AQ
570	4-BA	
571	4-AB	
572	4-AC	
573	4-BM	ex CEV
574	4-AF	
575	4-AO	
576	4-BP	
577	4-AN	
578	4-BQ	ex 4-BE
579		ex 3-JB
580	to Spain C11-01	ex 3-JE
583	4-BC	
584	4-BL	ex 3-IT, 3-II
585	4-BN	

586	4-BB	
587	4-AL	
588		ex 3-JE
589	Mirage 50	ex 3-JS, Mirage Milan S-01
590	4-BE	ex 4-AM, 3-IG
595	to Spain	ex 4-BM
598	to Spain	ex 4-BR, 4-BI
601	to Spain	ex 4-BS
605	ED/EPNER	ex CEV
606	W/o 22.10.71	ex 4-B.
607	4-AP	
608	4-BI	
609	4-BR	
610	4-AH	
611	4-BS	
612	4-AE	ex 118-AO, 3-JP
613	3-JQ	
614	4-AD	
615	4-BT	
616	4-AG	ex 4-BB
617	4-BJ	ex 4-BE
618	4-AI	
619	4-BO	
620	4-AJ	
621	4-BG	
622	W/o 18.3.76	ex 4-BJ, 4-AL
623	W/o 18.3.76	ex 4-AM
624	4-BF	ex 3-JN
625	4-AM	ex 3-JI

DASSAULT MIRAGE IIIR

The Mirage IIIR reconnaissance-fighter was produced by the addition of a camera-nose to two Mirage IIIA trials aircraft, the first of these conversions flying on 31 October 1961. All IIIR deliveries have been to ER 33, the last twenty to IIIRD standard with ER 3/33. The first production aircraft flew on 1 February 1963.

IIIR versions will be withdrawn in 1982, and the IIIRD is to follow in 1986. An unusual feature of the internal organisation of ER 33 is that aircraft transferred to a different squadron often return to their former unit and adopt the original code, e.g. No. 345 and No. 346 which have exchanged codes no less than three times.

C/n	Code/Status	Remarks
01	Preserved	
02	F-ZADY/CEV	
301	33-CV	ex 118-AQ, 33-NT, 33-NI
302	W/o 31.10.73	ex CEV, 33-NV
303	33-CK	ex 118-A., 33-TA, 33-NC
304	33-CQ	ex 33-NK, 118-AQ, 118-AV
305	W/o 25.2.64	ex 33-TA
306	33-CT	ex 33-TB,
307	W/o 9.4.75	ex 33-TC, 33-NO, 33-NG, 33-NB, 33-NC, 33-NV, 33-NC
308	33-CU	ex 33-TD, 33-CW, 33-CD
309	33-CA	ex 33-TE
310	33-ND	ex 33-TF, 33-NO
311	33-NL	ex 33-TG
312	W/o 25.5.73	ex 33-TH, 33-TW, 33-TJ
313	33-CM	ex 33-TK, 33-CV, 33-CM, 33-CV
314	33-NF	ex 33-TL, 33-NC, 33-NF, 33-NP
315	33-CL	ex 33-TM, 33-CW, 33-CJ
316	33-NN	ex 33-TN
317	33-NO	ex 33-TO, 33-NK, 33-NU, 33-NK
318	33-NA	ex 33-TP, 33-NA
319	33-NR	ex CEV, 33-TR
320	W/o 25.9.67	ex 33-TS, 33-NF
321	33-CJ	ex 33-NE, 33-NM, 33-CJ, 33-NM
322	33-NK	ex 33-NK, 33-NW
323	33-NS	ex 33-ND, 33-NS, 33-NK
324	33-ND	ex 33-NQ, 33-ND, 33-CK
325	W/o 12.3.69	ex 33-TA, 33-NF
326	W/o 20.3.65	ex 33-NG
327	33-NG	ex 33-NH
328	W/o 27.4.67	
329	33-NT	
330	33-NP	ex 33-NP, 33-NR
331	33-NE	ex 33-CC, 33-NE, 33-NL
332	33-NQ	ex 33-CA
333	33-CB	
334	33-CC	
335	33-CD	
336	33-CE	
337	Instructional	ex 33-CF, w/o 6.2.70
338	33-CG	
339	33-CH	
340	33-CI	
341	33-NI	ex 33-TT, 33-CJ, 33-ND, 33-NB, 33-CV
342	33-NM	ex 33-NL, 33-CK, 33-NL, 33-CJ
343	33-CP	ex 33-CL, 33-NM
344	Stored	ex 33-TR, 33-CM, 33-NN, Mirage Milan prototype
345	33-CN	ex 33-CN, 33-CO
346	33-CO	ex 33-NO, 33-CO, 33-CN
347	33-CF	ex 33-CP, 33-CF, 33-CH
348		ex 33-TW, 33-CQ, 33-CV
349	33-CR	ex 33-TZ
350	33-NB	ex 33-TB, 33-CS

Mirage IIIRD

C/n	Code/Status	Remarks
351	33-TT	ex 118-AP, 118-AR
352	33-TA	ex CEAM
353	33-TB	ex CEAM
354	33-TC	ex CEAM
355	33-TD	ex CEAM
356	33-TE	ex CEAM
357	W/o 4.2.77	ex CEAM, 33-TF
358	33-TG	
359	33-TH	
360	33-TI	
361	W/o	ex 33-TJ
362	33-TK	
363	33-TL	ex 33-TL, 118-AP
364	33-TO	
365	33-TM	
366	W/o 15.4.71	ex 33-TN
367	33-TP	
368	33-TQ	
369	33-TR	
370	33-TS	

Various other members of the Mirage III family have been built for trials purposes including the Mirage IIIF flown on 12.6.66, the IIIT first flown 4.6.64, both now instructional airframes; the IIIV of which four prototypes were built beginning with IIIV-01 first flown 12.2.65; Milan S No. 01 ex IIIE No. 589 first flown 29.5.70 and converted to Mirage 50 standard in 1975; and the Balzac V-001 converted from the original Mirage III and first flown on 13 October 1962 as France's answer to the P.1127/Harrier VTOL projects for NBMR-3.

DASSAULT MIRAGE IVA

A scaled up Mirage III, the IVA provides the French nuclear deterrent in conjunction with two escadrons of IRBMs and a growing fleet of nuclear submarines. The Mirage IV flew in prototype form on 17 June 1959, and was followed by three pre-production and 62 production aircraft, shared between EB 91, 93 and 94. As with the training, communications and flight-refuelling aircraft of these three Escadres, a system of central servicing is employed and the aircraft are given call-signs in a unified range, irrespective of the individual Escadrons to which they are allocated. For security reasons the CEAA call-signs F-THAA to HCI are used (though it is doubtful if they now fool anyone), the last two letters appearing on the nose. The force was declared operational in March 1968, and its authorised strength was nine escadrons of four aircraft, with the balance in reserve.

In June 1976, the FAS was re-structured with the result that only EB 91 and EB 94 now exist, each with three squadrons of four aircraft each. Approximately 15 have been lost in accidents and the remainder are being camouflaged, commencing with No. 4 in 1975. CIFAS 328 has four for training purposes, these fitted for reconnaissance.

The change of role from high- to low-level attack has brought about the camouflaging of the Mirage IVA, and in 1975 No.4 was the first to adopt these new colours followed by No.18. Little urgency has been attached to the task, with aircraft receiving paintwork at the time of their second-line servicing.

C/n	Code/Status	Remarks
01	W/o 13.2.63	
02	Preserved	ex F-ZADS/CEV
03		
04		
1		
2	AA	
3	AB	
4	AC	
5	AD	
6	AE	
7	AF	
8	AG	
9	AH	
10		
11	AJ	
12	AK	
13	AL	
14	AM	
15		
16	AO	
17		
18	AQ	
19	AR	
20	AS	
21	AT	
22		
23	AV	
24	AW	
25	AX	
26	AY	
27		
28	BA	
29	BB	
30		
31	BD	
32	BE	
33		
34	BG	
35		
36	BI	
37	BJ	
38		
39	BL	
40		
41	BN	
42	BO	
43	BP	
44	BQ	
45	BR	
46	BS	
47	BT	
48	BU	
49	BV	
50		
51	BX	
52	BY	
53	BZ	
54	CA	
55	CB	
56	CC	
57	CD	
58	CE	
59	CF	
60		
61	CH	
62	CI	

Note: Owing to frequent changes of base, no effort to identify individual units has been made. Thirteen aircraft have not been recently noted, although No. 33 was reported in April 1978 with no mention of a code. The fifteen crashes are thus likely to include most of those aircraft for which no code is shown.

DASSAULT MIRAGE 5F

Originally designated Mirage 5J, fifty Israeli Mirages, descendants of the original Mirage 5 first flown on 19 May 1967 were impounded by the French Government in 1970. After two years of storage they entered service with the newly-formed EC 3/13, whilst the balance remained with EAA 601 at Chateaudun until allocated to EC 3/3 late in 1974. In the spring of 1977 EC 3/3 converted to Jaguars and its Mirages re-equipped EC 2/13.

Mirage Formation. A Mirage formation from Dijon illustrates four variants of the basic type, four of the six unit insignia worn by the resident 2 Escadre and all three of its component squadrons. Early production Mirage IIIB trainer No.203 '2-FG' displays the 'Chimaera' badge of the OCU squadron ECT 2/2 to starboard and has to port (not visible) the 'Grim Reaper'. Mirage IIIBE No.269 '2-ZM' also of ECT 2/2 complements its 'Grim Reaper' by a seamew (again not visible) and Mirage IIIC No.7 '2-FD' has the 'Chimaera' and seamew to starboard and port respectively. This mixture of insignia illustrates the unique status of ECT 2/2 in having three escadrilles attached, their badges being applied in rotation, and not always to the same side of the fin. The photograph is completed by two Mirage IIIE of EC 3/2 (Alsace coat of arms) and EC 1/2 (stork). *(Armée de l'Air)*

Dassault Mirage IIIC No.50 '10-RP'. In contrast to ECT 3/2, the second squadron of EC 10 displays only one escadrille badge on both sides of the fin. No.50 was photographed at Tours in May 1972 before light blue/grey colours were applied overall to CAFDA fighters. *(E. Moreau)*

Dassault Mirage IIIC No.32 '10-SK'. The first squadron of EC 10 is represented by No.32 at Chateaudun in June 1977. Note that the nosewheel door carries the aircraft code 'K' and not the c/n as on the aircraft above. *(S.G. Richards)*

Dassault Mirage IIIA No.07. Believed to be the last of ten pre-production Mirage IIIA still flying, No.07 is pictured here on an early test flight, and now serves with the EPNER at Istres. The IIIA-01 made its first flight on 12 May 1958 and its last on 11 May 1976 before taking up a position in the Musée de l'Air at Le Bourget. Two others are preserved and the cockpit of a fourth acts as a mobile recruiting display. *(via A.W. Hall/ Aviation News)*

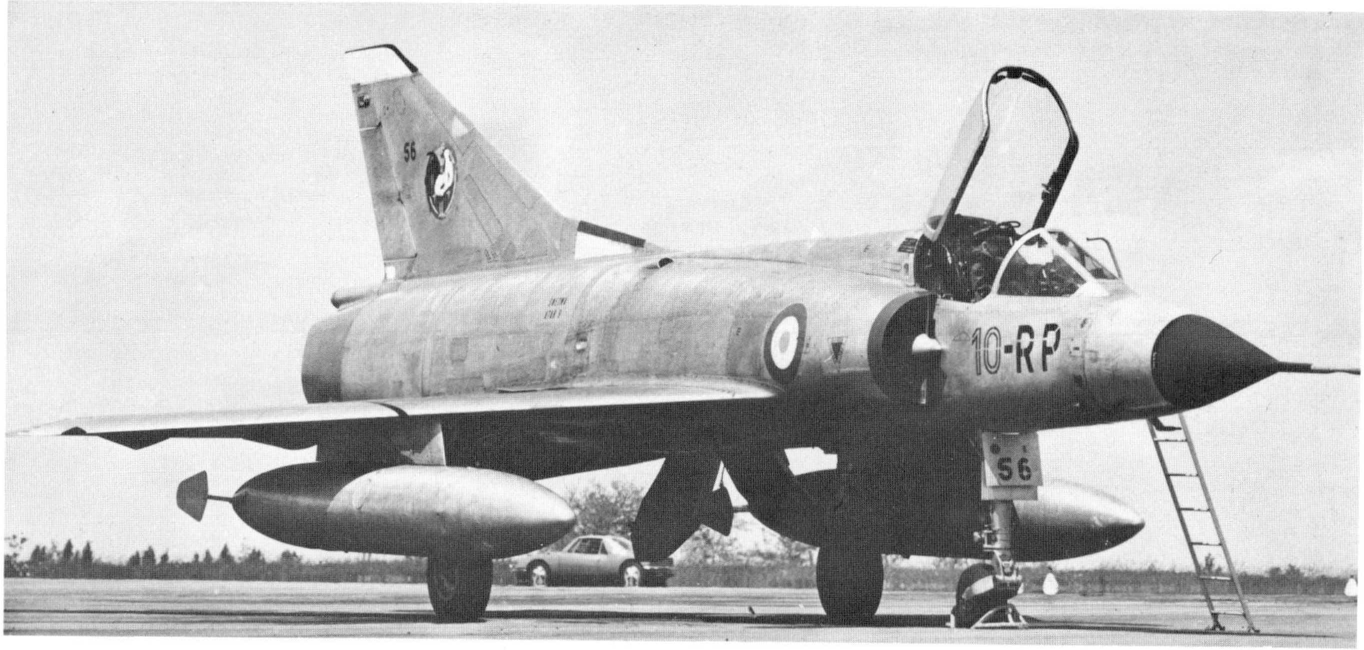
10-RP
56
56

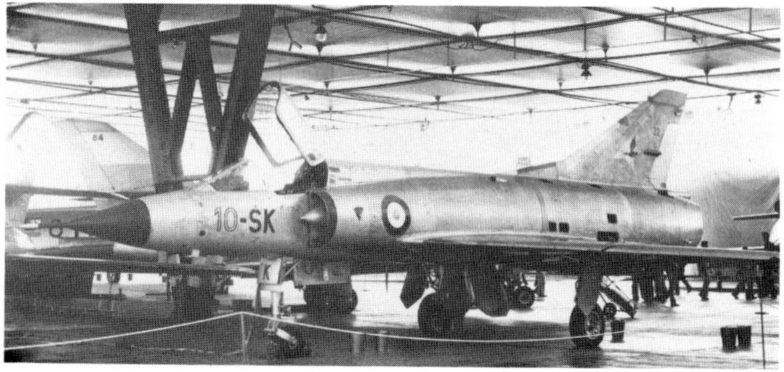
10-SK

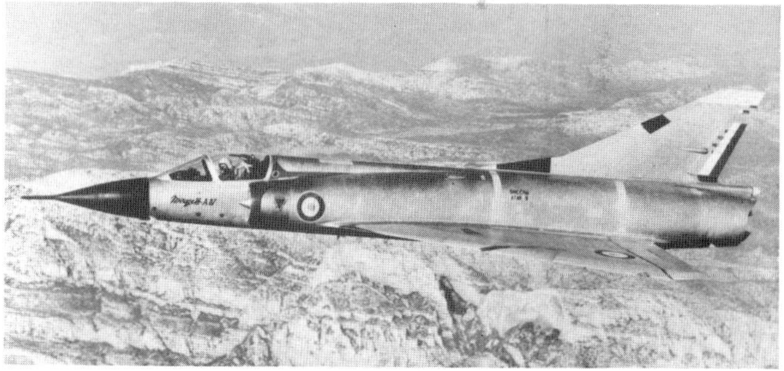

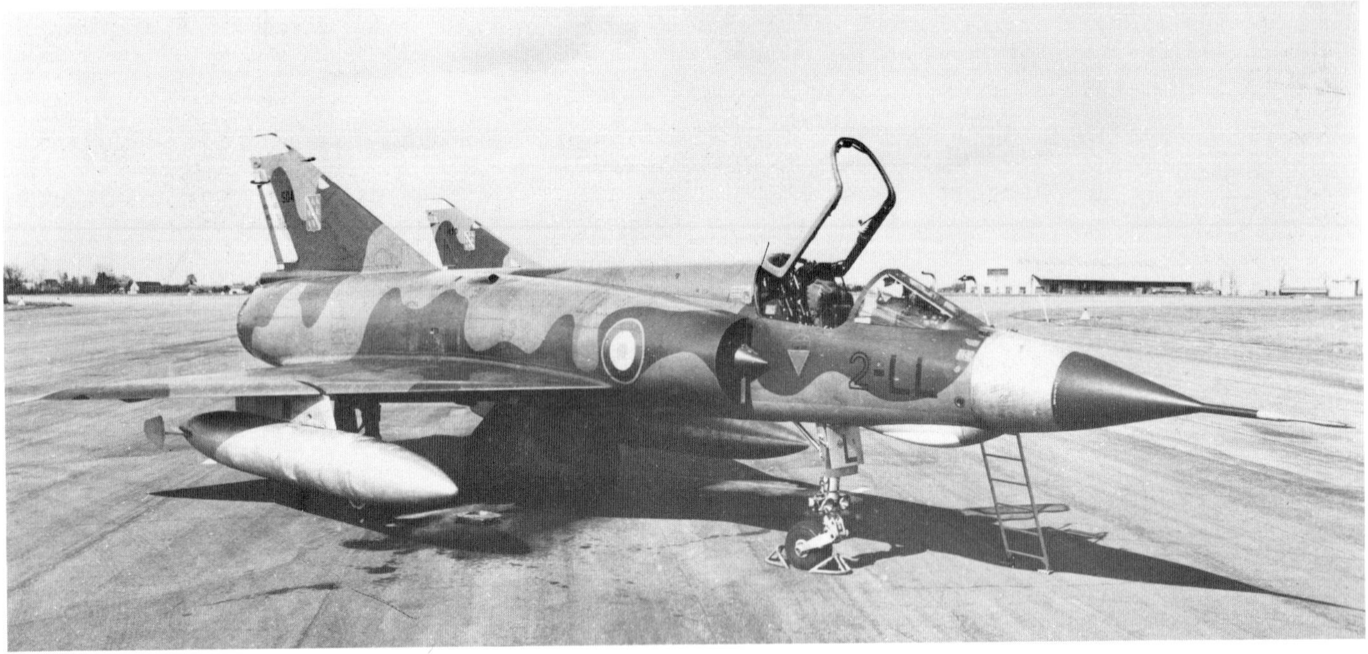

2-LL

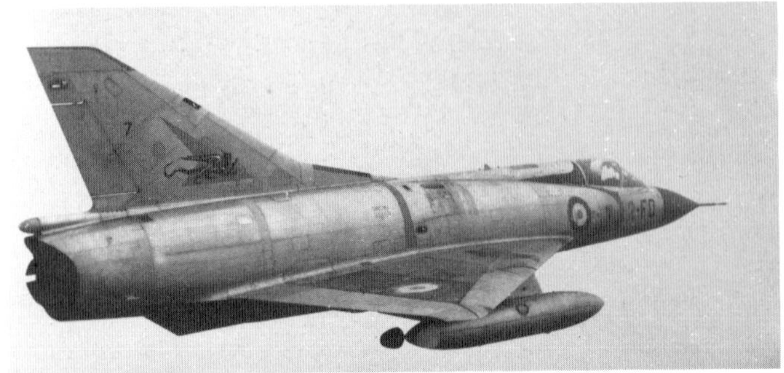

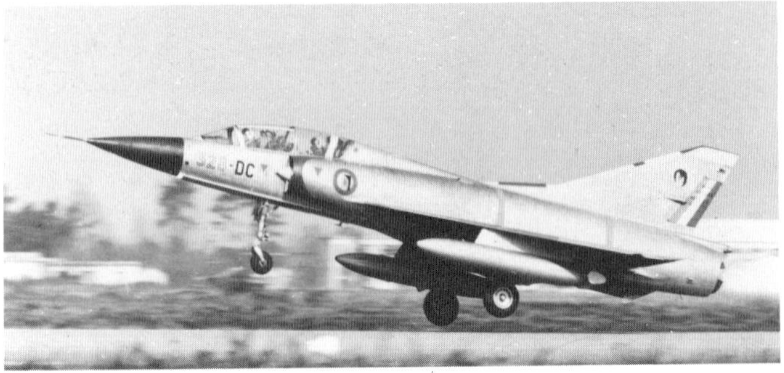

DC

Dassault Mirage IIIE No.504 '2-LL'. Photographed in 1972 during its period of service with EC 3/2, No.504 displays the insignia of the province of Alsace after which the squadron is named. *(E. Moreau)*

Dassault Mirage IIIC No.7 '2-FD'. Up to 1974, ECT 2/2 maintained a small flight of Mirage IIIC in addition to its main equipment of the IIIB, these being coded in the range 2-FA/2-FE. They were disposed of to either EC 10 or to Chateaudun when sufficient Mirage IIIBE became available. No.7 briefly became '10-RO' but has now been withdrawn. *(Armée de l'Air)*

Dassault Mirage IIIB No.201 '328-DC'. Operational training facilities for the strategic nuclear force are provided by CIFAS 328 at Bordeaux, to whom the first production Mirage IIIB belongs. It was originally practice to indicate the operating unit (91, 93, 94 or 328) as a code prefix, but aircraft now carry only the last two letters of their call sign. *(via A. W. Hall/Aviation News)*

Dassault Mirage IIIE No.432 '2-EA'. Perpetuating the traditions of the 'Cigognes' wing of the First World War, EC 1/2 is equipped with the Mirage IIIE as illustrated in this fine air-to-air photograph. Note that the aircraft is fitted with an appendage immediately above the rudder, presumably housing ECM or warning electronics package. *(Armée de l'Air)*

Dassault Mirage IIIR No.315 '33-TM'. 33 Escadre at Strasbourg operates the entire Mirage IIIR fleet, now totalling some 55 aircraft out of 70 delivered, the final twenty of which were the improved Mirage IIIRD which replaced the earlier models in ER 3/33. No.315 passed to ER 1/33 with whom it currently serves as '33 CL', but its rudder flashes have now been erased to conform with present-day practice. *(J-M. Lefebvre)*

129

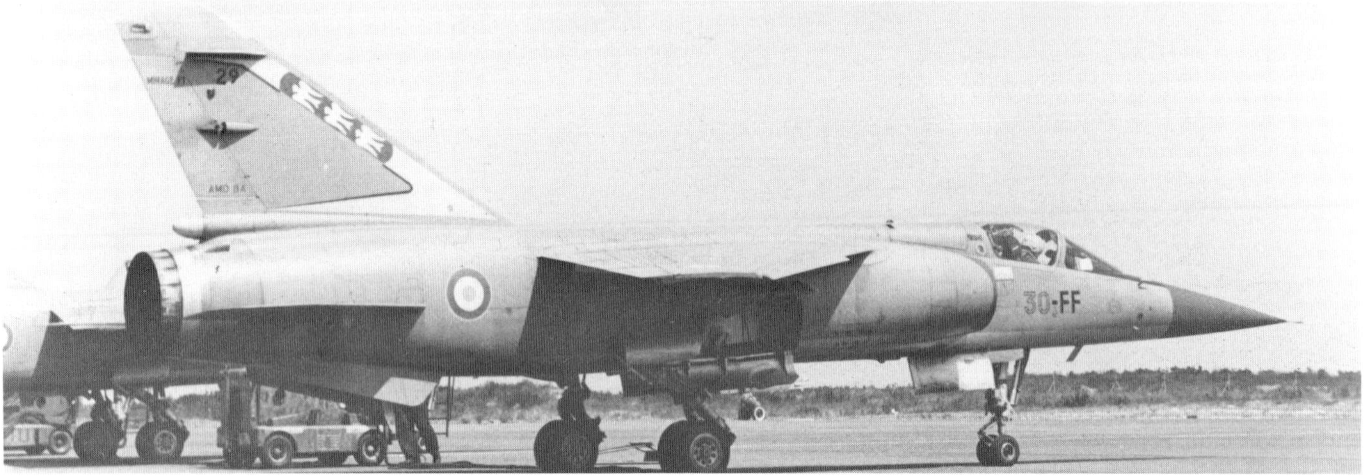
29
30-FF

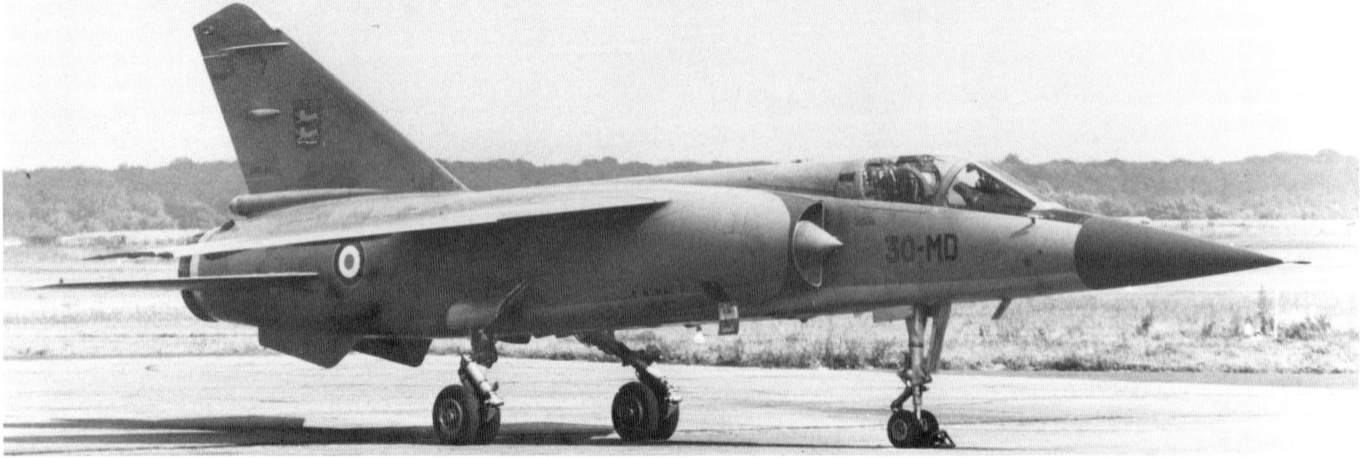
30-MQ

Mirage Miscellany. Representing the three current Mirage F1 wings (to which EC10 will soon be added) are No. 28 '30-FF' of EC 3/30 at Reims, No.7 '30-MD' delivered to EC 1/30 in December 1973 in the first batch to enter service and now an equally early write off, No. 44 '5-OC' of EC 2/5 in partly completed markings which lack three Fleur de Lys in the fin stripe, and No.100 '12-ZL' of EC 2/12 which re-equipped in 1976. *(R. Cram, 'FF & 'OC, J-L. Gaynecoetche)*

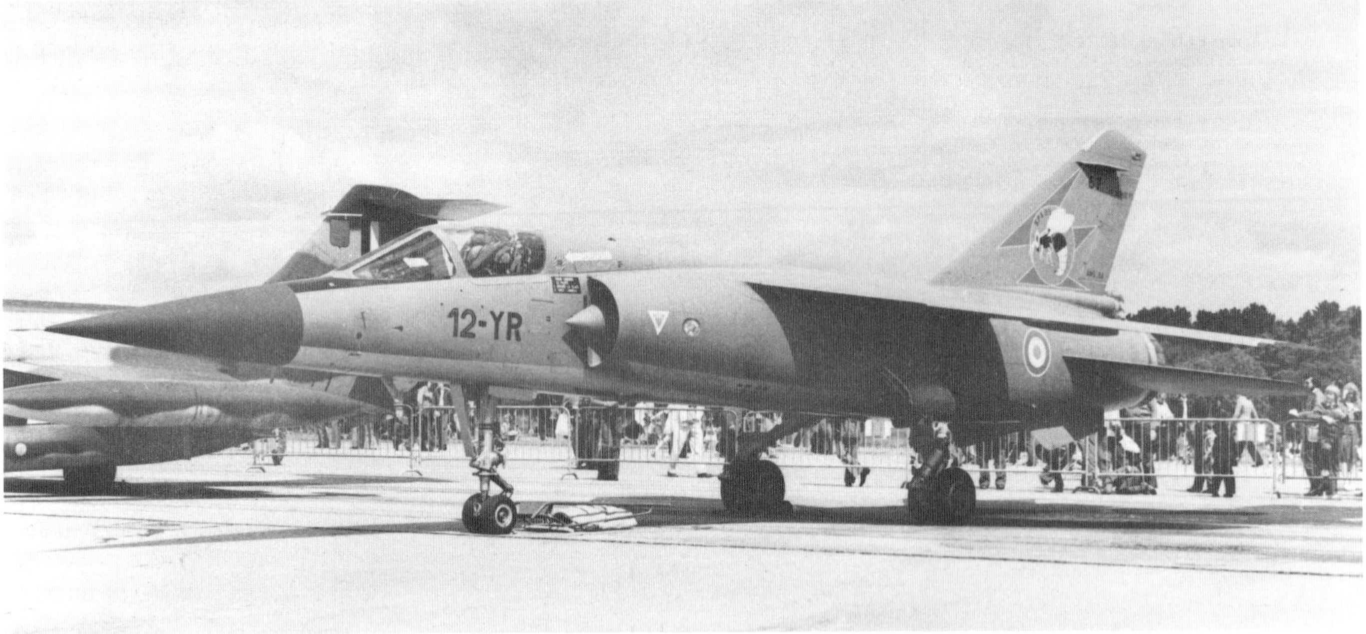
12-YR

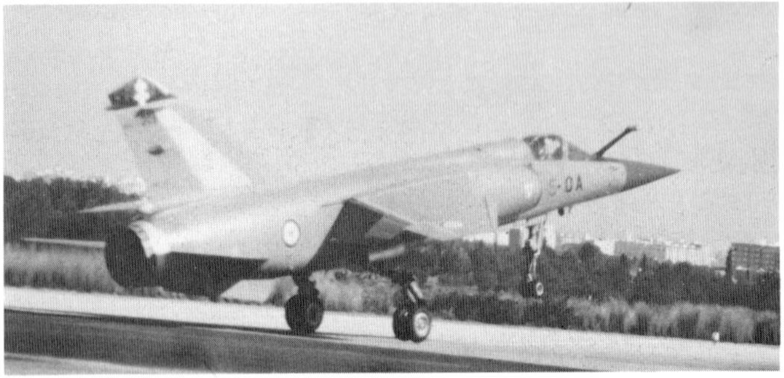

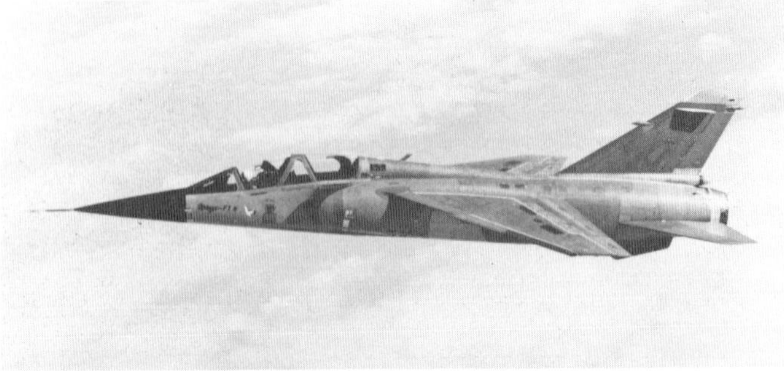

Dassault Mirage F1 No.67 '12-YR'. The first public showing of the Mirage in EC 1/12 markings was at Greenham Common in June 1977. *(S.G. Richards)*

Dassault Mirage F1 No.201 '5-OA'. During 1977, EC 2/5 received an issue of new Mirages in the '200' c/n range and equipped for in-flight refuelling. No. 201 is pictured approaching Manises-Valencia in Spain during February 1978 in full squadron insignia, but when seen three months later it had reverted to factory finish, and was entirely devoid of markings. *(S. M. Huertas)*

Dassault Mirage F1B No.01. First deliveries of the production F1B were to Kuwait, but a small number will equip the prospective ECT 3/5 which is to form as an OCU for home and overseas pilot training on the type, parallelling ECT 2/2 which operates the same service for the Mirage IIIE. *(via A. W. Hall/Aviation News)*

Dassault Mirage IVA No.56 'CC'. Approaching a C-135F tanker for a refuelling exercise, a Mirage IVA tactical nuclear bomber depicts the interim markings of this type. *(J-M. Lefebvre)*

Dassault Mirage IVA No.52 'BY'. Landing at Bordeaux in July 1976, No.52 is one of four Mirage IVA which are detached to instructional squadron CIFAS328, a unit which also operates the Mirage IIIB, Noratlas and T-33, all in support of the strategical force. *(H. de Ree)*

Dassault Mirage IVA No.20 'AS'. Commencing with No.4 in 1975, Mirages of the CFAS have received camouflage during major overhauls. When first in service, aircraft were in natural finish, but code letters were later introduced, running in numerical/alphabetical order beginning at 1/AA irrespective of squadron allocation. *(A.J. Brown)*

Dassault Mirage 5F No.22 '13-SS'. The Mirage 5 is a simplified version of the Mirage III featuring a modified nose profile and fewer electronics. The initial order was for 50 aircraft designated Mirage 5J for Israel, but French political favours changed, and their export was prohibited. After some years in storage, the batch was bought by the Armée de l'Air and re-designated Mirage 5F. No.22 belongs to the first unit to get the 5F, EC 3/13, its aircraft being rapidly camouflaged after entry into service.
(B. Marselis)

Dassault Mirage 2000 No.02 is seen here laden with two 374 gallon (1700 litre) fuel tanks, and is the second prototype of the latest single-engined fighter from the Dassault stable. It has been suggested that as many as 400 may eventually be ordered by the AdIA and Egypt has shown interest in it's license production. *(AMD-Breguet Aviation)*

C/n	Code/Status	Remarks
1	Stored	
2	13-SG	
3	Stored	
4	13-PE	ex 3-XA
5	Stored	
6	13-PG	ex 13-SM
7		ex 3-XB
8	Stored	
9	13-ST	
10	13-PA	ex 3-XC
11	13-SL	ex 3-XD
12		ex 13-SA, 3-X.
13	13-SQ	ex 3-XE
14	13-SJ	
15	13-SN	
16	Stored	
17	13-SH	
18		ex 3-XF
19	13-PJ	ex 3-XG
20	13-PB	ex 3-XH
21	13-PH	ex 3-XI
22		ex 13-SS
23	Stored	
24	13-ST	
25		ex 13-SM, 3-XM
26	W/o 8.10.75	ex 13-SI, 13-SM
27	13-SF	
28	13-SH	
29	13-PG	ex 3-XJ
30	13-PT	
31	13-PC	ex 13-SL
32	13-PD	ex 13-SC
33	13-SO	
34	Stored	
35	13-PL	ex 3-XK, 3-XR
36	13-SS	
37	13-SK	
38	13-SR	
39	13-PF	ex 3-XL
40	W/o 20.12.73	ex 13-SC
41	13-SE	
42	W/o 2.2.73	ex 13-SE
43	13-PK	ex 13-SN, 3-XN
44	13-SD	ex 13-SF
45	W/o 8.10.75	ex 13-SD
46	13-SP	
47	13-PM	ex 13-SQ
48	13-PO	ex 13-SH, 3-XO
49	13-PN	ex 13-SD, 3-X.
50	13-SB	

DASSAULT MIRAGE F1

The first of four prototypes of the F1 flew on 23 December 1966, and production began on 15 February 1973 with the first flight of F1-1. ECTT 30 equipped in 1974, EC 5 followed during 1974/75 and EC 12 in 1976/77. The current 5-year plan calls for the production of 109 aircraft, making an eventual total of 225. Of these, 123 will be delivered in the period 1977-82 and the final 23 in 1983. The total will probably include at least fourteen (1978 funding includes nine, and another five in 1979) of the twin-seat Mirage F1B, the first prototype having flown on 26 May 1976. The F1B has been delivered to Kuwait and will go to the new ECT 3/5 in 1980 when this is formed. The two prototypes are earmarked for AdlA evaluation in 1978. Following on from a batch of c/ns allocated to overseas deliveries, are a second series of aircraft equipped for flight refuelling. Their c/ns are irregular and interspaced with further exports. A number have replaced some earlier aircraft of EC 5, and are due to be supplied to EC 10, whilst a few have been produced by converting and re-numbering earlier aircraft. Deliveries to new units may be slowed down during 1979 by the decision to devote the majority of production to export, and only seven will be received by the AdlA in that year. Official figures give the total Mirage F1 deliveries to the end of 1978 as 105 aircraft indicating that all the c/n 200 series aircraft listed are re-serialled from earlier examples.

Mirage F1

C/n	Code/Status	Remarks
01	W/o 18.5.67	
02	CEV	
03	CEV	
04	CEV	ex CEAM

Mirage F1B

C/n	Code/Status	Remarks
..1		
..2		
..3		
..4		
..5		
..6		

(Six aircraft ordered 1978, and included in overall procurement of 225)

Mirage F1C

C/n	Code/Status	Remarks
1	r/s 201	ex CEV '1'
2	118-AK	
3	118-AL	
4	118-AM	ex CEV
5	CEV	
6	30-MA	
7	W/o 31.3.77	ex 30-MD
8	5-OQ	ex 30-ME
9	30-MF	
10	30-MJ	
11	r/s 224	ex 30-ML
12	5-OF	ex 30-MM, 5-NP
13	12-YA	ex 30-MO, 12-ZY
14	5-OP	ex 30-MP, 5-NO
15	30-MS	
16	5-ND	ex 30-MT
17	30-MU	
18	30-MI	
19	5-NQ	ex 30-MG
20	30-MK	
21	12-ZG	ex 30-MN
22	118-AN	ex CEAM
23	12-YB	ex 30-FA
24	5-NE	ex 30-FB
25	12-YC	ex 30-FC
26	5-NG	ex 30-FD
27	30-FE	
28	W/o	ex 30-FF
29	30-	ex 30-FG
30	30-FH	
31	30-FI	
32	30-FJ	
33	30-FK	
34	30-FL	
35	30-FM	
36	30-FN	
37	30-FO	
38	5-NB	
39	12-YD	ex 30-.., 5-NC
40		ex 5-NF, 5-OI
41		
42		
43		ex 5-NA
44	12-YO	ex 5-OC
45		ex 5-NM
46	12-YE	
47	30-MP	ex 5-NO
48	12-YF	ex 5-..
49	12-YG	
50	30-MB	
51		
52	12-ZH	ex 30-FP
53	12-YH	ex 12-ZH
54	12-	ex 5-NF

135

C/n	Code	Remarks
55	12-YI	ex 5-NJ
56		
57		
58	W/o 7.10.76	ex 5-
59		
60	12-YJ	ex 5-NQ, 12-YT
61		
62	30-MC	ex 5-OA
63	12-YK	ex 5-NE
64		ex 5-OD
65		
66		
67	12-YM	ex 5-NF, 12-YR
68	12-YN	
69		ex 5-NL
70		ex 5-OE
71	30-MM	ex 5-ND
72	30-MT	
73	30-MG	
74		ex 5-OO, 5-OC
75	5-NK	
76	30-MR	
77	30-MN	ex 5-NN
78	30-FG	
79	12-ZA	
80	12-ZB	
81	12-ZC	
82	12-ZD	
83	12-ZE	
84	12-ZF	
85	12-ZK	
86		ex 12-ZH
87	12-ZI	
88		
89		
90	12-ZJ	
91		
92	r/s 202	
93		
94	r/s 203	
95		
96		
97		
98	r/s 204	
99	r/s 208	
100	12-ZL	
101	12-ZM	
102	12-ZN	
103	12-ZO	

Second batch (known c/ns only)

C/n	Code	Remarks
201		ex No. 1
202	5-OR	ex No. 92
203	5-NJ	ex No. 95
204		ex No. 98
205	5-NA	
206	5-OA	
207	5-NP	
208	5-OJ	ex No. 99
209	5-NO	ex 5-OB
210	5-OD	
211	5-NH	
212	5-ON	
213	5-NE	
214	5-OG	
215	5-NR	
216	5-OL	
217	5-..	
218	5-OM	
219	5-NL	
220	5-OE	
221	5-NI	
222	5-OC	
223	5-NM	
224	5-OI	ex No. 11

Note: there is some evidence to suggest that re-numbered aircraft duplicate other Dassault allocations and are merely an AdlA device to produce a tidy batch. In support of this belief c/n 201 and 202 are reportedly Moroccan AF 210 and 211, whilst c/n 204 is Greek AF CG31.

DASSAULT MIRAGE 2000

The first of five prototypes of the air superiority Mirage 2000 made its first flight on 10 March 1978. Subject to Armée de l'Air satisfaction, an initial batch of 127 will be ordered, of which only the first ten will have been delivered before the end of 1982.
A second prototype was flown on 18 September 1978 to be followed by three AdlA experimental aircraft in 1979-80. The first production machine will go to the CEAM early in 1982 and the first squadron will form in the following year. Orders for the fighter variant will eventually total 200, and with production of interdictor and photo-reconnaissance marks now under consideration this figure may be doubled.

C/n	Status	Remarks
01	Dassault	
02	Dassault	
03	f/f .79	
04	f/f .80	
??	f/f .80	(2 seat)

DASSAULT MIRAGE 4000

A twin-engined fighter, the '4000' is as yet a private venture project without AdlA backing although there is little doubt that there will be a requirement for such an aircraft for French military service. Ground testing began on 13 November 1978, and it first flew on 9 March 1979.

DASSAULT MYSTERE IVA

The Rolls-Royce Nene-powered Mystère IV first flew on 28 September 1952, and an initial quantity of 225 (later 325) was ordered under US Offshore Procurement contracts. An eventual total of 421 was built, comprising 10 prototypes, 241 for the Armée de l'Air, 60 for Israel and 110 Indian aircraft. At peak strength the 2, 5, 7, 8, 10 and 12 Escadres used the IVA, but now only the 8th uses the type, the last of which will be replaced by Alpha Jets in 1980-81. With the flying schools, GI 312 and GE 314 have now withdrawn the Mystère. In the following list, recently retired aircraft are included as many were stored at Chateaudun prior to disposal. At least one example of the Mystère IVB all-weather fighter, No. 08 is used as an instructional airframe. Aircraft transferred to the USAF were delivered to Sculthorpe, commencing with No. 295 on 27 April 1976.

C/n	Code/Status	Remarks
04	Instructional	
07	Instructional	
08	Instructional	
09	314-ZH*	ex (314-)TL
11	Instructional	ex 314-TQ
12	314-ZX*	
14	314-TX	
15	USAF	ex 314-ZY, 312-US
16	314-ZA*	
17	USAF	ex (314-)UX, 314-TC
18	Withdrawn	ex (314-)TT
20	Instructional	
21	Withdrawn	ex (314-)TK
22	314-TG	
23	314-ZK*	
24	312-UT*	ex 314-ZT
25	8-NO*	ex 314-ZS, 314-ZZ
26	312-US*	ex 314-TW
27	Withdrawn	ex (314-)ZO
28	314-TY*	

#	Status	History
29	USAF	ex 8-MJ, 314-TB
31	Scrapped	ex 314-TA
32	USAF	ex 314-ZW, 312-UW
33	312-UR	ex (312-)UR
35	USAF	ex 312-UZ
36	314-TE*	
38	Instructional/Rochefort	
39	314-ZI*	
40	314-TT*	ex 314-TE
44	314-UU	ex 314-TX
45	314-TJ*	
46	312-UW	ex 8-MX
47	314-TB*	ex 314-ZK
48	Instructional	ex 314-TH
49	Withdrawn	ex (314-)ZK
50	314-TH*	
52	Instructional/Rochefort	
54	8-NO	ex (314-)TB
57	USAF	ex 5-NH, 312-UU, 8-MT
58	8-NN	
59	USAF	ex (314-)TH, 7-CV
60	8-NT	ex 314-ZQ, 7-AP
61	8-MI	ex 7-AP, 314-TN, 8-MY
63	Instructional	ex 12-YK, 10-RK
64	8-MS	
65	8-MU	ex 314-ZE
66	8-NX	ex 5-NF, 314-TV
68	8-ND	ex 5-OB, 314-ZG, 7-AM, 314-TU
69	Withdrawn	ex 314-TS
70	USAF	ex (314-)ZR, 7-AI, 314-TI, 8-NV
72	8-MH*	ex (314-)ZD, 314-ZQ, 7-AX
74	Instructional	ex 12-ZH
75	8-MW*	ex 8-NX
78	Instructional	ex 8-NP, 314-TC
79	USAF	ex 5-NJ, 314-TM, 8-NB
80	8-ML	ex (314-)TP, 314-ZQ, 8-NX
81	8-NS	ex 314-ZU, 7-CA
83	USAF	ex 314-TN, 8-MG, 8-MS
84	8-NY	ex 314-TD
85	8-MV	ex 332-BH
89	Scrapped	ex 314-ZN, 8-NQ
91	8-NR	
92	8-MX	ex 8-NT
93	8-MB	ex 8-MN
94	Preserved	
95	314-ZV*	
97	8-MG	ex 7-AV
99	8-NC	ex 8-MT
100	8-NP	ex 7-CH
101	8-MN	ex 7-CO, 8-MP
104	314-TL*	ex 5-NX
105	8-MZ	ex 12-XW, 314-ZM, 8-MV
106	Dump	ex 12-XX, 8-MP
107	Withdrawn	ex 12-XY, 8-MN
108	Withdrawn	ex 314-TR
111	8-NE	ex 12-XF, 314-ZO
113	8-MO	ex 314-TF
114	Instructional	ex 314-TO, 7-CR
116	8-MI	ex 7-AD
117	8-MZ	ex 7-AN
118	Instructional	
120	8-MP	ex 8-NE
121	8-MY	
122	Withdrawn	ex 7-AV
123	Withdrawn	ex 314-TS
124	Withdrawn	ex 7-AX
126	7-CC*	ex 7-AY
127	8-MD	ex 7-AS
129	8-ME	ex 7-AT
130	Withdrawn	ex 7-AU
133	8-MH	ex 7-AE
137	Withdrawn	ex 7-AL
139	8-MD	ex 7-AW, 7-CJ, 8-MR
141	Withdrawn	ex 7-AR
142	8-MB*	
145	8-NK	ex 7-CN
146	USAF	ex 8-NC
149	8-N.	ex 7-AB
153	8-NW*	ex 12-ZG
168	7-AO*	
177	8-NL	ex 7-AH, 8-NI
178	8-NK	ex 7-AA, 7-CW
179	Withdrawn	ex 7-CP
180	8-MG	
182	Instructional	ex 7-CE, 8-MZ
183	8-ND	ex 7-CH
184	8-NU	ex 7-CE, 7-CD
185	8-MN	ex 7-AY
186	8-NL	ex 7-CB
187	8-MU	ex 7-CW, 7-CU, 8-MU, 8-NS
188	Withdrawn	ex 7-CU
189	Withdrawn	ex 7-CX
190	Withdrawn	ex 7-AG
191	8-MO	ex 7-AC
193	8-MQ	ex 7-CS
194	8-MM	
195	Withdrawn	ex 7-AF
197	Withdrawn	ex 7-CK
198	Withdrawn	ex 7-CT
202	8-NQ	ex 7-CI
206	8-MX	ex 7-AK
207	8-NL*	
210	Scrapped	ex F-ZAGO/CEV
217	Withdrawn	ex 7-CL
234	8-NW*	ex 7-AO
235	8-NI	ex 7-CP, 8-NU
237	8-MA	ex 8-MR
241	8-NZ	ex 7-CQ
245	8-NN	ex 7-CW, 8-NB
276	8-NJ	
278	8-	ex 8-MA, 8-NW
279	8-NZ	ex 8-NV
282	8-MW	
283		ex 8-MU
285	8-MC*	
286	8-MD*	
287	8-ML	ex 8-ME
289	Preserved	ex 2-EY
290	8-MF	
291	8-NF	
293	8-NG	
294	8-NU*	
295	USAF	ex 8-NA
297	8-MH	
299	8-MR	ex 8-MJ
300	8-MK	
304	Withdrawn	ex 8-NK
305	8-NR	ex 8-ML
306	8-NK*	
307	Withdrawn	ex 8-MM
309	8-NP	ex 8-NI
312	Withdrawn	ex 8-MO
315	8-MQ	ex 8-NS
318	8-NM*	
319	8-ND	ex 8-MQ
320	Preserved/Brussels	ex 312-UQ
322	Dump	ex 8-NQ
324	8-NH	

Note: all aircraft marked * *were in store awaiting disposal in 1974-77.*

DASSAULT SUPER MYSTERE B.2 (†)

The prototype Super Mystère B1 flew on 2 March 1955 and was joined by the initial pre-production model on 15 May 1956. The first production B2 aircraft, No. 6, flew on 26 February 1957, and was followed by 174 further examples, 24 of which were supplied to Israel. The Super Mystère equipped EC 5, EC 10 and EC 12 at the peak of its career. Many of the aircraft retired from EC 10 were transferred to EC 12 to maintain the unit strength until the Mirage-F1 arrived. The last three aircraft (46, 148 and 151) were retired from EC 1/12 on 9 September 1977.

C/n	History
02	CEV
04	CEAM
5	CEV
9	CEV
11	12-ZU, 12-YQ, 12-ZW, Preserved
13	12-ZL, 12-ZG
16	12-YI*
17	Instructional
21	10-SR, 12-ZX*
22	12-YI, 12-ZL, 12-YE*, Instructional
23	12-ZC
27	12-ZN
41	10-SM
43	12-ZM, 12-ZC, 12-YJ
46	12-YR, 10-SS, 12-YW*, 12-ZY, Preserved
48	5-NV, 12-ZI, 12-YM*, Instructional
50	5-NC, 10-ST, 12-ZE
51	12-ZS, 12-YO
54	5-NO, 12-ZB, 12-YD*, Instructional
55	10-SP, 10-SH, 12-ZU, 12-YU*
59	10-ST, 10-SD, 12-ZS, Preserved
60	12-ZC, 12-ZH
61	12-SS, Scrapped
67	10-RD, 12-YE
69	12-YP, 12-ZN, 12-YQ, 12-YG
72	10-RY, 12-YY, 12-YO*, Instructional
73	10-SC, 12-ZI
74	12-YK, 12-ZK, 12-YS*, Instructional
77	12-ZM, 12-YW*, Instructional
79	10-ST, 12-YU
83	10-SQ, 12-ZT
85	12-ZR, 12-ZY, 12-YJ, 12-YF* Instructional
88	10-RB, 12-YD, 12-ZB, Preserved
89	12-YL, 12-YB
90	10-SE, 12-YB, 12-YR, 10-SE, 12-YQ
91	10-SN, 12-YF, 12-ZV
95	10-RG, 10-SK, 12-ZA
99	12-YB, 12-YJ*, Instructional
101	12-YJ, 10-SC
109	12-ZQ, 12-YL*, Instructional
111	5-NU, 12-YE, 10-SG, 12-YR*, Instructional
112	5-NA, 12-YM, 12-ZC, 12-YC*, Instructional
113	12-ZK, 12-YO*, Instructional
117	10-SL, 12-ZG
118	10-SC, 12-YS
121	12-YL, 12-YZ, 12-SF, Preserved as '5-OL'
124	10-SR, 10-SB, 12-YJ, 12-YX, Instructional
127	12-ZN, 12-YN*
132	12-ZB, 12-YC, 12-ZA
135	12-YP, 12-YB
136	12-ZN, 12-YH

139	12-YE, 10-RE, 12-ZF, 12-YB*, Preserved as '10-RS/10-SR'
140	12-YG, 332-BB, 10-SI
141	12-YP
145	12-ZK, 10-SR, 12-ZR
148	12-YP, 12-YH*
151	12-YN, 12-YG, 12-YM*
153	12-YP, 12-ZG, 12-ZF, 12-YY, Preserved
154	12-ZJ, 12-YA*
156	12-ZL, 12-YA, 12-YK*, Preserved as '21-HG'
158	12-YE, 10-SH, 12-ZP, 12-YP*
159	12-YC*
160	12-YR, 12-ZP
161	12-YS
166	12-ZP, 12-YE, 12-YT*, Preserved
167	12-YD
170	12-YW, 12-YJ, 10-SB
171	12-YX, 12-ZX
172	5-NA, 12-YL, 10-SL, 12-YV*, Preserved
173	12-YX, 12-ZO, 12-YP
175	12-ZM, 12-ZC, 12-YE
179	10-RU, 12-ZO, 10-SJ, 10-SY, 12-YN*

indicates final EC 12 aircraft 1976/77

DOUGLAS AD4 SKYRAIDER (†)

Between February 1960 and March 1962 the Armée de l'Air received 113 Skyraiders for service with EC 20 in Algeria, these later dispersing to EAA 21 and EAA 22 when French forces departed North Africa. In 1973, the squadrons on Madagascar and in Djibouti were disbanded and in October 1975 EAA 1/22 returned its aircraft to EAA 601 at Chateaudun, several receiving EC 70 codes in the range MA-MZ, whilst others were passed on to the Chad AF. During the first few months of 1977, a few aircraft received US civil registrations and were ferried to new owners over the Atlantic.

Serial	Ex USN	History
95	123789	20-LK, w/o 8.2.63
96	123797	20-QT, scrapped
107	123814	Stored, scrapped
97	123821	20-LX, scrapped
112	123828	20-.., scrapped
108	123832	20-.., scrapped
98	123833	20-QC, scrapped
109	123837	20-QB, scrapped
111	123846	20-LW, 21-LW, w/o 10.9.65
104	123854	Stored, scrapped
113	123884	Stored, scrapped

110	123859	20-LP, 20-FX, scrapped
100	123899	20-QZ, 20-FQ, scrapped
103	123920	20-FJ, scrapped
101	123950	20-FL, scrapped
7	124134	20-QF, 20-QE, 21-LA, scrapped
18	124140	20-QQ, 20-FB, Cambodia 24.11.64
15	124142	20-QN, w/o 22.10.63
14	124143	20-QM, 20-QQ, 20-FP 21-LL, 22-DA, MM/EdC 70, N91909 1977
5	124146	20-DD, 20-QG, w/o 25.9.67
30	124156	20-LF, 20-LA, 20-FO, 21-LF, 22-DI, ML/EC 70, N91935 1977
16	125714	20-QO, w/o 4.4.63
13	125715	20-QL, 20-QO, 20-FC, Cambodia 24.11.64
11	125716	20-QJ, 20-QL, 20-FX, 21-ZC, 22-DG EAA 601, Instructional
4	125717	20-QC, 20-FY, 21-LF, w/o 24.7.72
6	125718	20-QE, 21-LH, 22-DF, scrapped
89	125719	20-LL, scrapped
8	125721	20-QG, 20-QH, Cambodia 24.11.64
9	125722	20-QH, 20-FW, Cambodia 24.11.64
23	125724	20-LJ, 20-FK, Cambodia 24.11.64
10	125728	20-QI, w/o 23.10.60
27	125732	CEV, 20-FK, w/o 17.6.63
24	125734	20-LA, 20-LO, 20-FV, Cambodia 24.11.64
40	125735	20-FA, 21-Z., scrapped
12	125740	20-QK, w/o 7.5.62
86	125741	20-FZ, 21-LP, w/o 20.8.72
26	125744	20-LD, 21-LY, 22-D., scrapped
31	125746	20-LM, 20-FA, Cambodia 24.11.64
76	125749	20-FW, scrapped
32	125755	20-LL, 20-LU, w/o 30.6.69
39	125762	20-LQ, 20-FI, Cambodia 24.11.64
21	126877	20-LB, 20-FG, 21-LJ, 21-ZB, 22-DC, MN/EC 70, EAA 601, scrapped
69	126878	20-LT, w/o 7.3.62
34	126880	20-LG, 21-LN, 21-ZE, Chad 15.2.77
85	126882	20-QD, 20-FD, 22-DG, 21-LH, 21-ZG, N91945
58	126888	20-QI, w/o 9.8.63
35	126890	20-LK, Cambodia 24.11.64
33	126893	20-LN, scrapped
22	126894	20-QR, w/o 9.7.63
92	126897	20-Q., scrapped
57	126900	20-FN, 21-ZF, w/o 13.10.64
20	126901	20-QS, 21-LT, w/o 9.5.68
44	126903	20-FC, 20-FH, scrapped
75	126910	20-QW, w/o 6.11.61
62	126911	20-LU, 21-ZI, w/o 13.2.67
41	126912	20-FB, 20-QR, 20-FR, 21-L., 22-DJ, 21-LI, 22-DJ, Gabon 20.2.76

Dassault Falcon 20 No.268. Executive versions of the Falcon 20 are employed by ET 60, the Groupe des Liaison Aériennes Ministérielles, to which 268 belongs, and ET 65, the Groupe Aérienne d'Entrainement et de Liaison, the former wing having four on strength. No.268 may occasionally be seen at Northolt (and doubtless many other capital-city military airports) transporting high ranking officers and government ministers, usually forsaking its regular call-sign F-RAFK for a four-number identity in the range FM0001-0050. *(J-L. Gaynecoetche)*

Dassault Falcon 10MER No.32. The first of two such aircraft delivered to the Section Réacteur Léger at Landivisiau in mid 1975, and normally operates with the call-sign F-YETA. The SRL also flies the Paris as a continuation trainer, but the two Falcon 10s were obtained to act as radar trainers for the Super Etendard pilot training programme. Dassault hope for additional orders to replace the ageing Dakotas used by 56S. No.32 is pictured at Cognac in December 1975 functioning in its secondary role as a communications aircraft. *(J-L. Gaynecoetche)*

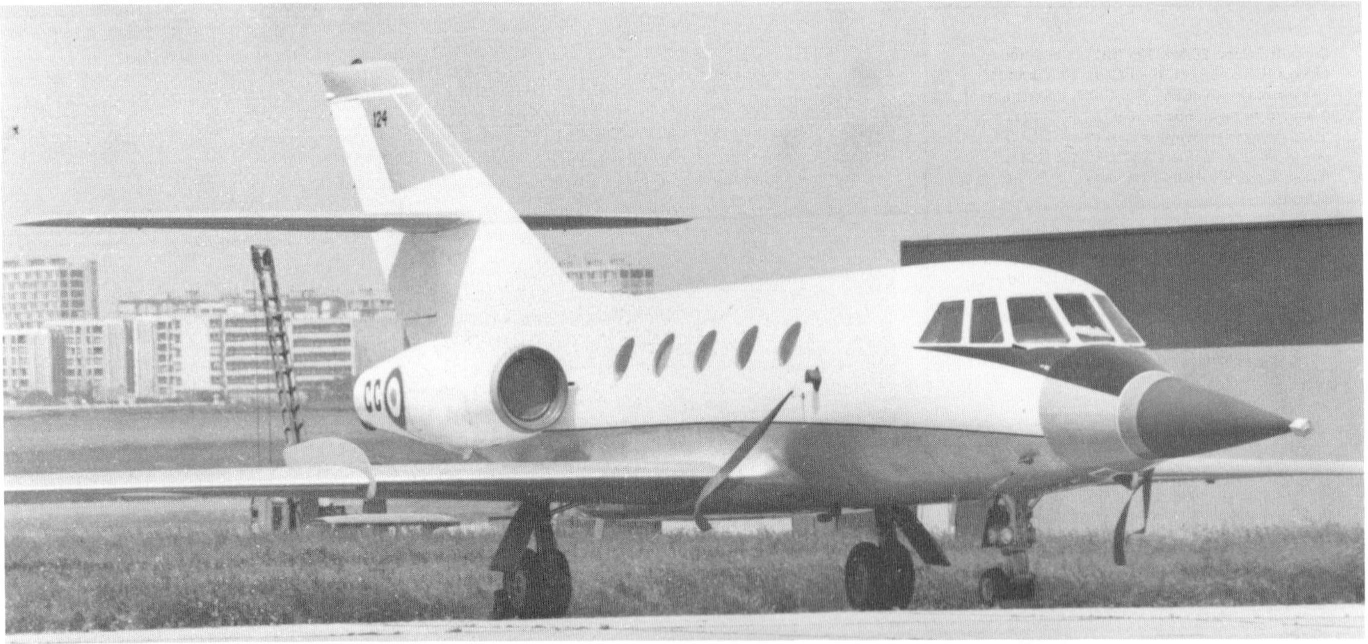
124
CC

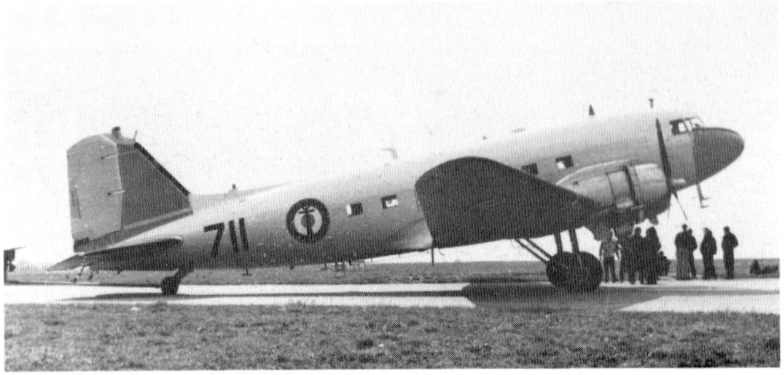
711

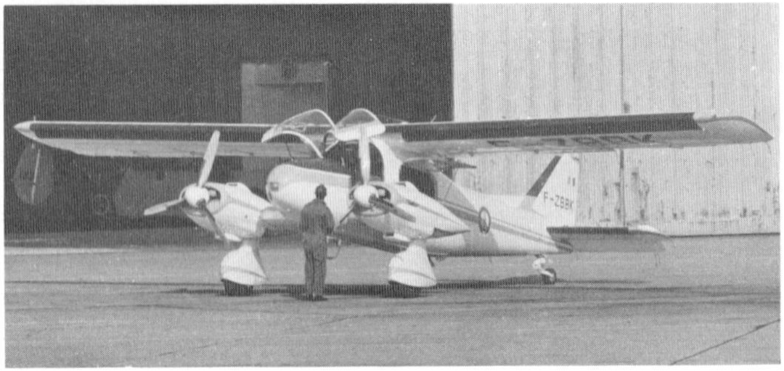
F-ZBBK

Dassault Falcon 20 No. 124 'CC'. In addition to being a VIP transport, the Falcon 20 is used as a test vehicle by the CEV. F-ZACC and sister aircraft CD are fitted with noseprobes, but should not be confused with two similar aircraft of CPIR 339 which are radar trainers with a Mirage IIIE radome giving an equally strange appearance. *(Jean-Marc Crozat)*

Douglas C-47D Dakota No.711. Nostalgia corner features an old favourite still actively employed in the Aéronavale training navigators for today's supersonic jets. The code '711' for this 56S aircraft is a contraction of its USAAF serial 44-77011 and before transferring to the Navy it served the Armée de l'Air for many years. *(J-L. Gaynecoetche)*

Dornier Do28B F-ZBBK. The registration series reserved for the Sécurité Civile also contains four Do 28 aircraft and two Alouette II helicopters used by the French customs. *(MAP)*

Douglas C-54E-20-DO No.49148 '48'. One of the longest serving French military aircraft, 49148 was delivered to the Armée de l'Air on 18 July 1945 and served with ET 60 before passing over to the Aéronavale's 11S at Le Bourget-Dugny to continue its VIP transport tasks. It is pictured here at Essendon in 1970 whilst with the Section de Liaison de Nouvelle Calédonie, call-sign F-YCIA, although its present status is unknown. *(via A.D. Annis)*

Douglas DC-6AC No.44063 '63'. A relatively recent military acquisition, No. 63 joined the Aéronavale's section de Liaison de Dugny late in 1973 as F-YEFA to replace the DC-4-10358 of the same call-sign. Now sporting the up-to-date 'MARINE' titling, it was photographed visiting Aberdeen in 1977. *(A.J. Brown)*

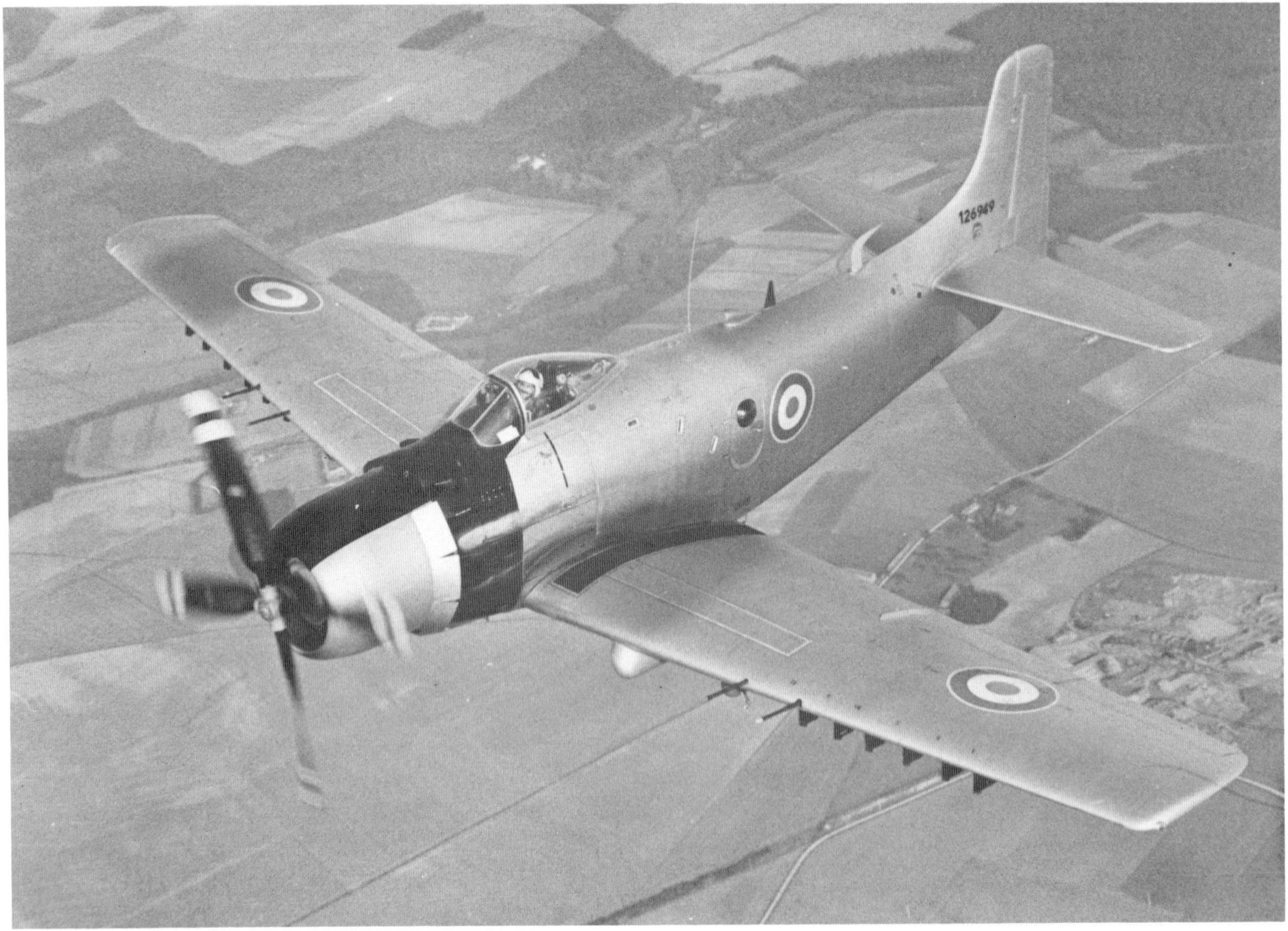
126949

Douglas AD4 Skyraider No.126949. Photographed on a test flight from Chateaudun, 126949 was returned to France after service with EAA 1/21 on Madagascar, and after overhaul was given to the Chad Air Force in April 1976. *(J-M. Lefebvre)*

Douglas DC-8F No. 45820. The first of five DC-8 freighters delivered to the Armée de l'Air, 45820 was received on the last day of 1965 for the newly formed ET 3/60 and allocated the call-sign F-RAFA, the last two of which appear on the nosewheel door. *(A.J. Brown)*

Douglas AD4 Skyraider No.126877 'MN'. Bearing a ferry code applied by EC 70, 126877 is displayed at Chateaudun in June 1976 having been previously attached to EAA 1/22, the last Skyraider squadron, disbanded late in 1975. *(S.G. Richards)*

144

Douglas DC-6AB No.43818 '82-PM'. Withdrawn in 1977, the Armée de l'Air DC-6 aircraft were collected at Le Bourget prior to disposal. No.43818 ex GAM 82 was photographed at Shannon on 30 March 1978 en route to Pat Air of St. Louis, in the ferry markings N72522. *(D. O'Mahony)*

Fouga CM170 Magister No.51 '4-WB'. Representative of the instrument-flying and continuation training aircraft of the SLVSVs, Magister '4-WB' is one of two attached to 4 Escadre. *(J-L. Gaynecoetche)*

Gloster Meteor NF.11 No.NF11-8. A small number of Meteors remain in use as trials installations 'chase' aircraft with the CEV. F-ZABG was seen at Cazaux in June 1975. *(H. de Ree)*

Douglas DC-7C No.45446 'CC'. Three DC-7 are employed by the CEV for missile tracking and other trials at the Landes range in Southern France or in the Pacific. *(J-L. Gaynecoetche)*

Jodel D140E No.206 'YH'. The Jodel 140 is used both as a glider tug and, in this case, as an air experience aircraft. No.206 is operated by the GAALEA 04/312, and wears the insignia of GI 312, the Ecole de l'Air. *(MAP)*

English Electric Canberra B.6 No.316 'AT'. Possibly now the last airworthy French Canberra, 316 is based at Cazaux by the CEV. *(H. de Ree)*

Fouga CM 175 Zéphyr No.12. The Aéronavale received 30 of its own navalised Magisters under the above designation, these serving principally with 59S, whose insignia No.12 wears on the forward fuselage. *(J-L. Gaynecoetche)*

Fouga CM 170 Magister No.443 '313-CE' transferred to its present markings in 1976, having been previously coded 312-AH. *(J-L. Gaynecoetche)*

145

90	126913	20-QV, scrapped	
25	126914	20-LC, w/o 17.9.60	
77	126920	20-QJ, scrapped	
74	126921	20-LW, 20-LE, scrapped	
42	126922	CEV, 20-QV, 20-FQ, 21-LS,21-ZD, 22-DK, Gabon 20.2.76	
46	126923	20-LS, 21-LC, 21-Z., scrapped	
19	126924	20-QT, 21-LF, 21-Z., 21-LD, 21-ZJ Gabon 20.2.76	
3	126927	20-QB, 20-QW, scrapped	
49	126929	20-FG, 21-L., w/o 26.4.69	
43	126931	20-LR, w/o 7.1.62	
51	126933	20-FH, scrapped	
28	126934	21-LD, w/o 28.5.65	
56	126935	20-FM, 21-ZE, 22-D., Chad 7.4.76	
87	126938	20-QS, scrapped	
17	126940	20-QP, 20-LJ, 21-ZB, w/o 1.12.67	
29	126942	20-LE, 20-FF, Cambodia 24.11.64	
93	126945	20-..,	
64	126949	20-LN, 21-ZJ, 21-LE, 21-ZI, Chad 7.4.76	
72	126952	20-LX, 20-FE, scrapped	
94	126954	20-QP, scrapped	
2	126955	20-QA, w/o 21.9.61	
45	126956	20-FD, 20-FY, 21-LB, 21-ZF, 22-DB, Gabon 20.2.76	
67	126957	Stored, scrapped	
47	126958	20-QR, 21-ZA, w/o 15.11.67	
50	126959	20-FI, 21-ZC, 21-Z., ME/EC 70, Chad 7.4.76	
52	126960	20-FJ, 20-FN, 21-ZD, 21-LA, 21-LC w/o 17.3.71	
91	126962	20-QK, 20-F., w/o 19.2.64	
73	126964	20-FV, scrapped	
54	126965	CEV, 21-QB, 21-LI, 21-ZA, Chad 7.4.76	
70	126966	20-FU, scrapped	
48	126969	20-FQ, 21-ZB, 21-L., w/o 14.6.69	
79	126970	20-LZ, 20-F., 21-LG, 21-Z., 22-D., 21-LJ, 21-ZC, 21-ZH, N91954	
55	126973	20-.., w/o 20.7.61	
53	126979	20-QA, CEV, 22-DD, MK/EC 70 Preserved	
36	126983	21-LO, 20-Q., 21-LP, 21-ZE, w/o 8.3.68	
71	126986	20-QH, 20-LG, scrapped	
59	126994	20-QU, 21-ZG, 21-Z., 22-D., w/o 19.6.70	
60	126995	21-FO, scrapped	
38	126996	20-FM, 21-Z., 22-D., MM/EC 70, N92023	
78	126997	20-LY, 20-FC, 21-Z., 21-ZK, 22-D., 21-LJ, 21-ZC, 22-DH,MK/EC 70, N92053	
37	126998	20-LC, 20-QX, 20-FE, 21-LB, MJ/EC 70, Chad 15.2.77	
61	127002	20-FP, 21-ZH, 21-L., 22-D., 21-LN, N91989	
63	127004	20-FQ, w/o 13.5.62	
1	127012	CEV 20-FS, scrapped	
99	127865	20-QF, scrapped	
80	127881	20-QX, w/o 20.4.63	
65	127888	20-QR, 20-FR, 21-LE, 21-ZA, 22-DE, MJ/EC 70, N92034	
82	127893	20-FX, w/o 18.7.62	
68	127894	20-FT, 21-ZF, 22-DC, N..... (US civil)	
88	127895	20-.., 20-FG, scrapped	
81	127900	20-QY, scrapped	
83	127903	20-F., w/o 25.3.62	
66	127919	20-QB, 20-ED, scrapped	
105	128932	Stored, scrapped	
84	128966	Stored, scrapped	
106	128968	Stored, scrapped	
102	129001	Stored, scrapped	

424	43-49824	27085 56S	ex KN219, K-24(Belg. AF), F-YDQS
468	43-49468	26729 F-SDLR/Ambassador Laos ex KK146, F-SCHL, F-ODEL	
485	43-48585	25846 56S	ex K-9(Belg. AF)
701	44-77101	33433 56S	
708	44-76708	33040 56S	
709	44-76209	32541 56S	ex K-C/AdlA
711	44-77011	33343 56S	
716	44-77116	33448 56S	ex F-YDQA
720	44-76420	32752 56S	ex 64-KQ/AdlA
721	44-76721	33053 56S	
725	44-76725	33057 56S	
726	44-76726	33052 56S	
729	44-76229	32561 56S	ex 316-FJ/AdlA
735	44-76835	33167 56S	ex KN555
771	44-77071	33403 56S	ex KN693, 61-ON, 64-KI/AdlA
919	42-93519	13440 SLNC	F-YEGC ex F-BFGF

The CNET national telecommunications agency use two Dakotas, the second of which is identified as '20423', which, of all things, is its C.of A. number.

13142	42-93251	13142	F-SEBD	ex F-BAXG
20423	43-93544	13467	F-SEBE	ex F-BEFN Scrap

Military callsigns are used, as the aircraft are maintained by the AdlA on behalf of the CNET.

In February 1979, France expressed interest in purchasing the British Aerospace 748 of which a small number would be allocated for navigation training, possibly as a Dakota replacement.

DOUGLAS C-47 DAKOTA

The Aéronavale continues to operate the Dakota, principally for training by 56S, but also with a few Sections de Liaison. Several have been transferred from the Armée de l'Air. Those aircraft used since 1970 have been:-

Serial	ex-US serial	C/n	Unit/ Status	Remarks
6	43-48406	25667	56S	ex 4X-AOA, F-YFGE/56S
10	42-32810	9036	SES,StR	ex EI-ACI, EI-ALS
11	42-23411	9273	Scrap	ex Sect. Liaison Saigon
23	Bu17233	13321	56S	ex 42-93412, F-YGGD
25	42-100825	19288	56S	ex OY-DDA, N9984F, N50V
35	43-30684	13835	56S	ex N88732, N48V, F-YFGB/56S
36	42-13936	9798	56S	ex OK-WZB, Sect. Liaison Dakar
59	43-15059	19525	56S	ex 5059(Czech AF), F-YGGA
71	42-92647	12471	56S	ex KG436, EI-ACT, EI-ALT
84	42-100521	18984	56S	ex N65384, N45V, F-YGGG
87	41-18487	4579	56S	ex EI-ACG, EI-ALR, F-YGGB, F-YFGC

DOUGLAS C-54 (†)

Three C-54 aircraft have served with the Aéronavale, and are given here in order of entry into French military service, respectively July 1945, 1961 and 1962.

49148 C-54E-20-DO c/n 27374 ex 44-9418, F-RAMA, F-RAFA, 11S, F-YCIA/9S. Possibly with Section de Liaison de Nouvelle Calédonie.
10358 C-54A-15-DC c/n 10358 ex 42-72253, LN-HAT, F-YEBB/31S, F-YCKG/11S, F-YCKE/11S, F-YCKA/11S, Section de Liaison de Dugny HQ Staff Flight as F-YEFA. Sold as F-BXOQ.
10454 C-54B-1-DC c/n 10454 ex 42-72349, NC34537, N34537, D-ABUL, D-ABEF. Served with 11S, and sold to the French Government in March 1969.

DOUGLAS DC-6B

Known to the US forces as the C-118, the DC-6 is a stretched C-54/DC-4 built in three versions: the DC-6 and 6A freighter, DC-6B passenger transport and DC-6C convertible freighter/passenger aircraft. The majority of French aircraft were withdrawn from ET 64 and GAM 82 in 1977 and stored at Le Bourget pending sale. No. 44697 was earmarked for the Musée de l'Air, but a replacement has been promised.

Current use

Serial	Status	Ex
44063	63/SSD	F-BGSK
45569	F-ZARK	TU-TCE

Withdrawn

Serial	Code/Callsign	Ex	Fate
43748	F-RAFB/GLAM	SE-BDR	W/o 9.3.68
43818	82-PU	F-BGTY	N72524
43819	82-PV	F-BGTX	N72539
43834	64-PI	F-BGOC	F-GAPK
44697	64-PJ	F-BHEF	N72522
45107	64-PI, 82-PZ	N3022C	TR-LXM
45108	64-PJ, 82-PY	N3023C	TR-LXN
45226	82-PW	F-BKPQ	N72532
45472	64-PK	N3025C	N72538
45473	64-PL	N3026C	N72534
45481		F-BLOE	W/o

DOUGLAS DC-7C/AMOR

Three aircraft are allocated to the CEV for experimental purposes connected with missile and armaments trials in the Pacific and the Landes range in the south of France. Callsigns are F-ZBCA/CC.

Serial	Code	Remarks
45061	CA	ex HB-IMK, LN-MOG
45367	CB	ex F-BIAQ
45446	CC	ex F-BIAR

DOUGLAS DC-8F

Five DC-8F serve ET 3/60 at Charles de Gaulle Airport, Paris, the first of which, 45820, was delivered on 31 December 1965. The last two, 45570 and 46043 were received in 1977, F-RAFE actually being operated by EE 51 as an ECM aircraft.

Serial	Callsign	Model	Remarks
45570	F-RAFE	DC-8-33	ex F-BIUZ, F-ZARC/CEV
45692	F-RAFB	DC-8F-55	ex N801SW
45819	F-RAFC	DC-8F-55	ex F-BNLD
45820	F-RAFA	DC-8F-55	ex F-BLKX
46043	F-RAFD	DC-8F-62	ex OH-LFS, OH-LFV

ENGLISH ELECTRIC CANBERRA B.6 (†)

Two batches, each of three English Electric built Canberras have been delivered to the CEV for experimental purposes. the first three were deleted from an RAF contract in 1954, having been intended as WJ763, WJ779 and WJ784; they entered French service as 763, 779 and 784. The other batch comprised 304, 316 and 318, purchased direct from the manufacturers in 1955. They were apparently laid down as WT304 etc, but replaced by other aircraft which then took up these serials in RAF service.
The aircraft served the CEV and EPNER as trial installation machines, pioneering the Turboméca Gazibo rocket motor and CSF Cyrano radar. Two aircraft remain airworthy with the CEV, No 316/AT fitted with a pointed nosecone and No 779/AN. Nos 304/AL and 784/AK were withdrawn at Bretigny in 1974, whilst No 763/AM is preserved at Le Bourget. A further aircraft appeared on the dump at Cazaux in 1975 and may be No 318/AU.

FOUGA CM170 MAGISTER

The prototype Magister first flew on 23 July 1952 and the last of the line appeared in December 1969. A total of 589 was built in France, including 437 production aircraft for the Armée de l'Air, and licence production has also been undertaken in Germany, Finland and Israel.
Deliveries to the Ecole de l'Air (later GI 312) began in 1956, and continued to the Ecole de Chasse at Meknes, Morocco from February 1958. The EdC aircraft left North Africa in February 1961 to establish the Escadron de Transition Réacteur 40/115 at Orange (from April 1962, Division T.R. 07/716) this becoming GE 315 at Cognac in July 1965. The Ecole des Moniteurs at Aulnat was likewise renamed DMP 07/745 and ultimately GE 313 in March 1966. Magisters have also been used by various base flights (SLVSVs), the Cazaux weapons school (CTB) and, of course the Patrouille de France. Surviving aircraft are being overhauled with a view to their remaining in service until 1990. Available airframe hours will be conserved by reducing Magister time from 70 to 50 hours for trainee pilots and the deficiency made up on the prospective Aérospatiale TB.30, immediately following the selection phase. As for a replacement, the Fanjet 600 and Fouga 90 (Magister development using a strengthened wing and the CM175 Zéphyr undercarriage) are both contenders, the latter (F-WZJB) flying on 20 August 1978.

Prototypes (all withdrawn)

C/n	Callsign	Remarks
001	F-ZWRO	
02	F-ZWRP	
03	F-ZWRQ	
04	F-ZWSK	
05	F-ZWSL	
06	F-ZWSM	
07	F-SDBC	ex F-ZWSN
08	F-SDBD	ex F-ZWSP
09	F-SSKK	ex F-ZWSU
10	F-SDBE	ex F-ZWSV
011	F-ZWSW	
012	F-ZWSX	
013	F-ZWSY	

Production

C/n	Code/Status	Remarks
1	AO/CEV	ex F-ZACL/CEV
2	DQ/CEV	ex BH/CEAM, TH/EdIA, 315-LI, (LD)/GAEL, 2-HJ
3	118-DD	ex TU/EdIA, TA/EdIA
4	5-MD	ex AD/EdIA, AF/EdIA, AC/GI 312
5	128-VM	ex TK/EdIA, TP/EdIA, 41-AU, 128-AU
6	11-QA	ex AM/EdIA, TV/EdIA, 30-QD
7	12-XJ	ex AG/EdIA, AA/EdIA
8	3-KD	ex AH/EdIA, 118-DD
9	W/o 30.1.57	ex AJ/EdIA
10	W/o 9.10.63	ex AK/EdIA
11	AR/CEV	ex AP/EdIA, TS/EdIA, 5-ME
12	W/o 2.4.57	ex AV/EdIA
13	13-TE	ex AX/EdIA, TG/EdIA

147

#	Status	Ex	#	Status	Ex	#	Status	Ex
14	Stored	ex AY/EdIA, AM/EdIA, 5-MD	68	W/o 31.10.58	ex EX/CIB 328	152	30-Q.	ex EdC, AJ/EdIA, TG/EdIA, 312-AJ, 12-XL
15	W/o 28.6.61	ex F-BHOF, TF/EdIA	69		ex TG/EdIA, Israeli AF, 315-...	157	W/o 20.3.72	ex EdC, BG/CEAM, 315-RL
16	W/o 9.6.59	ex TE/EdIA	70	11-OI	ex EZ/CIB 328, AD/EdIA	158	W/o 27.4.66	ex EdC, AK/EdIA
17	5-ME	ex EdC, UJ/EdIA, 30-QE, 7-JE	77	Moroccan AF 27.8.62	ex AL/EdIA, TI/EdIA, EB 2/92	160	128-AX	ex EdC, TE/EdIA, 315-RS, 41-AX
18	W/o 11.8.75	ex TL/EdIA, 3-KD	78	Stored	ex EdC, TX/EdIA, 315-.., OJ/CEV	162	118-DH	ex EdC, AY/EdIA, 315-..
19	11-OC	ex BD/EdIA, (LA)/GAEL, 30-QH	79	Irish AF (Instructnl.)	ex EdC, Attaché Stockholm, CEAM, TY/GI 312, 2-HJ, 3-KE, damaged 13.11.74	163	33-XC	ex EdC, AM/EdIA, 315-.., 4-WB
20	W/o 13.10.59	ex AA/EdIA				164	W/o 25.2.74	ex EdC, TZ/EdIA, 315-RB, 3-KC
21	Instructional 6.66	ex AB/EdIA, TU/EdIA	80	2-HB	ex EdC, TC/EdIA, 41-AW, 128-AW	165	3-KE	ex EdC, AZ/EdIA, RD/GE 315, 10-KM, 11-O.
22	W/o 19.3.68	ex TM/EdIA, 5-ME						
23	12-XM	ex TN/edIA, TH/EdIA, 30-QE	83	10-KG	ex EdC, AS/EdIA, 11-OG	166	10-KK	ex EdC, LC/GE 315, AG/EdIA, RE/GE 315, CEAM
24	2-HG	ex TQ/EdIA, AI/EdIA, 10-KI	85		ex EdC, 7-JG, 11-OD			
25	Instructional 6.66	ex TR/EdIA, AV/EdIA	89	Moroccan AF 27.8.62	ex EdC, UL/EdIA	167	312-TB	ex EdC, AE/EdIA, 315-RR, 41-AY, 128-AY
26	33-XE	ex TS/EdIA, 315-LO	96	AM/CEV	ex EdC, UK/EdIA, LP/GE 315			
27	W/o 5.9.57	ex TX/EdIA	97	Moroccan AF 27.8.62	ex EdC, AW/EdIA	168	Togo AF 1977	ex EdC, UE/EdIA, TZ/EdIA, 7-J., 315-PA
28	Stored	ex TZ/EdIA, AB/GI 312	98	W/o 10.2.60	ex EdC, GI 312			
29	Instructional 6.66	ex UU/EdIA, CEV	99	AA/CEV	ex EdC, UI/EdIA, 5-MF	169	315-PW	ex AK/EdC, UB/EdIA, EA/ETR 115
30	3-KC	ex TT/EdIA, 12-XM, 11-..	100		ex AZ/EdA, F-ZWSW, BF/CEAM, 10-KF			
31	30-QG	ex US/EdIA, 30-QK, 1-.., 7-..				170	W/o 2.2.70	ex EB 1/92, 315-QK
32	W/o 6.7.65	ex BR/EdIA, AO/EdIA, AT/EdIA	101		ex AH/EdC, BC/CEAM, 315-RJ, 2-HA	171	315-XM	ex EdC, CIB 328, EJ/ETR 115, 11-O.
33	W/o 23.9.74	ex BZ/EdIA, AF/EdIA, 5-MH, 33-XE	102	7-JE	ex EdC, TD/EdIA, 315-LA, 315-RM	172	313-CZ	ex BQ/EdC, UD/EdIA, RE/ETR 115, CIESS 343, 313-DM
34	10-KJ	ex UN/EdIA, TB/EdIA, 5-MD	103	118-DJ	ex AI/EdC, TF/EdIA, 315-LV, 5-RG	173	315-IA	ex EB 2/92, UA/EdIA, UJ/EdIA, 11-O.
35	2-HG	ex F-BHVS, CEV, CEAM						
36	Instructional 6.66	ex CEV, AO/EdIA	104	Fire aircraft	ex EdC, TS/EdIA, 315-RN, 10-KH	174	315-PG	ex EdC, EB/ETR 115, UG/EdIA
37	W/o 13.1.65	ex AC/EdIA				175	315-PU	ex EdC, CIB 328
38	30-Q.	ex AL/EdIA	111	HB/Solenzara	ex EdC, Attaché Madrid, TN/GI 312, CEAM	177	315-XH	ex EB 1/92, DY/CIB 328, 13-TD, 315-XG, 315-XA
39	AN/CEV	ex AN/EdIA						
40	Stored	ex AQ/EdIA, 12-XL	116	W/o 15.12.64	ex EdC, CEV	178	Instructional 9.70	ex EdC, CIB 328, 11-O.
41	13-TG	ex AR/EdIA, 315-LM, 11-O.	117	CEAM	ex EdC, AL/EdC, TA/EdIA, 315-LY, 315-RI	179	315-XI	ex EdC, EB 1/92, 13-TE, 315-PI
42	W/o 13.1.65	ex TI/EdIA						
43	12-XJ	ex AS/EdIA	119	10-KF	ex EdC, CEV, TQ/EdIA, ETR 115, AI/GI 312, 118-DD	180	313-PP	ex CIB 328, EN/ETR 115, 315-XJ, 313-DH
44	10-KI	ex AT/EdIA, 315-LJ						
45	2-HM	ex AZ/EdIA, 315-LE	124	-/EC 2	ex EdC, CEV, CEAM, CEV, CEAM, TR/EdIA, 315-IF, 2-HB, 2-HI	184	W/o 17.1.75	ex CEAM, UR/EdIA, ETR 115, 12-X., 10-K., 12-XK, 313-TF
46	AS/CEV	ex TO/EdIA						
47	W/o 5.6.61	ex AU/EdIA						
48	W/o 28.5.70	ex TP/EdIA, TV/EdIA, 12-X.	125	4-WA	ex EdC, EdIA, 10-K., 5-MF	185	W/o 22.11.63	ex AP/EdC, BY/EB 2/92
49	4-WA	ex AI/EdIA, 11-OF	126		ex EdC, EdIA, 315-.., 13-TE	191	315-IN	ex CEAM, AB/EdC, EB/ETR 115, 315-QD, 313-DC
51	4-WB	ex AF/EdIA, 118-DG	133	128-AW	ex EdC, EdIA, Israeli AF, AX/GI 312, 5-M., 118-DE			
52	HA/Solenzara	ex AG/EdIA, AI/EdIA, 315-LH				194	Scrapped 1.72	ex BI/CEAM, CTB, 8-OM
53	Moroccan AF 27.8.62	ex AJ/EdIA, CEV	134	7-JF	ex EdC, AJ/EdIA, 315-RA (LB)/GAEL, 10-KK	195	315-QI	ex OV/CTB, 8-O., 315-.., 8-OK, 13-TD
54	Moroccan AF 27.8.62	ex AA/EdIA						
55	AT/CEV	ex TJ/EdIA	135	118-DF	ex BG/EdC, UD/EdIA, UM/EdIA, 315-LD, 315-RK, 11-OH	196	8-ON	ex OX/CTB, 8-OA
56	Moroccan AF 27.8.62	ex AC/EdIA				197	315-IA	ex AT/EdC, ET/ETR 115, AG/GI 312, 315-QO, 313-DJ
57	13-TD	ex TK/EdIA, 315-.., 41-AW, Air Attaché, Rome	136	125-HG	ex EdC, UG/EdIA, UK/EdIA TP/GI 312, 315-RO			
60	315-PB	ex TW/EdIA, UF/Patrouille, TF/EdIA, 315-LQ, 315-PV	143	2-HA	ex EdC, CEAM, TJ/EdIA, 315-RQ	198	8-OB	ex CEAM, CEV
						201	8-OC	ex OY/CTB
61	DG/CEV	ex TA/EdIA, 118-DE				202	315-QO	ex OZ/CTB, 8-OO
62	2-HJ	ex TC/EdIA, AU/EdIA, 30-QF	150	11-OE	ex BH/EdC, AJ/EdIA, CIB 328, AO/EdIA, 315-RF	203	315-PD	ex BU/EdC, RU/ETR 115, TW/EdIA, 11-O., 313-..
63	Scrapped 5.23	ex TD/EdIA, Israel AF, 118-DG						
66	Moroccan AF 27.8.62	ex F-BIEZ, TE/GI 312	151	2-HE	ex EdC, CIB 328, TW/EdIA, 315-RT, 2-HI	204	W/o 23.9.69	ex BV/EdC, RV/ETR 115, 315-QI
67	Moroccan AF 27.8.62	ex AB/EdIA, CIB 328, Ecole de Chasse						

148

#	Code	Notes
205	315-QA	ex BW/EdC, RW/ETR 115
206	315-QX	ex BX/EdC, RX/ETR 115, TK/GI 312, 315-QU
207	W/o 22.4.68	ex BZ/EdC, RZ/ETR 115, 313-..
208	315-QS	ex AX/EdC, EX/ETR 115
209	315-QH	ex CEAM, CEV, AA/GI 312, ETR 115, 315-.., LA/GAEL
210	315-QF	ex EdC, RM/ETR 115, 315-LJ, 315-QW
213	315-QY	ex EdC, EW/ETR 115, CEV
214	W/o 8.8.69	ex BY/EdC, RY/ETR 115, 315-QH
215	315-QY 12.4.72	ex EdC, RE/ETR 115, 315-QC, 315-ID
216	315-PN	ex BS/EdC, RS/ETR 115, AW/GI 312, 315-PT, 313-CE
217	315-IC	ex BH/EdC, RH/ETR 115, 10-KF CC/GE 313, 315-PK, 8-OD
218	W/o 27.11.68	ex EdC, RL/ETR 115, AD/EdIA, 4-W..
219	315-QW	ex RN/ETR 115, 315-QY
220	315-PK	ex AR/EdC, ER/ETR 115, CEV, 315-QP
221	Stored	AA/EdC, EA/ETR 115, 313-CP 313-TH
222	315-IM	ex EdC, EC/ETR 115, 118-.., 313-.., 315-PD, 2-HJ
223	315-PV	ex EdC, ETR 115, 3-KC, 315-QW
224	315-PS	ex AE/EdC, EE/ETR 115, CQ/GE 313
226	315-QV	ex AH/EdC, EH/ETR 115
227	315-..	ex AF/EdC, EF/ETR 115, 4-WC, 315-XT
228	315-PG	ex ETR 115, 315-.., 33-XC
230	315-XK	ex AG/EdC, EG/ETR 115, CR/GE 313, QQ/GE 315
231	315-IT	ex AI/EdC, EI/ETR 115, TM/GI 312
232	315-PW	ex AJ/EdC, EJ/ETR 115, QT/GE 315, 4-WC
233	313-DD	ex AK/EdC, EK/ETR 115, 10-KG
234	W/o 31.10.68	ex UA/EdC, TI/EdIA, 5-MG
236	315-PO	ex EB 2/92, 315-PB
237	315-II	ex AL/EdC, EL/ETR 115, 10-K., 315-IE
238	W/o 30.10.69	ex AM/EdC, EM/ETR 115, 3-KD
239	Instructional 7.62	ex UB/EdIA, AW/EdIA, crashed 14.6.62
240	315-QE	ex UC/EdIA, TX/EdIA
241	315-QL	ex UD/EdIA, BS/EdIA, ETR 115, 7-JS
242	315-PT	ex UE/EdIA, AC/EdIA, 315-PR
307	315-QM	ex EB 2/92, 315-XI
308	W/o 25.3.74	ex CEV, TO/EdIA, 315-QC
309	315-QF	ex ETR 115, GE 315, 10-KH, 315-XT, GE 315
310	315-QO	ex DF/EdM, ETR 115, 30-QH 315-XN
311	W/o 26.8.61	ex EAA 601
315	315-PN	ex UN/EdIA, 2-HE
316	315-PQ	ex DG/EdM
320	315-PE	ex DH/EdM, DH/GE 313, 315-QQ
321	W/o 13.4.67	ex DI/EdM, DI/GE 313
324	315-QN	ex DJ/EdM, DJ/GE 313, PF/GE 315
325	315-PU	ex DK/EdM, DK/GE 313, 315-QM
326	315-PE	ex DL/EdM, DL/GE 313, 30-QG
328	315-QX	ex DM/EdM, DM/GE 313, DZ/GE 313
329	315-PE	ex DN/EdM, DN/GE 313, 315-QL
330	315-XK	ex DO/EdM, DO/GE 313, PB/GE 315, 313-TA
331	315-PP	ex DP/EdM, DP/GE 313
332	315-PL	ex DQ/EdM, DQ/GE 313, 315-XW
333	315-XS	ex DR/EdM, ETR 115, 313-CI
334		ex DS/EdM, DS/GE 313, PG/GE 315, 313-CD
335	315-IU	ex RC/ETR 40/115, QL/GE 315 QL/GE 315, 2-HE
336	315-IJ	ex ETR 115, QL/GE 315, 2-HE
337	W/o 2.12.69	ex DT/EdM, (LC)/GAEL, 315-QB
338	Stored	ex EQ/ETR 115, CT/EdM, CT/GE 313, 315-QI
339	W/o 17.2.66	ex ES/ETR 40/115, CU/EdM
340	315-PZ	ex DU/EdM, DU/GE 313, PF/GE 315, 118-DH
341	315-PI	ex EU/ETR 115, 41-AW, 315-PL
342	315-PM	ex EV/ETR 115, 30-QD
343	315-PY	ex DV/EdM, PH/GE 315, QG/GE 315, 118-DJ
344	315-..	ex DW/EdM, DW/GE 313, XX/GE 315, 12-XK
345	315-XB	ex DX/EdM, DX/GE 313
346	315-QK	ex DY/EdM, DY/GE 313, 313-CA
347	315-XM	ex EY/ETR 115, 41-AX, 315-PO
348		ex EZ/ETR 115, DT/EdM, 313-DT, 8-OJ, 315-..
349	315-IV	ex RA/ETR 115, GE 315, KW/CIESS 343, 313-DQ, 313-DB
350	315-PF	ex ETR 115, QE/GE 315
351	315-..	ex AW/EdIA, Attache London, CU/GE 313, 315-PJ
352	315-PX	ex AR/EdIA, LD/GAEL
353	—/EAA 601	ex UF/EdIA, 2-HA, 315-PY
354	315-XF	ex ETR 115, AY/EdIA, 30-QE, 315-PZ
355	315-XU	ex EH/ETR 115, QP/GE 315
356	315-XV	ex ETR 115, QH/GE 315, 313-CU, 315-PO
361	315-XU	ex CEAM, RD/ETR 115, GE 313, 313-CB, 315-PI
362	315-XH	ex TX/EdIA, Attache Rome, 2-HB
363	315-XL	ex TY/EdIA, UD/EdIA, Attache Naples, GE 313, XV/GE 315, XL/GE 315
369	315-QU	ex DF/EdM, DF/GE 313, 315-QF
370	315-QZ	ex RF/ETR 115, 315-QJ
371	315-QI	ex ETR 115, AG/GI 312, Attache Madrid, AG/GI 312, 30-QF
372	AP/CEV	
373	W/o 17.8.70	ex CIB 328, EB 92, 2-HG, 313-DD
374	315-XV	ex TZ/EdIA, 2-H.
375	W/o 8.1.73	ex 118-ID, 118-DG/CEAM, XA/GE 315, 315-XA/GE 315
376	AQ/CEV	
377	313-TE	ex CIB 328, QB/GE 315
378	315-XN	ex ETR 115, CIESS 343, 313-DK
379	315-QK	ex EB 2/92, 118-IH/CEAM
380	W/o 7.6.70	ex GV/CEV
381		ex EB 1/92, QJ/GE 315, 315-QZ
382	W/o 14.9.66	ex F-BLGG, AH/GI 312, 30-Q.
383	313-TG	ex F-BLGS, EdM, GE 313, XM/GE 315, 315-XH
384	AR/CEV	
385	118-..	ex ETR 115, XK/GE 315, 313-CY
386	W/o 2.2.67	ex ET/ETR 115, GE 315
387	315-PH	ex AR/EdIA, 30-QG
388	315-XR	ex XU/GE 315
393	315-QJ	ex EdIA, Attaché Stockholm, CIESS 343, PC/GE 315, 5-MC, 313-..
394	315-XO	ex XS/GE 315
395	315-XX	ex EdIA, 2-HJ
396	315-QP	ex XL/GE 315, 313-TH
397	315-XW	ex ETR 115, AZ/GI 312, 41-AY GE 315, 5-M.
398	315-QD	ex XM/GE 315
399	315-IR	ex EW/ETR 40/115, QF/GE 315, QF/GE 315
400	315-IB	ex XA/GE 315
401	W/o 10.5.66	ex EdM, GE 315

402	315-IS	ex 315-CX
403	315-XD	ex XG/GE 315
404	315-IL	ex 315-XT, 10-KG
405	312-TP	ex CEAM, CEV, 118-IC, 118-DI
406	315-ID	ex XI/GE 315, 313-DN, 315-QR
407	315-PX	ex XN/GE 315, 313-DO
408	315-PR	ex TR/GI 312, 5-MH, XX/GE 315
409	Stored	ex XO/GE 315, 7-JG, 13-TF
410	Instructional 4.66	ex XH/GE 315, Crashed 4.8.65
411	315-QC	ex XQ/GE 315, 315-QC
412	W/o 27.9.72	ex CY/GE 313, 315-IC
413	315-XQ	ex CZ/GE 313, 313-CZ
414	313-DN	ex XB/GE 315
415	315-XC	ex XC/GE 315
416	W/o 29.10.65	ex ETR 115, RK/GE 315
417	315-XA	ex XR/GE 315, 8-OA
418	315-CP	ex XP/GE 315
419	313-DA	ex DA/GE 313
420	315-XP	ex DB/GE 313
421	315-XY	ex DC/GE 313
422	315-XJ	ex F-BMCC, 41-AZ
423	315-XZ	ex AG/EdIA, 30-QK
424	315-QT	ex CV/GE 313, 313-CV
425	315-XE	ex DD/GE 313
426	313-CW	ex QA/GE 315
427	118-DE	ex XZ/GE 315, 313-DE
428	W/o 3.2.71	ex CW/GE 313
429	Stored	ex XY/GE 315, 315-XF
430	5-ME	ex DE/GE 313, 30-QH
431	315-QQ	ex XD/GE 315, 315-XD
432	315-XG	ex XJ/GE 315, 315-XJ
433	315-IO	ex XF/GE 315, 315-XF, 33-XD
434	315-XB	ex XE/GE 315, 315-XE
435	315-QG	ex XG/GE 315, 315-XG
436	313-CS	ex DR/GE 313, 313-DR
437	312-AM	ex UM/GI 312, 312-UM, 313-DU
438	312-AF	ex UN/GI 312, 312-UN, 313-DU
439	313-CJ	ex TA/GI 312, 312-TA
440	312-AO	ex TP/GI 312, 312-TP
441	W/o 4.2.66	ex AV/GI 312
442	312-AF	ex AB/GI 312, 312-AB, 312-AF, Attache Rome
443	313-CE	ex TU/GI 312, 312-TU, 312-AH
444	313-DP	ex AO/GI 312
445	312-AC	ex AH/GI 312, 312-AH
446	313-DV	ex AD/GI 312, 312-AD
447	312-TB	ex AM/GI 312, 312-AM
448	312-BF	ex AW/GI 312, 312-AW
449	313-DR	ex AX/GI 312, 312-AX
450	312-TE	ex AA/GI 312, 312-AA
451	313-CF	ex AN/GI 312, 312-AN
452	313-TL	ex AQ/GI 312, 312-AQ, 312-TH, 313-CG
453	W/o 14.4.71	ex AG/GI 312, 312-AG
454	313-CB	ex AT/GI 312, UH/PdF, UJ/PdF, 312-TA
455	312-BN	ex BY/GI 312, UI/PdF, UK/PdF, DH/GE 313, 313-DH, 312-AA
456	312-AU	ex DP/GE 313, 313-DP, 312-AB, HI/Bou S'fer (F-RHHI), 313-DY
457	312-AA	ex UH/PdF, UE/PdF, DS/GE 313, 313-DS
458	313-DI	ex BV/GI 312, UI/PdF, UF/PdF, DG/GE 313, 313-DG
459	312-TA	ex UO/GI 312, 312-UO
460	313-CI	ex UP/GI 312
461	312-TX	ex UQ/GI 312
462	312-AY	ex AF/GI 312
463	312-TC	ex TB/GI 312
464	312-TW	ex UT/GI 312, HA/Solenzara (F-RHHA)
465	312-TK	ex UI/GI 312, TK/GI 312
466	312-TG	ex AC/GI 312, 312-AX
467	312-AN	ex TC/GI 312
468	312-TG	ex AR/GI 312
469	Instructional 10.66	ex GI 312, Crashed 26.11.65
470	312-TR	ex AP/GI 312, 312-AP, 313-CO
471	312-TD	ex TD/GI 312
472	313-CQ	ex TI/GI 312
473	312-AW	ex GI 312, CE/GE 313, 313-CE, 313-CN
474	W/o 24.4.70	ex AU/GI 312
475	W/o 14.4.69	ex AZ/GI 312
476	312-TN	ex AY/GI 312
477	Instructional 5.66	ex AJ/GI 312, Crashed 22.12.65
478	312-TY	ex TG/GI 312, 312-TG
479	312-TM	ex TH/GI 312, 312-TH
480	312-AP	ex AI/GI 312, 312-TI
481	312-BB	ex TF/GI 312, 312-TF
482	312-AQ	ex TN/GI 312
483	312-BM	ex CEV, CR/GE 313, 313-CR
484	313-CT	ex TY/GI 312, 312-TY
485	312-AD	ex TZ/GI 312, HA/Solenzara
486	312-DX	ex UG/PdF, UB/PdF
487	312-TU	ex UE/PdF, UA/PdF, 313-CF
488	W/o 4.6.67	ex UA/PdF, UD/PdF
489	W/o 16.7.69	ex TT/GI 312
490	312-BY	ex AS/GI 312, 312-AS
491	W/o 18.8.67	ex UC/PdF, UF/PdF, UB/PdF
492	312-AJ	ex UF/PdF, UG/PdF, 313-DV
493	W/o 2.3.70	ex UC/PdF, UJ/PdF, TB/GE 313
494	312-AB	ex UD/PdF, UK/PdF, 313-DO
495	313-CC	ex AL/GI 312, 312-AL
496	312-BC	ex AJ/GI 312, HB/Solenzara
497	312-AS	ex TM/GI 312, Solenzara, 312-TM
498	312-UP	ex BW/GI 312, 312-BW
499	313-CR	ex BX/GI 312, 312-BX
500	313-CL	ex BZ/GI 312, 312-BZ
502	312-AE	ex AK/GI 312, 312-AK
504	313-TC	ex TJ/GI 312
507	312-TJ	ex TO/GI 312, 312-TO
508	312-TI	ex TR/GI 312, 312-AE
509	313-DS	ex TV/GI 312, 312-TV
510	312-TH	ex TW/GI 312, 312-TW
511	312-BA	ex DW/GE 313, 313-DW, 312-TB
512	313-DM	ex AJ/GI 312, Attaché Naples, 312-AJ, 312-AR
513	313-DK	ex DI/GE 313, 313-GI
514	312-BK	ex 313-TA, 313-TG
515	313-TC	ex DS/GE 313
516	312-UB	ex 313-TD
517	313-CK	ex DU/GE 313, CEV
518	W/o 5.12.72	ex DV/GE 313, 312-AV
519	312-AK	ex CN/GE 313, 313-CN
520	312-TQ	ex TX/GI 312, 312-TX
521	313-CA	ex 313-DF
522	312-TH	ex 313-DZ
523	312-TS	
524	312-AY	ex 312-TZ
525	312-TV	ex 312-AT
526	313-CI	ex 312-AI
527	VA/PdF	
528	312-BW	ex DJ/GE 313, 312-BY
529	VP/PdF	ex VB/PdF
530	312-AV	ex 313-DY
531	313-DW	ex UL/GI 312, UD/GI 312, 312-UD
532	313-DH	ex 312-AB
533	VI/PdF	ex 313-CG, VQ/PdF
534	VC/PdF	
535	VD/PdF	
536	W/o 30.7.64	ex VE/PdF
537	313-CH	ex CS/GE 313, 313-CS
538	VR/PdF	ex 312-TL
539	312-BD	ex CO/GE 313, 313-CO
540	W/o 10.9.69	ex VF/PdF
541	VG/PdF	
542	VH/PdF	
543	W/o 8.12.69	ex VI/PdF
544	VJ/PdF	
545	VK/PdF	
546	VL/PdF	
547	TR/ Attaché London	ex AE/GI 312
548	312-TS	ex 312-TQ, 313-CM
549	312-AH	ex UN/GI 312, 312-UN
550	312-BV	ex CL/GE 313, 313-CL
551	312-AL	ex CM/GE 313, 313-CM
552	W/o 2.5.69	ex CK/GE 313

553	313-DG	ex CJ/GE 313, 313-CK
554	312-BZ	ex CH/GE 313, 313-CH
555	VA/PdF	ex CI/GE 313, 313-CC
561	VI/PdF	ex VM/PdF
562	W/o 28.9.73	ex VI/PdF
563		ex VF/PdF
564	VO/PdF	
565	VP/PdF	
566	312-AR	
567	VF/PdF	ex 312-AM
568	312-AI	ex 312-AZ
569	312-AU	
572	312-AG	
573	312-UA	ex 313-DL
574	312-TT	ex 118-DF
575	312-TF	
576	VN/PdF	

FOUGA CM175 ZEPHYR

The CM.175 Zéphyr is a navalised version of the Magister flown under the original name of Esquif on 31 July 1956. The first of the thirty production aircraft made its first flight on 30 May 1959. The Zéphyr serves with 59S, the deck landing school at Hyères, which has a complement of fourteen; the others remaining in short-term storage though all are periodically rotated.

Prototypes (CM.170M)

01 Instructional
02 Instructional

Production (CM.175)

C/n	Status	Remarks
1		
2	59S	
3	59S	
4	59S	
5	59S	
6	59S	
7	59S	
8	W/o	
9	59S	
10	Instructional	ex 59S
11	59S	
12	59S	
13		
14	59S	
15		
16	59S	
17	59S	
18	59S	
19	59S	
20	59S	
21	59S	
22	59S	
23	59S	
24	59S	
25	59S	
26	59S	
27	SRL	
28	W/o	
29	59S	
30	59S	

GLOSTER METEOR

A small number of Meteors remain in use for experimental purposes with the CEV and as 'chase aircraft'. These are the survivors of 41 Meteor NF11 supplied to the Armée de l'Air for 30 Escadre prior to the availability of the Vautour. Unfortunately, the serial tie-ups are not known, but the following Meteors were delivered -

Meteor F.4
F-WEPQ/F-BEPQ ex EE523 of RAF High Speed Flight, delivered 1948.
RA491 (fitted with Mk.F.8 nose section), delivered 1952.

Meteor T.7
For CEV: No. 91 and No. 92 newly built, February 1951.
F-BEAR ex WA607/G-7-133, del. 1955. W/o 28.2.57.
For EC 30: Nos. F1 to F11. RAF serials (not in order) - WG997, WH136, WH228 in 1952; WL476, WL425, WL471, WH168, WF832, WN312, WL425 in 1953; WF776 in 1956.

Meteor NF.11
For CEV: NF11-1 to NF11-9
For EC 30: Nos. NF11-10 to NF11-41
Known RAF serials are WD619, WD628, WD631, WD669, WD674, WD683, WD698, WD701, WD756, WD783, WM153, WM164, WM235, WM243, WM265, WM296 to WM307, WN368 to WM371, WM375 to WM383 and possibly WD588. All delivered 1954-55.

Meteor NF.13
NF-F364 and NF-F365 to CEV 1956 ex WM364-WM365.

Meteor NF.14
NF14-747 and NF14-796 to CEV 1955 ex WS747 and WS796.

Meteor TT.20 (NF.14 conversion)
Six aircraft purchased for spares. WD649, WD652, WD780, WM242, WM255, WM293 delivered late 1974, all marked F-ZABD. The shells were sold as scrap in October 1975.

Surviving aircraft noted in recent years are:

NF11-1	BH	CEV
NF11-2		withdrawn ex BD/CEV
NF11-3	CA	CEV
NF11-8	BG	CEV
NF11-9	BF	CEV
NF11-24		Preserved
NF14-747	BM	CEV

ISSOIRE AVIATION E-75 SILENE

On 1 February 1978, Wassmer Aviation was re-born as Issoire Aviation and on 7 April delivered to the Armée de l'Air the third pre-production Silène, 03. Developed as the Cerva CE75, a prototype (F-CCFF) of this side-by-side two-seat glider trainer first flew on 2 February 1974, and was followed by three more pre-production examples. If found to be suitable for the AdlA gliding clubs, the Silène will replace the Wassmer Bijave (which see).

JODEL D.140E/R

The popular Jodel D.120 touring aircraft is operated by the Section Vol a Voile, GAALEA 4/312 at Salon-de-Provence as a glider tug replacing the M.S. Criquet. Following an order for 18 D.140E, a further 14 D.140R were delivered, the 'R' designation indicating 'Remorquer' = Tug.

D.140E Mousquetaire

C/n	Code/Unit
195	YD/GAALEA 4.312
196	YB/GAALEA 4.312
197	YC/GAALEA 4.312
198	YE/GAALEA 4.312
199	YF/GAALEA 4.312
200	YI/GAALEA 4.312
201	YJ/GAALEA 4.312
202	YK/GAALEA 4.312
203	YL/GAALEA 4.312
204	YP/GAALEA 4.312
205	YG/GAALEA 4.312

206	YH/GAALEA 4.312	
207	YM/GAALEA 4.312	
208	YN/GAALEA 4.312	
209	YO/GAALEA 4.312	
210	YQ/GAALEA 4.312	
211	YR/GAALEA 4.312	
212	YS/GAALEA 4.312	

Pseudo-military markings are also carried by DR.1051M c/n 252 F-ZWVY.

D.140R Abeille

C/n	Code/Unit	Remarks
507	XW/GALEA 4.312	ex YW/GALEA 4.312
508	XX/GALEA 4.312	ex YX/GALEA 4.312
509	QA/Solenzara	(F-ULQA)
510	FA/CVA 55.273	ex EA/Evreux (F-UMEA)
511	XY/GALEA 4.312	ex YY/GALEA 4.312
512	FB/CVA 55.273	ex VZ/Metz (F-TGVZ)
513	128-VZ/Metz	ex LA/Saintes (F-ULLA)
514	FC/CVA 55.273	ex Auxerre (F-RHAC), Solenzara
515	—/Evreux	ex LB/Saintes (F-ULLB), CVA 55.273
516	LA/Saintes	ex Metz (F-ULLA)
517	XZ/GALEA 4.312	
518	/CVA 55.273	ex Evreux (F-UMEB)
519	EPNER	(F-ZJOC)
520	CEV	(F-ZJFA)

LTV CRUSADER F-8E (FN)

The prototype F-8E (FN) Crusader 147036 flew on 27 February 1964 after conversion from F-8E standard. The aircraft was written off two months later on 11 April but 26 June saw the first production example make its initial flight. The 42 Aéronavale aircraft were allocated the USN serials 151732-773 but these were not carried. Additionally an F-8A has been obtained for ground instruction at Rochefort as '01'.

Serial	Unit/Status	Remarks
1	12F	ex 14F
2	14F	ex 12F
3	14F	ex 14F, 12F
4	12F	ex 14F, 12F, 14F
5	W/o 2.2.77	ex 12F, 14F, 12F
6	12F	ex 12F, 14F
7	12F	
8	12F	ex 12F, 14F
9	W/o 28.1.77	ex 12F, 14F, 12F
10	14F	
11	12F	ex 12F, 14F
12	12F	ex 14F
13	W/o 2.77	ex 12F, 14F
14	14F	ex 12F
15	Trials aircraft	
16	14F	ex 12F
17	12F	ex 12F, 14F
18		ex 12F, 14F
19		ex 12F, 14F
20	14F	ex 14F, 12F
21	W/o 24.7.68	ex 12F
22	12F	ex 12F, 14F
23	14F	ex 12F
24		ex 14F
25	12F	ex 14F
26		ex 14F
27	14F	ex 12F
28	W/o	
29	12F	
30	14F	ex 12F, 14F, 12F
31	12F	
32		ex 12F, 14F
33	12F	ex 14F
34	12F	
35	14F	ex 14F, 12F
36	W/o (with 14F)	
37	14F	ex 12F
38	W/o 14.1.78	ex 14F
39	14F	ex 12F, 14F, 12F
40	12F	
41	12F	ex 14F
42	14F	ex 12F

LOCKHEED P2V-7 NEPTUNE

All examples of the P2V-6 (126514/522/537/540, 134638-641, 643-650, 654-663) have now been withdrawn although 126522 is still used for ground instruction. The current version of the Neptune, the P2V-7/SP-2H has been partly retired, four examples having been transferred to the Dutch Navy in 1965, and others returning to the USA for storage at Davis-Monthan. Orion 152177 of the US Navy's VP-44 squadron underwent trials at Lorient in February 1976, and in January 1978 Fokker demonstrated F-27MPA PH-MPA (prior to delivery to Peru as AE561). However 42 improved Atlantics are on order to replace the Neptune from 1985 onwards.

Serial	Unit/Status	Remarks
144685	Instruc./Rochefort	ex 24F-1
144686	Withdrawn	ex 24F-2, 23F
144687	Withdrawn	ex 24F-3, 12S
144688	Instruc./Rochefort	ex 24F-4
144689	Withdrawn	ex 24F-5, 25F
144690	Withdrawn	ex 24F-6, 23F
144691	Dutch Navy 215	ex 24F-7
144692	Dutch Navy 216	
146431	Withdrawn	ex 23F
146432	12S	
146433	12S	(noseprobe)
146434	Dutch Navy 217	ex 25F-4
146435	Davis-Monthan	ex 23F
146436	Davis-Monthan	ex 23F
146437	Davis-Monthan	ex 12S
146438	Dutch Navy 218	ex 24F-9
147562	25F	ex 23F-4
147563	25F	
147564	25F	ex 24F
147565	Withdrawn	
147566	25F	
147567	25F	ex 23F
147568	25F	ex 24F
147569	12S(F-YDNA)	ex 23F-1, 25F
147570	25F	ex 23F-2
147571	Written off	
148330	25F	
148331	25F	ex 21F
148332	Withdrawn	ex 12S, 25F
148333	25F	ex 12S, 21F
148334	25F	
148335	25F	
148336	25F	ex 12S
148337	Withdrawn	

As a partial replacement for the Neptune in the overseas role with 12S, France was early in 1979 showing interest in four B.Ae.748 Coastguarder within an overall purchase of at least sixteen of the type for paratroop dropping and navigation training. These may additionally replace Atlantics based at Dakar and operating against Polisario guerillas in Mauritania, a role for which the Atlantic is 'over-equipped'.

152

LOCKHEED & CANADAIR T-33A

The Lockheed T-33 was supplied to the Armée de l'Air from both US and Canadian stocks. Most SLVSVs operate the type, in addition to training units CEVSV 338, and GE 314. The Armée de l'Air has regularly received additions to T-33 strength from USAFE, the last being the transfer of Norwegian aircraft in 1969. The first of the T-33s was received in 1951, and the type is due for replacement by the Alpha Jet from 1979 onwards. First returns to the USAF took place on 25 January 1978 when five aircraft were ferried to Sculthorpe for disposal by the 7519 Combat Support Squadron. The last of the type is expected to leave the service in 1983.

Lockheed T-33A

C/n	Serial	Code/Status	Remarks
5073	90923		ex 338-HI, 7-JB
5284	00431	Withdrawn	
5286	00433	Withdrawn	
5336	14042	Withdrawn	ex 314-YB
5338	14044	2-HC	ex 9-DB, 12-XC
5339	14045	314-VQ	
5354	14060	10-KX	ex 33-XX, 5-MB
5355	14061	Withdrawn	
5380	14086	—/CEVSV 338	ex 338-HI, WW(CIFAS 328)
5381	14087	Withdrawn	
5382	14088	Withdrawn	
5384	14090	Withdrawn	
5408	14114	30-WL	ex 30-QB
5409	14115	314-YM	ex (314-)YD
5410	14116	8-OH	ex 33-XB, 10-KZ, 10-KW, 12-XE
5447	14153	4-WH	ex 338-HQ, 314-YA, 314-WC
5448	14154	314-VL	ex 314-WE
5458	14164	Withdrawn	ex 338-HG
5486	14192	30-QB	ex 13-SB, 338-HA
5488	14194	Withdrawn	
5489	14195	Withdrawn	
5490	14196	Withdrawn	
5523	14229	Withdrawn	
5524	14230	314-VV	
5567	14272	314-VU	ex 314-WI, 314-YJ
5577	14282	314-VU	ex 30-QB
5578	14283	314-YJ	ex (314-)UH
5579	14284	13-TC	ex 338-HP, 7-JA
5580	14285	Withdrawn	
5581	14286	USAF 1978	ex WV, 8-OH
5582	14287	Withdrawn	
5643	14348	Withdrawn	
5644	14349	314-UQ	ex 314-UH
5645	14350	314-VM	ex 338-HP, 10-KY
5647	14352	USAF 1968	
5678	14383	338-HI	ex 12-XD, 338-HK
5680	14385	338-HP	ex 12-XE
5714	14419	USAF 1978	ex 30-QC, 338-HJ
5715	14420	314-UO	
5717	14422	Withdrawn	
5797	14502	338-HD	ex 314-WA, 30-QB
5798	14503		ex 12-XC, 8-OF
5799	14504	314-WA	
5848	16510	338-HF	
5852	16520	33-XG	ex WM, 314-WA, 338-HW
5856	16524	3-KB	
5857	16525	8-OF	ex 12-XF, 3-KA
5977	16645	W/o 29.10.65	
5980	16648	WY(CIFAS 328)	
5983	16651	Withdrawn	ex 314-WZ
6050	16718	314-UJ	ex 314-WF
6092	16760	W/o 12.5.71	ex 314-WK, 314-VP, 314-UH
6093	16761	314-UN	
6094	16762	314-VI	
6095	16763	314-YA	ex 314-WM
6096	16764		ex (314-)YA, WR(CIFAS 328)
6097	16765	Withdrawn	
6098	16766	Withdrawn	
6099	16767	314-VE	ex(314-)WH
6100	16786	314-VR	ex12-XC, 314-UJ, 314-YR
6101	16769	WA(CIFAS 328)	ex 12-XB
6102	16770	Withdrawn	
6103	16671	Withdrawn	
6104	16772	12-XA	ex DD, 338-HJ
6166	16834	338-HL	ex 7-JD, 314-WG, 338-HC
6197	16865	Withdrawn	
6198	16866	314-YD	
6200	16868	314-UE	
6201	16869	W/o 2.10.70	ex (314-)WL, 314-UD
6202	16870	314-VS	ex (314-)UD
6203	16671	Withdrawn	
6204	16872	(314-)YH	
6237	16905	WH(CIFAS 328)	ex 13-SA
6239	16907	Withdrawn	
6241	16909	338-HE	ex 33-XZ
6284	16952	338-HH	
6288	16956	WE(CIFAS 328)	ex 30-QC
6412	18628		ex 11-OE, 10-KY
6442	18658	338-HJ	ex (10-)KW
6477	18693	13-TF	ex 4-WG
6536	18752	338-HB	
6538	18754	8-OE	ex 10-KX
6551	18767	Withdrawn	ex (314-)WE, 314-WH
6556	18772	Withdrawn	ex 338-HJ
6604	18820	Withdrawn	ex 13-TC
6820	19036	USAF 1978	ex 7-JB, 2-HC
6931	19147	314-YC	ex 314-YA
6952	19168	WA(CIFAS 328)	
7034	19250	EC 5	ex HE, WG(CIFAS 328), EC 8
7039	19255	314-VY	ex 30-QA
7040	19256	Withdrawn	
7041	19257	Withdrawn	
7042	19258	Withdrawn	
7151	117412	338-HA	
7153	117414	338-HN	
7167	117428	4-WG	ex 314-WL
7186	29132	Withdrawn	ex 4-UD
7253	117462	Withdrawn	
7366	117472	Withdrawn	
7367	117473	314-UG	
7372	117478	Withdrawn	
7377	117483	314-VM	
7381	117487	Withdrawn	ex 13-SB, WF(CIFAS 328), 33-XG
7477	117497	338-HS	ex 338-HC
7483	117503	Withdrawn	
7582	117522	314-YE	ex R.Norwg.AF, 10-KZ 314-WH
7689	117544	10-KY	ex R.Norwg.AF, 2-HE, 314-WE
7691	117546	10-KW	ex R.Norwg.AF, 3-KB, 7-JA, 314-WB
7797	29901	5-MF	ex R.Norwg.AF, 10-KX, 314-WL
8144	29838	338-HK	ex 30-QZ
8173	29867	338-HY	ex 314-WL
8194	29963	USAF 1978	ex YB, 338-HC, WI, 5-MB
8195	29964	Withdrawn	
8204	29973	314-WJ	ex 338-HS
8206	29975	WX(CIFAS 328)	ex 338-...
8298	34959	338-HD	ex 338-HC, WO(CIFAS 328)
8300	34961	W/o	ex 12-XB
8394	35055	GC(EPNER)	
8399	35060	338-HG	ex 11-OD
8459	35120	338-HU	
8471	35132	338-HL	
8483	35144	WT(CIFAS 328)	
8486	35147	338-HR	
8550	35211	GH(EPNER)	
8621	35282	338-HM	ex 2-HC
8678	35339	12-XC	ex 314-WF
9087	35748	WB(CIFAS)	ex R.Norwg.AF, WQ WB(CIFAS 328)

153

LTV F-8E(FN) Crusader No.9. Now approaching obsolescence, the Crusader continues in front-line service as the Aéronavale's shipborne fighter, flying from the carriers Foch and Clemenceau. Approximately thirty of the 42 delivered remain, and they are operated by 12F and 14F, both based at Landivisiau. The Crusaders are allocated US Navy serials 151732-151773, but these are not carried, and instead the aircraft are numbered 1-42, to which a static instructional airframe F-8A 143719 has been added as '01'. Aircraft change between units from time to time, most having spent periods with both, including the example illustrated, which began its service with 12F in 1965, but was with 14F in 1971-74 before returning to its original owners. On 28 January 1977 it crashed near Landivisiau and was totally destroyed. *(E. Moreau)*

Lockheed P2V-7 Neptune No.147562. Retained by 25F after Atlantics re-equipped the remaining four maritime reconnaissance flotilles, the Lockheed Neptune additionally serves with 12S in the Pacific area. About seventeen Neptunes are currently on charge, others having returned to the USA or graduated to the Dutch Navy, which received four. No.562 commenced service with 23F with the markings '23-F-4' during the days when Aéronavale aircraft were helpfully coded. It was photographed at Greenham Common in 1973 and remains with 25F to date. *(S.G. Richards)*

Lockheed T-33A No.14114 '30-WL'. A recent change in aircraft coding involves the SLVSV of 30 (Mirage F1) Escadre at Reims as illustrated by T-33A 14114 in May 1978. Originally the flight used 'LA' to 'LZ' without number prefix, but with the disbandment of Meteor equipped OCU CIETT 346, a combination of the two brought into being EETT 12/30 with the continued use of the CIETT call sign range with '30-' substituted for '346-', viz '30-QA' etc. In 1972, the flight became an SLVSV once more and continued the established coding system until early 1978 when the first T-33A was seen in the new markings. *(J-L. Gaynecoetche)*

Lockheed T-33A No.14350 '314-WM'. Photographed in June 1977, a month after its twenty-fifth birthday, 14350 is on the strength of the principal T-33 operator, GE 314 at Tours. The school will begin to receive Alpha Jets in 1979 and gradually phase-out the 'T-Bird'. US-built T-33s are in the minority at Tours, as without exception, the sixty-one T-33AN diverted from Canadian stocks in 1959-62 were delivered to GE 314. *(S.G. Richards)*

Lockheed T-33A No.54439. The beginning of the end. No.54439 was in the first batch of five aircraft delivered to USAFB Sculthorpe for scrapping at the end of its operational life. The US government has decreed that all MDAP equipment, including Offshore Procurement aircraft built in France are to be returned to the American authorities when no longer required. Erased markings 'WI' of CIFAS 328 are still visible on the fuselage side, and the initial batch will doubtless be joined by many others in the next few years. *(D.M. Sargent)*

155

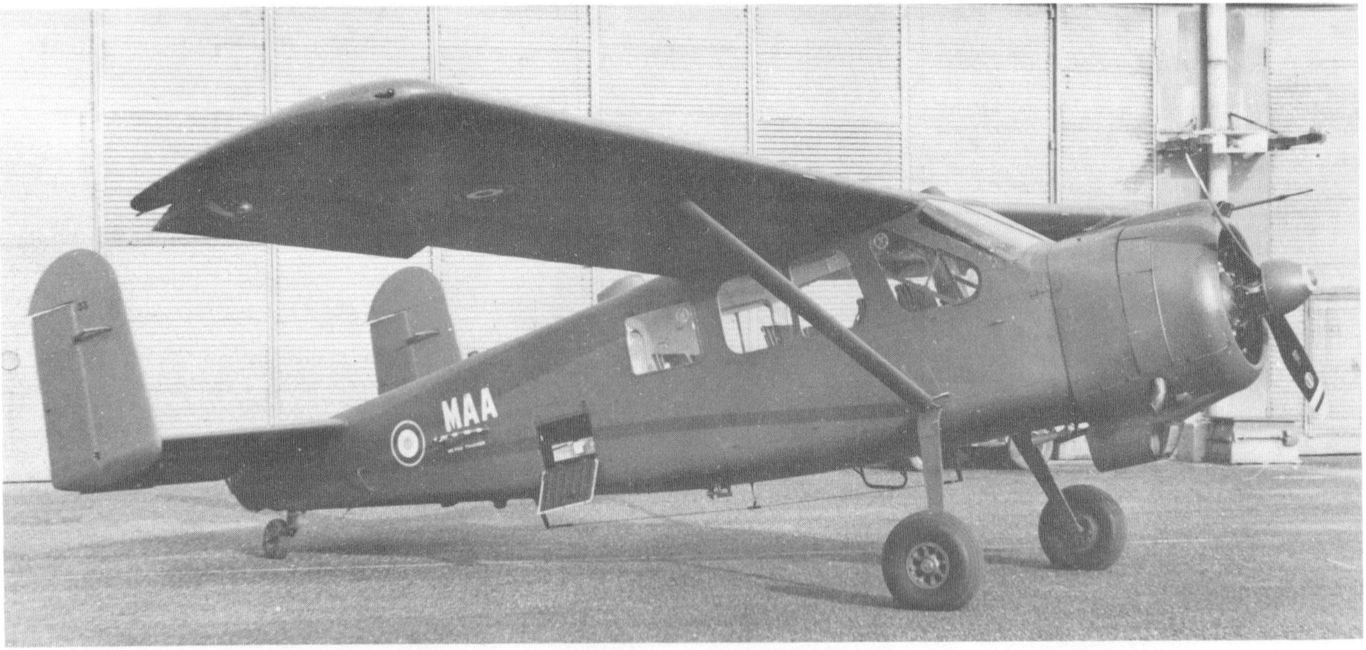
MAA

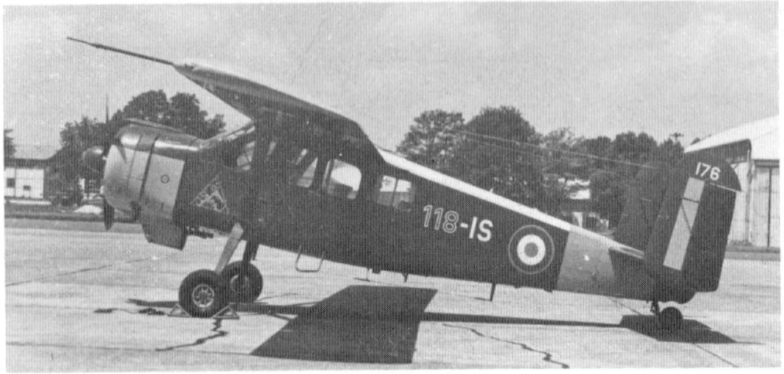
176
118-IS

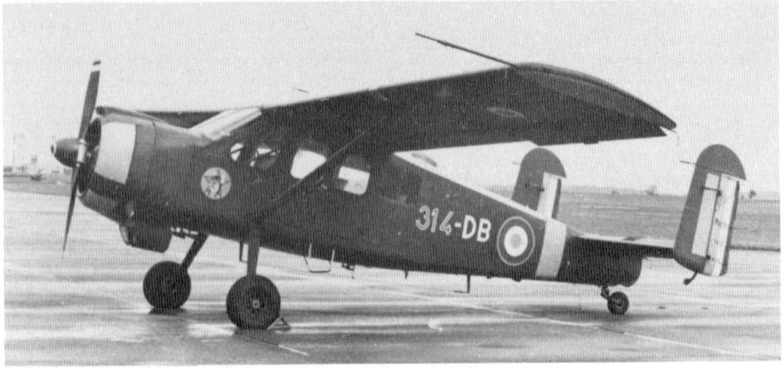
314-DB

Max Holste MH1521 Broussard 'MAA'. Little seen are the code letters of the Army's Direction Central du Matériel at Paris and Bourges. They are normally allocated to aircraft in stock or awaiting withdrawal, the Broussard together with Nord 3400 'MAB' and Gazelle 'MAG' appear to belong to a communications flight. Seen at Montauban in Dec. 1976. *(R. Cram)*

Max Holste MH1521 Broussard No.176 '118-IS'. Easily distinguised as an aircraft of the CEAM by its triangular badge, No.176 bears the coding of BA118, Mont-de-Marsan, the home of its current unit. The aircraft is used as a 'hack' and until recently served ELA 44 at Aix in a similar function. It was photographed at Cognac in June 1977. *(J-L. Gaynecoetche)*

Max Holste MH1521 Broussard No.015 '314-DB'. The communications flight of flying school GE 314 uses two Broussards and a Paris in the callsign range F-RHDA/F-RHDZ, a series not exclusive to GE 314 but allocated to 2 Air Region. Thus miscellaneous base-flight aircraft within one area employ the same callsigns with different prefixes. No.015 is a pre-production aircraft which first flew 24 March 1956. *(J-L. Gaynecoetche)*

Morane Saulnier MS760 Paris No.87. Aéronavale Paris communications aircraft are now concentrated in the Section Réacteur Léger as continuation and proficiency trainers in addition to their transport duties. No.87 is complete in the new Aéronavale 'MARINE' markings. *(J-L. Gaynecoetche)*

Nord N2501 Noratlas No.9 '118-IC'. Having spent much of its life as a trials and miscellaneous transport aircraft for the CEAM, as seen here visiting Sharjah in March 1967, No.9 was withdrawn to EAA 601 in 1970, transferring to Rochefort in 1974, where it now serves as an instructional airframe. *(MAP)*

158

Morane Saulnier Paris No.61 'LY' is one of the aircraft re-purchased from the Brazilian A.F. and now belongs to ET 65 at Villacoublay. *(R. Cram)*

Nord N2501 Noratlas No.125 'JF'. Although operated by GOM 88, the aircraft carries only the last two letters of its callsign. *(MAP)*

Nord N2501 Noratlas No.151 'CAR'. Unique amongst Armée de l'Air units, EdC 57 uses the last three of the callsign as a code and dispenses with a number prefix. *(J-L. Gaynecoetche)*

Morane Saulnier Paris No.36 '43-BD'. Small numbers of Paris are allocated to the Regional Communications Squadrons, as in this case of No.36, (at Cognac, Sept. 1977). *(J-L. Gaynecoetche)*

Nord N2501 Noratlas No.171 '316-FR'. The bulged Nord Noratlas is used by both CIFAS 328 for Mirage IVA bombardier training and navigation school GE 316, to whom the aircraft illustrated belongs. *(R. Cram)*

Nord N2501 Noratlas No.30 '44-GE'. Largest of any aircraft serving with the ELAs are the Noratlas of ELAS 1/44 at Solenzara, Corsica. This detachment of ELA 44 uses the type for SAR in conjunction with two Pumas. *(R. Cram)*

Nord N2501 Noratlas No.56 '312-BK' often acts as a support aircraft to the Patrouille de France. Photographed at Alconbury in June 1975. *(S.G. Richards)*

Nord N2504 Noratlas No.01. Doubly unique as the only N2504 and sole Naval Noratlas, the jet tipped 01 first flew on 17 November 1958 and served with 10S until the unit was re-named SES St Raphael in 1975. *(R. Peoc'h)*

Serial	Code	Status/Remarks			
9109	35770	Withdrawn			
9133	35794		ex R.Norwg.AF, WB(CIFAS 328)		
9137	35798	33-XC			
9174	41543	33-CY	ex 33-XW		
9179	41548	33-XT			
9180	41549	338-HG			
9184	41553	(ER 33)	ex 33-XU		
9264	41575	Withdrawn			
9265	41576	7-JA	ex 13-SC, 338-HO, 30-QP, 314-WK		
9266	41577	338-HO			
9268	41579	3-KA	ex 338-HO, 33-XG		
9269	41580	Withdrawn	ex 33-XT, 33-XY, 314-UM		
9270	41581	2-HF	ex 11-OE, 7-JC, 4-WH		
9632	53091	WP/CIFAS 328	ex 338-HD, 338-HE		
9633	53092	5-MA	ex 7-JA, 13-TC		
9634	53093	(ER 33)	ex 10-KZ, 11-OJ		
9636	53095	33-XH	ex 8-OG, 10-KZ		
9637	53096	314-WC	ex 7-JI		
9638	53097	Withdrawn			
9639	53098	314-YB	ex OY, YU, 314-VY, 314-UB		
9671	53101	Withdrawn			
9672	53102	Withdrawn			
9673	53103	314-VP	ex 13-SI		
9674	53104	314-VX	ex 5-MR, 314-UX		
9676	53106	11-OH	ex 13-SB, 9-DA, 8-OH		
9677	53107	8-OG	ex 12-XN		
9678	53108	WS(CIFAS 328)			
9974	54430	W/o 9.12.58			
9975	54431	Withdrawn	ex TI		
9976	54432	11-OJ	ex 338-HD, 338-HQ, 3-KB		
9977	54433	USAF 1978	ex WD, 338-HQ		
9978	54434	WV(CIFAS 328)	ex 30-QA		
9982	54438	314-VN	ex 3-KA		
9983	54439	USAF 1978	ex 1-DE, 2-HE, 338-HB, WI, 338-HK		
1332	70683	338-HT	ex 338-HS, 11-OA		
1333	70684	30-QA	ex R.Norwg.AF		

Canadair T-33AN delivered 1959-1962

Serial	Code/Status	Remarks
21002	314-UK	
21004	W/o 19.11.70	ex 314-YI
21006	314-US	To Instructional /Tours
21009	314-YP	ex 314-YM
21012	314-UH	ex 314-UU
21013	Withdrawn	
21015	314-VF	
21016	W/o 21.2.61	
21022	314-UB	
21027	314-YT	ex 314-YP
21028	314-UR	
21029	314-YG	
21031	314-YZ	
21032	314-VG	ex 314-YG
21033	Instr./Le Bourget	ex 314-YL
21036	Withdrawn	
21042	314-VT	
21049	314-VC	
21050	314-YQ	
21051	314-YF	ex 314-YH
21064	CEV-supercritical wing, ex 314-VP, 314-UP	
21077	Withdrawn	ex 314-YT
21081	314-YK	ex 314-YI
21088	314-UI	ex 314-YL
21105	314-YO	
21107	314-YX	
21111	W/o 1.65	ex 314-YZ, 314-UX
21112	314-VA	
21113	314-UV	
21116	Withdrawn	ex 314-YF
21117	Withdrawn	ex 314-YS
21121	Withdrawn	ex 314-YK, 314-YD, 314-VW
21127	314-UZ	
21128	Instr./Tours	ex 314-UB, 314-YY
21132	314-YV	
21138	Withdrawn	ex 314-VD
21140	314-VD	ex 314-UL
21152	314-YN	
21154	Withdrawn	
21155	314-UL	ex 314-UI
21172	314-UE	
21177	314-YS	ex 314-YT
21182	314-UW	
21185	Withdrawn	ex 314-YU
21195	314-YE	
21201	314-YW	
21211	314-VZ	ex 314-YK
21221	Withdrawn	
21247	314-VO	
21255	314-VH	
21267	314-UA	
21307	314-UT	
21330	Withdrawn	ex 314-UM
21372	W/o 9.10.70	ex 314-VJ, 314-VZ
21380	314-UX	ex 314-VT
21400	314-YY	ex 314-YS, 314-YU
21420	314-VK	
21439	314-VB	
21477	314-UC	
21485	314-YR	
21489	314-UF	

Note: T-33AN c/n is the 'last three' of the serial.

MAX HOLSTE MH1521M BROUSSARD

The prototype Broussard (Bushman) was built by Max Holste Aviation (now Reims Aviation) as F-WGIU and flown on 17 November 1952. Between 1955 and 1961 the type was delivered to the Armée de l'Air and ALAT, with an additional three, 43, 63, 66, going to the Marine National. Many were distributed to French African possessions when they were granted independence in 1960, and the remainder now serve with the SLVSVs, ET 65 and the ELAs, whilst those of the army are due for imminent withdrawal.
Broussard c/ns followed a complex pattern, and were suffixed M = Militaire or C = Civile.
Prototypes: 01, 02, (03 static test), 04M, 05M.
Pre-production: 06C, 07C, 06-022M.
Production: 1-5C, 20-55C, 62-65C, 79C, 212C, 1-316M.
Several MH1521C were diverted to overseas military use and received a new 'M' c/n, so that the grand total of aircraft built was approximately 370.
In 1975, six Rallyes were evaluated by the AdlA as a possible Broussard replacement, but no decision appears to have been reached. The 'OCU' for the type is a flight of GE 314.

C/n	Code/Status	Remarks
04M	Scrapped	ex 41-AG, OW
06		ex CEAM, F-SFPH/ELO, XC/ER 33
07	Preserved	ex 41-AI
08	11-OB	ex F-ZWTG, F-SCOL/ELA 55
010	Stored	ex F-BFKS, F-ZWTI, F-SFZB/ELO F-SFZD/ELO, 5-MQ
011	118-IU	ex ELA 56, F-SDLU/EAA 603
013	43-BM	ex F-RABS/CEAM, F-SDOL/ELA 56
015	314-DB	ex ZG/ELO, 43-BV
016	EF/	ex ZH/ELO, 43-BX
018	Scrapped 1975	ex ZZ/ELO
020	F-MAYU	ex F-ZWUA, F-MBCA, F-ZBBO
021	F-MAOC	
022	F-MAYS	ex F-ZBBP
5	L/ET 65	
6		ex 13-TB
7	2-HH	
11	41-AA	
16	BC/GI 312	
18	Stored	
23	F-MATR	
24	CB/ELA 44	ex 41-AE
27	Stored	
28	F-MCYB	

32	10-KE	
33	F-MAMT	
34	2-HD	
37	44-CI	
38	F-MMJA	
39	44-CF	ex DA, 314-DB
40	118-IZ	
42	F-MAGA	
50	44-CA	ex 5-MR
53	12-XF	
59	5-MQ	ex 5-MP
70	Bordeaux Base Flt.	
74	ALAT	
78	F-MCWP	ex F-MANE
84	118-IU	
91	8-OZ	ex 41-CK
93	F-MATQ	
94	Stored	ex F-MBPA
99	5-ML	
100	F-MAOB	
102	F-MBCB	
104	13-TB	
106	43-BU	
108	313-TD	
113	2-HH	ex HN/Salon Base Flt.
114	118-IW	
121	Stored	ex F-BMMO
124	41-AE	ex A/ET 2.60
128	HD/Nimes-Courbessac Base Flt. ex 44-CH	
137	44-CI	ex C/ET 2.60
138	65-CB	ex B/ET 2.60
142	10-KE	ex HN/Istres Base Flt.
144	CD/(ELA 44)	ex 7-JF
150	F-MAFR	ex F-MBCA
154	HE/Nimes-Courbessac Base Flt. ex 44-CC	
155	88-JV	ex 43-BL
156	88-JW	ex 10-KE
157		ex 44-CD
158	43-BO	ex 44-CB
159	118-IV	
163	Stored	ex 12-XI, Y/ET 2.60
164	4-WZ	
170		ex HG/GMT 59
172	XR	unit unknown
173	33-XB	
175	314-DA	
176	118-IS	ex 44-CC
179	5-MO	ex Q/ET 2.60, 44-CL
180	43-BT	
181	65-CD	
182	722-EA	
183	41-AB	
184		ex 8-OY

185	E/ET 65	
186	5-MP	
187	30-QN	
191	315-SK	
195		ex 43-BT, 13-TD
196	Scrapped	ex 315-SL
197	41-AC	
198	7-JI	
207	A/ET 65	ex 43-BL
211	Stored	ex Attaché New Dehli
214	44-CF	
218	Stored	
224	HR/Istres Base Flt.	ex GK/-, M/ET 2.60
228	41-AF	ex 722-EA, (33-)XB
235	Stored	
239	Stored	ex 5-MO
240	44-CJ	ex HF/GMT 59, 315-SK
244	44-CA	
247		ex 313-TY
250	41-AF	ex OL
251	44-CB	ex ST, 315-ST, 43-BL
253	5-MN	
254	313-TY	ex 315-TZ
256	43-BF	
258	DCAN(F-YEEH)	ex 41-AP, 41-AJ, CAN16/F-YCZP
259	Scrapped	ex HF/GMT 59
260	Stored	ex 070-MH
261	K/ET 65	
266	12-XD	ex M/ET 2.60
267	F-MAMS	
268	F-MCWM	ex F-MBCA
269	41-AI	
273	Scrapped	ex 315-SP
275	Scrapped	ex F-MAOA, F-MATQ, F-MAHQ
276	F-MMGA	ex F-MAGB
279	44-CL	
280	Scrapped	ex F-MAHR
281	F-MCWM	
283	Scrapped	ex F-MATQ, F-MATR, F-MAHP
284	XI/EC 12	
285	F/ET 65	
289		
290	41-AD	
291	315-ST	ex HF/Istres, 44-CG, 43-BL
292	65-CC	ex C/ET 2.60
294	F-MAYO	
296	(F-UMEC) 2 Region	
298	BA/GI 312	
299	F-MAOC	
303	315-SL	ex 44-CE
304	3-KY	
305	T/ET 65	
306	721-EP	

309	8-OY	ex 43-BS, 44-CE
311	H/ET 65	
312	113-DF	
315	070-MG	ex 5-MN

MS.760 PARIS

The MS.760 Paris serves as a light liaison jet with GAEL, the regional communications flights and Aéronavale training and communications sections. French military production was interspersed with civil aircraft and examples for Argentina and Brazil; most of these Brazilian aircraft were later purchased by the Armée de l'Air and are marked * in the list below. The prototype F-WGVO first flew on 29 July 1954 and the first production machine on 27 February 1958.

Prior to receiving two letter codes aircraft of the GAEL were marked with unique codes on the forward fuselage comprising the final letter of the callsign followed by the c/n, eg No.14 appeared as '140' and No.19 as '19P'. Several others were allocated to SLVSVs of fighter wings of CATac prior to the French departure from NATO.

C/n	Code/Status	Remarks
03	Withdrawn	
1	118-DB	
12	W/o 13.4.59	ex CEPA(Aéronavale)
14	LG/GAEL	ex O/GAEL
19	LX/GAEL	ex P/GAEL
20		ex Q/GAEL
23	CG/ELA 44	ex R/GAEL, 10-KY, 10-EC, CP/ELA 44
24	LW/GAEL	ex S/GAEL, 44-CZ, (44-)HM
25	118-DI	
24	LW/GAEL	ex S/GAEL, 44-CZ, (44-)HM
25	118-DI	ex T/GAEL, LQ/GAEL
26	LD/GAEL	ex N/GAEL, 33-XA, ELA 55
27	LF/GAEL	ex J/GAEL
29	43-BB	ex U/GAEL, 41-AQ
30	LI/GAEL	ex L/GAEL, 4-WB, 43-BC
31	Instr./Rochefort	ex Aéronavale, SLD
32	SRL Aéronavale	ex 2S
33	SRL Aéronavale	ex 2S
34	LE/GAEL	ex 5-GB, S/GAEL, 41-AP
35	(314-)DD	ex R/GAEL, 2-HC, 5-GH, 41-AP, LN/GAEL
36	43-BD	ex Y/GAEL, LU/GAEL, 10-EC
37	Withdrawn	ex LZ/GAEL

161

38	LO/GAEL	ex N/GAEL
40	SRL Aéronavale	ex 2S
41	SRL Aéronavale	ex SLD
42	SRL Aéronavale	ex 2S
44	LH/GAEL	ex X/GAEL, 41-AS
45	43-BC	ex 43-BA
46	SRL Aéronavale	ex SLD
47	Aéronavale	ex 2S
48	SRL Aéronavale	
51*	43-BA	
53*	LB/GAEL	ex LJ/GAEL
54*	LK/GAEL	
56*	LP/GAEL	
57*	LV/GAEL	
58*	332-DA	
59*	LR/GAEL	
60*	CN/ELA 44	ex LF/GAEL, LT/GAEL
61*	LY/GAEL	
62*	LZ/GAEL	
65*	41-AO	
68*	NB/CEV	
70*	070-MF	ex LB/GAEL
71*	Withdrawn	ex LC/GAEL
73	41-AS	ex 41-AQ
74*	Withdrawn	ex P/GAEL
75*	CO/ELA 44	
77*	41-AQ	
78*	LT/GAEL	
79*	LA/GAEL	
80*	LM/GAEL	
81*	LL/GAEL	
82*	41-AP	ex S/GAEL
83	NC/GAEL	
84	Withdrawn	ex Aeronavale, 11S
85	SRL Aéronavale	
87	SRL Aéronavale	ex 23S
88	SRL Aéronavale	ex 2S, SLD
91*	41-AT	ex M/GAEL, LN/GAEL
92*	41-AN	ex 41-AR
93*	LJ/GAEL	ex 118-DA
94	41-AR	ex V/GAEL, 41-AR, 41-AW, SLVSV 33
95	Withdrawn	ex W/GAEL
96	LU/GAEL	ex O/GAEL
97	CM/ELA 44	ex Y/GAEL, 41-AT
100	NG/CEV	
113	NI/CEV	
114	NJ/CEV	
115	OV/CEV	
116	ON/CEV	ex OP/CEV
117	AZ/CEV	
118	NQ/CEV	ex NQ/CEV, 118-DA
119	NL/CEV	

NORD 260/262/FREGATE

The Nord 262 and its predecessor the Nord 260 are well established in civil fields as medium transports. An initial order for the Series A comprised 16 for the Armée de l'Air and 15 Aéronavale, with 18 Series D going to the Air Force in 1971-73, followed by 6 for the transport conversion unit, CIET 340 in 1977-78. Naval strength was later increased by the transfer of the five remaining Series A aircraft of the GAEL (Nos. 45, 46, 51, 52 and 53). A small number of ET 65 aircraft were loaned to ELAs 41, 43 and 44 in 1975-77, and in the summer of the latter year, ELA 44 received a permanent allocation of four, and applied their unit insignia and code letters. Escadrille de Convoyage has applied their coding to two, both of which have returned to their former owners. The Nord 260 and 262 are also used in an experimental capacity by the CEV and ENSA, whilst some civil registered aircraft of Service de la Formation Aéronautique (SFA) (F-BLHX, 'PNS, 'PNT, 'PNU, 'PNV, 'PNX, 'OHH and 'SUF) have been seen in military markings, including F-BLHX in full Aéronavale colours and code 'HX'.

Nord 260

C/n	Code/Unit	Remarks
001	GG/EPNER	ex F-WJDV
6	MA/CEV	ex F-BLGP
7	MB/CEV	ex F-BLHN
8	MC/CEV	ex F-BLHO, LN-LME
9	ME/CEV	ex F-WLHP

Nord 262

C/n	Code/Unit	Remarks
01	DM/CEV	ex F-WKVR
3	OH/CEV	ex F-WLHR/F-BLHR
28	SLD	ex F-WNMP, SLD, 55S
43	55S	ex F-WOFE
44	W/o 21.1.71	ex OA/GAEL
45	2S	ex F-RBOB/GAEL
46	SSD	ex F-RBOC/GAEL
51	SSD	ex F-RBOD/GAEL
52	55S	ex F-RBOE/GAEL, SLD,
53	3S	ex F-RBOF/GAEL, SLD
55	MH/ENSA	(F-ZVMH)
58	MJ/ENSA	(F-ZVMJ)
59	55S	ex 3S, 2S, 3S
60	2S	ex SLD
61	2S	ex 55S
62	SSD	ex 3S
63	55S	ex 55S, 2S

64	AA/ELA 41	ex 118-IT, F-ZJYV, AA/GAEL
65	55S	
66	118-IT	ex AA/GAEL, AB/GAEL
67	MI/ENSA	(F-ZVMI)
68	CR/ELA 44	ex AC/GAEL
70	SSD	ex 55S
71	55S	ex 2S
72	55S	ex SLD
73	SSD	ex 2S, 3S
75	3S	ex 2S
76	AD/ELA 41	ex AK/GAEL, AD/GAEL
77		ex AE/GAEL, CS/ELA 44
78	AF/ELA 41	ex AF/GAEL
79	55S	ex 3S
80	070-MA	ex 118-.., AG/GAEL, CT/ELA 44
81	CS/ELA 44	ex AH/GAEL, 070-MA
83	AI/ELA 43	ex AI/GAEL
85	2S	
86	AJ/GAEL	
87	CU/ELA 44	ex AK/GAEL
88	AL/GAEL	
89	AM/GAEL	ex AM/GAEL, AM/ELA 44
91	AN/GAEL	
92	AO/GAEL	
93	AP/GAEL	
94	AQ/GAEL	ex AQ/GAEL, 070-MB
95	AR/GAEL	
105	HL/CIET 340	ex HM
106	/CIET 340	
107	HN/CIET 340	
108	/CIET 340	
109	HP/CIET 340	
110	/CIET 340	

Note: No.85 is fitted with a reconnaissance pod believed in connection with the Alizé modification programme.

NORD 1101 (†)

Production of the Messerschmitt 208 under German direction during the war was maintained after the liberation under the designation Nord 1101 Noralpha and its military version the Ramier. 200 Ramiers were built as communications aircraft, the final few serving the CEV until replaced by the Wassmer CE43 in 1974-75. Additionally, the DCAN communications flight of the Aéronavale maintains a small number, identified by their separate serialling system. Codes are prefixed 'F-ZJ' to give the full call-sign.

C/n	Code/Unit	Remarks
4	NN/CEV	
9	DC/CEV	
13	OA/EPNER	
15	NM/CEV	
16	DE/CEV	CN/CEV, scrapped
17	DF/CEV	Scrapped
29	NO/CEV	Scrapped
34	Scrapped	
35	BW/CEV	Scrapped
41	OE/EPNER	Scrapped
67	DK/CEV	CY, scrapped
75	DQ/CEV	Scrapped
77	NP/CEV	Instructional
87	BR/CEV	F-WZBI
88	DO/CEV	
94	OU/EPNER	Scrapped
113	PS/CEV	Scrapped
114	DW/CEV	
116	CP/CEV	
119	DG/CEV	
123	LW/CEV	
125	CAN 10/DCAN	Current 1978
132	CAN 9/DCAN	Current 1978
133	Scrapped	
139	CAN 11/DCAN	Current 1978
145	LV/CEV	
157	LB/CEV	Preserved
161	BO/CEV	Scrapped
170	BP/CEV	Scrapped
181	CAN 12/DCAN	Scrapped
183	LC/CEV	
184	CAN 13/DCAN	Scrapped
187	BT/CEV	Scrapped
190	Scrapped	
192	CAN 14	
197	CAN 15/DCAN	Current 1978

Note: F-BLQY/No.112 continues to fly from Etampes in its former military markings for displays etc.

NORD 2501 NORATLAS

Developed from the N2500-01 (F-WFKL) first flown on 10 September 1949, the initial example of five pre-production aircraft designated N2501 flew on 20 November 1950. The first production example took to the air on 10 September 1952 and was followed by a total of 425 aircraft including German-built airframes.

Several have been supplied to Israel, Portugal, Chad, Central African Republic and Greece (the latter ex Luftwaffe), but since 1973 the maintenance unit at Chateaudun has been storing many of the older aircraft, some of which were scrapped late in 1977. The remainder will continue in service until replaced by, presumably, a small extra quantity of Transalls in the 1980s. The first camouflaged aircraft appeared early in 1976, sometimes with only the two letters of the code applied. Examples of variants N2502, 2504 and 2506 are extant, as are the distinctive large-nosed N2501SNB navigation trainers used by CFAS 328. Civilianised aircraft in the F-BZC* series were sold via Le Bourget commencing May 1978.

N2501

C/n	Code/Status	Remarks
03	F-ZABT/CEV	
05	BS/CEV	ex 118-IG, 118-IB
1	Scrapped	ex 341-B, 340-HG
2	NV/CEV	(N2502C)
4	Instructional	ex 341-I
5	F-ZJNA/CEV	
6	Scrapped	ex 340-HH, 63-BB, 312-BJ
7	Scrapped	ex 340-HK
8	Scrapped	ex 341-K, 341-E, BD/GI 312
9	Instructional	ex 118-IC
10	Instructional	ex 340-HJ, BE/GI 312, 340-VD
11	Scrapped	ex BE/GI 312, 312-WO
12	Scrapped	ex 340-HN, 63-BL
13	Instructional	ex 340-HE, BD/GI 312, 340-VF
14	Instructional	ex BF/GI 312, 63-BJ, 340-VE
15	Stored	ex 340-HM, M-C/EC 70, 070-MC
16	Stored	ex 63-BC, BF/GI 312, 340-BY
17	Scrapped	ex BF/GI 312, 340-HS, 312-BF
18	CR (ELA 44?)	ex 340-HD, BG/GI 312, 312-BG
19	Scrapped	ex 340-HJ
20	Stored	ex BH/GI 312, 312-BH
21	Scrapped	ex 62-KF, XG/GAM 56
23	118-IE	ex 340-HK, 340-VC
24	312-BJ	ex 340-HI, 340-HT, 62-KA
25	–/EE 54	ex 62-KO, 61-NY, 62-WK
27	Scrapped	ex 62-WF, 62-WB, XG/GAM 56, 62-QA
28	–/EE 54	ex 340-MC
29	F-ZABJ/CEV	
30	44-GE	ex 62-KE, 62-KP
31	62-WB	ex 61-YI, 62-KM, 62-QB
32		ex XH/GAM 56, 64-BY
33	–/EE 54	ex 61-YZ
34	Instructional	ex N
36	340-VC	ex CEV, –/EE 54
37	62-WH	ex 62-WB, 62-KB, 62-WV, 62-WJ, OX/GAEL, OV/GAEL
38	Scrapped	ex 64-IA
39	Scrapped	ex –/EE 54
41	–/EE 54	ex 63-BT
42	–/EE 54	ex 62-KO
43	Scrapped	ex 62-WI, 340-VI
44	F-BZCK	ex 61-QQ, 63-BI, 64-BI
46	Stored	ex 61-NS, 62-WF, 59-CB
47	Stored	ex 63-BK, 64-IG
50	Museum	ex 62-KF, 64-BH
51	Scrapped	ex 340-HX, 340-HU, 62-WE, 59-CT
52	F-BZCL	ex 62-KW, XH/GAM 56, 64-BP, 44-GD
53	Stored	ex 59-CC
54		ex 62-KW, 62-WT, 61-QB, 64-IF, 312-BK, 64-BT, 44-GF
55	F-BZCM	ex 62-SG, 61-YM, 118-IC
56	F-BZCN	ex 63-BM, BK/GI 312, 312-BK
57	XC/GAM 56	ex 62-WP
58	F-BZCO	ex 61-NW, 64-IC, 64-IJ
60	F-BZCP	ex 62-.., 64-BX
61	Scrapped	ex 62-KP, 340-VJ
63		ex 62-KP, 63-BL, 61-NU, 64-IL, 312-BH
64	F-BZCQ	ex 61-QB, 63-BT, 64-BX, 62-KI
65	F-BZCR	ex 62-WH, 340-VO
66	–/EE 54	ex 62-WS, 62-KX
72	F-BZCS	ex 62-KI, 62-KT, 62-KD, 62-WD, XH/GAM 56, 62-WO
74		ex 341-B, 62-WJ, 61-NZ, XB/GAM 56, 62-WO
75	XH/GAM 56	ex 64-KC, 62-KS, 61-QS, XD/GAM 56
76	F-BZCT	ex 61-YT, 62-OW, 62-WD
77	Scrapped	ex 62-KT, 62-KI, 312-BG
78	Preserved	ex 62-KC, 340-HD, AD, 59-CD, 312-BE
79	62-QN	ex 62-WR, 61-YU, XH/GAM 56
80	64-BP	ex 61-QO, 62-KY, 64-IO
81	XK/GAM 56	
83	–/EE 54	ex 61-NO, 340-HO, 62-KN, 62-KF
84	340-VR	ex 62-KB
85	328-EA	ex 340-HA, 62-KC
86	62-QE	ex 61-OB, 63-IL, 61-NM, 62-OA, OY/GAEL, OX/GAEL, 62-KE, 88-JA
87	KA/ET 64	ex 61-OO, 61-QA, 61-QV, 88-JA
88	64-IX	ex 61-YW, 340-VS, 64-IX, 59-CU
89	KB/ET 55	ex 64-IC, OZ/GAEL, 62-QR
90	62-QW	ex 61-QH, 61-QO, 62-WV, 63-BR, 63-BK
91	62-QU	ex 62-WN, 62-KG, 62-KO, 62-KJ
92	64-IT	ex 62-KR, 62-KG, 62-WO, 64-BW, 64-BV
93	64-BD	ex 61-NK, 61-QG, 340-HV, 61-NF, 64-BG

163

#	Code	Ex
94	312-BI	ex 62-KJ, 62-WB, 50-WA
95		ex 61-NK, 63 BM, XJ/GAN 56, 328-EA
96	340-VH	ex 62-WG, 64-IK, 62-WK
97	340-VQ	ex 61-YY, 63-BN, 64-BN
98	64-BC	ex 64-IQ, 62-KI
99	62-KJ	ex 62-SJ, 62-KB, 62-KH
100		ex 61-NJ, 61-YH, 62-KK
101	64-KB	ex 64-IE, 61-YV, 63-BC, 64-BC
103	64-IB	ex 64-IR, 62-KC, 64-BF, 64-KD
104	328-EB	ex 340-HR, 64-YN, 340-HB, 64-IS, 62-KH
105	62-WW	ex 61-NH, 340-HY, 62-KW
106	JD/ETOM 82	ex 61-NE, 64-IK, 59-CN, 62-JC(sic), 62-WE
107		ex 62-WV, 62-KH, 64-IS, 64-IJ, 62-WG
108	118-ID	ex 61-NO, 61-NQ, 62-WM
109	62-QZ	ex 61-NM, 64-II, 64-IE
110	340-VS	ex 61-NK, 62-WV, 61-NL, 62-WZ
111	64-IC	ex 63-BP, 61-YH, 62-QC, 64-BA, 88-JF
112	64-BN	ex 63-AW, 61-QY, 61-NM, 62-QC, 64-BM, 64-BJ, 64-KO
113	64-BH	ex 61-NR, 61-DL, 61-DC, 63-BE, 61-NO, CAM/EC 57, 340-VZ, 64-BA
114	316-FQ	ex 61-YR
115	340-VA	ex 61-NO, 61-YL, 340-HF, XF/GAM 56, 64-BJ
116	64-BQ	ex 61-YM, 61-YJ, 64-IF, 62-WP, 62-WF
117	64-B.	ex 64-IO, 61-NV, 64-IZ
118	63-VG	ex 61-NE, 61-NH, 61-NA, 62-QI, CH/ET 59, 59-CS, 340-VG
119	KA/ETOM 55	ex 62-SK, 61-QD, –/GOM 88, 88-JD 340-VG
120	340-VZ	ex 62-KG, 62-WE, 62-KT, 64-BQ
121	64-IL	ex 61-YA, 64-IM, 64-IW, 62-KJ, 59-CM, 64-BM
122	62-KD	ex 62-SM, 62-WH, 61-QY, 340-VB, 62-KQ
123	312-BH	ex 61-NQ, 61-NF, 64-IP, 340-HD
124	Instructional	ex 61-YD, 64-IK, 61-NP, 63-BP
125	JF/ETOM 88	ex 61-NK, 61-NR, 64-IY
126		ex 61-QH, 62-KJ, 64-IE
127	328-EA	ex 61-NE, 64-IW, 62-QO
128	328-EC	ex 61-YH, 63-BU, 61-QJ, 62-WZ
129	316-FA	ex 64-IC
130	62-KI	ex 62-IH, 63-BD, XB/GAM 56, PM/GM 82, XB/GAM 56
131	340-VT	ex 62-WR
132	328-ED	ex 61-QK, 328-ER
133	62-KP	ex 62-QN, 62-KA, 340-HU, 62-WR, 62-QL, 62-KP
134	Stored	ex 61-YM, 61-NJ, XG/GAM 56
135	328-FE	ex 61-HC, 61-OM, 61-NI, 64-IJ, M-B/EC 70, 070-MB
136	62-WL	ex 61-QO, 61-NJ, 64-IK, 61-IF, 62-WN, MH/GAM 58, 58-MH
137	Scrapped	ex 63-BR, 64-BR, 64-BK, 316-FM
138	64-BG	ex 64-IQ, 63-BD, 63-BK, 64-BK
139	64-IE	ex 61-YF, 61-QM, 62-WP, 58-MI
140	340-VB	ex 64-IL, 62-WM
141	IJ (ETOM 88?)	ex 118-IG
142	KP/ET 64	ex 61-QP, 340-HZ, 64-II, 58-MJ, 62-WC, 62-KA
143	62-QP	ex 61-NO, 64-IN, 340-HP, 64-IN
144		ex 61-YO, XA/GAM 56
145	62-WA	ex 61-YC, 62-KV
146	64-KQ	ex 62-WE, 61-QR, CAG/EC 57
147		ex 64-IG, 64-QI, 62-QD, 50-WG, 62-WG, 62-QG
148	64-BK	ex F-OBDX, 61-QX, XI/GAM 56, 62-QM
149	64-IF	ex 61-YD, XF/GAM 56
150	62-KA	ex 61-NB, 61-NP, 88-JF, 62-JA, KA/ET 62, 59-CR
151	CAR/EC 57	ex 61-YP
152	Written off	ex 61-QQ, 64-II
153	62-QF	ex 64-IQ, 62-WL, 61-IQ, 62-KQ
154	328-EF	ex 340-HS, 62-WL
155	328-EG	ex 64-IF, 328-EQ
156	JE/ETOM 88	ex 61-YB, 88-JC, 62-KL, 64-IW
157	62-KS	ex 61-NG, 63-BW, 62-WI
158	64-IQ	ex 61-NH, 62-KD
159	312-BG	ex 61-YS, 62-WL, 64-BO
160	62-KK	ex 61-QE, 61-NF, 340-HO, –/EE 54, 88-JB
161	64-IM	ex 61-YK, 62-KL, 62-WM
162	64-II	ex 61-NM, 64-IO, 61-YU, 64-II, 62-WV
163	64-BF	ex 61-YK, 61-YO, 62-KM, 82-PO, 64-IO
164	63-VN	ex 62-SL, 61-YP, 64-IM, F-BPXR, 34-VN
165	63-VK	ex 61-YE, 61-YX, 63-VK
166	55-KD	ex 61-NA, 62-WQ, 64-BV, 62-KD, 64-IH
167	340-VB	ex 64-ID, 62-KU
168	62-KO	ex 64-IT, 340-HC
169	340-VU	ex 61-NC, 61-YN, 62-KZ, 64-IN
170	340-VY	ex 62-KB, 61-YX, 64-IC, 62-WU, CAP/EC 57
171	316-FR	ex 316-FT
172	XR/GAM 56	ex 64-IF, M-A/EC 70, 070-MA
173	62-WV	ex 61-QF, 62-WV, 64-II, 62-WU
174	XZ/GAM 56	ex 62-WV, 62-WO, 61-YO, 64-IH
175	328-EH	ex 61-QL, 64-ID, 61-QE, 340-VU, 64-BW
176	340-VV	ex 61-YP, 62-WA
177	64-IV	ex 61-NV, 64-IO, 62-KE
179		ex 61-QR, 61-YI, 50-WB, 62-QD 312-BE
180	328-EI	ex 64-IR, 340-VN, 64-IK
181	62-QC	ex 64-IJ, 64-IC, 63-BX, 50-WW, 64-IT
182	64-BR	ex 64-ID, 64-IE, 62-WY
183	64-BI	ex 64-IE, 61-NT, 63-BS, –/GAM 56
184	118-IF	ex 62-KZ, 62-KV, 118-IE
185	64-KV	ex 64-IG, 62-KZ, 118-IB, 58-MK, 62-WF
186	328-EJ	ex 61-QD, 328-EO
187	64-IS	ex 61-QA, 61-QK, 61-QN, XA/GAM 56, 61-QO, 82-PN, 64-BN
188	316-FS	ex 63-BU
189	316-FN	ex 61-QT, 62-WZ
191	JO/ETOM 88	ex 64-IA, 61-QK, 62-QJ
192	–/EC 57	ex 64-IB, 64-IA, CAL/EC 57
193	316-FU	ex 63-AE, 62-ST, 64-IE
194		ex 64-IB, 63-BW, 64-IB, 62-WL, 62-WC, 316-FP
195	070-MM	ex 62-KT, 62-KY, 64-IH, 59-CL, 340-VK
196	316-FO	ex 64-IB, 63-BC
197	Scrapped	ex 64-ID, 340-HK, 316-FV
198	64-IN	ex 62-KN, 64-IH, 62-KS, 59-CO, 64-IZ
199	64-KI	ex 61-YD, M-D/EC 70, 070-MD
200	328-EK	ex 61-QX, 328-ES
201	64-IG	ex 64-IZ, OY/GAEL, 62-KM
202	62-KM	ex 62-KI, 64-IH, 55-KB
203	328-EL	ex 61-YP, 62-WW, 328-EP
205	64-KE	ex 63-BY, 62-KS, 88-JC, 62-QI, 62-WD
206	62-KT	ex 61-NI, 64-IJ, 62-WE, 64-IR, 62-KA
207	XD/GAM 56	ex 61-NN, 62-KA
208	340-VX	ex 61-QH, 61-YG, 63-BY, 62-QF

N2504

01   F-YDEY/Section Experimental, St. Raphael, ex F-XCJG/10S

N2506

01   Instructional   ex F-WIEX, 118-IA

Note: 62- and 340- prefixes in the above listings are now redundant and are in the process of being changed to 64- and 63-.

NORD 3202 (†)

The low-wing, tandem-seat Nord 3202 was chosen as standard equipment for basic, aerobatic and blind-flying instruction by ALAT, replacing the Stampe SV.4. First flight was on 17 April 1957 and production deliveries of the first batch of fifty, with 240 hp engines, continued until 1961 when delivery of a further fifty with 260 hp engines commenced. Most served with the ESALAT at Dax, and were stored or dumped at La Ferte Alais in 1975-76.

C/n	Callsign	Remarks
2		
3		
4	F-MAIE	
5		
6		
7		To N2253B
8	F-MAJH	
9	F-MMDB	
11		
12		
13	F-MAJM	To N2253F
14	F-MAJB	
15	F-MAJV	F-WZBA
17		
18	F-MALB	
19	F-MAIC	
20	F-MAIE	
22		
23	F-MAIG	
24		
25		
26	F-MAJA	
27		
28		
29		
30	F-MAIV	To N2253J
31		
32		
33		
34	'JJ'	
35		
36		
38		
39		
40	F-MAIT	To N2253R
41	F-MAJB	To N2253W
43		
45	F-MAIC	To N2253Z
47		
48		
50		
52		
53		
54		To N22532
55	F-MAJV	To N22538
57	Preserved	
58	F-MAJQ	To N2254B
60		
62		To N2254R
63		To N2254U
65		To N2254X
66	F-MAJO	Preserved
68	F-MAJA	To N2254Z
69	F-MAJI	To N2254S
70	F-MAIX	To N22546
71	F-MAJT	Current as F-AZAD (civil)
72		To N22547
73	F-MAID	To N22549
77	F-MAIR	To N2255B
78		To N2255E
79	F-MAJI	To N2255F
80		To N2255N
81		To N2255P
82		To N2255Q
84		To N2255W
85	F-MAJG	To N2255Y
87	F-MAIM	To N2255Z
88	F-MAJU	To N2256B
91	F-MALD	To N2256V
92	Preserved	
93		To N2256U
94	F-MAJG	F-WZBB
97	F-MAIP	To N2256W
98		To N2256Y
101		To F-AZAI (civil)

NORD 3400 (†)

The Nord 3400 high-wing AOP aircraft was the winner of a design competition held in February 1957 and made its first flight on 20 January 1958. One hundred and fifty aircraft, numbered 01-03 and 4-150, were delivered to the ALAT, the last in March 1961. Relegated to use by training units in the latter days, the majority of the survivors were dumped at Rennes in 1973, although four continue in service with the Gendarmerie.

C/n	Callsign	Remarks
11		
13	F-MAYZ	
18		
21	F-MBTD	
23		
26		
28		
29		
40		
46	F-MMFA	
48		
49	F-MCUH	
60		
69		
73	F-MCAT	
74	F-MCBK	
79		
80	F-MCCS	
81	F-MCDA	
82	F-MCAR	
86	F-MCBP	
89	F-MCDG	
90		
91		
93	F-MMHA	
94		
95	F-MCCJ	
96	F-MJBV	Current
97	F-MCBN	
98	F-MCDB	
99	F-MJBW	Current
104	F-MCAX	
105	F-MJBX	Current
106		
107	F-MBTD, F-MCCN	
108	F-MJBY	Current
110	F-MMGB	
114	F-MAPC, F-MCCP	
115	F-MCCQ	
117	F-MCDF	
120	F-MBTD, F-MCAW	
128	F-MBTE	

NORTH AMERICAN F-100D/F SUPER SABRE

Principally operated by the USAF, the Super Sabre was supplied to Europe for the French, Danish and Turkish air forces, and remains in service with the latter two. The type

165

166

North American F-100 Super Sabre No.63935 '11-MQ'. The end of the line for an aircraft returned to the USAF at Sculthorpe for disposal. No.63935 wears th insignia of the Djibouti-based EC 4/11, but the '11-M*' code has been changed to 'MQ' (F-SDMQ) indicating the aircraft ferry unit EdC 70. *(D.M. Sargent)*

Robin DR300 F-ZVMG is a communications aircraft with ENSA. *(I. Burnett)*

Nord 3400 No.123 'BPI'. Like many army aircraft throughout the world, the N3400, now all-but withdrawn, features a high wing and plenty of glazing. The uncamouflaged 'BPI' served with GALDiv 11 at Pau. *(J-L. Gaynecoetche)*

Nord 262 Frégate No.73 is attached to the Headquarters communications squadron the Section de Soutien de Dugny at Le Bourget as a VIP transport. *(J-L. Gaynecoetche)*

Nord 3202 No.66 'AJO'. Large numbers of the Nord 3202 were sold in 1975-6, and many have found their way to La Ferte Alais under the ownership of Jean Salis. One which escaped civilianisation is 'AJO' preserved at Montauban. *(R. Cram)*

Nord 3400 No.100 at Montauban in December 1976 in olive drab colour scheme. *(R. Cram)*

Nord 260 Super Broussard No.8 'MC'. Differentiated from the Nord 262 by the lack of a dorsal fin is one of the four Nord 260 aircraft employed by the CEV, a fifth serving with the EPNER. *(J-L. Gaynecoetche)*

Nord 262 Frégate No.107 'HN' carries only the CIET 340 unit badge and the last two letters of the callsign on the nose. *(J-L. Gaynecoetche)*

Robin HR100-250 No.529 'PD'. The latest light aircraft aquisition for the CEV base at Istres is the Robin HR100, which entered service late in 1975, at least six having been delivered in the series F-ZJPA/PF. Taking into account the other types such as Cessna 310/411, and Guépard, the CEV has a considerable number of communications aircraft, which are of course also suitable for sport flying. A further two HR100 are used by the Naval Construction Board, the DCAN, also for communications. *(MAP)*

Piper PA-31 Navajo No.232. Last of the twelve Navajo communications aircraft delivered to the Aéronavale as Flamant replacements, No.232 serves with the SSD at Le Bourget, the other being distributed between this unit, 2S and 3S. Whereas the first ten of the order were delivered with civil registrations in the usual sequence, No. 232 and its sister aircraft, No.227, arrived a year later with special ferry registrations, F-ETBB and 'BC. As with the other Navajos, their c/n was abbreviated for presentation on the fin, the full identity of this example being 31-7401232. Despite the normal procedure of rapidly changing Aeronavale call signs, No.232 appears to have a preference for F-YEFU. *(J.-L. Gaynecoetche)*

was issued to EC 3 and EC 11 in 1958-59, but was concentrated in EC 11 from 1976 onwards.
Deliveries totalled 100, of which 12 were two-seat F-100F models, and when EC 11 began to re-equip with the Jaguar the survivors were ferried to the 7510 Combat Support Squadron at Sculthorpe, England for storage and scrapping, the first arriving in November 1975. Several have passed through Chateaudun and have received codes of the delivery unit EC 70, although retaining the '11-' prefix. As these clash with those of EC 2/11, as both are in the range 'MA' to 'MZ', the codes of EC 70 have been specifically designated. The final operational Super Sabre unit, EC 4/11 'Jura' codes 11-YA etc. was disbanded at Djibouti on 12 December 1978, but a small number will remain as target-towing aircraft at the same base.
The first batch was drawn from the USAF production run 54-2121/54-2303, c/n 223-1 to 223-183, block numbers F-100D-1-NA from 42121; F-100D-5-NA from 42133; F-100D-10-NA from 42152, and F-100D-15-NA from 42222; and the supplementary aircraft from F-100D-35-NH 52734/52743 c/n 224-1/224-10, and F-100D-40-NH 52745 c/n 224-12, with the two-seaters coming entirely from the F-100F-15-NA block 63920/64019 c/n 243-196/243-195. Later modification has raised most block numbers one unit upwards, eg 42128 is now an F-100D-2-NA.

F-100D Super Sabre

Serial	Status	Remarks
42121	W/o 10.66	ex 3-IE, 11-RT
42122		ex 3-IF, 11-RV
42123		ex 11-RQ, 11-MX
42124	W/o	ex 11-MQ
42125	11-YE	ex 3-JR, 11-RF, 11-MT, 11-MI
42128	USAF 6.1.76	ex 3-JT, 3-JA, 11-RG, 11-Y., 11-MJ/EC 70
42129		ex 3-JC, 11-RD
42130	11-YF	ex 11-RT, 11-MY
42131	Preserved	ex 11-RB, 11-MI, 11-MB, 11-MJ
42133		ex 11-EQ, 11-RC, 11-MX, 11-MJ/EC 70
42135	W/o	ex 11-EQ
42136		ex 11-EL, 11-EB
42137	W/o 1.64	ex 3-JM, 11-R.
42138	11-YM	ex 11-MD, 11-RH
42140	W/o 10.58	ex 11-M.
42141	W/o 9.59	ex 3-JA
42144	W/o 1.6.67	ex 11-MV, 11-RK, 11-RM
42146	USAF 10.2.76	ex 3-JB, 11-MG, 11-EB, 11-MK/EC 70
42148		ex 3-JA, 3-JC, 11-EY. 11-EM, 11-MK/EC 70
42149	USAF 10.8.76	ex 3-IB, 11-MH, 11-EA
42150	W/o	ex 3-JE, 11-EG
42152	USAF 2.3.76	ex 3-IC, 3-JP, 11-MT, 11-MH, 11-ML/EC 70
42154	11-YK	ex 11-MQ, 11-MN/EC 70
42156	11-Y.	ex 3-JD, 11-MD, 11-MT/EC 70
42157	USAF 24.5.77	ex 3-ID, 11-ER, 11-ML/EC 70
42158		ex 3-IF, 3-IJ, 11-RE, 11-MN
42160	USAF 22.2.77	ex 3-IF, 11-EC, 11-ET, 11-YF
42162	11-YG	ex 3-JG, 11-MI
42163	USAF 24.5.77	ex 11-ED, 11-YC
42164	11-YK	
42165	USAF 24.11.75	ex 3-IG, 11-MB, 11-ML/EC 70
42166	USAF 10.2.76	ex 3-JT, 3-JH, 11-ES, 11-MV/EC 70
42167	W/o	ex 11-ER, 11-EI, 11-MG
42168	USAF 2.3.76	ex 3-JG, 3-IJ, 11-MC, 11-EL, 11-EH
42171	Scrapped	ex 3-IS, 11-EQ
42174	USAF 22.2.77	ex 11-ES, 11-EE, 11-YI
42184	W/o 9.64	ex 3-JD
42185		ex 3-IG, 11-MO, 11-ED
42186		ex 3-JJ, 3-JL, 11-MJ
42187	W/o	ex 3-JK, 11-EA
42189	W/o	
42194	USAF 30.3.76	ex 3-IH, 11-RA, 11-MG/EC 70
42195	W/o	
42196	USAF 22.2.77	ex 11-ME, 11-YJ
42198	W/o 1.60	ex 11-MF
42203	USAF 30.3.76	ex 11-EV, 11-EM, 11-MW/EC 70
42204		ex 3-JE, 11-EH, 11-MO
42205		ex 3-IT, 11-MM
42210	W/o 13.9.66	ex 3-IJ, 3-IN, 11-MR
42211	USAF 6.1.76	ex 11-MA, 11-EJ, 11-MM/EC 70
42212	USAF 6.1.76	ex 3-IK, 11-EC, 11-MN/EC 70
42213	W/o	ex 11-M.
42215	W/o 12.64	ex 3-IL
42217	W/o	ex 11-MH
42220	W/o	ex 11-M.
42223	USAF 24.5.77	ex 11-RK, 11-RQ, 11-MK, 11-YK
42226	W/o	ex 11-M.
42231	W/o 10.64	ex 3-IM, 3-JA
42235	11-Y.	ex 11-EJ, 11-EV
42236	W/o 13.9.66	ex 3-IN, 11-MC
42237	W/o	ex 11-M.
42239	USAF 24.5.77	ex 11-EK, 11-YL
42243	W/o 8.63	ex 3-JH
42246		ex 11-EL
42247		ex 3-IO, 11-EP
42248	USAF 6.1.76	ex 3-JO, 11-MV, 11-MP/EC 70
42249	USAF 2.3.76	ex 3-IP, 11-MF
42252	W/o	ex 11-M.
42254	USAF 24.11.75	ex 3-IR, 11-RJ, 11-EG, 11-MJ/EC 70
42255	W/o	ex 3-IT
42257	W/o 12.64	ex 3-IM, 3-JP
42264		ex 11-EN
42265	USAF 30.3.76	ex 3-JG, 3-JR, 11-MY, 11-MP
42267	Instructional	ex 11-EO, w/o 1971
42269	USAF 30.3.76	ex 3-JI, 3-JS, 11-EO, 11-MW, 11-ER
42271	W/o 10.69	ex 11-E.
42272	USAF 24.11.75	ex 11-EF, 11-MK/EC 70
42273	W/o	ex 11-MP
42293.		ex 11-RL, 11-MB
42295		ex 11-MT, 11-RM, 11-MX/EC 70
52734		ex 11-EN, 11-RN, 11-EP, 11-RN
52736		ex 11-RO, 11-MR
52737	11-YC	ex 3-JJ, 11-RP
52738		ex 11-ET, 11-EA, 11-RR
52739		ex 3-JC, 11-CM, 11-RS, 11-MX, 11-MS/EC 70
52741	W/o 1972	ex 11-EQ, 11-ML
52745	W/o	ex 3-IN, 3-JN
63187	W/o	ex 11-EA

F-100F Super Sabre

Serial	Status	Remarks
63928		ex 11-EY
63935	USAF 6.1.76	ex 11-EN, 11-ED, 11-EW, 11-RI, 11-YH, 11-MQ/EC 70
63936	USAF 10.8.76	ex 3-IW, 11-EW, 11-MS, 11-RJ, 11-MA
63937		ex 11-EY, 11-RZ, 11-RK, 11-MT
63938	USAF 24.5.77	ex 11-EY, 11-MX, 11-RG, 11-EZ, 11-MU/EC 70
63939		ex 11-EM, 11-EZ
63940		ex 11-MZ, 11-MR
63941		ex 11-EX
64008	W/o	ex 3-JV
64009	USAF 10.8.76	ex 3-IX, 11-RW, 11-EI, 11-ES
64014		ex 3-IY, 11-RX
64017		ex 3-JY, 11-RY, 11-RW, 11-MZ/EC 70

On 30 March 1976, four aircraft flew direct from Toul to USAF bases other than Sculthorpe (the only ones so to do). 42194 and 42203 at Woodbridge and Alconbury respectively were used for fire practice; however 42269 has been preserved as '54-048/LN' at Lakenheath and 42265 is similarly '63000' at Wethersfield.
Early in 1978, several preservation groups were presented with Super Sabres, conditional upon them providing road transport. Those concerned may be found at the following locations: 42157 Usworth, 42160 Rhoose, 42174 Baginton, 42196 Flixton, 42223 Newark, 42239 Castle Donington and 63938 Torbay. Additionally 42165 went to the IWM at Duxford in 1976 and Sculthorpe have kept 42212 for themselves. Most USAF returns were made to 7519 Combat Support Squadron at Sculthorpe for scrapping.

PIPER SUPER CUB (†)

The Super Cub was withdrawn from ALAT service in the mid 'sixties, when vast numbers appeared on the Civil Registers of France and neighbouring countries. Details are-

Model	C/ns	Ex
L-18C	18-1009/1022	51-15312/15325
	18-1330/1344	51-15330/15344
	18-1354/1571	51-15354/15571
	18-1576/1653	51-15576/15653
	18-2077/2108	52-2477/2508
L-21B	18-2538/2549	52-6620/6231
PA-18-150	18-5322/5401	Direct order

PIPER PA-22 TRI-PACER (†)

Tri-Pacers were used exclusively by the French Army detachment at Djibouti, the final examples appearing at Montauban in 1976 prior to civilianisation.

C/n	Callsign	Remarks
22-5040	F-MKAA	To F-BJAB
22-5140	F-MKAB	To TU-BBB
22-5141	F-MKAC	To F-OCGZ, XT-AAH, G-AZRS
22-5143	F-MKAD	To F-OBDL
22-5147	F-MKAD	To F-BJAC
22-5148	F-MKAE	To TU-TDF
22-5153	F-MKAF	To XT-AAF, N11EE
22-5154	F-MKAG	To F-OCES, EL-AFE
22-5158	F-MKAH	To XT-AAG
22-5159	F-MKAI	To TU-TDE
22-5162	F-MKAJ	Written off
22-7490	F-MKAJ	Ex N3602Z. To F-BMHR
22-7631		
22-7632		To TZ-ACE
22-7633		To F-BXSJ
22-7634		To F-BJAL
22-7635		To TZ-ACL
22-7636		To F-BJAE
22-7637		
22-7638		To TZ-ACO
22-7639		
22-7640		To F-BJAK

PIPER PA-23 AZTEC

Two Piper Aztecs were taken on charge by the Armée de l'Air for use by GAM 82 in the Pacific area, but their current status is not known

C/n	Code/Unit	Remarks
27-2533	MD/GAM 58	ex N5488Y
27-2534	82-QB	ex N5489Y

PIPER PA-31 NAVAJO

The Piper Navajo replaced the Flamant in communications units of the Aéronavale. An initial order for ten delivered October 1972 to February 1973 was augmented by a further two in 1974. The aircraft are known by the last three of their c/ns; the main batch have full c/ns from 31-7300903 to 31-7300931, and the final two are 31-7401227 and '232.

Serial	Unit	Remarks
903	3S	ex 2S, 3S, SLD
904	2S	ex F-BTMS
906	2S	ex SLD
912	3S	ex 3S, SLD
914	3S	ex 2S
916	3S	
925	SLD	ex 2S
927	3S	ex SLD
929	3S	ex F-BTMT, SLD
931	2S	ex F-BTMU, 3S
227		ex F-ETBB
232	SLD	ex F-ETBE

One further example, F-ZBAA is used by the Sécurité Civile

ROBIN HR100/DR300/DR315

The theme of the popular Jodel range of light aircraft has been perpetuated by the firm of Avions Pierre Robin who have supplied the HR100-250 to the CEV and Aéronavale during 1975/76, and two earlier models to the CEV and ENICA at Toulouse. Some sources quote the HR100 order as thirty aircraft.

Robin HR100-250TR

C/n	Code/Unit	Remarks
503	PB/CEV	ex F-WVKG
525	PF/CEV	
526	PA/CEV	
527		
528	PC/CEV	
529	PD/CEV	
532	PH/CEV	
533	EK/DCAN(CAN 18)	
557	PL/CEV	

All CEV aircraft operated by the Istres detachment, using call signs F-ZJPB etc.

Robin DR300

615   F-ZVMG/ENICA

Robin DR315X

624/01   F-ZWRS/CEV

See also 'Jodel' main heading

SEPECAT JAGUAR

French requirements for the Jaguar (A = strike aircraft; E = trainer) total 160 and 40 respectively for three escadres, the first of these, the 7th having received its initial equipment on 24 May 1973.
The first of five French Jaguar prototypes flew on 8 September 1968, and the remainder joined the test programme in 1969, including the abortive Jaguar M, intended for the Aéronavale. Two have been written off to date, E-01 at Istres and A-03 at Tarnos as a result of a heavy landing. The first production example A-1 first flew on 20 April 1972 and from No. 80 onwards, the Jaguar A was fitted with the laser rangefinder pioneered by A4 in 1976. The 100th (of all versions) was delivered on 19 May 1976, by which time all 40 trainers were on charge. Next recipient of the Jaguar will be the fourth squadrons of the 7th and 11th Wings. Procurement will be raised to 174 by the delivery of sixteen Jaguars in 1979, the balance of twenty-six to be ordered later, although BAC Warton have already built their sections of these aircraft.

Prototypes

C/n	Code	Callsign	Remarks
E-01	'B'	(F-ZWRB)	W/o 26.3.70
E-02	'C'	(F-ZWRC)	BAC/BAe, ex CEAM

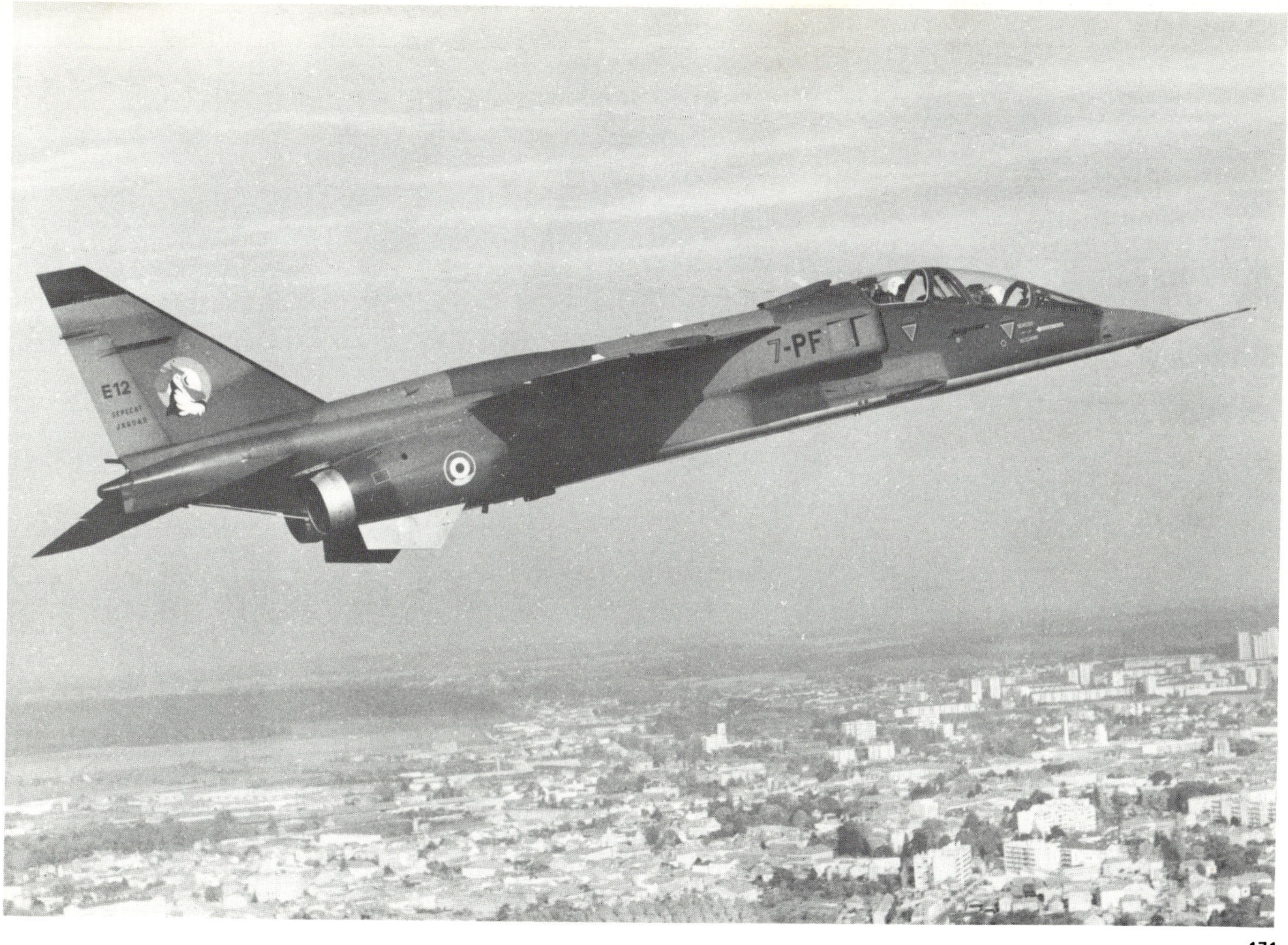
E12
7-PF

172

Sepecat Jaguar E No.E12 '7-PF'. A fine air-to-air photograph overleaf, of a Jaguar trainer flown by the OCU EC 2/7 at St. Dizier. *(J-M. Lefebvre)*

Sepecat Jaguar E No.E31 '11-RF' displays the snake insignia of SPA88 that is associated with 88 Squadron, RAF, which has a similar emblem. *(MAP)*

Sepecat Jaguar A No.26 '7-II' of EC 3/7 wears the motto "Qui S'y Frotte, S'y Pique" (Spiteful to those who touch it) is an apt warning to possible 'customers' of the Jaguar. *(J-L. Gaynecoetche)*

Sepecat Jaguar A No.A62 '3-XI'. The 3 Escadre is unusual in that it is comprised of two squadrons of Mirages and one of Jaguars. A second non-standard feature is the attempt by the unit to code all its aircraft in serial number order, a feat in which it has almost succeeded, placing it in a special group with EC 1/12 and EB 1/92. *(J-L. Gaynecoetche)*

Sikorsky H-34/HSS-1 No.932 'J'. The HSS-1 remains in use with the Aéronavale, those of the Armée de l'Air having retired some years previously. No.932 bears the conversion number '40' and served with helicopter trials squadron 20S with the call-sign F-YCTJ. It is now dumped at St. Mandrier. *(MAP)*

Sud Alouette III No. 1414 'BPU'. The Alouette II is gradually being withdrawn from front-line service with the ALAT in favour of the Gazelle. No. 1414 is operated by 11 GALDiv at Pau, a unit also responsible for amphibious and long-range intervention duties. *(MAP)*

173

A-03	'D'	(F-ZWRD)	W/o 14.2.72
A-04	'E'	(F-ZWRE)	CEAM
M-05	'J'	(F-ZWRJ)	CEV

Sepecat Jaguar A

C/n	Code/Unit	Remarks
A-1	Trials	
A-2	118-AF	ex 118-AE
A-3	Trials	
A-4	118-AG/CEV	Cazaux, laser trials
A-5	7-PK	ex 7-HD, 7-PK
A-6	7-..	ex 7-HB, 7-PY, 3-XA
A-7	3-XB	ex 7-HF, 7-PX
A-8	3-XC	ex 7-H., 7-PW
A-9	7-PV	ex 7-H.
A-10	3-XE	ex 7-IE, 7-PU
A-11	7-PJ	ex 7-HL, 7-PT
A-12	118-AV	
A-13	118-AI	
A-14	CEAM	
A-15	7-HP	
A-16	–/EC 1.7	ex 7-H.
A-17	11-MW	ex 7-HO, 11-RK
A-18		ex 7-HC
A-19	7-HE	
A-20	7-HF	
A-21		ex 7-HG
A-22	7-HH	ex 7-H. 7-I.
A-23	7-ID	ex 7-HI, 7-IK, 7-HI
A-24	7-HJ	ex 7-HJ, 7-IE
A-25	7-HK	
A-26	7-II	
A-27	7-IJ and 7-IK simultaneously	
A-28	7-HB	
A-29	3-XF	ex 7-H., 7-HL
A-30	7-IN	
A-31	7-IK	
A-32	7-IL	
A-33	7-IM	
A-34	7-HM	
A-35	7-HA	
A-36	7-IA	
A-37	7-PE	ex 7-IG
A-38	7-HN	
A-39	7-IO	
A-40	7-HD	
A-41	7-IP	
A-42	7-HC	
A-43	7-PB	ex 7-IQ
A-44	7-IH	
A-45	7-IF	ex 7-IB
A-46	7-IC	ex 7-IB

C/n	Code/Unit	Remarks
A-47	7-IB	ex 7-IC
A-48	11-RK	
A-49	11-RM	
A-50	11-RN	
A-51	3-XR	ex 11-RO
A-52	11-RQ	
A-53	11-RS	
A-54	11-RT	
A-55	3-XQ	ex 11-RV
A-56	11-..	ex 11-EA
A-57	7-PG	ex 11-EC
A-58	7-PH	ex 11-EF
A-59	7-PS	ex 11-EG
A-60	7-HO	ex 11-EH
A-61	3-XH	ex 11-EI
A-62	3-XI	ex 11-EJ
A-63	3-XJ	ex 11-EM
A-64	3-XK	ex 11-ER
A-65	3-XL	ex 11-ES
A-66		ex 11-EV, 3-XM, 11-MM
A-67	11-MH	ex 11-EB, 3-XN, 3-XM
A-68	3-XG	ex 11-RJ
A-69	11-RX	
A-70		
A-71	7-IE	ex 11-MB
A-72	11-ET	
A-73	11-EB	
A-74	11-EV	
A-75	11-ES	ex 11-MG
A-76	11-ER	
A-77	11-ED	
A-78	11-RA	
A-79	11-EC	
A-80	11-EM	
A-81	11-MA	
A-82	11-MB	
A-83	11-MC	
A-84	11-MD	
A-85	11-MF	
A-86	11-MG	
A-87	11-MH	
A-88	11-MM	
A-89	11-MO	
A-90	11-MP	
A-91	11-MQ	
A-92	11-MT	
A-93		
A-94	11-EF	
A-95		
A-96		
A-97		
A-98		
A-99	11-EV	

C/n	Code
A-100	
A-101	11-EJ
A-102	
A-103	
A-104	
A-105	
A-106	11-ES
A-107	
A-108	
A-109	
A-110	
A-111	
A-112	
A-113	11-YA
A-114	
A-115	
A-116	
A-117	
A-118	
A-119	
A-120	
A-121	
A-122	
A-123	
A-124	
A-125	
A-126	
A-127	
A-128	
A-129	
A-130	
A-131	
A-132	
A-133	
A-134	
A-135	
A-136	
A-137	
A-138	
A-139	
A-140	
A-141	
A-142	
A-143	
A-144	
A-145	
A-146	
A-147	
A-148	
A-149	
A-150	
A-151	
A-152	

A-153
A-154
A-155
A-156
A-157
A-158
A-159
A-160

Sepecat Jaguar E

C/n	Code/Unit	Remarks
E-1	CEV	ex 118-AI
E-2	3-XS	ex 118-AC
E-3		ex 118-AI
E-4	CEAM	
E-5	CEAM	ex 118-AJ
E-6	118-AH	
E-7	7-PA	ex 7-HA
E-8		ex 7-HB, 7-PB
E-9	7-IC	ex 7-HE, 7-PC
E-10	7-PD	ex 7-HH
E-11	7-PR	ex 7-HI, 7-IH, 7-PE
E-12	7-PF	ex 7-HM, 7-HN
E-13	7-PM	ex 7-HJ
E-14	7-PN	ex 7-HO
E-15	3-XO	ex 7-IA, 11-RW, 11-MT
E-16	3-XP	ex 7-IB, 11-RA, 11-MV
E-17	7-PI	ex 7-IC, 7-PH, 11-EO, 3-XG
E-18	11-ET	ex 7-ID, 11-EN
E-19	7-PI	ex 7-IF
E-20	7-PO	ex 7-IG, 7-HO
E-21	11-MW	ex 7-IK, 7-PJ
E-22	11-ME	ex 7-IL
E-23	11-RB	ex 7-IN, 7-PK
E-24		ex 7-IF, 7-PK
E-25	7-PL	
E-26	Believed w/o 26.3.75	
E-27	11-EL	
E-28		ex 7-·, 11-EI
E-29	11-EA	ex 11-RB
E-30	11-RC	
E-31	11-RF	ex 7-PF
E-32		ex 11-RG
E-33	11-RH	
E-34		
E-35	11-RG	ex 11-MW, 11-RV
E-36		ex 11-RX
E-37	11-ME	ex 11-RD, 11-ET, 11-RD
E-38	(EAA 601)	
E-39		
E-40	(EAA 601)	

Note: Rapid changes of codes, allied to the fact that aircraft in store/overhaul by EAA 603 retain their previous markings, has been responsible for the reporting of different aircraft bearing the same markings on the same date. Confused readers may take comfort in the fact that this practice is having a similar effect on the Armée de l'Air, for example '7-PE' was worn by both A37 and E11 in July 1978, whilst A27 was marked 7-IJ and 7-IK on opposite sides of the fuselage in August 1977. Also, the reverse of this situation obtained in Spring 1974, with at least A8, 9, 16, 17, 18, 19, 20, 21, 22, 23 and 25 flying simply as '7-H'. In 1977-78, No. A36 was marked 7-IA to port, but only '7-I' on the starboard side. Changes of unit likewise bring problems, for example No. A58 altered its code from 7-PH (EC 2/7) to 7-ID (EC 3/7) in July 1978, but at least a month later was still to be seen wearing the badges of its old squadron. Three Jaguars have been shot down in Africa during 1978

SIKORSKY & SUD H-34

The Aéronavale is now the principal operator of the H-34 following the withdrawal of the last Armée de l'Air aircraft, SA71, on 31 May 1976. Approximately fifty air force examples are in store at EAA 601, Chateaudun, but as most appear to be the licence-built version (although individual serials are known in only a few cases) it may not be possible for them to follow earlier examples to the USA for S-58T conversion. France received 135 US built H-34, plus a further 130 Sud Aviation assemblies in the c/n range SA51/SA185 of which SA145, 146, 181, 184 and 185 went to Belgium, SA1 to 50 being licence built H-19s. Air force helicopters served with EH 67 and EH 68 and were replaced by the Alouette III in 1973-74. Navy units still in commission are 31F and 33F.

Sikorsky-built, SKY prefix

C/n	Status	Remarks
248	Withdrawn	
266	Stored	ex 67-SR
267	Withdrawn	
280	Withdrawn	
281	Withdrawn	
299	Withdrawn	
300	Withdrawn	
318	Withdrawn	
320	Withdrawn	To N1143U
328	Withdrawn	To N1144U, HB-XDT
329	Withdrawn	
330	Withdrawn	To N1145U, C-FOKR
331	Withdrawn	ex SQ, To N1146U
334	Withdrawn	
335	Withdrawn	To N1147U
336	Withdrawn	To N1148U
337	Withdrawn	
340	Withdrawn	
354	Withdrawn	ex 67-SW, To N1149U
355	Withdrawn	
357	Withdrawn	
358	Withdrawn	
370	Withdrawn	ex 67-SM, To N1150U,
374	Withdrawn	To N1151U
375	Withdrawn	
376	Withdrawn	To N1152U
377	Withdrawn	
378	Withdrawn	To N1153U
379	Withdrawn	To N1154U
397	Withdrawn	
398	Withdrawn	
400	Withdrawn	
401	Withdrawn	
422	Withdrawn	ex EG, To N1156U
435	Withdrawn	
445	Aeronavale	Written off
447	88-JS	
453	A/31F	ex 'L'
454	Aeronavale	
455	Withdrawn	
469	Withdrawn	
478	Withdrawn	
479	Withdrawn	ex 67-SO
481	Withdrawn	ex 67-VU, To N1155U
487	Withdrawn	
488	Withdrawn	
494	Withdrawn	
500	Withdrawn	ex 67-SL
507	Preserved	ex 507-SV, 67-SV
512	Instructional	ex F-YCTN/20S
513	Withdrawn	
520	Withdrawn	
521	Withdrawn	
525	Withdrawn	ex 67-VX
533	Withdrawn	
541	Withdrawn	ex (67-)SS
549	Withdrawn	ex GAM 88
550	P/31F	
553	Withdrawn	ex LA
554	Withdrawn	
556	Withdrawn	ex 68-OE
561	Withdrawn	
567	Withdrawn	
576	Withdrawn	
582	Withdrawn	

175

C/n	Status	Remarks
584	Withdrawn	ex WJ, To N1157U, C-FOKW
585	Withdrawn	
586	Withdrawn	
587	Withdrawn	
593	Withdrawn	
594	Withdrawn	
595	Withdrawn	To N1158U
601	Withdrawn	To N1159U
602	Withdrawn	ex GU, To N1160U
603	Withdrawn	ex GAM 88
609	Withdrawn	ex (67-)ST, LW
610	Withdrawn	ex 67-SP
615	Instructional	ex 68-OK
635	Withdrawn	
636	Withdrawn	To N1161U
637	Withdrawn	
638	K/31F	
639	L/31F	
640	Instructional	ex 20S Aéronavale
641	Instructional	ex 33F Aéronavale
643	Withdrawn	ex MM, 68-OR
653	Withdrawn	ex 67-VL
659	Withdrawn	ex (67-)SU, GAM 88
670	Withdrawn	
680	Scrapped	ex 33F, 31F
681	Aéronavale	Written off
682	Withdrawn	
688	Instructional	ex 33F
689	Aéronavale	
693	Withdrawn	
705	Stored	ex XN, 68-OH
717	Withdrawn	ex 68-OT
729	Withdrawn	ex 31F
741	Withdrawn	
755	Withdrawn	
766	Withdrawn	
781	Instructional	
793	Withdrawn	ex (67-)SV, 68-ON, 68-04
819	Withdrawn	
832	Stored	ex 68-OX
922	33F	ex J/31F
932	Scrapped	ex 20S
944	33F	ex 32-F-8
954	Aéronavale	
956	Withdrawn	To N1162U, F-BVJI
961	33F	
971	33F	
977	Withdrawn	ex 977-ST, 67-ST, To N1163U
983	Scrapped	ex 33F
994	33F	
1001		ex XN-001, 1A
1002	002/33F	
1003	003/33F	
1004	33F	
1005	M/31F	
1006	F-YCTK/20S	ex S/31F
1007	Scrapped	ex F-ZKCO, 7/20S
1070	Withdrawn	ex XM, To N1168U
1071	Withdrawn	To N1169U. VH-UHX
1117	Withdrawn	To N1170U
1120	Withdrawn	To N1171U
1121	Withdrawn	
1122	Withdrawn	ex LY
1123	Withdrawn	ex GAM 88
1124	Withdrawn	To N1166U, N126GW
1126	Withdrawn	ex 67-SW, To N1167U
1128	Withdrawn	To N1164U, VH-UHV
1129	Withdrawn	To N1165U, VH-UHW
1376	PY/CEV	(F-ZJPY)

Note: the c/n plate of 638 gives '58-648'

Sud-built, SA prefix

C/n	Status	Remarks
54	Wfu 21.4.78	ex 67-VA, EPNER
55	Withdrawn	ex 68-OA
56	Scrapped	ex 68-OP
57	Preserved	ex XP, 67-VC, 68-OH
62	Stored	ex 67-XN, 68-ON
63	Withdrawn	ex 68-OV
64	Withdrawn	ex 68-OB
67	Withdrawn	ex 68-OQ
69	Stored	ex (68-)OQ
70	Withdrawn	ex 68-OK
71	Withdrawn	ex (67-)VI, 68-OX, 68-03, 44-GH
72	Withdrawn	ex 68-DB
73	Withdrawn	ex 68-OY
75	Withdrawn	ex (67-)VJ
76	Withdrawn	ex Bi-Bastan No. 01
79	Withdrawn	ex (67-)VF
83	Withdrawn	
84	Preserved	ex 67-VK, 67-OB
85	Instructional	
86	Preserved	ex 86-SU, 68-OR, 67-SS, 67-OY
90	Withdrawn	ex 67-VL
91	Instructional	ex 68-DK
92	Withdrawn	ex 67-VB, 68-OE
96	Withdrawn	ex 68-RB
98	Withdrawn	ex 68-RG, 67-XB, 68-DE, 68-DG 68-OF
99	Withdrawn	ex 67-XA, 67-SA
100	Withdrawn	ex 67-SX
101	Preserved	ex (67-)XB, 68-ON
102	Withdrawn	ex 67-SY, 68-DD
103	Withdrawn	ex (67-)VG
104	Withdrawn	ex 67-SN
106	Stored	ex 44-GF
107	Withdrawn	ex 68-OI
109	Stored	ex (67-)VM, 68-OZ
114	Withdrawn	ex 67-VH
115	Withdrawn	ex 44-GN, 67-QC, 68-DC
116	Withdrawn	ex 68-DA
117	Withdrawn	ex 67-SP
118	Scrapped	
119	J/31F	
121	Preserved	
122	/31F	ex E/31F, B/31F
123	F/31F	
124	Z/31F	ex G/31F
125	P/31F	ex H/31F, O/31F, 33F
126	33F	ex S/31F
128	G/31F	
129	33F	
130	H/31F	
132	T/31F	ex L/31F, Y/31F
134	R/31F	
135	N/31F	ex J/31F
136	/31F	ex A/31F
137	S/31F	
138	L/31F	
139	20S	ex C/31F
141	33F	ex G/31F, R/31F
142	Instructional	ex F/20S, P/31F
143	33F	ex H/31F
144	33F	ex U/31F
148	33F	
150	E/31F	
152	Instructional	ex 67-VC
153	Withdrawn	ex 68-OI
154	Withdrawn	ex 68-DI
155	Withdrawn	ex (67-)SM
157	Withdrawn	ex (67-)SN
158	Withdrawn	ex 68-OQ
160	Withdrawn	ex (67-)VS, 68-OW
162	Withdrawn	ex 68-OJ
163	Withdrawn	ex 68-OD
164	Stored	ex 67-SS, 68-DL
165	Withdrawn	ex 68-OC
167	Stored	ex 68-OC
168	Withdrawn	ex 67-VF
170	Withdrawn	ex (67-)XI
171	Withdrawn	ex 67-XG
172	Withdrawn	ex 67-SW
174	Withdrawn	
175	Withdrawn	ex 67-XO
178	Withdrawn	ex 67-OR
179	Withdrawn	ex 67-SZ
182	W/31F	
183	33F	ex X/32F

SUD AVIATION ALOUETTE II

Large numbers of Alouettes have been supplied to all three armed services in France, and to many overseas forces. The Alouette family evolved from the SE.3101 flown on 15 June 1948, to the SE.3120 first flown 31 July 1951 as the Alouette I, and the SE.3130 Alouette II first flown 12 March 1955. The revised designations are SA315/SA318.

Extreme care should be taken in the reporting of Alouette II identities, for in addition to its c/n, each Alouette received a production number commencing M1 for French military aircraft and C1 for the others. This number often appears as part of the aircraft's code and should not be confused with the c/n, eg c/n 1333/183-SF of EH 3/67. Where known, the operating unit is given, although in the past two years the wing prefix '67-' is being applied in place of the serial number. Gendarmerie aircraft have been obtained from both 'M' and 'C' ranges.

Naval aircraft are coded from either a part of the c/n, eg 1028 coded '28' of 23S, or the production number, eg 1182, coded '113'. Where no actual identity is known, the service employing an individual aircraft is given, thus - 'AA' - Armée de l'Air, 'MN' - Marine Nationale and 'ALAT' - Army.

Serial	C/n	Status	Remarks
	01	AS/EPNER	
1	1001	Stored	ex 1-DX
2	1002	AA	
3	1003	F-MCXA	
4	1004	04/20S	ex F-YCTB, 04-SA EH 3/67
5	1005	05-SB EH 3/67	ex F-RBSD
6	1006	F-MABG	ex F-MARG, F-MBVV
7	1007	67-SI	ex 7-SI
8	1008	F-MBBO	ex F-MACN, F-MBJF
9	1009	ALAT	
10	1010	10-DS	
11	1011	W/o	ex CEV
12	1013	F-MABZ	
13	1014	AA	
14	1015	F-MABB	
15	1016	F-SFIT	
16	1017	F-MAGF	ex F-MBJK
17	1018	Stored	ex AA
18	1019	F-MAGC	ex F-MBBC
19	1020	–/22S	ex 20-S-6
20	1021	ALAT	
21	1022	MN	
22	1023	67-SD	ex F-SFIA, 22-SJ
23	1024	W/o 1963	ex MN
24	1025	AA	
25	1026	F-MBAT	
26	1027	ALAT	
27	1028	28/23S	ex 23-S-25, 58-S-12
28	1029	W/o 20.2.61	ex AA
29	1030	ALAT	
30	1031	F-YCWY	ex 23-S-25
31	1032		
32	1033	F-MBSA	
33	1034	MN	
34	1035	W/o 13.1.60	ex AA
35	1036	F-MBVU	ex F-MBVW, F-MBGF, F-MBVI
36	1037	–/22S	ex F-YCWA
37	1038	F-MCAG	ex F-MASC, F-MBWT
38	1039		ex F-MAOW
39	1040	ALAT	
40	1041	MN	
41	1042	F-MBBJ	
42	1043	W/o	ex AA
43	1044	F-MBJS	
44	1045	341-RP	
45	1046	F-MBBI	
46	1047	AA	
47	1049	47-SH EH 3/67	
48	1050	F-MCXC	ex F-MBVN
49	1051	W/o 1965	ex MN
50	1052	MN	
51	1053	AA	
52	1054	MN	
53	1056	AA	
54	1058	ALAT	
55	1059	W/o 6.59	ex 20-S-9
56	1060	ALAT	
57	1071	57-MI	ex 57-SH EH 3/67
58	1073	F-MAGD	ex F-MBVR, F-MACN
59	1064	F-YCTI	
60	1074	To Peru	replaced by No. 182
61	1066	F-MBGG	
62	1067	W/o 15.1.60	ex F-MABH
63	1068	67-MC	ex 63-MC
64	1069	F-MMDV	
65	1070	65-SC EH 3/67	
66	1077	F-MADG	ex F-SDIT, F-MCVA
67	1076	67-MI	ex F-MBGJ, F-MBWM, F-MAZH
68	1080	67-SO	ex 68-SO EH 3/67
69	1078	F-MBBH	ex F-MBGK
70	1084	AA	
71	1081	F-MBNK	ex F-MBGL, F-MAZA
72	1079	AA	
73	1088	AA	
74	1089	ALAT	
75	1141		ex F-UJDA, F-SFIN
76	1091		ex F-SFIY
77	1142		ex F-SFXG
78	1093		ex F-MJAU
79	1095	AA	
80	1092	ALAT	
81	1094		ex F-MAOV
82	1101	AA	
83	1102	83-RT	
84	1103	F-MBBA	ex F-MBWS
85	1100	AA	
86	1104		ex F-UJDA
87	1105	AA	
88	1106	67-OH	ex F-MEXF
89	1111	89-RR GAM 82	
90	1143		ex F-SFIL
91	1113	–/22S	ex F-YCWD
92	1121	AA	
93	1122	ALAT	
94	1123	F-MCAH	ex F-MBGS
95	1131	F-MBGT	
96	1132	F-MBWN	
97	1133	F-MCXI	ex F-MABG
98	1134		ex F-RARZ
99	1144	AA	
100	1151	ALAT	
101	1152	F-MBUX	
102	1153	ALAT	
103	1154	F-YCVC	
104	1161	104-MK	
105	1162	162/20S	ex F-YCWC
106	1163	1163/23S	
107	1164	MN	
108	1171	AA	
109	1172	F-MACM	
110	1173	ALAT	
111	1174	F-MACP	
112	1181	F-MBJC	ex F-MBCK
113	1182	113/22S	ex F-YDKF
114	1189		ex F-UJDI
115	1190	F-MCXF	
116	1197	341-RZ	
117	1198	ALAT	
118	1199	ALAT	
119	1200	F-MAGG	
120	1204	AA	
121	1205	AA	
122	1206	AA	
123	1207	ALAT	
124	1211	Gendarmerie	
125	1212	F-MJAM	
126	1213	F-MBGH	
127	1214	F-MAZX	

128	1218	AA		179	1331	179-FW	ex F-MAZF, F-MAZU	229	1424	AA	
129	1219	67-SE	ex 129-SE EH 3/67	180	1332	F-MBWK	ex F-ZLAB, F-MAZR, F-MAFW	230	1425	ALAT	
130	1220	AA						231	1426	ALAT	
131	1221	131-SE EH 3/67		181	1096	AA		232	1427	F-MCVK	ex F-MABD
132	1225	F-MACO		182	1112	341-RR	ex 182-SL EH 3/67	233	1428	F-MBJO	
133	1226	AA		183	1333	183-SF EH 3/67	ex F-SFIQ, F-MJBA	234	1429	ALAT	
134	1227	F-MAZY	ex F-MCVC	184	1334		ex F-SFIX	235	1430	ALAT	
135	1228	F-MBVD	ex F-MACW	185	1335	F-MACN	ex F-MBWS, F-MAZH, F-MJAP	236	1440	67-DV	ex 236-DV
136	1232	AA						237	1441	F-MBBL	ex F-MCQE
137	1233	MN		186	1336	ALAT		238	1442	F-MBBD	
138	1234	F-MJAR		187	1342	ALAT		239	1443	F-MJAZ	
139	1235	F-MAPL		188	1343	ALAT		240	1444	Gendarmerie	
140	1239	AA		189	1344	F-MACJ		241	1445	F-MCXH	
141	1240	F-MCXJ	ex F-MEPV	190	1345	F-MCWR		242	1456	LA/ETOM 52	ex 242-SG EH 3/67, 242-RQ GAM 82
142	1241	AA		191	1346	F-MAZU					
143	1242	F-MBVG		192	1347	F-MBWN		243	1457	243-SJ EH 3/67	
144	1243	ALAT	ex F-RBME	193	1348	F-MBID		244	1458	F-MACW	ex F-MCVH
145	1247	F-MJBD		194	1354	67-DW	ex 194-DW	245	1459	AA	
146	1248	AA		195	1355	F-MAZS		246	1460	F-MBWU	ex F-MABA
147	1249	AA		196	1356	F-MBWO		247	1472	W/o 28.12.70	ex F-RADX
148	1250	Gendarmerie	ex F-UJDD	197	1357	F-MAZP		248	1473	AA	
149	1251	149-RV DPH 5/68	ex F-SDIW	198	1358	F-MAGE	ex F-MBWP, F-MBJD	249	1474	ALAT	
150	1252	AA		199	1359	F-MAGM	ex F-MBBF	250	1475	ALAT	
151	1253	151-DT	ex F-RARR, 151-DP	200	1360	F-MACV	ex F-MACU	251	1476	ALAT	
152	1258	152-DZ		201	1367	AA		252	1488	488/20S	ex F-YCVD, loan to Indian Navy
153	1259	AA		202	1368	F-MBVG					
154	1260	AA		203	1369	F-MBVT		253	1489	268-RH	
155	1261	AA		204	1370	F-MAZQ		254	1490	ALAT	
156	1262	AA		205	1371	F-MAZM		255	1491	F-MAGD	
157	1263	ALAT	ex F-SFIL	206	1372	F-MBJP	ex F-MAZL	256	1492	ALAT	
158	1264	F-MAZB	ex F-MBGJ, F-MBUJ, F-MBGH	207	1373	F-MBBM	ex F-MAZN	257	1504	AA	
				208	1381	67-SG	ex F-SFIR, 208-SG	258	1505	F-MCAG	
159	1270	F-MBNL	ex F-MBGU, F-MBMY	209	1382	F-MCFR		259	1506	F-MCAI	
160	1271	W/o 13.3.63	ex F-SFIG	210	1383	F-MAZJ	ex F-MBWO	260	1507	F-MCXG	
161	1272	ALAT	ex F-SFIF	211	1384	F-MAGL	ex F-MAZT, F-MBNP, F-MADW, F-MASD	261	1508	ALAT	
162	1273	AA						262	1509	ALAT	
163	1282	163-MA EH 2/67	ex F-RMMT, F-RBSD, 163-SI	212	1385	F-MBJE	ex F-MAZO	263	1510	ALAT	
				213	1386	F-MATW	ex F-MBUK	264	1520	AA	
164	1283		ex F-UJIB	214	1387	F-MBVR	ex F-MBIN	265	1521	AA	
165	1284	67-SN	ex F-SFIA, 165-SN	215	1395	W/o 26.7.61	ex F-SFIW	266	1522	ALAT	
166	1308	F-MCVY		216	1396	F-MBVZ		267	1523	F-MBVK	
167	1309	ALAT		217	1397	F-MAGJ	ex F-MAZA	268	1524	ALAT	
168	1295	F-MAOW	ex F-MBPZ	218	1398	F-MBMR	ex F-MBMM	269	1525	W/o 9.5.63	ex F-MAZE
169	1296	W/o 1.61	ex F-MAZA	219	1399	F-MBPZ		270	1526	ALAT	
170	1297	F-MAZC		220	1400	F-MAGF	ex F-MACN, F-MBIQ	271	1536	AA	
171	1306	AA		221	1401	F-MBMZ		272	1537	ALAT	
172	1307	F-MAZB		222	1409	AA		273	1538	ALAT	
173	1318	ALAT		223	1410	F-MBIR		274	1539	ALAT	
174	1319	F-MBJD	ex F-MAZE	224	1411	F-MBWP		275	1552	F-MATT	
175	1320	F-MBPU		225	1412	F-MCXB	ex F-MBWN	276	1553	F-MCQR	ex F-MATS, F-ZBAB
176	1321	F-MBPT		226	1413	F-MAGE	ex F-MBMK	277	1554	ALAT	
177	1322	F-MBMD		227	1414	F-MAGK	ex F-MACP	278	1555	67-DY	
178	1330	F-MAZI		228	1415	F-MAZC	ex F-MBGO	279	1540	ALAT	

280	1541	ALAT	
281	1568	AA	
282	1571	282-SP	ex 282-SD
283	1556	F-MACN	ex F-MCWV
284	1557	F-MACR	ex F-MBVF
285	1572	F-MBBJ	
286	1587	F-MCVB	ex F-MCVC
287	1588	F-MBBK	
288	1570	ALAT	
289	1569	ALAT	
290	1573	ALAT	
291	1584	ALAT	
292	1585	F-MCWV	
293	1586	F-MBWQ	ex F-MCWM
294	1604	F-MCWR	
295	1589	F-MAOV	
296	1600	F-MACK	
297	1601	F-MBWM	ex F-MCQJ
298	1602	ALAT	
299	1603	F-MBWJ	
300	1605	ALAT	
301	1616	ALAT	
302	1617	ALAT	
303	1618	ALAT	
304	1619	ALAT	
305	1620	ALAT	
306	1633	ALAT	
307	1634	ALAT	
308	1635	ALAT	
309	1636	ALAT	
310	1637	ALAT	
311	1650	ALAT	
312	1651	F-MATS	
313	1652	ALAT	
314	1653	ALAT	
315	1654	F-MJAG	
316	1667	ALAT	
317	1668	ALAT	
318	1669	ALAT	
319	1670	F-MBWL	
320	1671	F-MJAV	
321	1684	ALAT	
322	1685	F-MACZ	ex F-MCVQ
323	1686	ALAT	
324	1687	ALAT	
325	1688	ALAT	
326	1700	ALAT	
327	1701	ALAT	
328	1702	AA	
329	1703	329-ML	
330	1704	67-SB	ex 330-SB EH 3/67
331	1713	W/o 21.9.63	
332	1714	332-JL GOM 88	

333	1716	F-MJBA	
334	1717	F-MJAN	
335	1727	F-MJAP	
336	1728	336-RP/GAM 82	ex F-SFID, 336-MU
337	1729	337-SC EH 3/67	ex F-RBMV, 337-MV
338	1730	F-MJAL	
339	1731		ex F-MJAG
340	1741	F-YCTG	ex F-YCTB
341	1742	67-SC	ex 341-RS, F-BRPO
342	1743	67-OJ	ex 342-RN, loan Mexico
343	1745	AA	ex F-BRPR
344	1755	MN	
345	1756	W/o 15.8.67	
346	1757	AA	
347	1758	To Lebanon	ex AA
348	1759	F-MJAR	
349	1796	–/20S	
350	1770	W/o 11.10.69	ex AA
351	1771	F-MAHJ	ex F-MBGJ
352	1772	F-MAHZ	ex 1772-HU/GMT 59
353	1783	F-MJAT	
354	1784	ALAT	
356	1785	W/o 2.12.64	ex ALAT
357	1786	Gendarmerie	
358	1787	MN	
359	1797	F-MAHY	
360	1798	F-MAHX	ex 1798-HW/GMT 59
361	1799	ALAT	
362	1800	AA	
363	1801	F-MBWZ	
364	1806	F-MJBC	
365	1807	F-MJAX	
366	1808	67-JO	
367	1809	F-YCWF	
368	1907	F-ZBAT	
369	1927	F-ZBAU	
370	1940	F-MBIA/Gendarmerie (sic) ex Landes Test Centre	
371	1946	ALAT	
372	1949	1949-HX/GMT 59	ex ALAT
373	1952	ALAT	
374	1988	F-ZBDB	
375	2021	2021-HZ/GMT 59	ex ALAT
376	2022	F-MJAQ	
377	2028	F-MAHV	
378	2036	ALAT	
379	2037	W/o 16.6.72	ex ALAT
380	2043	F-MCQA	
381	2051	F-MBGL	
382	2052	ALAT	ex F-ZKBJ
383	2058	ALAT	
384	2066	F-MAES	
385	2067	F-MAHW	

386	2073	F-MAHL	
387	2081	ALAT	
388	2082	ALAT	
389	2088	ALAT	
390	2096	ALAT	
391	2097	ALAT	
392	2104	ALAT	
393	2111	F-MAHO	ex F-MCQE
394	2112	ALAT	
395	2117	ALAT	
396	2126	ALAT	
397	2127	ALAT	
398	2140	ALAT	
399	2145	ALAT	
400	2152	ALAT	
401	2153	F-MJAT	
402	2154	F-MJAI	
403	2156	ALAT	
404	2157	ALAT	
405	2160	ALAT	
406	2161	ALAT	
407	2164	ALAT	
408	2165	2165-HY/GMT 59	ex ALAT
409	2196	ALAT	
410	2197	ALAT	
411	2205	ALAT	
412	2206	ALAT	
413	2210	ALAT	
414	2211	ALAT	
415	2215	ALAT	
416	2216	ALAT	
417		ALAT	
418	2275	F-MCSI	
419	2280	F-MJBK	
420	2285	F-MAHT	

'Civil' production series

Serial	C/n	Status	Remarks
4	1057		
9	1075	Gendarmerie	
14	1087	F-MJAH	
16	1096	re-serialled 181M	
17	1097	F-MJAQ	
24	1112	re-serialled 182M	
26	1115	CNET	
28	1117	F-MJAW	
57	1165	F-ZBAA	
119	1285	F-MJAD	
128	1294	Gendarmerie	
187	1407	F-ZBAC	ex F-BJOI
255	1517	F-MJAY	
256	1518	F-MJBB	ex F-MJAV

179

180

Sud Alouette II 'ADX'. An unknown Alouette II of GALDiv 8 at Compiègne using a sequence of code letters now employed by Pumas. *(MAP)*

Sud Alouette II F-ZBAA. Dated by its titling, Alouette II F-ZBAA is now operated by the Sécurité Civile. *(MAP)*

Sud Alouette III No.2026 '341-EG' was coded '68-EG' until 1 May 1975, when its squadron became an OCU as CIEH 341. *(J-L. Gaynecoetche)*

Sud Alouette II No.1489 '268-RM' appears to be No.268, otherwise c/n 1524, an ALAT helicopter. The serial on the tailboom fairing reveals it to be actually No.253, i.e. c/n 1489, and although normally the code prefix was the helicopter's serial number, in this isolated case it apparently indicates EH 2/68, the ancestor of CIEH 341. Serial prefixes on Alouette IIs are now being removed in favour of the Escadre or OCU number, and No.1489 should now become '341-RM'. *(J-L. Gaynecoetche)*

Sud Alouette No.1731 '731'. An Alouette with a difference, No.731 is a naval example with a wheel undercarriage, operated by Aéronavale helicopter trials squadron, 20S at St. Raphael. *(MAP)*

Wassmer (CERVA) CE43 Guépard No.452 'LI'. Eighteen Guépard communications aircraft were delivered to the CEV in 1974/75 to be based at Bordeaux (illustrated) or Melun (codes 'DA' etc.) *(A.J. Brown)*

Sud Alouette II No.1654 'JAG' illustrates the Gendarmerie range F-MJAA.

Sud Alouette II No.1555 '67-DY' photographed in April 1977 wearing the new standard code presentation. *(J-L. Gaynecoetche)*

Sud Alouette III No.1075 'O'. The Groupe des Liaison Aériennes Ministérielles (ET 1/60) has a small flight of helicopters in addition to its Caravelle and Mystère 20s, these also for VIP transport. An unusual feature is the use of a single letter code, the Alouette IIIs, 'O', 'P' and 'Q' being followed by Pumas 'R' and 'S', (F-RAFO etc.). On both types the colour scheme makes a welcome change from the olive drab in which most helicopters are now seen. No.1075 was photographed at Villacoublay in May 1977. *(MAP)*

Sud Alouette III No.2054 '67-IC'. To replace the Sud-Sikorsky H-34, the Armee de l'Air ordered fifty Alouette III for the 67 and 68 Escadres, first deliveries being to EH 2/67 at Metz, followed by 3/67 at Villacoublay (illustrated), EH 1/68 at Pau (later Cazaux) and 2/68 at Chambery, the latter two becoming EH 1/67 and CIEH 341 in May 1975.

182

275	1550	F-ZBAE	
324	1628	F-MJAO	
325	1629	Gendarmerie	
338	1647	F-BYCX	ex F-WIET, F-ZBAF
351	1665	OK/EPNER	
402	1744	F-GBDT	ex F-ZBAK
421	1773	F-ZBBA	
447	1813	F-MJBO	
453	1819	Sold	ex F-ZBAM to Lama
	1819-11	F-GAMF	1819-11 F-GAMF
454	1820	F-ZBAN	
459	1825	825/23S (used by CERES)	
462	1828	F-ZBBB	
488	1854	F-BDZN	ex XC-FIB
501	1867	F-ZBAO	
509	1875	F-MJBH	
509	315-09	F-MCSH	(SA315 Lama, conversion of c/n 1875)

SUD AVIATION ALOUETTE III

Developed from the Alouette II, the mark III features an enlarged and covered fuselage, and was flown in prototype form on 28 February 1959. The designation SE.3160 has been revised to SA.316/319. Armée de l'Air aircraft from c/n 1968 onwards are from an order for 50 aircraft replacing the H-34 in service with EH 67, although some were used for a short time by EH 68 before its disbandment. At least four ex-Portuguese aircraft were obtained early in 1978 for the Sécurité Civile.

C/n	Status	Remarks
1006		
1013	W/o 21.11.73	ex F-YCVJ 22S
1014	14/23S	
1018	MN	
1029	W/o 16.9.78	ex 23S
1036	W/o 29.1.77	ex F-MCVM, F-ZBAL
1040	MN	
1041	–/22S	ex F-YCTE 20S
1042	AA	
1066	F-MCWB	
1073	F-MCVR	
1074	F-MCWB	
1075	O/GLAM	
1076	P/GLAM	
1088		
1089	F-MMDF	
1098	F-MJBF	
1099	F-MCVN	
1101	AR/EPNER	
1104	F-MCVM	ex F-MCVR, F-MCVO
1105		
1106	F-MCVQ	
1108		
1112	F-MCRC	
1115	Q/GLAM	
1121		
1122	F-MJBO	ex F-MJBG
1141	F-ZBDH	
1144	F-MBPS	
1160	F-MJBE	
1162	MN	
1170	F-MCRH	
1178	F-MAHH	ex F-MCVP
1185		
1192	F-ZBAV	ex F-ZBAS
1200	EPNER	
1212	212/23S	ex F-YCVN
1219	219/22S	ex F-YCTD
1220		
1221	221/23S	ex 221/22S
1222	W/o 1972	ex 222
1244	244/23S	ex Section Jeanne d'Arc
1245	245/34F	ex 245/23S
1265	AF/EPNER	
1273	F-MACA	
1278	278/23S	ex F-YDKI
1279	279/23S	ex 279/22S
1280		
1299	F-MBPG	
1306	UV/CEV (F-ZJUV)	
1318	F-MABC	
1328	F-MCWA	
1330		
1346	F-MCWB	
1353	F-ZBAB	
1354	F-MBSJ	
1435	F-ZBDC	
1444	MN	
1449	W/o 1971	ex MN
1450	W/o .7.78	ex F-YDKP
1455		
1517	F-ZBAG	ex EI-ATO
1559	W/o 22.5.74	ex F-YCTB
1566	F-YCWT	
1575		
1582	F-YCQW	
1583	F-YCQX	
1589		ex F-YCWB
1590	F-YCWB	
1594	MN	
1600	F-MCVP	
1602	MN	
1630	F-ZBDE	ex Portuguese AF
1646	F-ZBDF	ex Portuguese AF '9346'
1655	F-MCVQ	
1665		
1675		
1678	F-MJAK	
1692		
1693		
1707	AV/EPNER	
1718	–/EPNER	(F-ZAGO)
1731	731/22S	ex 731/20S
1749	F-ZBDG	ex Portuguese AF '9357'
1784	F-ZBDH	ex Portuguese AF '9366'
1791	F-ZBBC	
1793	F-ZBBO	
1795	F-ZBBP	
1798	F-ZBBQ	
1804	804/22S	
1806	806/34F	ex 806/22S
1809	809/22S	
1838	838/22S	
1842	842/22S	ex F-YDKT
1968	67-FA	
1972	Stored	
1978	F-ZBBS	
1997	997/22S	
2008	67-JE EH 5/67	
2009	F-MJBL	
2010	F-MJBM	
2020	67-IB	
2025	341-EC	ex 68-EC
2026	341-EG	ex 68-EG
2029	341-EE	ex 68-EE
2030	(341-)EB	ex 68-EB
2033	F-MJBN	
2041	341-ED	ex 68-SO
2042	67-FD	
2045	F-MJBO	
2053	67-IE	
2054	67-IC	
2057	F-MJBP	
2060	67-FE	
2061	67-IA	
2068	341-EH	ex 68-EH
2069	67-FA	
2076	67-FB	
2077	67-FC	
2082	–/20S	
2084	67-FF	
2085	67-FG	
2089	89/34F	ex F-ZKDA

Sud Caravelle No.141. Two Caravelles fly with the VIP communications squadron ET 1/60 at Villacoublay, of which No.141 is the first to be delivered, arriving in 1963. The aircraft normally uses the call-sign F-RAFG, and in 1977 was joined by the second example No.201/F-RAFH. Three other Caravalles have been recently delivered for use in the Pacific area. *(MAP)*

Sud Vautour IIB.1 No.620 '92-AM'. Being replaced by Jaguars of EC 7 and EC 11, the Vautours of EB 1/92, served at Bordeaux until EB 92 disbanded in September 1978. Six Vautours are expected to remain airworthy for use as target-tugs by the Centre de Tir et de Bombardement at Cazaux. *(MAP)*

2090	67-FH	
2091		ex 68-JA
2096	67-FI	
2097	67-ID	
2100	34F	ex 100/20S
2101	67-FJ	
2102	67-IF	
2106	106/34F	ex 106/20S
2111		ex 67-JB
2112	341-EI	ex 68-EI
2113	113/	ex 113/20S, 113/22S
2114	114/34F	ex 114/20S
2118	67-JE	ex 68-JE
2119	67-JC	ex 68-JC
2124	67-JG EH 5/67	ex 68-JG
2125	67-II	ex 68-JD, 67-JD
2131	67-IG	
2132	(341-)EL	
2137	67-JH EH 5/67	ex 68-JH
2138	67-JC EH 2/67	ex 68-EM
2145		ex 68-EN
2160	34F	
2161	161/34F	ex F-XCMG
2162	162/22S	
2164	F-ZBDK	
2234	Stored	
2244	244/23S	
2247	F-ZKBF	
2260	67-JD/EH 1/67	
2261	67-JB EH 1/67	
2262	262/34F	
2266	Stored	
2268	34F	
2306	F-ZBAW	
2309		
2313		
2314		
2361	34F	

The following aircraft of the Marine National have yet to be positively identified:

Code	Unit	Remarks
'13'	22S	W/o 21.11.73
'34'	34F	
'40'	22S	W/o 16.8.73
'41'	22S	
'85'	23S	
'89'	34F	
'91'	22S	
'92'	22S	
'219'	22S	
'279'	22S	

SUD-OUEST VAUTOUR

Three versions of the Vautour serve or have served with the Armée de l'Air, having been preceded by three prototypes and six pre-production aircraft. The prototype flew on 16 October 1952 and on 30 August 1956 was followed by the first of thirty Vautour IIA, nineteen of which were delivered to Israel. Seventy Vautour IIN, Nos. 301-370 served with EC 6 and later ECTT 30, and these were replaced by the Mirage F1 in 1974. The final Vautour variant, the IIB, attained a production run of forty aircraft, beginning on 31 July 1957 with the first flight of No. 601. All were delivered to EB 1/92 and 2/92, who in 1970 rationalised their codes into one sequence. Strength has been maintained by the transfer of surplus Vautour IIN from ECTT 30. The IIB was due to be withdrawn late 1978/early 1979 when EB 92 disbanded and is replaced by the Jaguars of EC 4/7 and EC 4/11. However, during 1979, six aircraft will be formed into a target-towing flight within 3 Region for the use of the Cazaux gunnery school, although in view of its proximity to Bordeaux, the Vautours may remain at their old base.

Vautour IIN

The recently retired aircraft of ECTT 30 are included, as most are still in existence prior to being scrapped.

C/n	Code/Status	Remarks
304	DR/CEV	
306	Scrapped	ex 6-QA, 30-MA
307	DF/CEV	
308	Preserved	ex 6-QC, 30-MC
310	Stored	ex 30-MM, 30-MI
314	Stored	ex 30-OC, 30-MB
315	Scrapped	ex 30-MD
318	Stored	ex 30-MF
320	Scrapped	ex 30-OM
321	Stored	ex 30-OG, 30-MH
324	Scrapped	ex 30-ME
330	Preserved	ex 30-ML
333	Scrapped	ex 6-QQ, 30-MQ, 30-MW
334	Stored	ex 30-MN, 30-MK
336	Scrapped	ex 30-OK, 30-FW, 30-MO
337	DN/CEV	
338	Preserved	ex 30-MN
339	Scrapped	ex 30-MB, 30-MM
340	Scrapped	ex 30-OL
343	92-AL	ex 30-MR
345	Preserved	ex 30-MP
347	Preserved	ex 30-FB
348	CEV	ex 30-FC
349	92-AE	ex 30-FD
350	Scrapped	ex 30-FE
354	92-AA	ex 30-FI
355	CEV	ex 30-FJ
356	Scrapped	ex 30-FK
357	92-AD	ex 30-FL
358	CEV	ex 30-FM
362	Scrapped	ex 30-FQ
363	DE/CEV	ex 30-FR, 30-OD
364	92-AY	ex 30-FS, 30-OM, 30-FF
365	Scrapped	ex 30-FT, 30-FD
366	92-AG	ex 30-FU, 30-FG
367	Stored	ex 30-FV, 30-FH, 30-MI, 30-FH
368	Preserved	ex 30-FW, 30-OJ, 30-FK
369	Scrapped	ex 30-FX, 30-OH, 30-FN
370	92-AZ	ex 30-OY, 30-FA, 30-MN, 30-FA

Note: 337, 348 and 363 are fitted with a pointed Mirage nose. 322, 325 to 329 went to Israel in 1960.

Vautour IIB

C/n	Code/Status	Remarks
601	Scrapped	ex 92-AJ, 92-AA
602	92-AB	ex 92-AK
603	Scrapped	ex 92-AL, 92-AC
604	Withdrawn	ex 92-AM, 92-AD
607	Withdrawn	ex 92-AO, 92-AE
610	92-AF	ex 92-AQ
611	Withdrawn	ex 92-AR, 92-AG
612	92-AH	ex 92-AS
613	92-AI	ex 92-AT
614	92-AJ	ex 92-AU
615	92-AK	ex 92-AV
619		ex 92-AW, 92-AL
620	92-AM	ex 92-AX
621	92-AN	ex 92-AY
623	92-AO	
627	W/o 20.12.76	ex 92-BB, 92-AP
629	92-AQ	
631	92-AR	ex 92-BE
632	92-AS	ex 92-BF
633	92-AT	ex 92-BG
634	92-AU	ex 92-BH
635	Withdrawn	ex 92-BI, 92-AV
636	92-AW	ex 92-BJ
637	W/o 20.12.78	ex 92-BK, 92-AX
640	CEV	

Note: 616, 624 and 628 went to Israel in 1958.

185

SUD SE210 CARAVELLE

The first Caravelle to enter military service was No. 141 delivered to ET 60 on 13 September 1963 as a presidential communications aircraft followed by No. 158 to the same unit for VIP duties. Two experimental examples have served with the CEV, No. 116 sold by SAS on 19 October 1964 and No. 193 delivered in 1973 and flown with an M53 engine to starboard. Withdrawal of the DC-6 has brought Nos. 240, 251 and 164 into service with ETOM 82 in 1976 followed by No. 201 for ET 60 in 1977.

C/n	Code/Unit	Callsign	Srs.	Remarks
116	CE/CEV	F-ZACE	III	ex OH-LED
141	GLAM	F-RAFG	III	ex F-BJTK
158	Sold		VIR	ex F-BLHY, F-RAFA, To 5Y-DAA
193	CF/CEV	F-ZACF	III	ex SE-DAH, F-BRIM
201	GLAM	F-RAFH	10R	ex F-BNRA
240	PR/ETOM 82	F-RBPR	11R	ex 9Q-CLC
251	PS/ETOM 82	F-RBPS	11R	ex 9Q-CLD
264	PT/ETOM 82	F-RBPT	11R	ex EC-BRJ

TRANSALL C-160

A product of the TRANSport ALLiance, the C-160 serves jointly with the Luftwaffe and the Armée de l'Air. The first (German) prototype flew on 25 March 1963 and the first production aircraft (F1) on 13 April 1967. The aircraft for France were built by Nord at Bourges, VFW/Fokker at Lemwerder, and MBB/HFB at Finkenwerder, as indicated in the first column of the following list, and delivered to ET 61. Operating on a centralised servicing system, the three escadrons of the unit use only the codes 61-MA/MZ and 61-ZA/ZZ. Four aircraft are currently civil - registered for night postal work, where they carry 45% of all night mail, and several have previous German flight-test serials.

Aérospatiale re-opened the French production line in December 1976 using parts fabricated in Germany, to assemble twenty five further aircraft for the Armée de l'Air, and hopefully at least forty more civil sales to ensure a profitable run. The first is expected to fly at Toulouse late in 1979, and by the end of 1982, fourteen will be in service, the balance following in 1983-84. The first recipient is to be ET 2/64, the previous operator of the Sahara and DC-6. Three additional new aircraft will be delivered to the Night Postal Service which already operates four in civilian markings.

Mftr.	C/n	Code	Remarks
N	V1	Instruc'l	ex D-9507, F-ZADK, D-ABEX, F-ZWWV, F-ZADK
VFW	V2	Luftwaffe	ex D-9508, F-ZADH/CEV, Luftwaffe 5001 (ntu), YD/CEV
VFW	A02	61-MI	ex D-9526, F-ZWWS, 118-BS
N	A04	'61-BI' *	ex D-9527, F-ZWWT, 118-BT, 61-ZA
MBB	A06	61-ZB	ex D-9529, F-ZWWU, 118-BU
VFW	F1	61-MA	ex KM101
MBB	F2	61-MB	ex KA201
N	F3	61-MC	
VFW	F4	61-MD	ex KM102
MBB	F5	61-ME	ex KA202
MBB	F11	61-MF	ex KA203
N	F12	61-MG	
VFW	F13	61-MH	ex KM105
MBB	F14	61-MI	ex KA204
N	F15	61-MJ	
VFW	F16	F-BUFP	ex KM106, 61-MK, F-WUFP
MBB	F17	61-ML	ex KA205
N	F18	61-MM	
MBB	F42	61-MN	ex KA206
VFW	F43	61-MO	ex KM108
MBB	F44	61-MP	ex KA207
N	F45	61-MQ	
VFW	F46	61-MR	ex KM109
N	F47	F-BUFQ	ex 61-MS, F-WUFQ
N	F48	61-MT	
MBB	F49	F-BUFR	ex KA208, 61-MU, F-WUFR
VFW	F50	F-BUFS	ex KM110, 61-MV, F-WUFS
N	F51	61-MW	
VFW	F52	61-MX	ex KM111
MBB	F53	61-MY	ex KA209
N	F54	61-MZ	
N	F55	61-ZC	
MBB	F86	61-ZD	ex KA210
N	F87	61-ZE	
MBB	F88	61-ZF	ex KA211
N	F89	61-ZG	
MBB	F90	61-ZH	ex KA212
VFW	F91	61-ZI	ex KM112
MBB	F92	61-ZK	ex KA213
N	F93	61-ZK	
VFW	F94	61-ZL	ex KM113
MBB	F95	61-ZM	
N	F96	61-ZN	
VFW	F97	61-ZO	
MBB	F98	61-ZP	
N	F99	61-ZQ	
VFW	F100	61-ZR	
N	F153	61-ZS	
N	F154	61-ZT	
N	F155	61-ZU	
N	F156	61-ZV	
N	F157	61-ZW	
N	F158	61-ZX	
N	F159	61-ZY	
N	F160	61-ZZ	

Hybrid code; actually F-ZABI of CEV

WASSMER SAILPLANES

Three variants of Wassmer sailplanes are in use by weekend glider pilots of all Armée de l'Air ranks, in a similar manner to those of the RAFGSA in Britain.

The Standard Class WA21 Javelot II is, as the designation suggests, a development of the WA20 Javelot I, and made its first flight on 25 March 1958. A further progression brought about the WA22 Super Javelot high performance glider, first flown on 26 June 1961, which was again a single seater. Two-seat advanced training is undertaken by the WA30 Bijave, a Javelot variant flown on 17 December 1958. See also Issoire Aviation.

WA21 Javelot II

C/n	Code/Base	Remarks
51	XG/Salon	

WA22 Super Javelot

C/n	Code/Base	Remarks
112	XA/Salon	
114	XB/Salon	
119	XC/Salon	
126	128-VK/Colmar	(Metz code)
133	–/Evreux	
134	XD/Salon	
151	XF/Salon	
155	–/Evreux	
156	XG/Salon	
157	XH/Salon	

WA30 Bijave

C/n	Code/Base	Remarks
151	XI/Salon	
159	–/Evreux	
162	XG/Salon	
165	128-VA/Colmar	(Metz code)
171	XK/Salon	

Transall C-160 No.F97 '61-ZO'. ET 61 flies the majority of the Armée de l'Air Transall fleet detaching some of its aircraft to the Antilles and Réunion in support of French units there.
The wing uses a centralised coding system, the three squadrons having codes only in the ranges '61-MA' etc. and '61-ZA' etc. making identification of individual aircraft and squadrons impossible. *(J-L. Gaynecoetche)*

Westland 01B Lynx HAS2(FN) No.XZ260. Following two pre-production aircraft, deliveries of the Lynx to the Aéronavale began on 20 June 1977 with XZ260. Curiously, the helicopters seem to be retaining their British military serials and not adopting the c/n as an identity, as would be normal practice. *(Westland Helicopters, via Avia Press)*

187

175	–/Evreux
228	XL/Salon
232	XM/Salon

The three gliders 'XG' were all in simultaneous use in 1974.

WASSMER CE43 GUEPARD

The CE43 Guepard (Cheetah) was developed from the wooden Wassmer WA4/21 by the Consortium Européen de Réalisation et de 'Ventes d'Avions - CERVA - formed in 1971 out of Wassmer and Siren. The Guepard made its first flight on 18 May 1971 and entered limited production for the CEV in 1974-75.

C/n	Code/Unit	Remarks
439	DA/CEV	
441	DE/CEV	
442	DH/CEV	
443	DN/CEV	
444	DK/CEV	
445	DL/CEV	
446	DM/CEV	
447	DP/CEV	
448	LE/CEV	ex F-WVKC
449	LF/CEV	
450	LG/CEV	
451	LH/CEV	
452	LI/CEV	
453	LJ/CEV	
454	LK/CEV	
455	LL/CEV	
456	LM/CEV	

Aircraft coded D* are based at Melun, the L* batch at Bordeaux.

WESTLAND WG.13 LYNX HAS2 (FN)

The Lynx prototype flew for the first time on 21 March 1971 and of a pre-production batch of thirteen helicopters, an initial quantity of two were delivered to France making their first flights on 6 July and 18 September 1973 respectively, and transferring to Aérospatiale at Marignane a few weeks later. They were preceded by a static test rig c/n 3/15, used for trial installation of Aéronavale electronics at Yeovil, whilst Royal Navy example XX510 conducted trials on the *Tourville* off the French coast in April 1974.

Production began in 1976 for the British forces, Holland, Brazil, Argentine, Denmark, Qatar etc, and the first for France flew on 4 May 1977, and was delivered on 20 June. Twenty six are on order of which the final fourteen purchases were made under the 1977-82 plan. All deliveries from Britain have been initially to Marignane from where 04 was delivered to 20S, the Aéronavale trials squadron, in May 1978, the first to enter military service in France. Total procurement is expected to be forty aircraft.

Pre-production

	C/n	Unit	Remarks
03	05-03	20S	ex XX904/F-ZKCU
04	05-04	20S	ex XX911/F-ZKCV and CEPA

Note: 03 and 04 were used as serials

Production (Model 01B)

Serial	C/n
XZ260	WA015
XZ261	WA027
XZ262	WA031
XZ263	WA039
XZ264	WA040
XZ265	WA045
XZ266	WA046
XZ267	WA051
XZ269	WA054
XZ270	WA057
XZ271	WA059
XZ272	WA063
XZ273	WA066
XZ274	WA068
XZ275	WA071
XZ276	WA074
XZ277	WA078
XZ278	WA081
XZ620	WA087
XZ621	WA092
XZ622	WA095
XZ623	
XZ624	
XZ625	
XZ626	
XZ627	

Note: Serial XZ268 not allocated. Early aircraft held at Marignane, off Aéronavale charge. F-ZARL was undergoing trials at the CEV, Bretigny, late in 1978.

Space for notes

Space for notes

Appendices

A — Principal French Military Airbases 1979
B — Former Overseas Bases
C — Overseas Military Bases 1970-79
D — French Callsign Blocks
E — 'F-Z' Registration Series
F — Unit Names
G — Named Squadrons
H — Escadrille Numbers in Current Use
J — Export Aircraft
K — Keeping Up-To-Date

APPENDIX A

Principal French Military Airbases 1979

#	Base	Service	Unit	Aircraft
1	Aix	AdlA	ELA 44	Various types
2	Ajaccio-Aspretto	MN	55S	Nord 262
3	Avord	AdlA	GE 319	Flamant
4	Baden-Baden/Oos	ALAT	ECCFFA	Various types
5	Bordeaux-Merignac	AdlA	ELA 43	Various types
			EB 92	Vautour
			CIFAS 328	Various types
		ALAT	4 GHL	Gazelle/Alouette
6	Brétigny		CEV	Various types
7	Cambrai-Epinoy	AdlA	EC 12	Mirage F 1
8	Cazaux	AdlA	EC 8	Mystère IVA
			EH 1/67	Alouette/Puma
			EB 2/91	Mirage IVA
9	Chambéry/Aix-les-Bains	AdlA	CIEH 341	Alouette
10	Chateaudun	AdlA	EAA 601	Maintenance unit
			EC 70	Various types
11	Clermont Ferrand-Aulnat	AdlA	EFIPN 307	CAP.10
			GE 313	Magister
12	Cognac	AdlA	GE 315	Magister
13	Colmar-Mayenheim	AdlA	EC 13	Mirage III/5
14	Compiègne	ALAT	6 RHC	Gazelle/Puma
15	Creil-Senlis	AdlA	EC 10	Mirage III
16	Cuers	MN	DCAN	Various types
17	Dax	ALAT	ES	Various types
18	Dijon-Longvic	AdlA	EC 2	Mirage III
19	Etampes-Mondesir	ex ALAT		
20	Evreux-Fauville	AdlA	GAM 56	Various types
			ET 64	Noratlas
21	Freiburg-Bremgarten	ALAT	2 RHC	Gazelle/Puma
22	Hyères-La Palyvestre	MN	17F	Etendard
			3S/59S	Various types
23	Istres-le Tube	AdlA	EPNER	Various types
			EB 1/94	Mirage IVA
			ELA 44(Dt)	Various types
			EH 5/67	Alouette/Puma
			ENSA	N262/Caravelle
24	Landivisau	MN	11F	Etendard
			12F/14F	Crusader
			16F	Etendard
			SRL	Paris/Falcon
25	Lanvéoc-Poulmic	MN	32F	Super Frélon
			34F	Alouette III
			22S	Alouette II/III
			SVSEN	Rallye
26	Le Bourget-Dugny	MN	SSD	Various types
26	Paris-de Gaulle	Civil	ET 3/60	DC-8
27	Les Mureaux	ALAT	1 GHL	Gazelle/Alouette
28	Lille-Lesquin	ALAT	2 GHL	Gazelle/Alouette
29	Lorient/Lann-Bihoué	MN	4F	Alizé
			23F/24F	Atlantic
			25F	Atlantic
			2S	Various types
30	Luc-le Cannet	ALAT	EA	Gazelle/Alouette
31	Luxeuil-St. Saveur	AdlA	EC 4	Mirage III
			EB 3/94	Mirage IVA
			CPIR 339	Falcon
32	Lyon-Corbas	ALAT	5 GHL	Gazelle/Alouette
33	Marignane		Aérospatiale test field	
34	Metz-Frescaty	AdlA	ELA 41	Various types
			EE 54	Noratlas
			EH 2/67	Alouette
35	Mont-de-Marsan	AdlA	CEAM	Various types
			EB 1/91	Mirage IVA
36	Mulhouse	ALAT	ex 7 GALDiv	
37	Nancy-Essey	ALAT	11 GHL	Gazelle/Alouette
37	Nancy-Ochey	AdlA	EC 3	Mirage/Jaguar
			CEVSV 338	T-33

192

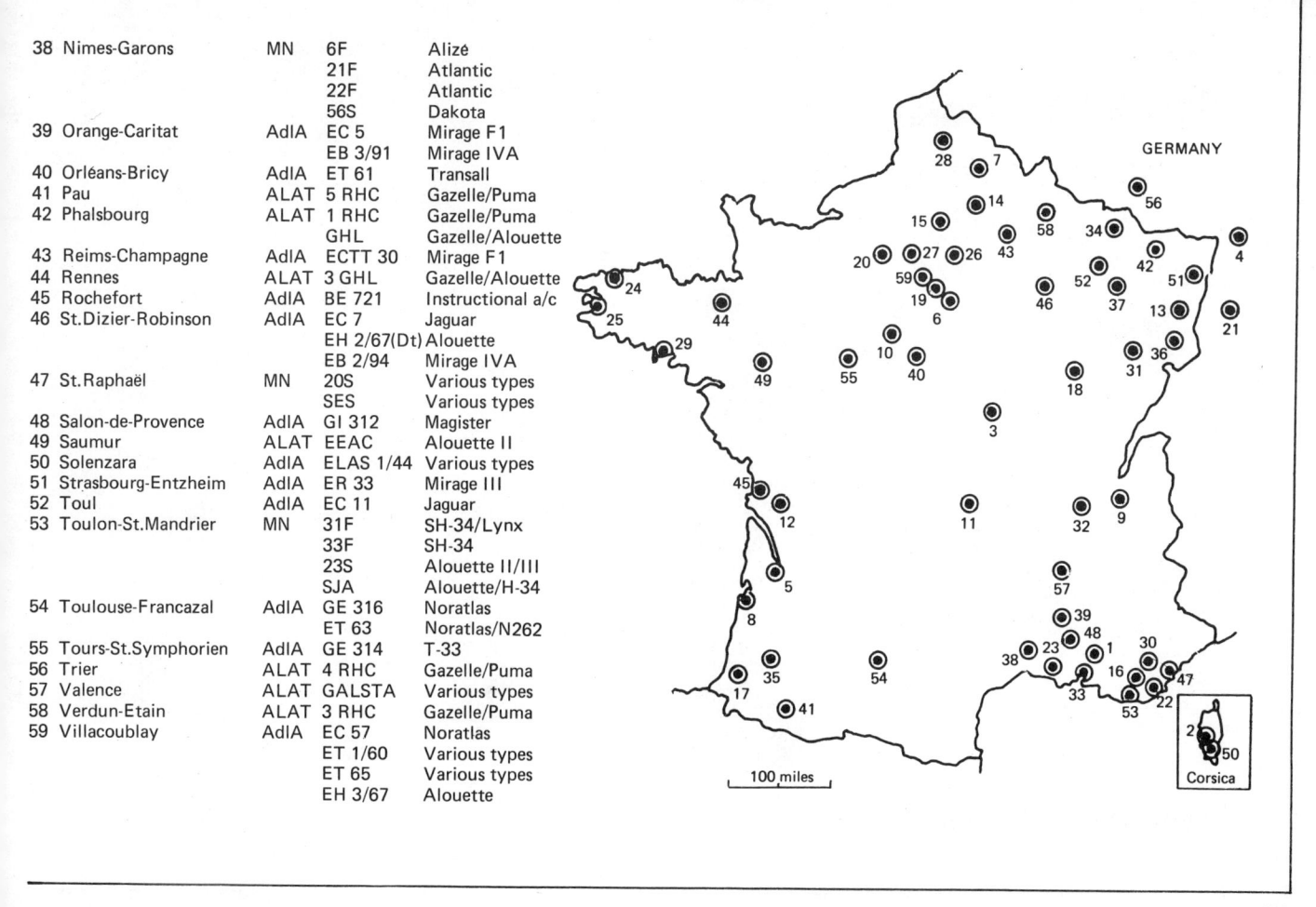

38	Nimes-Garons	MN	6F	Alizé
			21F	Atlantic
			22F	Atlantic
			56S	Dakota
39	Orange-Caritat	AdlA	EC 5	Mirage F1
			EB 3/91	Mirage IVA
40	Orléans-Bricy	AdlA	ET 61	Transall
41	Pau	ALAT	5 RHC	Gazelle/Puma
42	Phalsbourg	ALAT	1 RHC	Gazelle/Puma
			GHL	Gazelle/Alouette
43	Reims-Champagne	AdlA	ECTT 30	Mirage F1
44	Rennes	ALAT	3 GHL	Gazelle/Alouette
45	Rochefort	AdlA	BE 721	Instructional a/c
46	St.Dizier-Robinson	AdlA	EC 7	Jaguar
			EH 2/67(Dt)	Alouette
			EB 2/94	Mirage IVA
47	St.Raphaël	MN	20S	Various types
			SES	Various types
48	Salon-de-Provence	AdlA	GI 312	Magister
49	Saumur	ALAT	EEAC	Alouette II
50	Solenzara	AdlA	ELAS 1/44	Various types
51	Strasbourg-Entzheim	AdlA	ER 33	Mirage III
52	Toul	AdlA	EC 11	Jaguar
53	Toulon-St.Mandrier	MN	31F	SH-34/Lynx
			33F	SH-34
			23S	Alouette II/III
			SJA	Alouette/H-34
54	Toulouse-Francazal	AdlA	GE 316	Noratlas
			ET 63	Noratlas/N262
55	Tours-St.Symphorien	AdlA	GE 314	T-33
56	Trier	ALAT	4 RHC	Gazelle/Puma
57	Valence	ALAT	GALSTA	Various types
58	Verdun-Etain	ALAT	3 RHC	Gazelle/Puma
59	Villacoublay	AdlA	EC 57	Noratlas
			ET 1/60	Various types
			ET 65	Various types
			EH 3/67	Alouette

APPENDIX B

Former Overseas Bases

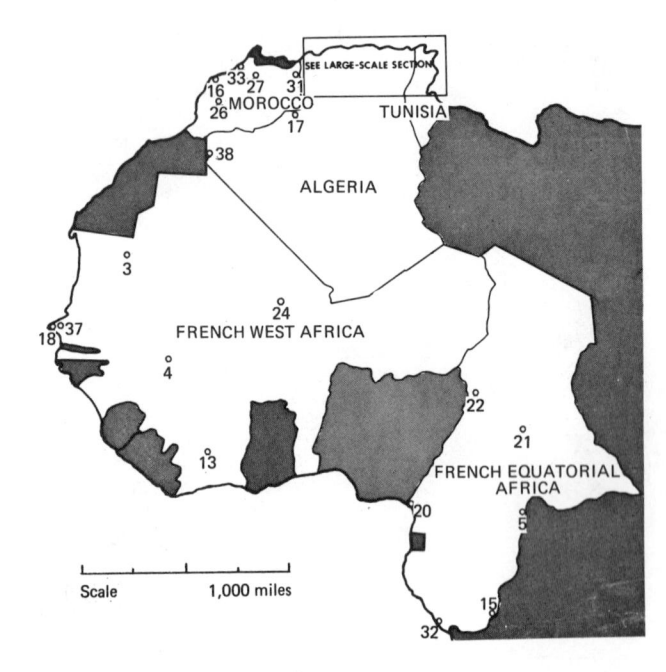

1	Ain Oussera	21	Ft. Archamboult
2	Algiers-Maison Blanche	22	Ft. Lamy
3	Atar	23	Gabes
4	Bamako	24	Gao
5	Bangui	25	Laghouat
6	Batna	26	Marrakech
7	Beja	27	Meknès
8	Bir Rabalou	28	Oran/La Sénia
9	Biskra	29	Orléansville
10	Bizerte	30	Oud Zenata
11	Blida	31	Oujda
12	Bône	32	Pointe Noire
13	Bouake	33	Rabat/Salé
14	Boufarik	34	Sétif
15	Brazzaville	35	Tebessa
16	Casablanca/Mediouna	36	Thiersville
17	Colomb Béchar	37	Thies
18	Dakar	38	Tindouf
19	Djelfa	39	Tunis
20	Douala		

North Africa - Mid-Century

Inset from opposite map

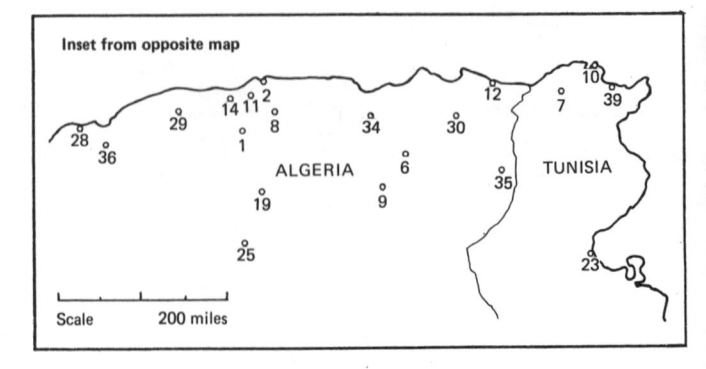

Cochinchina (Vietnam) - Mid-Century

The Levant - Mid-Century

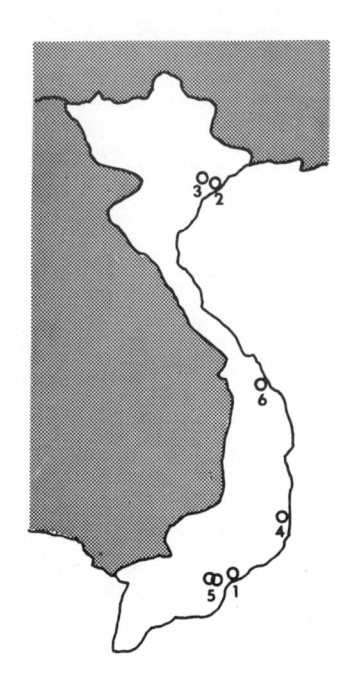

1. Cap St. Jacques
2. Haiphong
3. Hanoi
4. Nha Trang
5. Saigon (Bien Hoa and Tan Son Nhut)
6. Touraine

1. Aleppo
2. Baalbek
3. Beirut
4. Damascus
5. Deir ez Zor
6. Homs-Hamidiye
7. Palmrya
8. Rayak

APPENDIX C

Overseas Military Bases 1970-79

1. Abidjan (Ivory Coast)
2. Cayenne (French Guyana)
3. Dakar/Thies (Senegal)
4. Djibouti (Terr. des Afars & Issas)
5. Fort Lamy (Chad)
6. Hao (Tuamotu)
7. Ivato (Madagascar)
8. Noumea (New Caledonia)
9. Papeete (Tahiti)
10. Pointe-a-Pitre (Guadeloupe)
11. St. Denis (Réunion)

APPENDIX D

French Callsign Blocks

F-AZAA to ZZZ		Restricted CofA (from 1976)
F-ABAA to SAB		Pre-war civil series.
F-BAAA to ZZZ		Civil registrations for aircraft with a full Certificate of Airworthiness. Series used since 1940.
F-CAAA to ZZZ		Current gliders. F-CRxx used for those with restricted Certificate of Airworthiness only.
F-DAAA to AGA		Used for Moroccan aircraft. Now replaced by CN-.
F-EAAA to ZZZ		Originally used for test aircraft, and then allocated for the French West Indies, but not used. F-EXAA was used 1963-4 by a Paris for export, and since 1974 the series F-ETxx has been used for deliveries of Piper types.
F-GAAA to ZZZ		Current civil register, following from F-BZZZ.
F-KHAA to HAD		Used for Cambodian aircraft. Now replaced by XU-.
FL-AAA to ZZZ		Free French (World War 2).
F-LAAA to ZZZ		Used for Laotian aircraft. Now replaced by XW-.
F-MAAA to CZZ		Army Aviation (ALAT).
F-MJAA to JZZ		Gendarmerie
F-MKAA to KCZ		ALAT overseas.
F-MMAA to MJZ		Army Aviation (Direction Central du Matériel).
F-OAAA to ZZZ		French overseas civil aircraft. The series F-OTAN- followed by a number was used by NATO clubs in France but this practice is no longer current.
F-PAAA to ZZZ		Current CNRA register, for aircraft with restricted Certificate of Airworthiness. Those based overseas use the F-POAx series.
F-RAAA to ZZZ		Armée de l'Air transport wings.
F-SAAA to ZZZ		Armée de l'Air liaison and evaluation units.
F-TAAA to ZZZ		Armée de l'Air training groups.
F-UAAA to ZZZ		Armée de l'Air fighter wings.
F-VAAA to AZZ		Recently introduced for civil delivery flights.
F-VNAA to NBU		Used for Vietnamese aircraft. Replaced by XV-.
F-WAAA to ZZZ		Manufacturers marks for experimental prototypes.
F-XAAA to ZZZ		Aéronavale first line units.
F-YAAA to ZZZ		Aéronavale second line units.
F-ZAAA to AZZ		C.E.V. types for evaluation.
F-ZBAA to BBZ		Sécurité Civile.
F-ZBCA to BCZ		Space research - satellite tracking.
F-ZBDA to BDZ		Sécurité Civile, Police Nationale & Customs.
F-ZJAA to JZZ		C.E.V. support aircraft.
F-ZKAA to KZZ		Manufacturers' test registrations.
F-ZLAA to LAZ		E.P.N.E.R. (trials unit).
F-ZVMA to VMZ		E.N.S.A. (trials unit).
F-ZWAA to XZZ		'Class B' registrations.

APPENDIX E

'F-Z' Registration Series

The first part of the series is allocated principally to the CEV at its various bases, the EPNER and ENSA. Current and recent allocations are given below, although they are shortened to the 'last two' on the aircraft. An asterisk appears after an aircraft type where that example is known to have been withdrawn.

Reg'n	Aircraft type	C/n
F-ZABC	Meteor NF11	11-5
F-ZABD	Meteor NF11	11-2
F-ZABG	Meteor NF11	11-8
F-ZABH	Meteor NF11	11-1
F-ZABI	Transall	A04
F-ZABJ	Noratlas	29
F-ZABM	Meteor NF14	14-747
F-ZABP	Meteor NF11	11-7
F-ZABT	Noratlas	03
F-ZABV	Meteor NF11	11-14
F-ZABY	Bretagne*	44
F-ZABZ	Bretagne*	37
F-ZACA	Meteor NF11	11-3
F-ZACB	Meteor NF11	11-22
F-ZACC	Falcon 20	124
F-ZACD	Falcon 20	131
F-ZACE	Caravelle	116
F-ZACF	Caravelle	193
F-ZACG	Falcon 20	86
F-ZACH	Mirage IIIB	31
F-ZACI	Mirage IIIB	32
F-ZACJ	Mirage IIIB	33
F-ZACK	Mirage IIIB	34
F-ZACL	Mirage IIIB	35
F-ZACM	Meteor NF11	11-24
F-ZACN	Bretagne*	39
F-ZACR	Falcon 20	138
F-ZACS	Meteor NF11	11-20
F-ZACV	S. Mystère B2	02
F-ZADA	Dakota* (ex 44-76222)	
F-ZADE	Vautour IIN	363
F-ZADF	Vautour IIN	307
F-ZADG	Magister	61
F-ZADH	Transall*	V2
F-ZADK	Transall*	V1
F-ZADM	Nord 262	01
F-ZADN	Vautour IIN	337
F-ZADQ	Magister	2
F-ZADR	Vautour IIN	304
F-ZADS	Mirage IVA	02
F-ZADY	Mirage IIIR	02
F-ZAEA	Mirage IIIB	202
F-ZAED	Mirage IIIE	605
F-ZAGA	Puma	
F-ZAGG	Nord 262	01
F-ZAGH	T-33A	(ex 35211)
F-ZAGQ	Alouette III	1718
F-ZAGT	Mirage IIIB	234
F-ZAGV	Bretagne*	380
F-ZAGX	C-45*	1395
F-ZARL	Lynx	
F-ZJAA	Magister	99
F-ZJAB	Cessna 411	03
F-ZJAC	Cessna 411	01
F-ZJAD	Cessna 411	06
F-ZJAE	Cessna 411	08
F-ZJAJ	C-45*	(ex 44-7591)
F-ZJAK	C-45	(ex 35700)
F-ZJAM	Magister	96
F-ZJAN	Magister	39
F-ZJAO	Magister	1
F-ZJAP	Magister	432
F-ZJAS	Magister	46
F-ZJAT	Magister	55
F-ZJAU	Cessna 310	0045
F-ZJAV	Cessna 310	0046
F-ZJAW	Cessna 310	0242
F-ZJAX	Cessna 310	0244
F-ZJAZ	Paris	117
F-ZJBG	Cessna 310	193
F-ZJBH	Cessna 310	194
F-ZJBI	Cessna 310	186
F-ZJBJ	Cessna 310	187
F-ZJBK	Cessna 310	188
F-ZJBL	Cessna 310	190
F-ZJBM	Cessna 310	192
F-ZJBO	Nord 1101*	161
F-ZJBP	Nord 1101*	170
F-ZJBT	Nord 1101*	187
F-ZJBW	Nord 1101*	35
F-ZJDA	CE43	439
F-ZJDC	Nord 1101*	9
F-ZJDE	CE43	441
F-ZJDF	Nord 1101*	17
F-ZJDG	Nord 1101*	119
F-ZJDH	CE43	442
F-ZJDJ	Nord 1101*	34
F-ZJDK	CE43	444
F-ZJDL	CE43	445
F-ZJDM	CE43	446
F-ZJDN	CE43	443
F-ZJDO	Nord 1101*	88
F-ZJDP	CE43	447
F-ZJDQ	Nord 1101*	75
F-ZJDW	Nord 1101*	114
F-ZJFA	Jodel 140	520
F-ZJLE	CE43	448
F-ZJLF	CE43	449
F-ZJLG	CE43	450
F-ZJLH	CE43	451
F-ZJLI	CE43	452
F-ZJLJ	CE43	453
F-ZJLK	CE43	454
F-ZJLL	CE43	455
F-ZJLM	CE43	456
F-ZJMA	Nord 260	6
F-ZJMB	Nord 260	7
F-ZJMC	Nord 260	8
F-ZJME	Nord 260	10
F-ZJNA	Noratlas	5
F-ZJNB	Paris	68
F-ZJNC	Paris	83
F-ZJNH	Paris	101
F-ZJNI	Paris	113
F-ZJNJ	Paris	114
F-ZJNL	Paris	119
F-ZJNM	Nord 1101*	15
F-ZJNN	Nord 1101*	4
F-ZJNO	Nord 1101*	29
F-ZJNQ	Paris	118
F-ZJNV	Noratlas	2
F-ZJNZ	Paris	117
F-ZJOA	Nord 1101*	13
F-ZJOD	Flamant (SAR)	130
F-ZJOE	Nord 1101*	41
F-ZJOH	Nord 262	03
F-ZJOK	Alouette II	1665
F-ZJON	Paris	116
F-ZJOQ	Meteor NF11	11-6
F-ZJOU	Nord 1101*	94
F-ZJOV	Paris	115
F-ZJPA	HR200/250	526

Reg'n	Aircraft type	C/n		Reg'n	Aircraft type	C/n		Reg'n	Aircraft type	C/n		Reg'n	Aircraft type	C/n
F-ZJPB	HR200/250	503		F-ZLAK	Canberra*	784		F-ZKBK	Alouette II	1744		F-ZWSL	Magister	05
F-ZJPC	HR200/250	528		F-ZLAL	Canberra*	304		F-ZKBL	Puma	1003		F-ZWSM	Magister	06
F-ZJPD	HR200/250	529		F-ZLAM	Canberra*	763		F-ZKBL	Puma	1122		F-ZWSN	Magister	07
F-ZJPF	HR200/250	525		F-ZLAN	Canberra*	779		F-ZKBM	Super Frélon	133		F-ZWSP	Magister	08
F-ZJPH	HR200/250	532		F-ZLAR	Alouette III	1101		F-ZKBM	Super Frélon	141		F-ZWSU	Magister	09
F-ZJPK	Canberra*	(ex 784)		F-ZLAS	Alouette II	01		F-ZKBO	Super Frélon	313		F-ZWSV	Magister	10
F-ZJPL	HR200/250	557		F-ZLAT	Canberra*	316		F-ZKBT	Puma	1093		F-ZWSW	Magister	11
F-ZJRK	Breguet 941*	01		F-ZLAU	Canberra*	318		F-ZKCH	Puma	1019		F-ZWSX	Magister	12
F-ZJRL	Breguet 941*	02		F-ZLAV	Alouette III	1707			(Portuguese AF 9506)			F-ZWSY	Magister	13
F-ZJRM	Breguet 941*	03		F-ZLAW	Puma	1251		F-ZKCO	H-34	1007		F-ZWUC	Alizé	01
F-ZJRN	Breguet 941*	04		F-ZLAX	Puma	1204		F-ZKCU	Lynx	05-03		F-ZWUN	Mirage III	06
F-ZJTA	Falcon 10	2		F-ZLAY	Mirage IIIA	06		F-ZKCV	Lynx	05-04		F-ZWVY	Jodel DR1051	252
F-ZJTJ	Mirage F1B	5		F-ZVMB	Broussard*	23C		F-ZKCW	Gazelle	(XW844)		F-ZWWA	Atlantic	01
F-ZJTK	Mirage F1E	10		F-ZVMF	Rallye	11438		F-ZKDA	Alouette III	2089		F-ZWWB	Atlantic	02
F-ZJTS	Alpha Jet	01		F-ZVMG	Jodel DR300	615		F-ZKLO	Puma	1006		F-ZWWD	Merville D63	01
F-ZJUV	Alouette III	1306		F-ZVMH	Nord 262	55		F-ZWRA	Gazelle 340	02		F-ZWWE	Super Frélon	01
F-ZLAA	Alouette II			F-ZVMI	Nord 262	67		F-ZWRB	Jaguar	01		F-ZWWF	Super Frélon	02
F-ZLAB	Alouette II*			F-ZVMJ	Nord 262	58		F-ZWRC	Jaguar	02		F-ZWWG	Atlantic	03
F-ZLAD	Alouette II	02		F-ZVMV	Constellation*	2503		F-ZWRD	Jaguar	03		F-ZWWH	Super Frélon	03
F-ZLAF	Alouette III	1265						F-ZWRE	Jaguar	04		F-ZWWI	Super Frélon	04
								F-ZWRF	Gazelle 340	01		F-ZWWJ	Super Frélon	05
								F-ZWRH	Gazelle 341	01		F-ZWWK	Super Frélon	06

Manufacturer's test registrations form the second part of the 'F-Z' series. Aircraft in these markings will carry either the final letter of the registration, or in some cases the full lettering. Many of the aircraft below are no longer current.

Reg'n	Aircraft type	C/n		Reg'n	Aircraft type	C/n		Reg'n	Aircraft type	C/n		Reg'n	Aircraft type	C/n
								F-ZWRI	Gazelle 341	02		F-ZWWL	Potez 94	
								F-ZWRJ	Jaguar	05		F-ZWWM	Atlantic	04
								F-ZWRK	Gazelle 341	03		F-ZWWN	Puma	01
								F-ZWRL	Gazelle 341	04		F-ZWWO	Puma	02
				F-ZKBG	Super Frélon	105		F-ZWRM	Sea King	WA801		F-ZWWP	Puma	03
F-ZKAC	Cessna 411			F-ZKBG	Super Frélon	118			(Pakistan 4514)			F-ZWWQ	Puma	04
F-ZKBA	Puma	1114		F-ZKBG	Super Frélon	137		F-ZWRO	Magister	001		F-ZWWR	Puma	05
F-ZKBA	Puma	1257		F-ZKBG	Gazelle	1069		F-ZWRP	Magister	02		F-ZWWS	Puma	06
F-ZKBB	Super Frélon	159		F-ZKBH	Super Frélon	149		F-ZWRQ	Magister	03		F-ZWWS	Transall	A02
F-ZKBC	Super Frélon	132		F-ZKBH	Gazelle	1070		F-ZWRR	MD312B	001		F-ZWWT	Puma	07
F-ZKBD	Super Frélon	134		F-ZKBJ	Alouette II	2052		F-ZWRR	SA.361H	1003		F-ZWWT	Transall	A04
F-ZKBE	Super Frélon	102		F-ZKBJ	Puma	1015		F-ZWRS	Jodel 315X	624-01		F-ZWWU	Transall	A06
F-ZKBF	Super Frélon	103		F-ZKBJ	Puma	1115		F-ZWRV	Alpha Jet	03		F-ZWZG	Djinn	014
F-ZKBF	Puma	1121		F-ZKBK	Super Frélon	140		F-ZWRX	Alpha Jet	04		F-ZWZH	Djinn	015
F-ZKBF	Alouette III	2247		F-ZKBK	Super Frélon	142		F-ZWSK	Magister	04				
F-ZKBF	Puma	(Libya 6029)		F-ZKBK	Puma	1063								
				F-ZKBK	Puma	1123								

APPENDIX F

Unit Names

Most Armée de l'Air squadrons are given a name in addition to their numerical title, this usually being geographical, and with a preference toward the historic provinces of France. Only those in current use are listed here.

Name	Unit
Alpes	EC 2/13
Alpilles	EH 5/67
Alsace	EC 3/2
Anjou	ET 2/64
Arbois	EB 3/94
Argonne	EC 2/7
Ardennes	EC 3/3
Artois	EC 1/13
Aubrac	EE 54
Aunis	ERV 1/93
Auvergne	EC 3/13
Béarn	ET 1/64
Beauvaisis	EB 3/91
Belfort	ER 1/33
Bigorre	ET 2/63
Bretagne	EB 2/91
Cambrésis	EC 1/12
Cevennes	EB 3/91
Champagne	EC 2/3
Cigognes	EC 1/2
Commercy	EC 57
Cornouaille	EC 2/12
Corse	EC 3/11
Côte d'Or	ECT 2/2
Dauphiné	EC 1/4
Dunkerque	EE 54
Durance	EH 4/67
Estérel	ET 3/60
Franche Comté	ET 2/61
Gascogne	EB 1/91
Guyenne	EB 1/94
Gevaudan	GE 313(EFIPN)
Ile de France	EC 2/5
Jura	EC 4/11
La Fayette	EC 2/4
Languedoc	EC 3/7
Landes	ERV 2/93
Lorraine	ECTT 3/30
Luberon	EMS 1/200
Marne	EB 2/94
Maurienne	CIEH 341
Mistral	ELA 44
Moselle	ER 3/33
Nice	ET 2/8
Normandie	ECTT 2/30
Ouessant	ETOM 55
Parisis	EH 3/67
Poitou	ET 3/61
Provence	EC 1/67
Pyrénées	EH 1/67
Rambouilliet	ET 2/65
Roussillon	EC 1/11
Saintonge	EC 1/8
Savoie	ER 2/33
Seine	EC 2/10
Sologne	ERV 3/93
Touraine	ET 1/61
Valmy	EH 2/67
Valois	EC 1/10
Vaucluse	GAM 56
Vendée	EC 1/5
Vendome	ET 1/65
Verdun	ELA 41
Vexin	EC 3/10
Vosges	EC 2/11

Some formations have alternative titles, by which they are occasionally known:

Name	Unit
Ecole de l'Air	GI 312
Ecole de Chasse	GE 314
Ecole des Moniteurs	GE 313
GAEL (Groupe Aérien d'Entrainement et de Liaison)	ET 65
GLAM (Goupe des Liaison Aériennes Ministérielles)	ET 1/60

APPENDIX G

Named Squadrons

Not intended as an exhaustive reference, this section lists Squadrons recently disbanded or those previously associated with current units, to which reference should be made for details. It should be borne in mind that some of the fighter squadrons in this section will in all probability be re-formed to operate the third escadrons of those two-squadron wings shortly to be increased in strength. 'Comtat Vanaissin' has recently been selected to once more become EC 3/5. Bomber and Transport units often have a combined squadron insignia which is shown where applicable.

'Ain' ex EAA 1/22. The device is known as a 'Ramel', which was also the unit's radio callsign.

'Aquitaine' ex EB 2/92. 1 escadrille 4B3, an owl; 2 escadrille GB 1/25-2e, a bison.

'Aures Namentcha' ex EAA 1/21. Previously the insignia of Esc. Entrainement et Calibration 1/17 and EC 1/20.

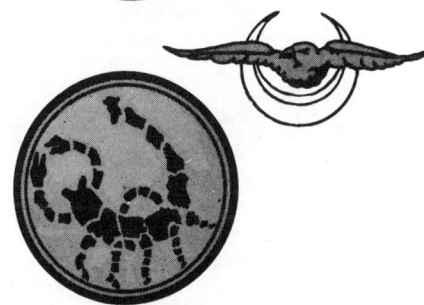

'Beauvaisis' ex EB 3/91. Scorpion - F554 (GB 2/63-4e), Bird - SAL558 (GB 2/68-3e).

'Bourgogne' ex EB 1/92.

201

'Comtat Venaissin'   ex EC 3/5. Dragon - SPA171; Sword and pennant - ERC 571.

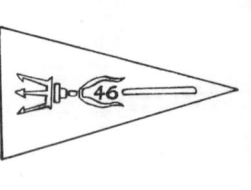

'Loire'   ex ECTT 1/30 and EM 85; the latter using the C-46 insignia only.

'Bourbonnais'   ex EB 1/94. Cat - BR29; Dragon - BR123.

'Flandre'   ex EC 3/4. Devil - SPA160; Running man - SPA155.

'Limousin'   ex EC 1/9. No World War 1 connections. Bird is a crow (GC1/9-1e); the animals head a 'Fennec' (desert fox) (GC1/9-2e).

'Camargue'   ex ECTT 2/30. A bull - GC3/13-5e.

'Hautvillers'   ex EE 12/30, previously CIECTT 346.

'Maine'   ex ET 2/64.

202

'Morvan' ex EC 2/1. Fighting Cock - GCII/1-4e; La Fauche le Mort - SPA94. Latter (only) current with ECT 2/2.

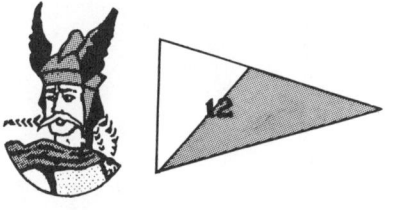

'Picardie' ex EC 2/12. Parrot - SPA172; diving bird - SPA173.

'Sahara' ex GT 3/62. (Noratlas).

'Oranie' ex EC 1/6 and later EC 3/20. Pennant - SPA12; Gallic warrior - SPA96.

'Ventoux' ex ET 3/62 (Breguet 941).

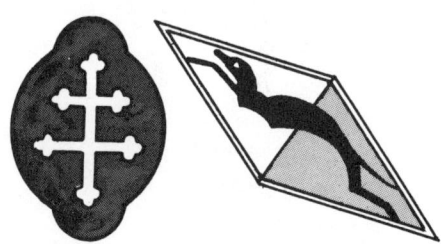

'Orleans' ex GMT 59.

'Sambre' ex EB 3/93. Scarab - C56; Chick - BR226.

'Vercors' ex ET31/62. Lorraine cross - SAL8; Greyhound - SPA55.

APPENDIX H

Escadrille Numbers In Current Use

World War I Escadrille numbers still in use are shown against the current units.

3	EC 1/2	48	EC 2/7	84	EC 1/10	125	EB 3/91
6	ER 2/33	54	ERV 2/93	85	EC 3/13	126	EB 2/94
7	EB 1/92	55	ET 1/62	88	EC 3/11	127	EB 3/94
10	ERV 1/93	56	EB 3/93	89	EC 1/12	128	EB 3/94
11	ER 3/33	57	EC 2/2	91	EC 2/11	129	EB 1/94
14	ET 1/61	65	EC 2/2	94	EC 2/2	137	EMS 1/200
15	EC 1/7	66	EB 1/94	95	EC 1/3	153	EC 1/3
22	ERV 2/93	67	EC 2/3	96	EAA 2/21	158	EC 4/11
26	EC 1/5	69	EC 3/11	97	EC 2/11	162	EC 1/12
28	EB 1/91	73	EC 2/8	99	EH 3/67	167	EC 2/4
29	EB 1/94	75	EC 2/3	100	EC 1/13	226	EB 3/93
31	EC 2/7	77	EC 1/7	103	EC 1/2	277	ERV 1/93
33	ER 1/33	78	EC 2/8	107	EB 2/94	465	ERV 3/93
35	EB 1/92	79	EB 1/91	109	EB 3/91	554	EB 3/91
37	EC 1/4	81	EC 1/4	113	ET 1/61	558	EB 3/91
38	EC 2/7	83	EC 1/13	123	EB 1/94		
44	ERV 3/94	84	EC 1/10	124	EC 2/4		

The following World War II numbers are used also -
GCIII/7-5e   GAM 82
GCII/9-4e   EC 3/13
GCIII/10-3e   EC 2/10

Three former Aéronavale numbers are in current use -
3C-1   EC 3/7
3C-2   EC 2/8
4C-1   EC 2/8

Current Escadres with no ancestry of insignia (Fighter units only): EC 3/3, EC 2/5, EC 2/12, EC 2/13, ECTT 2/30, ECTT 3/30.

APPENDIX J

Export Aircraft

To complement the production lists of French-designed types, details are given here of military export examples of certain more modern aircraft. It should be borne in mind that serial blocks are not necessarily complete and serial numbers are only quoted for those aircraft whose c/ns are known. Licence-built and second-hand aircraft are not included with the exception of British built Pumas and Gazelles, which have integrated c/ns.

DASSAULT-BREGUET-DORNIER ALPHA JET

Luftwaffe examples built at Oberpfaffenhofen begin at A1 (c/n 0001) serial 9833, first flown 12.4.78. A2 flew 26.6.78, but A3 and A4 will initially be static instruction airframes. Belgian aircraft commence with French-built AT-01 flown 20.6.78, and the remaining thirty two will be assembled by SABCA. Exports will be French-built, and expressed, in terms of overall production, the delivery positions are:
Morocco 24 (between aircraft Nos. 23 and 215);
Ivory Coast 12 (between aircraft Nos. 96 and 227);
Togo 5 (between aircraft Nos. 151 and 210).

MORANE-SAULNIER PARIS

Brazilian Air Force: c/ns 02, 52 to 68, 70, 71, 74 to 82. **Argentine Air Force:** serials A-01 to A-12; c/ns 3, 4, 7, 10, 11, 13, 15 to 18, 21, 22. **Civil:** c/ns 01, 2, 5, 6, 8, 9, 28, 39, 43, 49, 50, 69/Swiss AF J-4117, 72, 86, 89, 90, 98, 99, 102 to 109, 111, 112.

SUD SA321 SUPER FRELON

Israeli Air Force: c/ns 104 (F-WMHH), 107 (4X-FJM), 108, 110, 117, 125, 126, 130, 131 (4X-FJR), 136, 138, 146. **South African Air Force:** serials 301 to 316; c/ns 109, 111, 115, 119, 121, 124, 127, 128, 129, 130 (F-ZKBC), 131 (F-ZKBN), 135. **Libyan Air Force:** serials LC-158 to LC-158; c/ns 150 to 158. **Iraqi Air Force:** 10 aircraft; c/ns 177 onwards. **Civil:** c/n 113.

SUD AVIATION ALOUETTE II SERIES

Israeli Air Force: c/ns 1063, 1963 ('10'), 1969 ('12'), 2090?, 2146?, 2147?. **Portuguese Air Force:** serials 9201 to 9207; c/ns 1082, 1107, 1108, 1738 to 1740, 1754. **Swiss Air Force:** serials V-41 to V-70, c/ns 1110, 1119, 1120, 1184, 1229 to 1131, 1236 to 1238, 1929 to 1931, 1897, 1898, 1902 to 1904, 1908 to 1910, 1914 to 1916, 1919 to 1921, 1924 to 1926. **Austrian Air Force:** serials 3D-XR to 3D-XZ, c/ns 1124 to 1126, 1155 to 1157, 1376, 1377; serials 3D-XJ to 3D-XP, c/ns 1906, 1911, 1912, 1917, 1922, 1932, 1935. **Swedish Air Force:** are 02-101 to 02-113, c/ns 1168 to 1170, 1175, 1254, 1246, 1256, 1268, , 1148, 1158, 1830, 1831; serials 02-401 to 02-403, c/ns 1176, 1177, 1269; serials 02-201 to 02-212, c/ns 1278, 1279, 1303, 1302, 1316, 1290, 1291, 1255, 1317, 1323, 1435, 1436. **German Army:** c/ns 1166*, 1178, 1179*, 1180, 1188, 1191, 1192*, 1193 to 1196, 1215 to 1217, 1257, 1265 to 1267, 1274 to 1277, 1286 to 1289, 1298 to 1301, 1310 to 1313; 1324 to 1327, 1337 to 1340, 1349 to 1352, 1361 to 1364, 1388 to 1391, 1392, 1402, 1403, 1404*, 1405, 1406, 1416 to 1420, 1431 to 1434, 1437, 1446*, 1447*, 1448 to 1450, 1461 to 1466, 1477 to 1482, 1493, 1494*, 1495 to 1498, 1511 to 1516, 1527 to 1530, 1531*, 1532, 1533, 1543 to 1549. 1559 to 1564, 1574*, 1575 to 1580, 1590 to 1593, 1608 to 1613, 1622, 1623, 1625, 1627, 1630, 1632, 1638 to 1643, 1655 to 1660, 1672 to 1674, 1675*, 1678, 1690 to 1694, 1697, 1698, 1705 to 1708, 1709*, 1712, 1718 to 1722, 1732 to 1735, 1736*, 1737, 1746 to 1749, 1750*, 1751, 1760 to 1762, 1763* 1664, 1665, 1774, 1775*, 1776 to 1779, 1788 to 1790, 1814*, 1816, 1817*, 1832 to 1834, 1835*, 1836, 1839 to 1843, 1846 to 1850, 1853 to 1855, 1856*, 1857, 1858, 1860*, 1861 to 1865, 1868 to 1873, 1876 to 1880, 2008, 2015 to 2017, 2027, 2031, 2032, 2040, 2041, 2046, 2047, 2054 to 2056, 2061, 2062, 2069 to 2071, 2076, 2077, 2084 to 2086, 2091, 2092, 2098 to 2101, 2105 to 2108, 2113 to 2116, 2118 to 2123, 2128 to 2132, 2134 to 2137, 2248. These originally wore various codes. With the exception of aircraft marked * the remainder were re-serialled 7501 to 7778 in c/n order. **British Army:** serials XN132 to XN133, c/ns 1184, 1185; serials XP966 and XP967, c/ns 1499 and 1500; serial XR232, c/n 1503; serials XR376 to XR387, c/ns 1558, 1567, 1582, 1583, 1596, 1606, 1607, 1621, 1644, 1645, 1663, 1664. **Dutch Air Force:** serials H-1 to H-8; c/ns 1201 to 1203, 1208 to 1210, 1501, 1502. **Dominican Air Force:** serials 3005 to 3008; c/ns 1245, 1281, 2141, 2195. **Moroccan Air Force:** c/ns 1292, 1795. **Belgian Army:** serials A-01 to A-03; c/ns 1293, 1304, 1305; serials A-51 to A-53; c/ns 1341, 1365, 1366; serials A-04 to A-81; c/ns 1377, 1378, 1422, 1423, 1467, 1468, 1534, 1535, 1565, 1566, 1581, 1594, 1595, 1614, 1624, 1626, 1646, 1661, 1662, 1666, 1695, 1696, 1710, 1711, 1752, 1753, 1766,

1767, 1780, 1781, 1791, 1792, 1802, 1803, 1810, 1851, 1956, 1958 to 1962, 1964, 1986 to 1987, 1989, 1990, 1992, 1993, 1995, 1996, 1998, 1999, 2009, 2010, 2018, 2019, 2034, 2035, 2049, 2050, 2057, 2064, 2065, 2068, 2072, 2079, 2080, 2083, 2087, 2094, 2095, 2110, 2124, 2133, 2138, 2139, 2142. **Belgian Rijkswacht:** serials A-90 to A-96; c/ns 1991, 1994, 2003, 2004, 2102, 2103. **Laotian Air Force:** c/ns 1314, 1315. **Cambodian Air Force:** c/ns 1380, 1393, 1804, 1805, 1957, 1979, 1981. **Madagascar Air Force:** c/n 1838. **Peruvian Air Force:** serials 60-601 to 60-605, c/ns 1421, 1438, 1439, 1484, 1485, 1486; serial EP312; c/n 2344; serial EP315; c/n 2345; EP318, c/n 2350; serial EP321. c/n 2351; serial EP329, c/n 2356; serial EP334, c/n 2357; serial EP337, c/n 2358; serial EP341, c/n 2362. **South African Air Force:** serials 15 to 21; c/ns 1452 to 1455, 1469 to 1471. **Lebanese Air Force:** serials L-201 to L-203; c/ns 1597 to 1599. **Brazilian Air Force:** serials 1648 and 1649; c/ns 1648 and 1649. **Tunisian Air Force:** c/ns1793, 1795, 1811, 1821, 1822, 1881, 1882, 1885. **Indonesian Air Force:** serials ALV-421 to ALV-423; c/ns 1889, 1892, 1893. **Mexican Air Force:** HBRA-1101 and HBRA-1102; c/ns 1894, and 1895. **Congolese Air Force:** serial TN303; c/n 2245. **Argentine Air Force:** serials H-61 to H-66; c/ns 2267, 2282, 2299, 2302, 2327, 2328. **Indian Air Force:** c/ns 2266, 2271, 2283, 2290, 2304, 2310, 2311, 2318, 2326, 2332, 2339, 2340, 2346, 2353, 2354, 2360.

SUD AVIATION ALOUETTE III SERIES

Burmese Air Force: c/ns 1001 to 1003, 1114, 1179, 1180, 1210, 1277, 1284, 1436. **South African Air Force:** serials 30 to 73, c/ns 1010, 1004, 1005, 1012, , 1020, 1022, 1023, 1026 to 1028, 1033 to 1035, 1039, 1043 to 1057, 1062 to 1064, 1147 to 1149, , , 1157, 1479, 1480, 1491 to 1493; serials 23 to 29, c/ns 1395, 1403, 1410, 1459, 1462, 1463, 1478; serials 101 to 120, c/ns 1604, 1605, 1627, 1628, , , , 1695, 1696, , 1719, 1720, , 1829, 1844, , , , ,1861. **Rhodesian Air Force:** serials 500 to 507; c/ns 1015 to 1017, 1037, 1038, 1131 to 1133. **Danish Navy:** serials M-019, M-030, M-070, M-071, M-072, M-388, M-438, M-439; c/ns 1019, 1030, 1070 to 1072, 1388, 1438, 1439. **Peruvian Air Force:** c/ns 1024, 1025, 1031, 1032, 1486. **Peruvian Navy:** serial N410; c/n 1845. **Indian Air Force:** c/ns 1058 to 1060, 1065, 1077, 1078, 1143, 1145, 1146, 1171 to 1175, 1231, 1238, 1262, 1270, 1276, 1286, 1290, 1297, 1309, 1315, 1326, 1327, 1334, 1335. **Indian Navy:** c/ns 1313, 1314, 2014. **South Vietnamese Air Force:** serial as c/ns 1061, 1068. **Lebanese Air Force:** serials L-220 to L-232; c/ns 1393, 1069, 1085, 1086, 1118, 1119, 1448, 1876, 1963, 1981, 1930, 1931, 1938. **Portuguese Air Force:** serials 9251 to 9313, c/ns 1079, 1091 to 1094, 1110, 1111, 1116, 1117, 1124, 1129, 1130, 1136 to 1138, 1102, 1103, 1163, 1232,

205

1233, 1250, 1294 to 1296, 1311, 1312, 1316, 1331 to 1333, 1355 to 1357, 1368 to 1370, 1384 to 1386, 1396, 1397, 1400, 1532, 1533, 1551 to 1553, 1556 to 1558, 1572, 1573, 1579 to 1581, 1584, 1585, 1598, 1599, 1601, 1612, 1613, 1620; serials 9332 to 9401, c/ns 1631, 1632, 1641 to 1643, 1661 to 1663, 1666, 1672 to 1674, 1682, 1683, 1646, 1648, 1699, 1705, 1706, 1709, 1732, 1733, 1740 to 1742, 1749 to 1752, 1757, 1758, 1764, 1765, 1768, 1774 to 1777, 1800 to 1803, 1805, 1815, 1818 to 1820, 1835 to 1837, 1839, 1840, 1855 to 1858, 1878 to 1882, 1894 to 1897, 1913 to 1917; Also known are c/n 1234, 1621, 1622, 1630. **Mexican Navy:** serials HOP-210 to HOP-212; c/ns 1134, 1135, 1142; serial HMR-132; c/n 2045. **Malayan Air Force:** serials FM1077, FM1098, FM1099; c/ns 1150, 1591, 1592. **Irish Air Corps:** serials 194 to 196, 202, 211 to 214; c/ns 1194, 1151, 1153, 1973, 1983, 1984, 2116, 2121. **Tunisian Air Force:** c/ns 1154 to 1156, 1263. **Singapore Air Force:** serials 200 to 207; c/ns 1593, 1607, 1618, 1619, 1637, 1638, 1644, 1698. **Swiss Air Force:** serials V-201 to V-224; c/ns 1196 to 1199, 1161, 1186, 1187, 1213, 1340, 1341, 1347, 1361, 1362, 1371, , , 1392, 1401, 1402, 1408, 1409, , 1417. **Australian Air Force:** serials A5-165, A5-166, A5-167; c/ns 1165, 1166, 1167. **Netherlands Army:** serials A-177 etc (last three of c/n); c/ns 1177, 1208, 1209, 1217, 1218, 1226, 1227, 1235, 1236, 1246, 1247, 1253, 1254, 1260, 1261, 1266, 1267, 1274, 1275, 1281, 1282, 1292, 1293, 1301, 1302, 1307, 1319, 1324, 1336, 1342, 1343, 1350, 1351, 1366, 1374, 1382, 1383, 1390, 1391, 1398, 1399, 1406, 1407, 1414, 1415, 1451 to 1453, 1464, 1465, 1470, 1471, 1482, 1483, 1488, 1489, 1494, 1495, 1499, 1500, 1514, 1515, 1521, 1522, 1528, 1529, 1535, 1536, 1542, 1543, 1549, 1550. **Netherlands Air Force:** serials H-08 etc (last two of c/n); c/ns 1308, 1320, 1367, 1375, 1381. **Venezuelan Air Force:** serial 0085; c/n 1201. **Ivory Coast Air Force:** c/ns 1205 and 1206. **Jordanian Air Force:** serials 309 to 311, 215; c/ns 1239, 1240, 1237, 1501; also c/ns 1472, 1498. **Hong Kong Police:** serials HKG-1 and HKG-2; c/ns 1241 and 1242. **Saudi Air Force:** c/ns 1268, 1269, 1288, 1289. **Congolese Air Force:** serials 359 and TN-KHH; c/ns 1359 and 1920. **Austrian Air Force:** serials 3E-KE to 3E-KK; c/ns 1419, , 1461, , , 1546, 1547. **Pakistan Army:** serials as c/ns 1454, 1457, 1468, 1821, 1823, 1898, 1900, 1948, 1950, 2072, 2073, 2078, 2151. **Pakistan Air Force:** c/ns 1456, 1458, 1477, 1525, 1843, 1862. **Argentine Navy:** serials 4-H-23, 3-H-11, 3-H-12; c/ns 1624, 2345, 2346. **Libyan Air Force:** serials as c/ns 1715, 1716, 1808, 1810. **Libyan Army:** serials as c/ns 2281, 2288, 2289. **Belgian Navy:** serials M-1 to M-3; c/ns 1812, 1816, 1817. **Tunisian Air Force:** c/n 1891. **Nepalese Army:** serial RAN12; c/n 1926. **Abu Dhabi Air Force:** serials 101 to 105; c/ns 1990, 1992, 1994, 1996, 1998. **Greek Navy:** serials 01 to 04; c/ns 2210, 2220, 2221, 2267. **Spanish Air Force:** serials Z16-1 to Z16-8; c/ns 1952, 1961, 2048, , 2227, 2241, 2256, 2274.

SA341/342 GAZELLE

British Forces: serial XW276, c/n 03; serials XW842 to XW871, c/ns 1002, 1004, 1005, 1007, 1009, 1011, 1013, 1016, 1019, 1021, 1024, 1033, 1045, 1050, 1078, 1081, 1089, 1091, 1100, 1101, 1104, 1114, 1116, 1118, 1120, 1128, 1130, 1132, 1146, 1148; serials XW884 to XW913, c/ns 1150, 1152, 1157 to 1161, 1163, 1165, 1167, 1173, 1174, 1177, 1178, 1191, 1192, 1195, 1196, 1199, 1208, 1209, 1212, 1213, 1216, 1217, 1227, 1228, 1230, 1231, 1233; serials XX370 to XX419, c/ns 1236, 1237, 1240, 1241, 1244, 1253, 1254, 1257, 1258, 1261, 1268, 1269, 1272, 1273, 1276, 1283, 1284, 1287, 1288, 1291, 1298, 1299, 1302, 1303, 1306, 1313, 1314, 1317, 1318, 1321, 1328, 1329, 1332, 1333, 1336, 1343, 1344, 1347, 1279, 1351, 1358, 1359, 1362, 1309, 1366, 1367, 1370, 1371, 1344, 1381; serials XX431 to XX462, c/ns 1382, 1385, 1386, 1389, 1401, 1402, 1405, 1406, 1409, 1184, 1418, 1221, 1235, 1248, 1435, 1436, 1439, 1440, 1443, 1449, 1450, 1453, 1454, 1457, 1464, 1465, 1468, 1469, 1472, 1484, 1485, 1488; serials XZ290 to XZ349, c/ns 1489, 1492, 1502, 1503, 1506, 1507, 1510, 1520, 1521, 1524, 1525, 1528, 1538, 1539, 1542, 1543, 1559, 1560, 1563, 1564, 1577, 1578, 1581, 1582, 1595, 1596, 1599, 1600, 1609, 1610, 1613, 1614, 1630, 1631, 1634, 1635, 1647, 1648, 1651, 1652, 1661, 1662, 1665, 1666, 1673, 1674, 1676, 1677, 1682, 1683, 1691, 1692, 1697, 1698, 1704, 1705, 1710, 1713, 1719, 1720; serials XZ930 to XZ942, c/ns 1727, 1728, 1734, 1735, 1736, , 1743 etc. **Yugoslav Air Force:** serials 12001 to 12021; c/ns 1030, 1048, 1049, 1062, 1079, 1093, 1106, 1121, 1127, 1139, 1140, 1162, 1164, 1183, 1202, 1203, 1220, 1222, 1242, 1243, 1247. **Trinidad and Tobago Defence Force:** serial '3'; c/n 1044. **Kuwait Air Force:** serials 501 to 524; c/ns 1085, 1086, 1112, 1126, 1256, 1305, 1322, 1323, 1325, 1330, 1331, 1339, 1340, 1341, 1342, 1345, 1349, 1350, 1352, 1364, 1365, 1368, 1379, 1380. **Qatar Police:** serials QP1 and QP2; c/ns 1141, 1156. **Egyptian Air Force:** c/ns 1346, 1357, 1395, 1396, 1442, 1444, 1478, 1479, 1496, 1497, 1514, 1532, 1533, 1553, 1554, 1568, 1569, 1571, 1572, 1585, 1589, 1590, 1603, 1604, 1623, 1624, 1632, 1633, 1650, 1653, 1667, 1684, 1685, 1686, 1696, 1699, 1700, 1701, 1709, 1714, 1715, 1716, 1763, 1769, 1773, 1774, 1776 to 1787. **Kenya Air Force:** c/ns 1393, 1394. **Iraqi Air Force:** c/ns 1397, 1398, 1428, 1429, 1445, 1446, 1460, 1461, 1480, 1481, 1498, 1499, 1516, 1534, 1535, 1555, 1556, 1573, 1574, 1591, 1592, 1606, 1607, 1625 to 1627, 1636, 1640, 1641, 1654 to 1656, 1668 to 1670, 1687, 1688. **Syrian Air Force:** c/ns 1493 to 1495, 1550 to 1552, 1570, 1586 to 1588, 1620 to 1622, 1637 to 1639.

SUD SA330 PUMA

Royal Air Force: serial XW241, c/n 08; serials XW198 to XW237, c/ns 1039, 1042, 1048, 1054, 1061, 1068, 1074, 1080, 1086, 1091, 1095, 1096, 1101, 1106, 1111, 1116, 1120, 1125, 1129, 1134, 1139, 1144, 1148, 1152, 1157, 1161, 1166, 1170, 1175, 1178, 1183, 1191, 1195, 1199, 1205, 1206, 1213, 1217, 1220. **Portuguese Air Force:** 9501 to 9512; c/ns 1001, 1002, 1004, 1009, 1011, 1019, 1035, 1040, 1046, 1050, 1059, 1065. **South African Air Force:** serials 121 to 140; c/ns 1016, 1022, 1030, 1033, 1045, 1053, 1058, 1064, 1070, 1076, 1077, 1083, 1089, 1090, 1097, 1104, 1105, 1110, 1118, 1119. **Abu Dhabi Air Force:** serials 111 to 115; c/ns 1113, 1127, 1169, 1224, 1233. **Gabon Air Force:** serial TR-KCA; c/n 1132. **Chilean Air Force:** serial H-98; c/n 1181. **Pakistan Army:** serials as c/ns 1194, 1398, 1401, 1406, 1408, 1414, 1415, 1443, 1458, 1523, 1525, 1528, 1530, 1531, 1533, 1534, 1535, 1538, 1540, 1543, 1555, 1558, 1561, 1564, 1566, 1568. **Belgian Rijkswacht:** serials OL-G01 to OL-G03; c/ns 1225, 1237, 1265. **Ecuadorian Air Force:** serials 226 and 227; c/ns 1226 and 1227. **Spanish Air Force:** serials Z19-01 to Z19-03; c/ns 1230, 1245, 1254. **Ethiopian Air Force:** serial 850; c/n 1240. **Kuwait Air Force:** serial 551; c/n 1274. **Nigerian Air Force:** serials 530 to 536; c/ns 1318, 1330, 1324, , 1497, 1501. **Moroccan Air Force:** serials CN-ARH/8 to CN-ARL/12; c/ns 1353, 1356, 1360, 1359, 1372.

APPENDIX K

Keeping up-to-date

Enthusiasts of squadron and serial-number data will find much to interest them in the monthly publications listed hereunder. These cover developments throughout Europe, and will be of assistance in keeping this book up-to-date.

AIR FAN - A smart new 52 page military monthly, with many photos (some in colour), mainly French text but with English captions etc. Articles predominantly on French Military Aviation. First published in November '78 - all back issues available, single copies £1.65 (£1.80 non UK). Annual subscription £19.80 (£21.60 non UK) inclusive of postage.

FLASH - An A4 Dutch enthusiasts magazine with military aviation news, photos and articles. Ten copies per year at 70p each (80p non UK) plus one at 85p (£1.00 non UK). Back issues July/August '77 issue to-date Annual subscription £7.85 UK, (£9.00 non UK) inclusive of postage.

MILITARY AVIATION REVIEW - A lavishly illustrated A4 monthly with news and articles, first published May '76. Stocks of some back issues are now low or out-of-print, so alternatives should be quoted when ordering. Single copies 60p UK (70p non UK). Annual subscription £7.20 (£8.50 non UK) inclusive of postage and packing.

The following two publications are also highly recommended:

British Aviation Review
8 Nightingale Road
Woodley, Berkshire
RG5 3LP
England

South East Air Review
18 Green Lawns
Southbourne Gardens
Eastcote, Ruislip
Middlesex, England

Aviation Publications

Midland Counties Publications is engaged upon the publication of a range of works of reference for the aviation historian and enthusiast.

Our growing series on **Military Air Arms** is acknowledged by reviewers and enthusiasts the world over, for the depth of original research, quality (and quantity) of illustrations and accuracy of content; also for the high standard of presentation and production in a subject-suited landscape format.

Although the contents vary slightly, according to subject, usually included are: a history of the air arm involved; its organisation; unit histories; also considerable detail on the individual aircraft - including unit allocations and codes, constructors numbers and fates etc. This is backed-up by extensive photographic coverage, detailed drawings of unit markings, plus various appendices.

Titles offered (subject to availability) in both softback (glossy card cover) and hardback (cloth cover, silver blocked), are:

		Softback	Hardback
GERMAN MILITARY AVIATION 1956-76	152pp	£3-45 ea	£5-45 ea
BELGIAN MILITARY AVIATION 1945-77	120pp	£3-45 ea	£5-45 ea
SPANISH & PORTUGUESE MIL. AVIATION	128pp	£3-45 ea	£5-45 ea
DUTCH MILITARY AVIATION 1945-78	134pp	£3-45 ea	£5-45 ea
FRENCH MILITARY AVIATION (2nd Edn.)	208pp	£3-95 ea	£5-95 ea

Other titles published by MCP include:

BEAGLE AIRCRAFT - A production history. Details all the types produced by the Company, from the early 6A right through to the Pup. £0-90

LOCKHEED AEROBATIC TROPHY 1955-65 compiled by Tony Lloyd. A close look at the men and machines which took part in these contests. £1-00

BRUSH AIRCRAFT - Production at Loughborough - an illustrated account of the aircraft constructed and overhauled (includes Avro 504s and Rapides) at this Midlands factory during two world wars. Glossy card cover £1-20

AIRSHOWS 1978 - David Sargent has compiled this comprehensive checklist of upwards of 11,000 aircraft that attended the 200-plus air events throughout the UK (and Europe) during the 1978 'Airshows' season. It is profusely illustrated with 120 carefully selected photographs and also contains details of Squadron Exchanges and European Deployments etc. Glossy paper, A4 size. £1-95

BRITISH CIVIL AIRCRAFT REGISTERS, 1919-1978 (John Appleton / Ian Cave) This invaluable reference book, contains a mammoth alphabetical listing of the 21,000-odd aircraft which have appeared on the registers, featuring for the first time the previous identity, construction number and cancellation details for each aircraft (where known). Also included are the BGA and Irish Registers, plus several useful Appendices. Available in Softback (glossy card cover) for £3-95 or in the Hardback cased style (cloth covered card covers, silver blocking, coloured dust jacket) for £5-95.

MYSTERE FALCON 20 - a production history - compiled by Brian Gates. A thoroughly researched new monograph on this most successful Biz-Jet by the author of the well-known 'Biz-Jet' annual. Produced to the same high standard as the 'Military Air Arm' series, within its 134 pages it contains individual histories of the 370-odd examples produced at the time, with f/f and delivery dates, owners, registrations and bases. It is illustrated by 127 photographs and offered in two versions: Softback binding (glossy colour card cover) for £3-60 or in Hardback (cloth covered covers, silver blocking, colour dust jacket) for £5-75.

All the titles listed on this page are available from specialist bookshops or alternatively direct (post-free) from the publisher's address below. Subject only to continuing availability or any price increase beyond our control.

AVIATION BOOKS BY POST

In addition to publishing their own range of aviation reference books, MCP have established a world-wide mail-order service that currently offers over 600 aviation books, over 100 vinyl 'stickers' and a range of wallcharts and postcards. For full details of our service (including how you can get your order sent post-free - and details of our monthly prize-draw) either 'phone or send us a SAE (or IRC from overseas). We take extra care when packing (including water-proofing) and we turn most orders round within 48 hours of receipt. Why not give us a try for your next order ?

MIDLAND COUNTIES PUBLICATIONS (Aerophile) LIMITED
24 The Hollow, Earl Shilton, Leicester, LE9 7NA, England. Tel: (0455) 47256